MW00611344

AMERICA
FIRST

ALSO BY H. W. BRANDS

T.R.

The First American

The Age of Gold

Lone Star Nation

Andrew Jackson

Traitor to His Class

American Colossus

The Man Who Saved the Union

Reagan

The General vs. the President

Heirs of the Founders

Dreams of El Dorado

The Zealot and the Emancipator

Our First Civil War

The Last Campaign

Founding Partisans

AMERICA FIRST

Roosevelt vs. Lindbergh
in the Shadow of War

H. W. BRANDS

DOUBLEDAY

New York

Copyright © 2024 by H. W. Brands

All rights reserved. Published in the United States by Doubleday, a
division of Penguin Random House LLC, New York, and distributed in
Canada by Penguin Random House Canada Limited, Toronto.

www.doubleday.com

DOUBLEDAY and the portrayal of an anchor with a dolphin are
registered trademarks of Penguin Random House LLC.

Book design by Michael Collica
Jacket images: (left to right) President Franklin D. Roosevelt,
Hulton Archive/Getty Images; Nazi flags, Heinz Dorn/ullstein bild/
Getty Images; Charles Lindbergh, Bachrach/Getty Images
Jacket design by Oliver Munday

Library of Congress Cataloging-in-Publication Data
Names: Brands, H. W., author.
Title: America first : Roosevelt vs. Lindbergh in the shadow of war / H. W. Brands.
Description: First edition. | New York : Doubleday, a division of Penguin
Random House LLC, [2024] | Includes bibliographical references and index.
Identifiers: LCCN 2023050744 | ISBN 9780385550413 (hardcover) |
ISBN 9780385550420 (ebook)
Subjects: LCSH: Roosevelt, Franklin D. (Franklin Delano), 1882–1945—Political
and social views. | Lindbergh, Charles A. (Charles Augustus), 1902–19744—
Political and social views. | World War, 1939–1945—United States. | World War,
1939–1945—Diplomatic history. | Isolationism—United States—History—20th
century. | Intervention (International law)—History—20th century. | United
States—Politics and government—1933–1945. | Political culture—United States—
History—20th century. | United States—Foreign relations—1933–1945.
Classification: LCC D742.U5 B73 2024 | DDC 940.53/73—dc23/eng/20240521
LC record available at https://lccn.loc.gov/2023050744

MANUFACTURED IN THE UNITED STATES OF AMERICA

1st Printing
First Edition

Contents

AMERICA FIRST

Prologue

THE CROWD STARTED gathering in the late afternoon. Some came to cheer, others to protest. Most knew they wouldn't get inside the Manhattan Center, the old opera house once so successful the rival Metropolitan Opera paid to shut it down. Tickets were reserved for the most important people in the city—those of them, at any rate, inclined to be associated with the controversial group sponsoring the evening's event.

The America First Committee, they called themselves. Established just seven months earlier, in September 1940, they claimed half a million members, with thousands more swelling the ranks of the committee's hundreds of local chapters each week. Headquarters were in Chicago, far from the coast and even farther from the wars being waged in Europe and Asia. Midwesterners, including descendants of German immigrants, were well represented among the members; so were socialists, who preached international brotherhood; anticommunists, who said Russia was the greater threat than Germany; xenophobes and nationalists, who distrusted foreigners and disdained to include them in calculations of American interest; Republicans reflexively opposed to anything Franklin Roosevelt supported; open and closeted admirers of Hitler and Mussolini; Irish-Americans unwilling to lift a finger to help the British, their homeland's historic oppressor; industrialists who feared the nationalization of their businesses should America go to war again, as their businesses had been nationalized in the World War; and young men who didn't want to become the kind of cannon fodder their fathers had been in that first war.

And now their ranks included Charles Lindbergh, the celebrity-hero of the age in America. The famous aviator—conqueror of the Atlantic in 1927, feted around the planet since—had long spoken against American involvement in the affairs of Europe and Asia. But until a week ago he had done so on his own, as befitted the one his admirers called the Lone Eagle. His decision to close ranks with the other antiwar activists reflected an apparent increase in America's momentum toward war. Roosevelt had been elected to a third term, thereby giving his critics a new argument: that war would be Roosevelt's excuse to make himself dictator or at least president for life. He had persuaded Congress to fund American military aid to countries fighting the Axis powers: Germany, Italy and Japan. His latest scheme was to furnish naval convoys for goods crossing the Atlantic.

Congress hadn't approved the convoys, and "the American First Committee" was determined to keep the lawmakers from doing so. Wasn't it obvious what Roosevelt intended? He was provoking German submarines to fire on American ships and kill American seamen; when they did, he would demand and doubtless receive a declaration of war.

This was what Lindbergh was going to say this evening. America was on the brink of war; only a concerted effort by peace-loving and right-minded Americans could pull the country back. Lindbergh and the others were tarred as "isolationists" by their interventionist opponents; he and the others embraced the label if it meant they aimed to isolate America from the madness consuming Europe and Asia. Some in the group were pacifists, but most were not. Lindbergh was not; he contended that a security perimeter close to American shores, proclaimed at once and defended as necessary, was most likely to bring real and lasting security.

He rose to speak. The audience inside the Manhattan Center fell silent and leaned forward to listen. As they did, the shouts from the throng outside became audible. The police had closed Thirty-fourth Street to vehicles and pushed the crowd back from the doors of the building, but they hadn't been able to keep the protesters and counter-protesters from exchanging epithets and blows. To those inside, the violence in the street sounded a warning against the much greater violence they aimed to avert.

RADIO CARRIED LINDBERGH'S address, and millions tuned in. Franklin Roosevelt did not. The president knew what the aviator was going to say. It was what the isolationists had been saying for two decades—since, indeed, they torpedoed the Treaty of Versailles in the Senate at the end of the World War. Their opposition to foreign commitments had intensified since then, and it kept the United States out of the League of Nations, signaling to the enemies of freedom that they could have their way with the countries they trampled and brutalized.

Politics had prompted Roosevelt to hold his tongue during his first eight years in office. He knew that by riling the isolationists he would imperil the New Deal and spoil his chances of alleviating the domestic distress of the country. But the outbreak of war abroad had increased demand for the products of American farms and factories and revived the economy. And his election to a third term gave him a mandate for stronger action internationally. The Lend-Lease program Congress had recently passed was heartening the British, the Chinese and others fighting the Axis. American convoys would ensure that the American-made weapons and provisions reached their intended destinations.

Roosevelt rejected much of what Lindbergh and the isolationists were saying. He had to admire their cleverness in claiming the label "America First," which implied that their opponents had dubious priorities. Roosevelt considered himself as much an America-firster as Lindbergh and the others; he simply had a clearer view of where America's interests lay. Their policy was really "America alone," at a time when the United States needed all the help it could get in dealing with the existential challenge of militant fascism. Those in the Lindbergh crowd who weren't outright apologists for Hitler underestimated the degree to which the Nazi regime required war to maintain its legitimacy. Hitler wouldn't stop until he came after the United States, and if he controlled all of Europe by that time, America would be truly—and terrifyingly—alone. Aid to Britain wasn't for the sake of Britain; it was for America's sake, to keep Britain's fleet afloat and Britain itself viable as a launchpad for fighting Hitler on the eastern side of the Atlantic rather than the western.

Yet Roosevelt silently acknowledged an essential part of the isolationists' argument: that American aid to countries fighting the Axis made America's direct intervention more likely. In public Roosevelt said the opposite: that America sent guns to the wars in Europe and Asia so it wouldn't have to send soldiers. He hoped this might be so, but he didn't believe it. Hitler and the warlords of Japan wouldn't stop till they met an immovable object, and American military power was the only such object left to oppose them.

By the time Lindbergh addressed the America First meeting, Roosevelt had concluded that sooner or later America would have to take on Germany and Japan, and sooner would be better than later. Yet the isolationists might still frustrate his design. They were more dangerous than ever now that Lindbergh was their charismatic spokesman, which was all the more reason for Roosevelt to keep his conclusions to himself.

PART ONE

The Allure of Neutrality

I

A MORE TERRIBLE THING couldn't have happened to a
more admirable man.

Such was the reaction of Americans as they read that the
infant son of Charles Lindbergh had been kidnapped. Lindbergh
had become America's hero five years earlier when he accomplished
the historic feat of leaping the Atlantic in a single bound of flight.
The twenty-five-year-old aviator paired the courage of the explorer
with the technical know-how of the inventor: he was Lewis and
Clark and Edison rolled into one. That he was handsome—tall and
rangy, with the blond hair and blue eyes of his Swedish forebears—
made Lucky Lindy irresistible to the newsreel cameras that were just
beginning to bring important events to mass audiences almost as
they happened. His natural shyness made him the more appealing;
amid the din of the Roaring Twenties, his diffidence was endearing.
He seemed the boy next door, if the boy next door were also inven-
tive, brave and famous.

His wedding to Anne Morrow, the charming and talented daughter of a Wall Street banker turned diplomat, filled the tabloids and
respectable papers alike. In due course the couple were blessed with
a child, christened Charles and immediately called Little Lindy by
the headline writers. Lindbergh built a home in rural New Jersey for
his small family; in the late winter of 1932 they spent time there even
though it wasn't quite finished. On March 1 Anne and the child's
nurse put him to bed around seven; Lindbergh was reading in the

study below. At ten the nurse checked on Little Lindy before she went to bed. She didn't find him in the crib.

At first she thought the mother or father must have picked up the twenty-month-old and taken him to another room. When she checked with Anne and saw no baby, she began to be alarmed. When Lindbergh didn't have him either, her alarm turned to panic.

Lindbergh dashed up the stairs to the bedroom. Seeing the empty crib, he searched the other rooms, on the chance young Lindy might suddenly have learned to climb out of the crib. Then he searched outside the house, realizing the possibility of finding the baby there was minuscule. He finally called the New Jersey state police. His son was missing, he said.

If American hearts had swelled with pride on watching the newsreels of Lindbergh in Paris, standing in front of *The Spirit of St. Louis* and receiving from France's president the Cross of the Legion of Honor, those same hearts were wrenched by worry on reading of the disappearance, and on seeing newsreel clips from home movies Lindbergh had made of Little Lindy. Lindbergh and Anne had tried to shelter the baby from public view, but now they were persuaded to let the world into their home so that the public might assist in identifying and rescuing the child.

The home movies touched the heartstrings of every audience member in every theater where the newsreels played. Little Lindy was an angelic junior version of his father; the toddler's smiling blue eyes, framed by golden curls, smiled sweetly and innocently into the camera. Millions of Americans felt as if their own child or grandchild or younger sibling had been stolen. Men from hundreds of miles around joined the search; people all across the country offered up prayers for the child's safe return. More than a few vowed vengeance against the perpetrators should any harm befall the darling boy.

Government officials ordered their agencies to join the search. President Herbert Hoover put his best men on the job. Governor Franklin Roosevelt of neighboring New York state likewise stepped up. "I am personally deeply interested, because I know both Colonel and Mrs. Lindbergh," Roosevelt said from Albany. "My daughter, Mrs. Curtis Dall, was at school with Mrs. Lindbergh."

The worry over the missing child turned to agony when, after weeks of investigation and negotiation, and the futile delivery of fifty thousand dollars in ransom money to someone claiming to speak for the kidnappers, the decomposing body of Little Lindy was found under a pile of brush a few miles from the Lindbergh home.

Lindbergh and Anne were devastated, although Lindbergh held himself together long enough to identify the remains of his child. Parents all over America shuddered in sympathy, imagining how they would feel in his circumstances. Lucky Lindy didn't seem so lucky anymore; the man to whom so much had been given was now deprived of even more. People had admired Lindbergh as an ideal type; suddenly they identified with him in the shared humanity of suffering.

Individuals reached out, writing letters, sending telegrams, making phone calls. Herbert Hoover reiterated the backing of the federal government in the search for those who had taken—and killed—the baby. New York's Roosevelt declared, "No crime has so moved the country during the last generation as has this one." The governor added, "Every agency at my command has been instructed to bring the fiendish murderers to justice."

AT THE TIME Roosevelt spoke, his promise was worth more than Hoover's. Or rather, it would be if the manhunt took longer than a few months, as the lack of leads suggested it might.

By the summer of 1932 America knew that Hoover would not be reelected president. The stock market crash of 1929 hadn't been his fault, most Americans acknowledged, but many blamed the Republican president for failing to pull the economy out of its post-crash dive, and for ignoring the pleas for help from the millions of Americans rendered jobless and homeless by the collapse of the economy the Republicans had spent the previous decade boasting about. Whoever won the Democratic nomination would surely defeat Hoover. And Roosevelt was the Democrats' favorite.

Roosevelt didn't know Lindbergh as well as his comment about his daughter—Anna Roosevelt Dall—and Anne Lindbergh suggested. Yet the trajectory of his life paralleled Lindbergh's in certain respects. No one ever called Roosevelt "Lucky Frank," though he too was blessed with good looks and sufficient wealth to pursue his interests—in his case, politics. He was vigorous and athletic, preferring sailboats to airplanes, and he charmed people with his winning smile and warm personality. Fortune smiled on him as he advanced through the ranks of the Democratic party, to the point where he was made his party's nominee for vice president in 1920. In a Republican year, the ticket lost, but Roosevelt emerged unscathed—indeed, more appealing than ever. He was widely spoken of as a contender for the top of the ticket next time.

But in 1921 he contracted infantile paralysis, as polio was then called. He went to bed one evening feeling unusually tired; he woke up the next day paralyzed from the neck down. As word got out, Roosevelt received sympathy cards and letters from all parts of the country. Everyone wished him well; a few dared to pray for a speedy recovery. Most assumed his public life was over; cripples, to use the term of the time, were expected to stay home and out of sight if they could afford to. Fortunately for Roosevelt, he could; the family estate at Hyde Park, in the Hudson Valley, would be an appropriate retirement retreat.

Roosevelt retreated to Hyde Park, but he didn't retire. He maintained his ties with Democratic leaders in New York and beyond, corresponding with them, speaking to them by phone and hosting them when they could visit Hyde Park. His wife, Eleanor, served as his proxy to local groups at first, then others farther afield.

He spent months at a time in Warm Springs, Georgia, a spa renowned for its soothing waters. While there he got to know the locals: humble whites and blacks often overlooked by one or both political parties.

People familiar with Roosevelt thought the experience of polio made him more empathetic. Before polio most of what he wanted came easily; afterward everything was harder. Therapy and time restored the use of his arms, but he never was able to walk again without braces and the supporting arm of an adult son or assistant. Yet he didn't complain; his typical expression was a broad smile; the hearty hello with which he greeted visitors boomed louder than ever. If there had been a complaint against him before, it was that he was shallow, or seemed to be. Nothing had tested his mettle. People had admired him, but few had identified with him. What could he know about the travails of ordinary life, about the fact that bad things happen to good people through no fault of their own? After Roosevelt contracted polio, no one asked that question anymore.

Roosevelt's ability to appreciate the problems of ordinary people, and Hoover's perceived inability to do so, emerged in sharp relief during the summer of 1932. Unemployed veterans of the World War—as it was called before the second one—gathered in Washington to petition Congress for early payment of a pension bonus they had been promised. They argued that the bonus would boost the economy and that, on present trends of distress, some of them might not live long enough to receive the bonus when its scheduled date arrived. Congress, on the advice of Hoover, rejected the petition. Some of the veterans returned whence they had come, but many others, without money for travel and with nothing much to return to, remained in Washington, in an encampment near the Anacostia River.

Most of the vets weren't political, but radicals circulated among them preaching the overthrow of the government. Hoover took fright and ordered the "bonus army" dispersed. Douglas MacArthur, chief of staff of the U.S. Army, personally led a column of regular troops against the vets. The result was a political fiasco: newsreels around the country showed the bonus camp in flames, women and children fleeing the violence, and the nation's senior soldier grimly approving.

Roosevelt watched from New York. He turned to adviser Felix Frankfurter and said, "This will elect me."

It did elect him, aided by his refusal to say anything specific about almost any issue before the public. The election was Roosevelt's to lose, and he stuck to the path of hopeful banality. He promised a "new deal" between government and the ordinary people of America, without elaborating. He let voters imagine what they wanted, and most imagined he couldn't be worse than Hoover.

Roosevelt steered especially clear of foreign affairs. He understood that most Americans cared about other people and countries only intermittently. At a time when their jobs, life savings and futures were in peril, they wanted to hear what their government would do about *their* concerns, not those of folks far away. Roosevelt appreciated that America's depression was aggravated by the global slump, which might best be remedied by coordination among the major trading powers, including the United States. But coordination required putting foreigners ahead of Americans on some matters, and Roosevelt wasn't going to ask Americans to make that sacrifice.

An economic conference in London in the summer of 1933 gave the new president a chance to wave the flag of American nationalism. He kept the delegates in suspense; they knew that with a single sentence he could blast their hopes for a collective approach to the international slump. They labored for weeks devising a scheme to align exchange rates; all that remained was a signal of American cooperation. Roosevelt delivered just the opposite. The United States would insist on the status quo, he declared, no matter the havoc it did to other countries. "The sound internal economic system of a nation is a greater factor in its well-being than the price of its currency in changing terms of the currencies of other nations," the president declared. Every nation must look out for itself, and devil take the hindmost.

2

THE SEARCH FOR the killer of the Lindbergh baby moved slowly, but in September 1934 the police arrested Bruno Richard Hauptmann, an immigrant from Germany living in the Bronx. The trial commenced the following January, and while it held promise of justice for the murdered child, it compelled his parents to relive the horrible moments of his disappearance and death. The Lindberghs found themselves at the center of a media circus, with print reporters and newspaper photographers competing with radio broadcasters and newsreel teams for a glimpse, the more heartrending the better, of the suffering couple. The jury delivered a verdict of guilty, and the judge pronounced a sentence of death. Hauptmann was duly executed.

Lindbergh and Anne hoped the scrutiny would ease after the case closed, but it didn't. The Lindbergh story meant profits for the newspapers and newsreels, and they weren't going to let it go. Photographers followed them and harassed Jon, their younger son. On one occasion Jon's teacher was driving the child home from school when a car full of glowering men pulled alongside and forced the teacher's car to a stop. The teacher knew of threats against Jon the Lindberghs had been receiving, and, fearing the worst, she tried to shield the boy with her body. That the men were photographers rather than kidnappers, and that they contented themselves with pushing cameras rather than guns into Jon's face, hardly eased the terror the teacher felt or the anger Jon's parents experienced on learning of the incident.

By late 1935 Lindbergh had had enough. He spirited Anne and Jon away on a liner to England, informing only one reporter, whom he swore to secrecy until after the ship had cleared American waters. "Colonel Charles A. Lindbergh has given up residence in the United States and is on his way to establish his home in England," the front-page story said. "With him are his wife and 3-year-old son, Jon. Threats of kidnapping and even of death to the little lad, recurring repeatedly since his birth, caused the father and mother to make the decision. These threats have increased both in number and virulence recently." The authorities could do little against the threats, given America's emphasis on freedom and the First Amendment. "And so the man who eight years ago was hailed as an international hero and a good-will ambassador between the peoples of the world is taking his wife and son to establish, if he can, a secure haven for them in a foreign land."

AT THE TIME Lindbergh left America, the American verdict on the World War was overwhelmingly negative. Woodrow Wilson had led the country into the war proclaiming that America's participation was necessary to make the world safe for democracy; the struggle was touted by its supporters as the war to end all wars. The American side won but began to fall apart at the peace conference, which imposed punitive and humiliating conditions on Germany that all but guaranteed German resistance. Economic disruption in several countries during the 1920s led to political turbulence that intensified amid the depression of the 1930s. By the middle of that decade democracy, which the World War was supposed to have saved, had been bludgeoned to death in Germany and Italy and was imperiled elsewhere. War, which the World War was supposed to have ended, once more loomed.

Americans concluded that they had been played for suckers—that the hundred thousand of their compatriots who died in the war had lost their lives to capitalist greed and imperialist folly. The capitalists were the American bankers and arms manufacturers who made a killing from all the killing; the imperialists were the leaders of Britain and France who expanded their empires in Asia and Africa by the victory secured with American blood and treasure. The Senate's rejection of the Versailles treaty and membership in the League of Nations had been controversial in the immediate aftermath of the war; a decade and a half later, that shunning of Europe was celebrated and being projected forward. Americans had tried once to rescue Europe from its folly and failed; they would not repeat the mistake.

Gerald Nye led the campaign against involvement in future wars. The North Dakota Republican headed a Senate special committee investigating the munitions industry. For nearly two years the Nye committee called witnesses, heard testimony and wrote multiple drafts of a report. The final draft blistered the arms dealers directly and the American government obliquely. The report quoted a witness, an agent for the Colt firearms company, who testified that wartime arms sales "brought into play the most despicable side of human nature; lies, deceit, hypocrisy, greed, and graft occupying a most prominent part in the transactions." Speaking in its own voice the Nye panel called the practices of the arms dealers "highly unethical, a discredit to American business, and an unavoidable reflection upon those American governmental agencies which have unwittingly aided in the transactions so contaminated." The committee pointed to numerous instances of bribery and corruption and declared, with more restraint than the evidence required, "The constant availability of munitions companies with competitive bribes ready in outstretched hands does not create a situation where the officials involved can, in the nature of things, be as much interested in peace and measures to secure peace as they are in increased armaments."

The Nye committee inspired and reflected a literature of denunciation of America's role in the World War. Such titles as *Merchants of Death* and *Iron, Blood and Profits* wore their indictments on their covers; subtler works like *America Goes to War* and *The Road to War* allowed greater nuance. The more charitable contributions to the genre accounted American intervention a mistake; the harsher called it a crime. Almost no one defended American participation in the war. Even veterans of the war—*especially* veterans of the war—regretted their service and vowed not to let their sons do anything so deluded.

Congress caught the drift and wrote the conventional wisdom into statute. The legislature approved a series of neutrality laws designed to keep the country from being led astray again. The laws forbade the sale of weapons to belligerents in future wars, the entry of American vessels into war zones, and travel by American nationals on ships flying belligerent flags. Each of the proscribed actions had contributed to the American entry into the World War; each ban was intended to preempt pressure for American entry into the next war.

IN THE MID-1930S that next war seemed imminent. By some interpretations it had already started. Japan had fought a war against China in the 1890s and won, with its booty including Taiwan and Korea. In 1931 Japan struck again, seizing the Chinese province of Manchuria, which it turned into a puppet state. The world, including the United States, disapproved of the seizure but with insufficient vigor to make Japan disgorge its prize. If anything, the feckless response tempted the generals and admirals in Tokyo to take more of China, which appeared unable to defend itself.

In Europe, Italy led the way toward militarism and war. Benito Mussolini's Fascist party provided a name and model for the bellicose nationalism that emerged in several countries; Fascist Blackshirts fought street battles against their foes, seized the offices and revenues of government, and boasted of reviving the Roman empire, with Il Duce—Mussolini—as the modern Caesar. To that end Mussolini launched a war of conquest against Abyssinia, or Ethiopia, one of the few parts of Africa not already claimed by a European empire.

In Spain, Francisco Franco led a revolt against his country's republican government, sparking a civil war that drew fascists from other countries to Franco's side and pulled communists, the sworn foes of the fascists, to the side of the government. The Spanish conflict seemed a portent for Europe and perhaps the world, as the fascists and communists locked in a death embrace of rival despotisms.

German fascists marched under banners of the National Socialist, or Nazi, party. They made their stiff-armed salutes to Adolf Hitler, an eerily magnetic veteran of the World War and an Austrian native who became more German than the Germans. Hitler wasn't the first German to rail against the Versailles treaty and the burdens it placed on Germany, but he was the first to fully exploit the politics of German grievance. He assumed the chancellorship at almost the same moment Roosevelt became the American president. Hitler soon made himself dictator. His initial reforms focused on Germany itself; flouting the Versailles treaty, he reoccupied the industrial Rhineland and rebuilt the German military. Then he began looking outward. Complaining that Germany had been robbed of essential parts of the fatherland at the end of the war, he promised the German people he would take those territories back. The fact that other countries claimed the territories made his promise sound like a predated declaration of war.

ROOSEVELT KEPT HIS distance. He had been an internationalist during the World War, convinced that American interests and world peace required an active role for the United States in international affairs. As assistant secretary of the navy in the internationally minded Wilson administration, he could hardly have thought otherwise. Roosevelt made the internationalist cause his own in the election campaign of 1920. The Democrats' defeat failed to disabuse him of the theoretical advisability of a large role for the United States in the world, but it convinced him of the political impracticability of such a role until the backlash against the war diminished.

It hadn't done so at the time Roosevelt became president; hence his refusal to join the international effort to adjust exchange rates. Nor did it diminish during his first term, when Hitler ranted in Berlin and Gerald Nye raged on Capitol Hill. Roosevelt kept his head down during debate over the neutrality legislation. He fretted about encroachment on presidential prerogative but mounted no serious opposition.

After his 1936 reelection he occasionally raised a finger to test the wind. In the summer of 1937 Japan's militarists escalated their occupation of Manchuria into a regular war against China. The brutality of Japan's campaign appalled many in America; Roosevelt thought it might weaken the hold of isolationism on the American mind.

On a trip to Chicago, the epicenter of American isolationism, he gave a rare—for him until now—speech on foreign affairs. "The political situation in the world, which of late has been growing progressively worse, is such as to cause grave concern and anxiety to all the peoples and nations who wish to live in peace and amity with their neighbors," Roosevelt said. "The present reign of terror and international lawlessness began a few years ago. It began through unjustified interference in the internal affairs of other nations or the invasion of alien territory in violation of treaties; and has now reached a stage where the very foundations of civilization are seriously threatened. The landmarks and traditions which have marked the progress of civilization toward a condition of law, order and justice are being wiped away." Accepted methods of peace had been supplanted by a new mode of war. "Without a declaration of war and without warning or justification of any kind, civilians, including vast numbers of women and children, are being ruthlessly murdered with bombs from the air," Roosevelt said. "Nations are fomenting and taking sides in civil warfare in nations that have never done them any harm. Nations claiming freedom for themselves deny it to others. Innocent peoples, innocent nations, are being cruelly sacrificed to a greed for power and supremacy which is devoid of all sense of justice and humane considerations."

Roosevelt, as he typically did, avoided identifying the objects of his criticism by name. But his listeners would have had no difficulty recognizing the Japanese in China, the Italians in Ethiopia, and Franco's fascists and their allies in Spain. Roosevelt wouldn't have complained had they prospectively added Hitler's Germany to his list. Careful listeners noticed that all the violence Roosevelt described was happening in Europe, Asia and Africa—not in the Americas. He aimed to puncture their complacency. "If those things come to pass in other parts of the world, let no one imagine that America will escape, that America may expect mercy, that this Western Hemisphere will not be attacked," he said.

When bad men rampaged, good men must ally against them. "Those who cherish their freedom and recognize and respect the equal right of their neighbors to be free and live in peace must work together for the triumph of law and moral principles in order that peace, justice and confidence may prevail in the world. There must be a return to a belief in the pledged word, in the value of a signed treaty. There must be recognition of the fact that national morality is as vital as private morality."

Likening war to a contagion, Roosevelt proposed a remedy. "When an epidemic of physical disease starts to spread, the community approves and joins in a quarantine of the patients in order to protect the health of the community."

He didn't clarify what he meant by a quarantine. Diplomatic non-recognition? Economic sanctions? Ouster from international forums?

He pressed on: "War is a contagion, whether it be declared or undeclared. It can engulf states and peoples remote from the original scene of hostilities. We are determined to keep out of war, yet we cannot insure ourselves against the disastrous effects of war and the dangers of involvement. We are adopting such measures as will minimize our risk of involvement, but we cannot have complete protection in a world of disorder in which confidence and security have broken down."

He concluded earnestly but no more specifically. "America hates war. America hopes for peace. Therefore, America actively engages in the search for peace."

3

JOSEPH KENNEDY WAS an unlikely pick for American ambassador to Britain. He had been an even more improbable choice to head the Securities and Exchange Commission when Roosevelt tapped him for that spot. Kennedy had made a bundle on Wall Street and managed to survive the crash of 1929. Rumors swirled of corners he'd cut and rules he'd bent. And now he was going to *set* the rules? Roosevelt reasoned that if anyone knew where existing law needed bolstering, it was Kennedy. And Roosevelt thought himself clever enough to keep Kennedy in line.

Kennedy's performance pleased Roosevelt sufficiently that when America required a new ambassador in London in early 1938, the president chose him. Kennedy's Irish ancestry made him suspicious of the British; Roosevelt wanted a skeptic in the London post. The British had been playing the diplomatic game longer than Americans had, and they had a habit of winning American envoys to their cause. With an Irish chip on his shoulder, Kennedy wouldn't succumb.

Kennedy went to Hyde Park to receive final instructions from the president. "He discussed the foreign situation in general and the break between Eden and Chamberlain in particular," Kennedy recorded in his diary. Anthony Eden and Neville Chamberlain were leading Conservatives, or Tories; Eden had just resigned as foreign secretary, while Chamberlain continued as prime minister. "He indicated his firm intention of keeping our country out of any and all involvements or commitments abroad," Kennedy continued, of Roosevelt. "He considered the situation too uncertain for the United

States to do anything but mark time until things have settled down. He did not seem to resent the position Chamberlain has taken of trying to make deals with Germany and Italy in order to fend off a crisis, but he seemed to regret Eden's passing from the picture."

London had never hosted an American ambassador of Irish descent, and the appointment raised concerns. Some were silly: whether Kennedy would wear traditional knee breeches or trousers when he presented his credentials at Buckingham Palace. He chose trousers.

Some were more substantive. A few weeks after his arrival in London, Kennedy spoke at the annual Pilgrim's Day Dinner, an Anglo-American lovefest. He started on a light note, saying that ferrying his brood of nine children across the Atlantic made him feel like a Pilgrim father himself. His audience chuckled.

He turned serious. "In taking up my duties here I am moved by one prime consideration," he said. "That is that we"—Americans and British—"of all peoples in the world, must be frank and straightforward with each other. I conceive it to be my duty to tell you, individually and collectively, as accurately as I possibly can, what is in the minds and hearts of my countrymen."

He started with foreign affairs. "The average American has little interest in the details of foreign affairs," Kennedy told his British audience. Americans had other things to worry about, especially at present. "The everyday business of making a living has recently become harder for our people, following a period which they had begun to breathe a little bit more easily." Backsliding in the economy, begun the previous year, had erased many of the gains since the worst of the depression. "The average man wants to know whether he will be able to keep his job and his savings. The possibility of losing job and savings is of immediate and visible interest to him, whereas international developments, regardless of their importance, appear to be vague and far away."

Kennedy told a story from his time at the Securities and Exchange Commission. "One of the first things I had to do was make a comprehensive study of the operation of the various exchanges and speculative activities of our country. I learned, among other things, that speculation in foreign exchange is almost nonexistent in the United States. The arbitrage dealers and the skilled professionals have this field practically to themselves."Things were very different in Europe. "There, in addition to professional operators, thousands of merchants large and small are forced to speculate in foreign exchange as a normal part of their business. Even the general public—the barber, the bootblack, the taxicab driver—will occasionally take a fling at foreign exchange dealing. As they speculate or back their individual judgments, they are forced to take an active and continuing interest in the affairs of the country in whose currency they are dealing."This was one aspect of a broad phenomenon. "Over here, men's minds inevitably incline toward their neighbors' affairs. In my country, this is not true, and our collective interest in other nations is correspondingly less."

Occasionally Americans looked up from their narrow concerns. When they did, they often mistook what they saw. A decision by President Roosevelt to bolster the American navy had got the country's attention. "People understand battleships. They may not know or care about the exchange of notes or other diplomatic formalities, but they do know about warships. There they are. They can see them; they have to pay for them; their children serve on them. Moreover, to most people a battleship is synonymous with war. Why, they ask themselves, is it necessary to build these costly engines of destruction if we are not contemplating war? Does the president know of some danger which is not apparent to the ordinary citizen?"

The average American had two worries, Kennedy said. "He fears he may lose his job and he fears his country may get into a war." America's elected officials needed to keep this in mind if they wished to remain elected. Cordell Hull, the secretary of state, had been appointed to that position, but he had served in Congress for many years. He understood politics. Hull had recently described the preservation of peace as the cornerstone of American foreign policy. "In that statement he was thoroughly sincere," Kennedy said. "And he spoke the mind of his fellow countrymen. Let there be no doubt whatever on that score. The United States desires peace, not only for itself but for the rest of the world."

Americans were willing to assist in the search for peace. But they would do so on American terms. "Nations, like men, do not consider undertaking business transactions unless they are convinced a common interest exists. We are careful and wary, and I think rightly so, in the relationships we establish with foreign countries." Kennedy hoped his audience was listening carefully. "It would be better for all of us if this traditional American attitude were more clearly understood. Nothing constructive can be built on false hopes." He reiterated: "Any stand the American people take will be based primarily on the fundamental and firm ground of national interest, which is the soundest basis for relations between nations."

Non-Americans, perhaps including some at this dinner, must rid themselves of false expectations regarding America. "My country is unwilling to bind itself to any course of action in the future without an opportunity to examine the situation in the light which then envelops it," Kennedy said. This American attitude did not seem to be well understood. "In some quarters it has been interpreted to mean that our country would not fight under any circumstances short of actual invasion. That is not accurate in my opinion, and it is a dangerous sort of misunderstanding to be current just now. Others seem to imagine that the United States could never remain neutral in the event a general war should unhappily break out. That, I believe, is just as dangerously conceived a misapprehension as the other."

Kennedy repeated that Americans would judge any situation on its merits. "We have no way of knowing what position the United States would take under circumstances which cannot now be foreseen." Americans had not concluded that war in Europe was inevitable. "We prefer to believe that the common sense of the peoples of the world will prevent it. Therefore we do not approach world affairs in the spirit of fatalism." If war did come, Americans would choose the course that seemed best for America at the time. "That is the policy we have followed in the past. It will undoubtedly be our policy in the future."

Americans were appalled by the possibility of war. "We cannot see how armed conflict can be expected to settle any problems or to bring happiness and contentment to any nation. There certainly was no winner in the World War, we can all see now. If another general conflict should unhappily break out, the resulting destruction of man power and painfully accumulated capital wealth would bankrupt the world to a point where a new civilization and a new form of society would have to be slowly and haltingly evolved—something of which we have no conception today."

Kennedy stressed that Britons and others must not take the wrong lesson from America's decision to strengthen its defenses. "As a prudent guardian of his country's safety, President Roosevelt has urged a rearmament program. In doing, so, he stated specifically that he knew of no one corner from which danger is to be expected. He was actuated only by the obvious state of the world around us and the very apparent uncertainties of the future. His recommendation did not mean, by any stretch of the imagination, that he believes a general war to be inevitable." The president didn't think America would be going to war. "The United States has no intention of attacking anyone. It does not expect to be attacked. It is now, and intends to remain, on friendly terms with every country in the world. If the force of events should make it impossible for us to follow this policy, my country will decide, when the time comes, what to do to preserve the welfare of its own citizens."

4

APERS CARRY REPORTS of German invasion of Austria,"
Charles Lindbergh wrote in his journal within days of Kennedy's wake-up call to the British. "Sources too mixed to permit any accurate conclusions. Hope England and Germany can find
some way of working together. If they could do so, there need be no
major war in Europe for many years to come. If they fight again, it
will be chaos."

The union of Austria and Germany—the *Anschluss* that Austrian pan-Germans had called for at the end of the World War
when the empire of Austria-Hungary broke up, and which Hitler
had turned to his own purposes—was accomplished by subversion,
threat and the sincere support of Austrian Nazis. The other European powers—chiefly Britain, France and Italy—stood by, having no
treaty obligations to Austria and scant inclination to step between
the two German-speaking countries.

Lindbergh was relieved that the moment passed without larger
consequence. Yet he was sure Europe's troubles hadn't ended. Hitler
wouldn't be satisfied so easily. "Will there be a major war in Europe?"
he asked himself at the start of April. "If there is, will America be
involved?" Lindbergh's time in England had convinced him that
Britannia's great days were over. "How much longer can this trend
toward mediocrity continue?" he wrote. "What has happened to the
English?"

As the most famous aviator in the world—and one who had traveled the globe since his Paris flight—Lindbergh had been given

the run of aircraft production facilities in every country he visited. His hosts wanted to impress him even as they sought his advice. No one came to know more about the warplanes of the major powers: America, Britain, France, Germany, Italy, Russia, Japan. The British lagged badly, Lindbergh concluded. "The contrast between an English aircraft factory and an American or German factory is un-understandable," he wrote. "The English simply do not seem to have equivalent ability along those lines. God! How they will have to pay for it in the next war. This country has neither the spirit nor the ability needed for a modern war. And the worst of it is that countless Englishmen will die needlessly because of a lack of training and equipment."

He detected a larger failure of the British spirit. "It is not only in aviation that they are behind. I sometimes wonder if history will not eventually show that the British Empire has already passed its greatest period. I cannot see the future for this country." The British thought of themselves as apart from Europe, safe behind their Channel moat. They failed to appreciate the revolution in air combat. "The value of the Channel is passing with every improvement in military aircraft."

At each opportunity Lindbergh told the British what they were up against. But their complacency was impenetrable. "When an Englishman is stating his opinion, anything you say has about as much effect as spray on a rock," he observed. "There is a combination of bluff and vanity in the English that leaves them extremely vulnerable to an enemy who knows these characteristics. Personally, I believe the assets in English character lie in confidence rather than ability; tenacity rather than strength; and determination rather than intelligence."

Lindbergh met Joseph Kennedy at a luncheon hosted by Lady Astor. He discovered a similarity in their views. "It was one of the most interesting lunches I ever attended," Lindbergh wrote. "Always several conversations, each of which I wanted to listen to." The American ambassador surprised him. "Kennedy interested me greatly. He is not the usual type of politician or diplomat. His views on the European situation seem intelligent and interesting. I hope to see more of him."

One reason Roosevelt had sent Kennedy to Europe was to get

him out of the United States, where he might be tempted to run for president in 1940. Lindbergh enthusiasts had been talking of their hero as a presidential candidate; now Roosevelt tried to lure the flyer *back* from Europe to America, where he could keep his eye on him. In June, Lindbergh received a telephone call from New York. Juan Trippe, founder of Pan American Airways, asked him if he would accept the chairmanship of the newly formed Civil Aviation Authority. "Trippe said the request came from headquarters, which means Roosevelt. I wonder what is behind it."

Lindbergh wasn't attracted by the offer. "The appointment would be for six years. They would probably be the six unhappiest years I ever spent." He declined. "I told him that I did not think it advisable to move my family back to America under present circumstances, and that, consequently, I did not see how it would be possible for me to accept the position."

He crossed the Channel and again toured French aircraft facilities. He wasn't encouraged. "France seems to be in worse shape from an aviation standpoint than I believed, and I knew conditions were bad. There are not enough modern military planes in this country to even put up a show in case of war. In a conflict between France, England, and Russia on one side, against Germany on the other, Germany would immediately have supremacy of the air. Even if the present French program is carried out during the next two years, there will be a relatively small number of planes available for service. Germany has developed a huge air force while England has slept and France has deluded herself with a Russian alliance."

What made this most worrisome was that Britain and France had pledged to defend the Versailles settlement against German challenge. They had failed to do so in the matter of German rearmament, and the failure made it more difficult for them to withstand future German offenses—efforts to reverse the territorial transfers imposed by the peace treaty, for example. Lindbergh supposed Britain and France would have to draw the line somewhere. On present trends they wouldn't be able to hold that line. Their irresolution invited aggression; their lack of preparation made aggression's success all too likely.

IN AUGUST 1938 Lindbergh returned to Russia. "Great change in the city since we were last here in 1933," he wrote of Moscow. "Much brighter appearance. Better streets and buildings. People better dressed. Many more motorcars, trucks, and buses." The subway was a showpiece. "Between the museum and the embassy we were given a ride in Moscow's new subway, recently built and probably the best in the world today. Roomy stations and good trains. The cleanest thing I have seen in Moscow." Yet all was not well. "The faces of the people did not seem happy and gave the impression of an underfed body." The government had the first claim on talent. "Best people seemed to be in army and government offices."

He observed the country's latest warplanes in flight. "The Russian air demonstration was rather slow and indicated much less aviation development than exists in the United States, Germany, or England." He examined the fighter planes closely and drew a mixed conclusion. "In general these planes are not as good as the similar designs of the United States, Germany, and England. However, they are good enough to be effective in a modern war."

Lindbergh later learned more about the Soviet Union from Igor Sikorsky, a Russian aircraft designer who had fled the Bolshevik revolution and wound up in America. Sikorsky kept abreast of conditions in Russia even as he conceived new aircraft, including the helicopter, in America. "Sikorsky expects the present system to break down, 'maybe in one year, maybe in a generation,'" Lindbergh wrote. "I think he is right. Conditions in Russia are too bad to continue indefinitely, and the present system cannot work. It kills ability, and that is fatal to the system which causes it. Sikorsky estimates the executions which have taken place in Russia since the war to be in the millions and claims that between 30 and 40 million people have been killed directly or indirectly as a result of the Revolution. Says he knows of one concentration camp where about one hundred people are being executed each day at the present time. He did not state the source of this information."

IN EARLY SEPTEMBER, Lindbergh visited Czechoslovakia, the country then in Hitler's crosshairs. Czechoslovakia had been constructed from the wreckage of Austria-Hungary, and it included territory inhabited by ethnic Germans. A consistent theme of Hitler was the unification of the German-speaking peoples, and Czechoslovakia's Sudeten Germans, as they were called, were next on his list after the Austrians. He demanded cession of the Sudetenland to Germany. The government of Czechoslovakia, headed by Edvard Beneš, resisted, and took some comfort from a guarantee it thought it had from Britain and France to prevent such strong-arming. Yet only *some* comfort, for the British and French appeared to be wobbling on their guarantee.

Lindbergh met with Beneš on September 3. "He asked about modern aircraft and their effectiveness. We spoke of the war in Spain, of the Russian air fleet, of Czechoslovakian aviation. Obvious that he had been, and was, under tension."

Lindbergh wished Beneš and his country well. But they were badly overmatched in any contest with Germany. In his journal Lindbergh wrote, "Czechoslovakia is not well equipped in the air. Her pursuit planes are too slow to be effective against the fast German bombers, and she has only a few fast bombers for counterattack. These have been obtained from Russia." There was no assurance Russia would replace them if doing so risked Hitler's disfavor.

5

THE CRISIS OVER Czechoslovakia intensified during the following weeks, and it provided the chief topic of discussion during a lunch at the American embassy in London. Joseph Kennedy had been watching Lindbergh from a distance and thought it time to sit down with the aviator and hear his views. "Talked with Ambassador Kennedy for an hour after lunch," Lindbergh recorded. "We discussed the crisis and the aviation and general military situation in Europe. Everyone in embassy is extremely worried. Hitler is apparently ready to invade Czechoslovakia and has his divisions on the border. Hitler told Chamberlain"—according to Kennedy—"that he (Hitler) would risk a world war if necessary. Kennedy says England is ready to fight, even though not prepared. Chamberlain realizes the disastrous effects of a war with Germany at this time and is making every effort to avoid one. English opinion"—again according to Kennedy—"is pushing him toward war. It is a terrible situation. The English are in no shape for war. They do not realize what they are confronted with. They have always before had a fleet between themselves and their enemy, and they can't realize the change aviation has made. I am afraid this is the beginning of the end of England as a great power. She may be a 'hornets' nest' but she is no longer a 'lion's den.'"

Later that day Kennedy visited Lindbergh at the latter's hotel. "We talked together for another half hour. Chamberlain is going to meet Hitler again. If Hitler makes more demands, the feeling here is that England will declare war. God knows what the result will be. There is already great criticism of Chamberlain for making concessions to Hitler in regard to Czechoslovakia and the Sudeten territory."

KENNEDY FOUND LINDBERGH to be as interesting as Lindbergh found Kennedy. He asked Lindbergh to put his thoughts on air-power into a form Kennedy could send to Washington. Lindbergh obliged.

Kennedy attached a cover letter to Lindbergh's report, explaining its provenance. "I venture to repeat below the substance of an interesting talk I had yesterday with Colonel Lindbergh regarding the present relative air strength of the great European powers as he sees it, which he has confirmed today in a memorandum," Kennedy wrote to Cordell Hull. "Lindbergh has had unusually favorable opportunities to observe the air establishments of the countries he discusses and has in fact just returned from a trip to Russia. You may feel that this confidential expression of his personal opinion may be of interest to the President and to the War and Navy Departments."

Lindbergh's report was succinct, and sobering to those who hoped to contain German power. "Without doubt the German air fleet is now stronger than that of any other country in the world," he declared. "The rate of progress of German military aviation during the last several years is without parallel. I feel certain that German air strength is greater than that of all other European countries combined, and that she is constantly increasing her margin of leadership. I believe that German factories are now capable of producing in the vicinity of 20,000 aircraft each year. Her actual production is difficult to estimate. The most reliable reports that I have obtained vary from 500 to 800 planes per month.

"The quality of German design is excellent and the extensive research facilities which have been built in that country are a guarantee of continued progress in the future. The Germans long ago established their ability in the design, construction and operations of aircraft. I believe they have the greatest ability of any European nation in the field of aviation. In fact I believe that the United States is the only country in the world capable of competing with Germany in aviation. At present however, Germany is rapidly cutting down the lead we have held in the past. In numbers of fighting planes she is already ahead of us. In time of war, her weakness would undoubtedly lie in her supply of raw materials.

"Germany now has the means of destroying London, Paris, and Praha"—Prague—"if she wishes to do so. England and France together have not enough modern war planes for effective defense or counter attack. France is in a pitiful condition in the air. England is better off but her air fleet is not comparable to Germany's. France is probably now building in the vicinity of 50 planes per month; England probably in the vicinity of 200 first line aircraft. I understood that France hopes to have about 2500 first line planes by the spring of 1940.

"Czechoslovakia has no completely modern aircraft except those obtained from Russia. I saw a number of Russian built bombers on the field at Praha. The Czechoslovakians have excellent machine guns and anti-aircraft guns.

"It is not possible to estimate the Russian air strength. The Russians have copied American factories and purchased American machinery of the most modern type. If operated on American standards these factories might place Russia next to Germany in military aviation. The production is certainly much less on Russian standards. Judging by the general conditions in Russia, I would not place great confidence in the Russian air fleet. However, Russia probably has a sufficient number of planes to make her weight felt in any war she enters. Her aircraft are not the best but their performance is good enough to be effective in modern warfare. I believe the Russian weakness lies in inefficiency and poor organization."

Lindbergh summarized the advantage the Germans had over their potential foes. "Germany has such a preponderance of war planes that she can bomb any city in Europe with comparatively little resistance," Lindbergh wrote. "England and France are far too weak in the air to protect themselves."

6

ROOSEVELT KEPT AMERICA aloof from the crisis over Czechoslovakia. The response to his "quarantine" speech had been tepid at best. Americans remained as disinclined to engage with Europe as Joseph Kennedy had described them to the British as being. Roosevelt, moreover, had elections for Congress to worry about. He had squandered his big win of 1936 on a failed attempt to reform the Supreme Court by adding new justices; following the "court-packing" clunker, the president's hopes for achieving anything substantive in his second term depended on a good showing in the 1938 elections.

Yet he felt he had to say something. So he wrote a letter to the governments of Germany, Czechoslovakia, Britain and France, urging them to continue to talk. "The fabric of peace on the continent of Europe, if not throughout the rest of the world, is in immediate danger," Roosevelt declared. "The consequences of its rupture are incalculable. Should hostilities break out the lives of millions of men, women and children in every country involved will most certainly be lost under circumstances of unspeakable horror."

He moved beyond platitude to explain America's position and signal its intentions. "The United States has no political entanglements. It is caught in no mesh of hatred. Elements of all Europe have formed its civilization. The supreme desire of the American people is to live in peace. But in the event of a general war they face the fact that no nation can escape some measure of the consequences of such a world catastrophe."

At this point in his message, Roosevelt's readers might have thought he was going to offer to mediate. Why else proclaim America's impartial concern? "The traditional policy of the United States has been the furtherance of the settlement of international disputes by pacific means," Roosevelt continued. "It is my conviction that all people under the threat of war today pray that peace may be made before, rather than after, war."

But he made no offer of mediation. He simply counseled further negotiation. "Whatever may be the differences in the controversies at issue and however difficult of pacific settlement they may be, I am persuaded that there is no problem so difficult or so pressing for solution that it cannot be justly solved by the resort to reason rather than by the resort to force," Roosevelt said. "During the present crisis the people of the United States and their Government have earnestly hoped that the negotiations for the adjustment of the controversy which has now arisen in Europe might reach a successful conclusion."

He repeated: "So long as negotiations continue, differences may be reconciled. Once they are broken off reason is banished and force asserts itself. And force produces no solution for the future good of humanity."

HITLER ANSWERED ROOSEVELT with the same argument the Nazi chief had been making for years. "In 1918, the German people laid down their arms, in the firm confidence that by the conclusion of peace with their enemies at that time the principles and ideals would be realized which had been solemnly announced by President Wilson and had been just as solemnly accepted as binding by all the belligerent powers," Hitler said. "Never in history has the confidence of a people been more shamefully betrayed, than it was then. The peace conditions imposed on the conquered nations in the Paris suburbs treaties have fulfilled nothing of the promises given. Rather have they created a political regime in Europe which made of the conquered nations world pariahs without rights and which must be recognized in advance by every discerning person as untenable."

The Sudeten issue was part of this untenable regime. "One of the points in which the character of the dictates of 1919 was the most openly revealed was the founding of the Czechoslovakian State, and the establishment of its boundaries without any consideration of history and nationality. The Sudeten land was also included therein, although this area had always been German, and although its inhabitants, after the destruction of the Hapsburg monarchy, had unanimously declared their desire for annexation to the German Reich. Thus the right of self-determination, which had been proclaimed by President Wilson as the most important basis of national life, was simply denied to the Sudeten Germans."

All Germany sought at present was a rectification of this historic mistake. His government had negotiated in good faith, Hitler said. But the Czechoslovakian government had not. Fault for the present impasse lay in Prague. "It is not Germany who is to blame for the fact that there is any Sudeten German problem at all, and that the present unjustifiable circumstances have arisen from it. The terrible fate of the people affected by the problem no longer admits of a further postponement of its solution." The future was out of his hands, Hitler said. "It does not rest with the German Government, but with the Czechoslovakian Government alone, to decide, whether it wants peace or war."

7

LINDBERGH PREPARED FOR the worst. "Went to Morgan Grenfell this morning and cashed $500.00 check," he wrote on September 23, referring to the London bank. "It will be necessary to have an amount of ready money if trouble starts. Five hundred dollars will not go far, but it will be enough to travel on for a few days." Londoners were nervous. "People on streets are talking war. I hear bits of their conversation as I pass by." Other actions were more sobering still. "Makes one think, to see gas masks being fitted in the center of London."

Attitudes changed by the hour. "News seems a little better tonight," Lindbergh wrote the next day. "The fact that the German troops have not yet entered Czechoslovakia is an encouraging sign." Lindbergh let his optimism have a moment. "I still think there is a reasonable chance that we will not have war this year."

It was all up to Germany. "Hitler is in a unique position. No one is going to start fighting before he does. Consequently, he can do about as he wishes without danger. He probably enjoys having the fate of the world in his hands, especially after the way the world treated Germany after the war. I cannot blame him too much for making France and England worry a bit, but I cannot believe he will throw Europe into a major war over the present situation. It would take a madman to do that. Hitler is a mystic and a fanatic, but his actions and results in the past do not lead me to believe he is insane."

Londoners argued both sides of the Czech crisis. Oswald Mosley, a baronet by inheritance, had entered British politics as a Conservative, defected to Labour, become disillusioned there too, and finally founded the British Union of Fascists. He and his followers wanted nothing to do with a war against Germany, especially over Czechoslovakia. Meanwhile British Communists, like communists elsewhere, judged Hitler the devil incarnate and demanded he be stopped.

Lindbergh ventured out to hear the arguments. "To get to the Mosley meeting I had to pass through a Communist meeting two or three blocks away," he recorded. "The Mosley meeting was much larger (both were street meetings, and the speakers stood on top of light trucks containing amplifiers). The street was jammed for nearly a block. I listened to Mosley for a few minutes. He was speaking against war with Czechoslovakia, and his statements were not too intelligent. However, Mosley's meeting, and even his speech, was of a much higher quality than that of the Communists. It always seems that the Fascist group is better than the Communist group. Communism seems to draw the worst of men."

Lindbergh had thought no news was good news. Now he wondered. "Conditions look very bad," he wrote on September 25. "Everything still hung on Hitler. "I can't believe he wants to start a general European war, but I wish I felt better."

"Opinion is hardening in England and France," Lindbergh wrote the next day. "No tendency apparent for more concessions." He heard that trenches were being dug in Hyde Park.

Another day increased the tension. "Everyone depressed. Seems less hope every hour." Lindbergh was as depressed as anyone. "Hitler is actually mad if he starts a general war under these circumstances. No one can win anything worth having. The best blood of Europe will be dead when it is over. The last war took more than we could afford to lose."

Nighttime offered no respite. "Kept waking up at intervals during the night, thinking about England being bombed," Lindbergh wrote. The next day he went to the embassy to receive one of the gas masks the U.S. Army had sent for distribution to American nationals. "Returned to hotel and adjusted and tested my mask."

Better news arrived. "Headlines on press billboards say Hitler, Mussolini, and Chamberlain are to meet in Munich," Lindbergh wrote. "War is *probably* avoided for the time being, at least. Am not surprised, but very much relieved." If war was indeed avoided, Lindbergh trusted that Britain had learned a lesson. "If she does not wake up now, there is no hope."

Joseph Kennedy gave Lindbergh more reason for optimism. "Everything is looking better," Lindbergh wrote after speaking with the ambassador the next day. Lindbergh credited Kennedy in part. "Kennedy has been very active during the last few days. He had several American cruisers sent to England simply for effect on Germany. He went to see Chamberlain one day on business, and then went back a second time for no reason at all except to have it known that the American Ambassador went twice on the same day to see the Prime Minister about the crisis."

EVENTS PROVED KENNEDY right. At Munich, Britain's Chamberlain and France's Edouard Daladier accepted Hitler's demand for control of the Sudetenland. Edvard Beneš was informed that if he and his government refused to agree, Czechoslovakia would have to fight Germany alone. Hitler and Chamberlain affirmed their mutual desire to resolve all their countries' differences peacefully.

Chamberlain treated the Munich deal as a triumph. He returned to London and announced that he had achieved "peace with honor." The agreement would last. "I believe it is peace for our time." The crowds that greeted Chamberlain with cheers took him at his word.

Beneš and many Czechoslovakians viewed the bargain differently. So did Winston Churchill, a member of Chamberlain's Tory party but a harsh critic of the prime minister. Churchill said he understood the relief the British people felt at the passing of this crisis. But they should know the truth. "They should know that we have sustained a defeat without a war, the consequences of which will travel far with us along our road; they should know that we have passed an awful milestone in our history, when the whole equilibrium of Europe has been deranged, and that the terrible words have for the time being been pronounced against the Western democracies: 'Thou art weighed in the balance and found wanting.' And do not suppose that this is the end. This is only the beginning of the reckoning. This is only the first sip, the first foretaste of a bitter cup which will be proffered to us year by year unless by a supreme recovery of moral health and martial vigour, we arise again and take our stand for freedom as in the olden time."

8

LINDBERGH WAS IN Paris when he learned of the Munich accord. He had received an invitation from William Bullitt, the American ambassador to France, to come for a visit. The embassy elicited memories of his first time in France, at the end of his famous flight. "Seems very strange to be in the room I had in 1927, when Herrick"—Myron Herrick, the ambassador then—"invited me to stay in the embassy, and to gradually remember some of the old surroundings: the court in front, the staircase, the corner parlor. The rooms have been changed a great deal, but there are still many familiar things. There is a brass plate on the bed I slept in eleven years ago."

Lindbergh discovered that Bullitt had invited him to Paris because he needed help in circumventing America's neutrality laws. Bullitt's scheme was for American manufacturers to build warplanes in Canada, whence they might be shipped to France and Britain without regard to American law. Lindbergh knew the manufacturers and they respected him; Bullitt wanted Lindbergh to pitch the plan to them.

Lindbergh responded coolly. "While it is of great importance for England and France to build up their military strength, especially in the air, there are more immediate and pressing problems," he wrote in his journal, paraphrasing what he had told Bullitt. "These consist of, first, the need for a different spirit among the people and, second, the absolute necessity of a changed attitude toward Germany if a disastrous war is to be avoided in the future." The French grossly overestimated their ability to make Germany bend to their will. They needed to reduce the gap between their diplomatic desires and their military strength. There was no shortcut to the latter. "Strength is necessary for character and for survival, but strength cannot be bought by gold, except temporarily, and with the danger of bringing greater demoralization at a later date. Strength is an inherent quality in a people. No amount of foreign aircraft will give France the security she wishes." France needed to learn to build her own planes. "The purchase of aircraft abroad would be second only to the hiring of soldiers—the last act of a dying nation."

Lindbergh had another objection. For American companies to build factories in Canada for the purpose Bullitt described would give the companies a perverse incentive. "Those who take part in the establishment of factories in Canada for the production of warplanes for France will be considered successful only in case a war is fought. Therefore, success would depend upon the destruction of European civilization."

Lindbergh had a counterproposal. "I suggested that France purchase some bombers from Germany. Of course, this astounded everyone at the table, but it was accepted with more calmness than I expected (after the first laugh, when they took the suggestion as a joke)." But Lindbergh wasn't joking. Trade would tend to ease tension between the two countries, he judged, and cooperation between their military professionals would counteract the rivalries of their politicians.

"I intend to carry this idea further," Lindbergh said. If nothing else, the response of the interested parties to his idea would reveal their sincerity. "I believe this would depend very largely upon Germany's future intentions and the attitude of France and England in regard to them."

While in Paris, Lindbergh reviewed France's air force. He flew one of the latest French planes and found it disappointing. "The most amazing fact, however, is that if war had come last week, France did not have a single modern pursuit plane ready for the defense of Paris! There was not, and is not, in France one fighting plane as fast as the latest German bombers! The French air fleet is almost nonexistent from the standpoint of a modern war. And many people in France and in England were advising their governments to declare war!"

WITH ANNE HE proceeded to Germany. If a war had broken out, he wouldn't have had such freedom, but peace had held, and he wanted to take the opportunity while he still could. "Berlin has greatly changed," he wrote. "Much more activity of every kind; buildings going up, great increase in traffic, store windows more attractive. In fact, Berlin has lost the air of tenseness I noticed in 1936 and now has the appearance of a healthy, busy, modern city (if the word 'healthy' can be applied to a modern city)." Lindbergh didn't like cities.

He spoke with officials of Lufthansa, Germany's flag airline. He visited an antiaircraft regiment and battery on the outskirts of Berlin. He toured a factory that made engines for warplanes, and another that produced finished bombers. Of an example of the latter he wrote, "This is an excellent light bomber. Undoubtedly one of the best in existence." He flew a Messerschmitt fighter. "The plane handled beautifully."

He was shown plans for the modernization of Berlin. "They are to take from ten to fifteen years to complete, and contemplate tearing down and rebuilding huge areas. The proposed architecture is simple and attractive. This is undoubtedly the greatest city-building project of modern times."

Lindbergh thought the Germans were on to something. "I am anxious to learn more about this country. The Germans are a great people, and I believe their welfare is inseparable from that of Europe. The future of Europe depends upon the strength of this country. It cannot be kept down except by war, and another European war would be disastrous for everyone."

Lindbergh attended a dinner at the British embassy in Berlin. The British ambassador, Nevile Henderson, asked Lindbergh's opinion of German aviation. Lindbergh told him it was the best in Europe. The ambassador agreed and said he hoped Lindbergh would convey that message to government officials back in Britain. "He said they did not believe him when he described it."

He was invited to a dinner at the American embassy. "Marshal Goering, of course, was the last to arrive," Lindbergh noted of Hermann Goering, the fighter ace from the World War who had become Hitler's right-hand man and head of the air force. "I was standing in the back of the room. He shook hands with everyone. I noticed that he had a red box and some papers in his hand. When he came to me, he shook hands, handed me the box and papers, and spoke a few sentences in German." Lindbergh did not speak German. "I found that he had presented me with the German Eagle, one of the highest German decorations, 'by order of der Führer.'"

Lindbergh's decoration would become notorious; at the time, he hardly noticed it.

"Later in the evening Goering came over and suggested that we go into the next room and talk," Lindbergh wrote. The air marshal had heard that Lindbergh and Anne had been in Russia. "Goering asked me why we had gone to Russia; what the hotels were like; whether many Russians stayed in the hotels; how the Russian cities compared to other cities; and many other questions. I talked to him frankly about what we saw in Russia and the impressions we had during our trip."

Goering turned the talk to aviation. "He spoke of the performances of present military planes and of the quantity of production. He said the new Junkers 88 bomber (which no one we know has seen) is far ahead of anything else built, and that he would arrange that it be shown to me. Goering said the Junkers 88 did 500 kilometers per hour and that it was not 'a magazine figure,' but an actual speed of 500 kilometers. He said they expected to have a plane which would make 800 kilometers per hour in the near future (at critical altitude)."

Lindbergh couldn't tell if Goering was boasting. On the basis of what he himself had seen, he thought not, or not much.

Goering grew philosophical. "He spoke at length on the ability of a man to attack any problem, regardless of his previous experience. Said there was too much tendency to think a man had to be a specialist before he could understand a problem, while the fact was that a specialist is often the worst man to put in charge. Goering referred to his own experience with German financial problems. Said that at one time he knew so little about finance that he couldn't even keep his own pocketbook filled. Goering said he told Hitler he would be willing to take on any problem in Germany except the religious problem." That was for others. "He did not know how to solve the religious problem."

9

OTTO TOLISCHUS WAS born in Prussia in the late nineteenth century and emigrated to America as a young man in the early twentieth. He labored as a factory hand before enrolling in Columbia University's school of journalism shortly after that institution launched its effort to transform journalism from a craft into a profession. Tolischus returned to Europe as a correspondent in the 1920s and reported the rise of the Nazis in Germany in the 1930s. He covered the transcription of Nazi anti-Semitism—a foundation of the party's ideology—into German law. He recounted the exclusion of Jews from the German civil service and German professions; he explained the meaning and portent of the "Nuremberg laws"—so-called from their unveiling at a Nazi rally in Nuremberg in 1935—depriving Jews of German citizenship and political rights and barring them from marrying non-Jews. Tolischus was in Berlin in November 1938.

"A wave of destruction, looting and incendiarism unparalleled in Germany since the Thirty Years War and in Europe generally since the Bolshevist revolution, swept over Great Germany today as the National Socialist cohorts took vengeance on Jewish shops, offices and synagogues for the murder by a young Polish Jew of Ernst Vom Rath, third secretary of the German Embassy in Paris," Tolischus wrote in a cabled report to the *New York Times*. "Beginning systematically in the early morning hours in almost every town and city in the country, the wrecking, looting and burning continued all day. Huge but mostly silent crowds looked on and the police confined themselves to regulating traffic and making wholesale arrests of Jews 'for their own protection.'"

The violence lasted many hours. "All day the main shopping districts as well as the side streets of Berlin and innumerable other places resounded to the shattering of shop windows falling to the pavement, the dull thuds of furniture and fittings being pounded to pieces and the clamor of fire brigades rushing to burning shops and synagogues. Although shop fires were quickly extinguished, synagogue fires were merely kept from spreading to adjoining buildings."

The campaign concluded when it ran out of targets. "By nightfall there was scarcely a Jewish shop, café, office or synagogue in the country that was not either wrecked, burned severely or damaged," Tolischus wrote.

Joseph Goebbels, the Nazi minister of information, rationalized the violence. "The justified and understandable anger of the German people over the cowardly Jewish murder of a German diplomat in Paris found extensive expression during last night," Goebbels declared. "In numerous cities and towns of the Reich retaliatory action has been undertaken against Jewish buildings and businesses." Goebbels called off the thugs even as he hinted at the government's next step. "A strict request is issued to the entire population to cease immediately all further demonstrations and actions against Jewry, no matter what kind. A final answer to the Jewish assassination in Paris will be given to Jewry by way of legislation and ordinance."

LINDBERGH WAS IN Paris when he read about what came to be called "Kristallnacht," or "Night of Broken Glass." The violence puzzled and dismayed him. "I do not understand these riots on the part of the Germans," he wrote. "It seems so contrary to their sense of order and their intelligence in other ways. They have undoubtedly had a difficult Jewish problem, but why is it necessary to handle it so unreasonably? My admiration for the Germans is constantly being dashed against some rock such as this. What is the object in this persecution of the Jews? Do the Germans feel that in this way they can frighten all Jews sufficiently to prevent such incidents as the Herr vom Rath shooting? Or is this a countermove to the Jewish pressure on Germany? Or, by bringing up the Jewish issue and forcing German Jews into other countries, do the Germans hope to create an international anti-Jewish movement? Or is it simply German hatred of the Jews—at least on the part of members of the present government? Probably a combination of these and other factors."

Erhard Milch was a top aide to Goering. Lindbergh encountered him in Paris and learned more about the violence—perhaps. "Milch told me that the recent anti-Jewish demonstrations 'were not done by Goering and were not done by Hitler,'" Lindbergh recorded. "I suppose this means that Himmler and Goebbels were responsible. The general feeling in Berlin seems to be that Goering was very much opposed to what has happened and leads the 'element of moderation' in the party. The German people seem to be definitely anti-Jewish but ashamed of the violence with which the last demonstrations were carried on." Lindbergh had some confidence in what he was hearing, but not complete confidence. "In the contacts I have had up to date in Germany no officer has lied to me or attempted to mislead me. Of course, it is always necessary to consider such a possibility."

Germany's anti-Semitism distressed Lindbergh. The Germans were models of restraint and civilized behavior in nearly all areas but this. "During the days I was in Berlin I tried to obtain a better understanding of the German mind in regard to the Jewish problem. Germans all seem to be anti-Jewish, but in varying degrees. I did not talk to a single person who I felt was not ashamed of the lawlessness and disorder of the recent demonstrations. But neither did I talk to anyone who did not want the Jews to get out of Germany, even though they disagreed with the methods now being used. The Jew, according to the German, is largely responsible for the internal collapse and revolution following the war. At the time of the inflation the Jews are said to have obtained the ownership of a large percentage of property in Berlin and other cities—lived in the best houses, drove the best automobiles, and mixed with the prettiest German girls."

To his French contacts Lindbergh preached the need to reach some kind of accord with Germany. "I told la Chambre that the Germans I talked to seemed to strongly favor a better understanding with France. I told him I felt there was more chance of an understanding with Germany now than there had been previously and that if it were possible for France and Germany to work together, peace could be maintained in Western Europe for an indefinite period."

Lindbergh feared for Western civilization if Europe went to war again. Germany had to be accommodated in some way. "I think it is of vital importance to come to some understanding with Germany. In fact, I believe the future welfare of Western civilization depends largely upon the strength of Germany and the avoidance of a major war in Western Europe."

THE NEW YEAR—1939—BROUGHT no immediate new crisis but neither did it furnish cause for comfort. "European affairs are becoming more disturbed. England is, I believe, in desperate situation," Lindbergh wrote in London in January. "She has been asleep too long, and in the changed conditions of the modern world I am afraid her old position of leadership has gone. Aviation has largely destroyed the security of the Channel, and her superiority of manufacture is a thing of the past. The conditions which built the British Empire were far different than those of today."

His opinion was sought by the well-connected. "Lord Astor asked me what I would do if I were the Prime Minister and had to come to some agreement with Germany on air disarmament. He placed his question in two parts: 1) What ratio should England demand of Germany in limiting air power, and what ratio would give her safety, i.e., one to one, one to two, or what? 2) Should there be an attempt to abolish bombers completely, and if so, how could they be described?" In the 1920s the great powers had curtailed naval fleets according to agreed ratios; could the same be done with air fleets?

Lindbergh appreciated the understanding that informed the question, and also the difficulty of finding an answer. Without careful study, he told Astor, he could offer only an imperfect plan. "I told him that my observations had led me to believe that Germany was the natural air power of Europe, that her record in the design, construction, and operation of aircraft spoke for itself, and that in addition it was necessary to realize that Germany had certain geographical advantages which England lacked. I told Lord Astor that if I were a German I would demand a minimum of two to one with England in the air. I told him I would be surprised if the Germans did not demand the same superiority in the air that England has on the sea, i.e., three to one."

Lindbergh confessed he didn't know enough of British air strategy to say what would be acceptable to Britain. "I would not attempt to suggest what ratio the Prime Minister should agree to, or what ratio would give England safety from air attack. I brought out the point that even if England had equal numbers with Germany, London was much more vulnerable to attack than Berlin because of her population, centralization of government and industry, and proximity to the border. Berlin is less centralized, and attacking aircraft would have to fly over hundreds of miles of German territory, which is thoroughly organized with listening posts, antiaircraft, and pursuit squadrons. Then there are the added difficulties of training pilots in England— worse weather and smaller area."

As for the elimination of bombers, this would be very hard, not least because of definitional problems. "It would be extremely difficult to abolish bombing completely or to describe a bomber accurately enough for effective limitation. I mentioned the fact that a commercial transport could be transformed very quickly to a bomber, especially if it had been designed with that transformation in view. Then, a two-engine pursuit plane could be turned into a fast light bomber by the simple installation of wing bomb racks. Also, factories can start the production of bombers with great rapidity if plans are laid for doing so in advance. On the whole, bombing aviation is far more difficult to define and limit than battleships, which are far different than merchantmen and which require years to build."

Lindbergh added that a prerequisite to negotiating arms control in planes was a political consensus in Britain on what to do if negotiations failed. "I told Lord Astor that it seemed to me necessary to consider how far England could and would compete with Germany in military aviation before deciding what ratio she would be willing to accept in a disarmament program."

He met Neville Chamberlain, who looked "amazingly young and well." The prime minister's appearance belied his nearly seventy years. "I would not have judged him to be over sixty, and one would never believe that he has been going through one of the most difficult periods in British history."

At the Astors' Lindbergh met Lord Lothian, soon to be ambassador to America. "He has just come back from a trip to the United States and knows America exceptionally well for an Englishman. We discussed the possibility of war this year. It is the subject of most conversations. He feels, as I do, that a general war in 1939 is unlikely and that a lasting peace is by no means impossible provided 1) that Germany is given a reasonable opportunity for trade and influence; 2) that German leadership does not go mad with the feeling of power and destiny."

Lindbergh shared the hope, and the fear. "I think I have a little more confidence in the sanity of German leadership than he has. What I am most afraid of is that a combination of stupid moves on both sides may make each seem mad in the eyes of the other. He agrees with me that France, England, and America are just as responsible for present conditions in Germany as the Germans are themselves."

Lothian described the danger to democracy from the present European situation. "Said it was essential for the United States to take part in preserving it and that England could not carry on longer alone, as the cost was too high for her to bear. He advocates some sort of organization among the democratic nations."

Lindbergh thought this was casting the net too widely. "I told him that I regarded alliances of strength as necessary in these times, but that I did not think a world-wide democracy either desirable or possible. I said that I thought any attempted organization should be confined to Western European peoples (in the sense that would include America) and that such an organization would be difficult enough to bring about. I told him I felt democracy's danger was internal and not external."

Lindbergh liked the time he spent at the Astors' yet suspected he was experiencing the end of an epoch. "Cliveden gives one the feeling of stepping back a century into the feudal days of England. The great halls, filled with paintings, tapestries, suits of armor, and fireplaces, do not seem to belong to the modern world. The house sometimes makes me think of a dinosaur which has outlived its age, to give the people of a new era the opportunity of tasting the life of the old one. But is England herself not in the same position? I wonder if someday Jon and Land"—his sons—"will see Cliveden open as a museum for the public, with felt-covered ropes holding curious hands away from the beds and chairs and tables."

LINDBERGH SPENT MORE time with Joseph Kennedy. "I cannot help liking Kennedy. He is an unusual combination of politician and businessman. He has, I believe, raised a good family, and he has apparently given his children an important place in his life. I admire and greatly respect this quality in his character. He has great vanity, but he also has ability. He does not seem to like the press, yet seems fascinated by it, and, I understand, keeps his own public relations representative. I am not sure whether he enjoys being in the spotlight of publicity or whether he simply considers it a necessity in present conditions. I doubt that he knows himself. However, I place him among the men who are a constructive influence in this so-called modern world. Kennedy does not expect war this year and feels that Chamberlain has handled the situation well."

The question was: What would Germany do next? And would Italy follow Germany's lead? "No one seems to know that," Lindbergh remarked. "I wonder if Hitler and Mussolini do themselves. I, personally, do not see how Germany and Italy can move effectively against France or England without too high a cost (i.e., from a military standpoint). The English fleet, the Maginot Line, and the French Army form a combination which will be difficult to overcome." Common sense appeared to preclude another war. "The only cause I can see for a general European war at this time would be if Germany desires one for retaliation for the last, and I do not think that is the case. Why should she try to move west at great expense when the Danube basin and the East are open to her desires? I look for Germany to 'dig in' on the western border and continue her eastward expansion." Hitler was the key; Mussolini would take his cue from the German leader. "What Italy does must conform to German policy."

Lindbergh asked Kennedy if he could see any other path for Germany. "He could not, he said, although Germany might be mad enough to want a European war."

Meanwhile Britain seemed to be sleepwalking. Lindbergh

attended a play in London. "The acting was excellent and the play reasonably well written," he wrote. Its theme was timely, in a way the playwright perhaps had not intended. "It left me with the impression of a rather decadent English family struggling on for one more generation. In a strange way it depressed me, for it reminded me so much of present-day English life—loss of spirit and hope and spark, nearing the end of a great era, without more than vague realization, and with a sort of dazed complacency. Everything done too late—marriage, children, the feel of life, and then that desperate attempt to catch up, to bring back lost opportunity, and the feeling that they have succeeded in bringing back true life by that gesture. A great past, a failing present, a gallant but aged attempt—England, the only hope resting in another generation, which by some Mendelian law may inherit the spark of genius which built this empire."

Britain's decline preoccupied Lindbergh, not least since the British appeared oblivious to it. "I think that Chamberlain has done a good job with the material and conditions he had to work with. His acceptance of the facts and conditions which existed is, I think, one of the greatest things about him." But the narrow escape from war hadn't prompted the necessary reforms. "England is making a great effort only by her own comfortable, accepted standards of life, and that is not enough these days. Effort, like everything else, is relative. England's standard of effort should be that which is being made against her. She is, of course, being influenced by the German Reich, but she is not able to assess properly anything which is not British and, consequently, is unable even to assess properly that which is. England is surrounded by military power, yet will not even change her ways enough in these critical times to enforce universal military training."

Germany had learned the lessons Britain taught the world better than the British had. "It is a strange fact that the country which started the industrial revolution seems singularly ill-adapted to the results of industrial life," Lindbergh wrote. "The English mind seems more attuned to the age of ships than to the age of aircraft. Now that action is quick and time short, it seems to me the Englishman is at a fatal disadvantage."

Lindbergh feared what Britain's decline, and Britain's slowness to recognize its decline, augured for others. "I am afraid that the readjustment which must result will bring great hardship. The important thing is to avoid letting this readjustment overthrow our entire civilization. One danger is that people do not yet fully realize that the balance of power has changed among nations." The Germany of 1939 was not the Germany of 1919, and the Germans must not be treated as though it was. "Their rights have changed accordingly. If these rights cannot be asserted by peaceful means, war will probably be resorted to."

10

IN JANUARY 1939 an airplane crashed in a parking lot near Los Angeles. The plane was a fighter built by the Douglas Aircraft Company, based in Santa Monica. The pilot died in the crash, but a passenger survived. The company identified the passenger as a mechanic for the firm. This proved to be incorrect. Reporters learned and their papers printed that he was a representative of the French government, sent to examine the Douglas plane with an eye to purchasing the model for the French air corps.

The French connection to American aircraft manufacture had not been revealed previously. An administration spokesman felt obliged to say that, yes, President Roosevelt was aware of the connection and had approved the sale of Douglas planes to France. In fact the administration was facilitating the sale.

The news produced an outburst of criticism against Roosevelt and the secret foreign policy he was said to be conducting. To stem the criticism Roosevelt summoned the seventeen members of the Senate military affairs committee to the White House. For more than an hour the members heard Roosevelt expound on what American defense required and how it would best be secured.

The session was supposed to calm things, but it had the opposite effect. Those in attendance were sworn to secrecy, a requirement that made the allegations of a secret policy the more plausible. Yet the swearing didn't stop some attendees from relating, in vague and suggestive terms, language that had been discussed. "Mr. Roosevelt, it was said, had outlined in gloomy terms the military position of Brit-

ain and France, and had given the impression that, short of actual
military support in time of war, he intended to give those democratic
nations all possible aid, particularly in the form of planes, munitions
and war machinery," the *New York Times* said. "Most sensational
of all, it was reported that the President had asked the Senators to
regard America's frontier, in any war involving the dictatorships and
the democracies, as 'in France.' This remark, in paraphrase of Stanley
Baldwin's historic statement a few years back that henceforth Britain's frontier would be on the Rhine, soon was being interpreted as
meaning that America's frontier also was on the Rhine." Baldwin was
then British prime minister.

Roosevelt tried again to calm the furor. At a press conference on
February 3, he gave his version of what had been related at the meeting with the senators. He said that nothing had changed in America's
foreign policy, and that nothing important was being withheld from
the American people. The fuss was much ado about nothing, the
result of cynical misinformation. "A great many people, some members of the House, some members of the Senate, and quite a number
of newspaper owners, are deliberately putting before the American
people a deliberate misrepresentation of fact—deliberate." These
self-interested parties were trying to score political points ahead of
the 1940 election. Roosevelt gestured toward a pile of newspapers on
his desk. "There isn't one story or one headline in all of those papers
that does not give, to put it politely, an erroneous impression. Not
one. It is a rather interesting fact. These things have been manufactured by deliberate misrepresentation of facts, existing facts."

"The foreign policy has not changed and it is not going to change,"
Roosevelt continued. Going on the record, he spelled it out: "Number 1: We are against any entangling alliances, obviously. Number 2:
We are in favor of the maintenance of world trade for everybody—
all nations, including ourselves. Number 3: We are in complete sympathy with any and every effort made to reduce or limit armaments.
Number 4: As a nation—as American people—we are sympathetic
with the peaceful maintenance of political, economic and social
independence of all nations in the world."

Roosevelt went off the record again. "Now, that is very, very simple," he said. "There is absolutely nothing new in it. The American
people are beginning to realize that the things they have read and

heard, both from agitators of the legislative variety and the agitators of the newspaper owner variety, have been pure bunk—b-u-n-k,
bunk; that these people are appealing to the ignorance, the prejudice
and the fears of Americans and are acting in an un-American way.
You will also notice that quite a number of them are receiving the
loud acclaim, the applause, of those governments in the world which
do not believe in the continued independence of all nations."

A reporter asked if Roosevelt could be more explicit about what
took place at the meeting with the senators, especially in light of the
stories that were being circulated about it. Was the secrecy surrounding the meeting really necessary?

"I will ask you a question," Roosevelt responded. "Suppose I had
information which came in through the intelligence service, that
such and such things were going on in such and such a country.
There are no names, no way of proving the information before a
court, and yet it is information which, because it has been checked
from two or three different sources, looks to be, as far as we can tell
now, reasonably true. Now suppose I held a press conference every
day and gave out information of that kind to the public. In the first
place, we are not definitely sure of it; it would be almost like certain
stories that you read—many of them are true, many of them turn out
later on not to be true. In the second place, giving out information of
that kind would completely terminate the getting of future information, because the sources of the information would be immediately
blocked.

"Now, in that conference the other day, I told them of some things,
information of that type, which at the present time we believe to be
true, but it is not the kind of thing to write a newspaper story about
because it may not be true. It is merely our best slant as of today. It
may be changed two weeks or a month from now by other information." That was the extent of the secrecy of the meeting with the
senators. "The rest of the conference related solely to what I have
just given you."

A reporter zeroed in on the explosive claim about the meeting.
"You are supposed to have told some of the conferees that the Rhine
was our frontier in the battle of democracies versus fascism," the
reporter said.

"Shall I be polite or call it by the right name?" responded Roosevelt.

"Call it by the right name."

"Deliberate lie."

"May we quote that?"

"Yes."

II

A MID THE CRISIS over Czechoslovakia in the autumn of 1938, Hitler had said the Sudetenland was the limit of his territorial ambitions. The unification of the German-speaking peoples was his aim; in others he had no interest. Either he had been lying then or his appetite grew with the eating, for in March 1939 he declared that he must have the rest of Czechoslovakia. He mobilized his troops and tanks and planes for an invasion. The dispirited government of Czechoslovakia, receiving no sign of help from Britain or France, gave way to the pressure and told its troops to stand down. German forces rolled in, extinguishing the twenty-year-old country and creating a puppet state in its place.

Neville Chamberlain was embarrassed by Hitler's mendacity and his own gullibility. The British prime minister drew a new line, declaring that if Hitler moved against Poland, the most likely next target, Britain would fight on Poland's behalf. The French government announced it would do the same.

FRANKLIN ROOSEVELT WEIGHED in more ambiguously. The president made no move to stop the seizure of Czechoslovakia, but in its wake he called on Hitler to stop using threats of force against Germany's neighbors. "Hundreds of millions of human beings are living today in constant fear of a new war or even a series of wars," Roosevelt said in a letter released to the newspapers. Threats eroded the trust on which civilization rested. "If such threats continue, it seems inevitable that much of the world must become involved in common ruin. All the world, victor nations, vanquished nations, and neutral nations, will suffer."

Roosevelt refused to accept this as humanity's fate. "On the contrary, it is clear that the leaders of great nations have it in their power to liberate their peoples from the disaster that impends. It is equally clear that in their own minds and in their own hearts the peoples themselves desire that their fears be ended."

Hitler had claimed that Germany did not want war. "If this is true there need be no war," Roosevelt said. Remarking that America had no stake in the quarrels of Europe, the president offered to forward a message of conciliation from Germany to its frightened neighbors. "I trust that you may be willing to make such a statement of policy to me as head of a nation far removed from Europe in order that I, acting only with the responsibility and obligation of a friendly intermediary, may communicate such declaration to other nations now apprehensive as to the course which the policy of your government may take."

Roosevelt challenged Hitler to prove his good faith. "Are you willing to give assurance that your armed forces will not attack or invade the territory or possessions of the following independent nations"—he listed some thirty countries of Europe and the Middle East. "If such assurance is given by your government, I shall immediately transmit it to the governments of the nations I have named and I shall simultaneously inquire whether, as I am reasonably sure, each of the nations enumerated will in turn give like assurance for transmission to you."

For America's part, Roosevelt proposed to devote his government to disarmament, in order to reduce the risk of a disastrous war, and to trade expansion, to promote cross-border connections.

Roosevelt reiterated that responsibility for world peace fell on the leaders of the great powers. "Heads of great governments in this hour are literally responsible for the fate of humanity in the coming years. They cannot fail to hear the prayers of their peoples to be protected from the foreseeable chaos of war. History will hold them accountable for the lives and the happiness of all—even unto the least. I hope that your answer will make it possible for humanity to lose fear and regain security for many years to come."

HITLER RESPONDED IN a speech to the Reichstag. Pointedly observing that Roosevelt's letter had been published in America before it reached him in Berlin, Hitler said he deemed it appropriate to give his answer to the representatives of the German people before Roosevelt got it.

Hitler defended the territorial changes he had set in motion. "The present Greater German Reich contains no territory which was not from the earliest times part of this Reich, not bound up with or subject to its sovereignty. Long before an American continent had been discovered—to say nothing of settled—by white people, the Reich existed, not merely in its present extent but with the addition of many regions and provinces which have since been lost." Hitler proceeded from this reference to the Holy Roman Empire to a repetition of the tale of Germany's betrayal at the Paris peace conference and in the Versailles treaty. He recounted the financial burden placed upon the German people, a burden unfair and beyond the capacity of any people to repay. He described the "senseless dismemberment of peoples and states" that led to the impoverishment of the German-speaking regions of Europe during the postwar years.

He justified the annexation of Austria as rejoining the two great German states. "I should have sinned against my call by Providence had I failed in my own endeavor to lead my native country and my German people of Ostmark"—the Nazi name for Austria as a province—"back to the Reich and, thus, to the community of German people." The seizure of Czechoslovakia corrected the cynical designs of the Paris victors in planting a satellite state in the heart of Central Europe.

He professed no hostility toward Britain; quite the opposite. "The Anglo-Saxon people have accomplished immeasurable colonizing work in the world. For this work I have sincere admiration." Yet Britain must accord Germany comparable respect. "I regard it as impossible to achieve lasting friendship between the German and Anglo-Saxon peoples if the other side does not recognize that there are German as well as British interests, that not only is preservation of the British Empire the meaning and purpose of the lives of Britishers, but also that for Germans freedom and preservation of the German Reich is their life and purpose." Germany wouldn't tamper with Britain's empire; Britain must not stand in the way of Germany's revival of the German empire.

Hitler reiterated that he and the German people were merely reclaiming what had been German in times past. "We do not want anything that did not formerly belong to us, and no state will ever be robbed by us of its property." But Germany would not be deprived of its due. "Whoever believes that he is able to attack Germany will find himself confronted with a measure of power and resistance comparable to which that of 1914 was negligible."

Finally getting around to Roosevelt's letter, Hitler noted the president's solicitude for people living under the shadow of war. But who was really casting the shadow? During recent decades the United States had repeatedly occupied countries of Central America and the Caribbean. Was the president speaking of the people there? The American president had stated that war had serious and lasting consequences. Hitler responded, "No one knows this better than the German people." They had been living with the consequences of the World War since 1918. Roosevelt had said countries should go to war only in defense of their home territory. Why had the United States not followed this rule in the World War?

The American president had declared that international problems could be solved at the council table. If so, why had the United States boycotted the League of Nations? And why had America not submitted its own disputes to international arbitration? "The freedom of North America was not achieved at the conference table any more than the conflict between the North and the South was decided there," Hitler observed. "I will say nothing about the innumerable struggles which finally led to the subjugation of the North American continent as a whole."

Roosevelt had asked for a German pledge to respect the sovereignty of a list of nations. These included Ireland. Hitler said he had just read a speech by Eamon de Valera, the Irish leader. "Strangely enough, and contrary to Mr. Roosevelt's opinion, he does not charge Germany with oppressing Ireland, but reproaches England with subjecting Ireland to continuous aggression at her hands." Likewise Palestine. "The fact has obviously escaped Mr. Roosevelt's notice that Palestine is at present occupied not by German troops but by the English; and that the country is having its liberty restricted by the most brutal resort to force, is being robbed of its independence and is suffering the cruelest maltreatment for the benefit of Jewish interlopers."

Roosevelt had said that the leaders of the great powers were, at this critical hour, responsible for the fate of humanity. "Mr. Roosevelt!" said Hitler sarcastically. "I fully understand that the vastness of your nation and the immense wealth of your country allows you to feel responsible for the history of the whole world and for the history of all nations." Germany was not so large or wealthy.

Yet it was enough for the Germans. "My world, Mr. Roosevelt, in which Providence has placed me and for which I am therefore obliged to work, is unfortunately much smaller, although for me it is more precious than anything else, for it is limited to my people."

12

Y ET *WAS IT* enough? Would Hitler be satisfied with the bites he had taken out of the Versailles settlement, or had his appetite merely been piqued? He had previously said he was satisfied and then changed his story. Would he change his story again? This was the question on which the fate of Europe hung.

Lindbergh didn't believe Hitler. Lindbergh acknowledged that Chamberlain had no choice but to draw a line against further German aggression. All the same, the prospects were alarming. "If England and France attempt to stop the German eastward movement there will be war, a war in which England and France will have to attack. That would mean the loss of many of the best men in Europe. A general war now will be disastrous, yet it is coming closer and is considered inevitable by many people. Why in heaven's name did not England move in 1934 if she intended to stop Germany? These last five years of indecision may well bring the end of her empire, if not of all Europe."

Lindbergh's dismal opinion of Britain declined further. "The more I see of modern England and the English people, the less confidence I have in them. She took part in Versailles. She stood by and watched Germany rearm and march into the Rhineland. She imposed sanctions against Italy. She advised a Czech mobilization last spring. She advised them to surrender to Germany last fall. She recognizes Franco after originally opposing him, at least unofficially. And now she wants to guarantee Polish integrity. And Lord knows what else. Where is the long-range vision, the stability, and the strength that we were brought up to believe lay in Great Britain? Her present actions seem desperate."

Lindbergh thought the British had placed themselves at Hitler's mercy. "This man, damned almost everywhere except in his own country, called a fanatic and a madman, now holds the future of Europe in his hand. Civilization depends upon his wisdom far more than on the action of the democracies. Whether he now desires to or not, Hitler can dominate all of the Eastern Hemisphere if he uses intelligence and lays his plans well. I am more than ever depressed by the shortsightedness and vacillation of democratic statesmen. Much as I disapprove of many things Germany has done, I believe she has pursued the only consistent policy in Europe in recent years. I cannot support her broken promises, but she has only moved a little faster than other nations have in breaking promises. The question of right and wrong is one thing by law and another thing by history." At the moment, Hitler was the one making the history.

LINDBERGH AND ANNE decided to return to America. With Europe on the edge of war they sought a safer place for their children. They had been away for three years; they hoped the newsreels and scandal sheets had found others to harass. He went first to find a house to rent; Anne would bring the children over later.

He wasn't encouraged by his reception at the pier in New York. "Both sides of the corridor and stairs were lined with cameramen and flashing, blinding lights," he wrote. "They started shoving and blocking the way in front of us. The police immediately formed a wedge and pushed them out of the way. There were dozens of uniformed police in addition to many plain-clothes men. All the way along the deck the photographers ran in front of us and behind us, jamming the way, being pushed aside by the police, yelling, falling over each other on the deck. There must have been over a hundred of them, and the planks were covered with the broken glass of the flashlight bulbs they threw away. I have never seen as many at one time before, even in 1927, I think. It was a barbaric entry to a civilized country."

He took the train to Washington and reported to the Army Air Corps, headed by Henry Arnold, called Hap. Everyone wanted to talk to him. Some wanted to keep him to themselves. Arnold escorted him to a meeting with Henry Woodring, the secretary of war. "Discussed military aviation in America and Europe. Woodring seems very anxious for me not to testify before any of the congressional committees." Lindbergh didn't object to the ban on speaking to Congress. "As a matter of fact, I prefer not to do so," he remarked. "But I wonder just what politics are working in his mind."

Arnold seemed a straight shooter. "General Arnold impresses me more as I get to know him better. I think our relationship will be a very pleasant one. And I am already beginning to see ways in which I can be of help."

Woodring's boss wanted a piece of Lindbergh. A summons came from the president. Apparently Roosevelt wanted to be seen with the famous flier. "A crowd of press photographers at the door and inane women screeching at me as I passed through—a disgraceful condition to exist on the White House steps," Lindbergh recorded. "Roosevelt was behind with his appointments (as usual, I understand), so I waited for about three-quarters of an hour for mine. Meanwhile, I talked to the Congressmen who were also waiting for appointments—very political they were, but quite interesting and pleasant."

Lindbergh had never met Roosevelt. "He was seated at his desk at one end of a large room. There were several models of ships around the walls. He leaned forward from his chair to meet me as I entered, and it is only now that I stop to think that he is crippled. I did not notice it and had no thought of it during our meeting. He immediately asked me how Anne was and mentioned the fact that she knew his daughter in school. He is an accomplished, suave, interesting conversationalist. I liked him and feel that I could get along with him well. Acquaintanceship would be pleasant and interesting. But there was something about him I did not trust, something a little too suave, too pleasant, too easy. Still, he is our President, and there is no reason for any antagonism between us in the work I am now doing."

Lindbergh studied the president as they talked. "Roosevelt gave me the impression of being a very tired man, but with enough energy left to carry on for a long time. I doubt that he realizes how tired he is. His face has that gray look of an overworked businessman. And his voice has that even, routine tone that one seems to get when the mind is dulled by too much and too frequent conversation. It has that dull quality that comes to any one of the senses when it is overused: taste, with too much of the same food day after day; hearing, when the music never changes; touch, when one's hand is never lifted. Roosevelt judges his man quickly and plays him cleverly. He is mostly politician, and I think we would never get along on many fundamentals. But there are things about him I like, and why worry about the others unless and until they necessitate consideration? It is better to work together as long as we can; yet somehow I have a feeling that it may not be for long."

LINDBERGH RETURNED TO the War Department, where he met the press scrimmage a second time that day. The experience revived bad memories. "The meeting room was packed with photographers—motion picture and still. They lined one entire end of the room." Lindbergh said he would enter the room after the pictures had been taken. He was informed *he* was the one they wanted to photograph. "I replied that I would not pose for press pictures there or anywhere else. They came back with the proposition that they would let me alone in the future if I would let them take one picture, that they would give their word of honor. Imagine a press photographer talking about his word of honor! The type of men who broke through the window of the Trenton morgue to open my baby's casket and photograph its body—they talk to me of honor." Lindbergh made his opposition stick. The photographers were shown out.

Lindbergh's message to the officers he spoke with was that the United States needed to intensify its research efforts in aviation. "I asked how we expected to catch up with military developments abroad in aviation research with our present facilities. I pointed out that we had fallen behind while the foreign facilities were even less than they are today, that even with the full appropriation for the new Sunnyvale"—California—"experimental station, we would be far behind a country like Germany in research facilities, and that we really needed the full Sunnyvale appropriation and much more besides. I made the point that while we could not expect to keep up with the production of European airplanes as long as we were on a peacetime basis, we should at least keep up in the quality of our aircraft."

AMERICAN READERS WERE as curious about Lindbergh as ever. Or so editors of the country's newspapers and magazines thought. A profile in the *New York Times* declared, "America's number one air man is back in his own country." The article continued, "Recalled to active duty in the army recently and put to work studying the aviation research facilities at the United States, Charles A. Lindbergh took up a task for which he is preeminently fitted." America was lucky to have him. "Of all the men actively engaged in aviation, there is none who surpasses Colonel Lindbergh in absorbing information, and few who have had such a wide opportunity of learning what is going on abroad." His talents were distinctive, and distinctively American. "Colonel Lindbergh's great value to his country lies in his prestige, and in the fact that being a good pilot, a practical engineer and practical research worker, as distinguished from research men in advanced aeronautic science, he can direct his abilities with such concentration that he is able to solve many difficult problems. And all his infinite capacity for detail will be called upon in his present job."

The article traced the rise of the young Lindbergh, noting the youthful charm that had made him such a favorite. Time and exposure showed their effects. "That good-natured Lindbergh has all but disappeared. What was reticence has become a fear of intrusion so sharp that it aggravates the very condition he seeks to avoid. His modesty, which, first endeared him to the world, has become a vain flight from the inescapable light of publicity. He is just as loyal and American as he ever was, just as interested in his profession, just as desirous of doing something worthwhile in the world. But he constantly avoids contact with the public."

Yet what mattered was what he brought to the discussion of American security. "There have been constant warnings from army officers, and from civilian engineers engaged in aviation research, that this country is in danger of falling behind European countries. They want to remedy that condition, and there is no name quite so potent as that of Lindbergh to focus national attention on this condition."

THE ROOSEVELT ADMINISTRATION didn't succeed in keeping Lindbergh to itself. Congress summoned Lindbergh to hearings on a proposal to increase American defense spending. He spoke in confidence to a House subcommittee, which declined to publish his testimony. The members were impressed. One especially valued Lindbergh's steadiness. "He gave us a calm, dispassionate picture of affairs abroad," said Albert Engel, a Michigan Republican. "In the face of all the wild reports of what Germany, Italy and Russia are doing in aviation, he emphasized that we should not try to match them in numbers." Instead America should focus on quality. Numbers could come later.

A subsequent session was more open. To the House appropriations committee, Lindbergh reiterated the need for quality over quantity. Until the mid-1930s the United States had led the world in both military and commercial aviation, he said. "But during the past five years, the lead in military aviation has been taken away from us." While America built commercial planes, Germany built warplanes. America would require a few years to catch up in military aircraft, if it spent its money wisely. Wisdom began in design. Manufacturers were clamoring for contracts, and members of Congress wanted the assembly lines in their districts to add workers. Lindbergh said the American military needed better designs first. "I do not believe it is either practicable or advisable for this country to attempt to compete with Europe in the quantity production of military aircraft under present conditions."

HAP ARNOLD SENT Lindbergh on the road—or in the air, rather—to visit army air bases and research facilities around the country. The journey reminded him what he liked about flying and what he didn't like about civilization. "Flew over an uninhabited country broken now and then by a dirt road and, during the latter portion of the flight, by a railroad," he wrote about West Texas. "Civilization has spread greatly in the Southwest since I made the survey flights for the central transcontinental air route (Transcontinental Air Transport) in 1928 and '29. Somehow I feel every road and oil well is an imposition, an intruder on the solitude which was once mine as I flew over it. The great western plains and deserts are giving way rapidly to the marks of men. And looking down on them from the air, those marks seem like a disease—a rash spreading slowly over the earth's surface."

The Rocky Mountains were majestic. "The high peaks are so close to Denver that I had to climb the plane almost at its maximum rate to get over them without circling. The peaks were snow-capped and clear except for an occasional rain cloud hiding one of them here and there. Above, the sky was broken, with scattered clouds at different altitudes all the way up to 20,000 feet." He remembered again what he loved about flying. "I climbed through them and rode on top like a god—the cloud-strewn sky, the white-capped peaks, the rain-filled valleys, mine. I owned the world that hour as I rode over it, cutting through my sky, laughing proudly down on my mountains, so small, so beautiful, so formidable. I could dive at a peak; I could touch a cloud; I could climb far above them all. This hour was mine, free of the earth, free of the mountains, free of the clouds."

BACK IN WASHINGTON he consulted with more elected officials. Harry Byrd of Virginia was the leader of Democratic conservatives in the Senate; he disliked Roosevelt's New Deal and distrusted Roosevelt himself. "Taxi to Capitol for appointment with Byrd," Lindbergh wrote in his journal. "We went into Garner's office adjoining the chamber"—John Nance Garner of Texas was vice president, which made him president of the Senate—"and talked for fifteen minutes about the tension which is developing in Europe and the course the United States should take if war should start over there. We are both anxious to avoid having this country pushed into a European war by British and Jewish propaganda, of which there is already too much."

Lindbergh didn't begrudge the British or American Jews their opinions. Both had reason to dislike and fear Hitler and both wished to enlist American power against him. But Lindbergh didn't think a foreign government or a small minority in America ought to dictate the policy of the United States. "I can understand the feeling of both the British and the Jews, but there is far too much at stake for us to rush into a European war without the most careful and cool consideration. We over here, 3,000 miles away, have a false and immature conception of most European problems. Those problems cannot be solved by American good will and idealism; they are far deeper, and I am not sure that our participation in another European war would help the solution in the end." One world war had nearly destroyed civilization; a second general conflict would be more calamitous still. "I think it would be more likely to throw the entire world into chaos than to 'save it for democracy.'"

Roosevelt made another play for Lindbergh. The White House offered him the chairmanship of the National Advisory Committee for Aeronautics. Lindbergh declined, saying his gifts lay elsewhere.

Hap Arnold took him aside. "Do you mind if I ask you a personal question?" he said.

Lindbergh told him to go ahead.

"What are you shooting at? Have you set a goal for yourself, or do you just take life as it comes?"

Lindbergh said he wasn't shooting at anything. Life was too confusing to try to chart a future. "I told him I did not want political office or any special reward for what I did, and that while I often worked toward an objective it was usually one which was not so very far in the future. I said I liked to feel my way along as I lived and let life have a hand in guiding its own direction."

Arnold didn't object, not in words. "Arnold told me he had always followed somewhat the same policy and that he, too, had never set a definite objective as his life's work (although it seems to me that an Army career is a pretty definite objective)."

13

T HE FIRST THUNDERCLAP of the summer of 1939 came at the end of July, when Hitler and Joseph Stalin concluded a nonaggression pact. For two decades Europe's fascists and its communists had been each other's sworn enemies. The Nazis rose to power promising Germans protection against communism. The Spanish civil war had devolved into a proxy battle between Germany and the Soviet Union. More than a few democrats, in Europe and America, hoped the two dictators would fight to the death of one and the debility of the other.

The nonaggression agreement shattered this hope. Hitler was removing the one impediment to Germany's eastward advance. He had been ranting about *Lebensraum*—living space—and in his formulation it lay to the east. The people of Poland, who had regained a country of their own after the World War, following a century of partition, had hoped the enmity between Russia and Germany would create a standoff that would let them survive between the two great powers. The nonaggression pact all but killed this hope.

"EUROPEAN CRISIS BECOMING extremely tense," Lindbergh wrote on August 18. "Germany is not bluffing and will fight if necessary to gain her ends in the East." Two days later: "Can't keep mind off war. It is just like the Munich crisis last year except that we"—Lindbergh, Anne and the boys—"are in America this time and do not feel the atmosphere of preparation, apprehension, and depression there was in London a year ago. The German-Russian pact did not surprise me, but I believe it has greater significance than appears on the surface at this moment."

The tension grew worse. "There is talk of war everywhere," Lindbergh wrote on August 23. "The press is full of it. Reminds me of Europe last September." He met with William Castle, an aide to Harry Cohn at Columbia Pictures, and Fulton Lewis, a radio broadcaster. "The three of us had dinner together and discussed the European situation and the action this country should take if war breaks out over there. We are disturbed about the effect of the Jewish influence in our press, radio, and motion pictures. It may become very serious. Lewis told us of one instance where the Jewish advertising firms threatened to remove all their advertising from the Mutual system if a certain feature were permitted to go on the air. The threat was powerful enough to have the feature removed."

At the War Department the next day he spoke with Truman Smith, an army attaché and intelligence officer recently stationed in Berlin. "We discussed the European crisis. There seems to be about an even chance of war. I cannot believe that England and France will attack Germany under present conditions. It would be suicide to attack the German 'Western Wall,' and what else can they do? England can clear the sea of German shipping but that in itself will not win a war. Poland is beyond help under any circumstances. The German Army will close the Corridor"—Poland's outlet to the Baltic Sea—"within a few days after it attacks, and there is no other way for England and France to get to Poland. They can't go through Rumania or through one of the northern Baltic countries. Of course, there is the question of what Italy will do. But whether she joins Germany in war or stays neutral, the problem is not much simplified as far as France and England are concerned."

"Constantly thinking about war," Lindbergh wrote on August 30. "Seems impossible to keep it from one's mind or conversation. Have been considering whether anything I could say in a radio address would be of constructive value, even in a minute way. I am afraid events have gone too far on the other side for words to have any effect. Better not to speak at all in that case."

On August 31: "General Arnold and Truman Smith came for dinner. We talked about the Army, the Air Corps, conditions in America and in Europe. As we were talking, extras were out on the streets, carrying headlines to the effect that Poland had refused Hitler's offer for a peaceful settlement."

PART TWO

Distant Guns

14

T HE WAR HAS begun!" wrote Lindbergh in his journal on
September 1. Radio news reported that German forces
were streaming into Poland. He didn't think the Polish
army had much chance. The question was whether other countries
would come to Poland's rescue. "What will England and France do?"
If they declared war, they might discover they'd taken on more than
they could handle. "If they try to break the German Western Wall,
I think they will lose unless America enters the war." Lindbergh
assumed American entry was precisely what the British and French
were counting on.

This would be no solution, Lindbergh judged. The political and
economic turmoil of the last two decades had demoralized and ener-
vated Europe, and an extended war—the inevitable result of American entry—would finish it off. "If we go in, Europe will be still more
prostrated after the war is over."

Lindbergh blamed bad decisions in London and Paris. "Why
did England and France get themselves into such a hopeless position?" They had failed to resist German rearmament and had let
Hitler gain momentum and confidence in international affairs. They
allowed him to have his way with Czechoslovakia, which they could
have defended, and then they committed to keep him from taking
Poland, which they almost certainly couldn't defend. "If they wanted
to fight a German eastward movement, why in heaven's name pick
this particular set of circumstances to fight over? They are in a hopeless position militarily, and Danzig, Poland, and the Polish Corridor

are not banners which will encourage the Allied armies to attack on German soil. And the English talk of stupid *German* diplomacy!"

The war was in Europe, but it was on every American mind. "I went out for a twenty-minute walk along Fifth Avenue and some of the side streets," Lindbergh wrote. "There seems to be a somewhat subdued atmosphere. The war news has affected everyone." It preempted other subjects of conversation. "Anne and I discussed the war situation. Will it be long or short? It is too early to tell. We spent the evening in the parlor, thinking and listening to radio reports. The latter are excited, speculative, and superficial, with few exceptions. The future of the human world hangs in the balance today. This war will change all of our lives."

No one followed the news more closely than Lindbergh. "The radio commentators are beginning to ask why England and France have not declared war," he wrote on September 2. "Why indeed! They're in no position to fight one. The question is why they ever made this alliance with Poland. There are reports—fairly direct ones—that Chamberlain did not consult his general staff before he made the Polish alliance. I told Anne that England and France seemed hesitant about declaring war in spite of their promises to Poland. 'Maybe they've talked to a general,' she said."

The essential question for Lindbergh was the American response. "What stand should America take in this war?" he asked himself. "This is now our most pressing issue. We have enough internal problems without confusing them with war." The depression still blighted much of the American countryside, and American democracy had yet to prove it was up to the challenges the depression put in its way. "I see trouble ahead even in times of peace. War would leave affairs chaotic."

15

ROOSEVELT HAD RESPONDED to the German-Soviet non-aggression pact with another letter to Hitler urging restraint. Hitler ignored the counsel and proceeded with his designs against Poland. The German invasion on September 1 caused the world to wonder if America would take any stronger action. Reporters asked Roosevelt at a press conference that day what the new fighting in Europe meant for America. One said, "I think probably what is uppermost in the minds of all the American people today is, 'Can we stay out?' Would you like to make any comment at this time on that situation?"

"Only this," Roosevelt replied, "that I not only sincerely hope so but I believe we can, and that every effort will be made by the administration to do so."

"May we make that a direct quote?" Under the rules at the time, the president could not be directly quoted without his express permission.

"Yes."

He said no more just then, awaiting further intelligence. Two days later Britain and France declared war on Germany. That day, September 3, was a Sunday, the day of the week on which Roosevelt typically delivered the radio addresses known as "fireside chats." In the evening he went on the radio for his first chat in more than a year.

"Tonight my single duty is to speak to the whole of America," he said. "Until four-thirty this morning I had hoped against hope that some miracle would prevent a devastating war in Europe and bring to an end the invasion of Poland by Germany." This had not happened; the war had come, despite American diplomacy at previous moments of crisis. "It is right that I should recall to your minds the consistent and at times successful efforts of your government in these crises to throw the full weight of the United States into the cause of peace." America would continue to press for peace. "It seems to me clear, even at the outbreak of this great war, that the influence of America should be consistent in seeking for humanity a final peace which will eliminate, as far as it is possible to do so, the continued use of force between nations." America in the 1920s had led efforts to get governments to abjure war. These efforts had failed to prevent the current conflict, but Roosevelt hoped they might be revived.

The president acknowledged that Americans were being bombarded with information and opinion on the unfolding events. Without mentioning the proven disinformation that had preceded American entry into the World War, he warned conveyors and consumers of news to be careful what they heeded. "It is of the highest importance that the press and the radio use the utmost caution to discriminate between actual verified fact on the one hand, and mere rumor on the other," he said. "I hope the people of this country will also discriminate most carefully between news and rumor. Do not believe of necessity everything you hear or read. Check up on it first."

Amid the storm of news, mostly bad, Americans would be tempted to turn away from world affairs. This would be a grave mistake, Roosevelt said. "You must master at the outset a simple but unalterable fact in modern foreign relations between nations. When peace has been broken anywhere, the peace of all countries everywhere is in danger." It would be tempting to dismiss foreign troubles as too distant to concern America, and to conclude that if America ignored them the troubles would resolve themselves. Americans must resist the temptation. "Passionately though we may desire detachment, we are forced to realize that every word that comes through the air, every ship that sails the sea, every battle that is fought, does affect the American future."

Yet by no means must that future include engagement in the new conflict. "Let no man or woman thoughtlessly or falsely talk of America sending its armies to European fields," Roosevelt declared. In fact, the United States was about to announce its intention to stay out of the war. "At this moment there is being prepared a proclamation of American neutrality." The president acknowledged he wasn't a free agent in making the proclamation; the existing neutrality law bound him. Yet he would have acted in the same manner regardless. "This would have been done even if there had been no neutrality statute on the books, for this proclamation is in accordance with international law and in accordance with American policy."

Roosevelt remembered—and he supposed many in his audience remembered—that President Wilson, in proclaiming American neutrality at the outset of the European war in 1914, had asked Americans to be neutral in their thoughts as well. Roosevelt said he himself would make no such request. "This nation will remain a neutral nation, but I cannot ask that every American remain neutral in thought as well. Even a neutral has a right to take account of facts. Even a neutral cannot be asked to close his mind or his conscience." The president didn't name Germany as the aggressor, yet no one listening mistook his meaning.

While reluctant to engage in Europe, America would defend itself closer to home. "We have certain ideas and certain ideals of national safety, and we must act to preserve that safety today, and to preserve the safety of our children in future years," Roosevelt said. "That safety is and will be bound up with the safety of the Western Hemisphere and of the seas adjacent thereto. We seek to keep war from our own firesides by keeping war from coming to the Americas." Roosevelt cited America's first chief executive in distinguishing the security of the Americas from that of Europe. The tenure of George Washington had been a time of European war, and he had issued a proclamation of American neutrality. Roosevelt would take similar action regarding the current hostilities. "It is our national duty to use every effort to keep them out of the Americas."

The president reaffirmed his opposition to war of any sort. "I have said not once but many times that I have seen war and that I hate war. I say that again and again." He hated the present war no less than other wars. "I hope the United States will keep out of this war. I believe that it will. And I give you assurance and reassurance that every effort of your government will be directed toward that end."

16

I T WAS A better talk than he usually gives," Lindbergh granted. He was pleased that Roosevelt had emphasized America's neutrality, even though the neutrality law gave him little choice in the matter. The president had uttered the right words in saying he hated war. But his manner still left Lindbergh doubtful. "I wish I trusted him more."

He thought he himself could do better. Lindbergh had never been publicly political, though politicians had tried to capitalize on his fame, to the point of suggesting he run for office as a candidate of their parties. Politics ran in the Lindbergh family. His father had been a congressman from Minnesota, and his grandfather had served in the legislative assembly of Sweden. Lindbergh's father was a Republican who liked Theodore Roosevelt and disliked Woodrow Wilson; he backed Roosevelt against Wilson and President William Howard Taft in 1912, and when Wilson won anyway, he opposed Wilson's Federal Reserve system in 1913. The elder Lindbergh was especially unpersuaded by Wilson's rhetoric about an American obligation to save the world for democracy; he denounced American participation in the World War with such vigor that federal agents raided the publisher that was printing his book *Why Is Your Country at War?* and destroyed the printing plates. The stillborn book blamed the powers of the media for stampeding America toward war. "It is impossible according to the big press to be a true American unless you are pro-British," Lindbergh's father wrote. "If you are really for

America first, last and all time, and solely for America and for the masses primarily, then you are classed as pro-German."

This unpopular stand ended his political career. The younger Lindbergh observed and took note. He admired his father's insistence on principle and perhaps concluded that it contributed to his father's early death, in 1924. It certainly soured the son on politics. And after the American consensus swung around to Lindbergh senior's belief that the American role in the war had been a con job in the service of big money and the British, his son couldn't help concluding that a prophet was indeed never honored in his own country, at least if that country was America.

Doubtless he thought of his father as he watched Europe go to war again. Possibly he felt he could redeem his father posthumously by keeping their country from making the same mistake again. Perhaps that desire was what overcame his distaste for politics and the public scrutiny it entailed.

"I have now written one article and two radio talks," Lindbergh noted in his journal on September 7. Unlike Roosevelt, Lindbergh couldn't command the radio waves at a moment's notice. And the situation on the ground overtook his pen. "Events have moved so rapidly that the first two are already out of date." Still, he would persevere. "I do not intend to stand by and see this country pushed into war if it is not absolutely essential to the future welfare of the nation. Much as I dislike taking part in politics and public life, I intend to do so if necessary to stop the trend which is now going on in this country."

He arranged to speak over the Mutual Broadcasting radio network on September 15. The Mutual executives knew Lindbergh would attract an audience, despite the years he had spent away from America. If anything, absence had made many hearts grow fonder. Nearly all were curious to hear what the famous aviator had to say. Mutual considered a Lindbergh speech a scoop.

Lindbergh recognized that his opinions might cause trouble for Hap Arnold, who was known in Washington to be his confidant. He informed the general of his speaking plans.

Arnold said he understood Lindbergh's views. He agreed with some of them. He observed that Lindbergh had the right as an

American to express those views. But given their political nature, Arnold thought Lindbergh should resign his reserve position in the air corps.

Lindbergh didn't object. "The matter was of minor importance," he wrote. "My main concern was to avoid causing the Air Corps any embarrassment." He especially didn't want to make Arnold's life difficult. "He is a grand fellow. Said he did not like to see me go, but fully understood the situation. I told him I would be glad to help him or the Air Corps in any way I could in the future, regardless of my status."

Lindbergh offered to let Arnold read his speech ahead of the broadcast. Arnold said he'd like to. Lindbergh gave him a copy. "Arnold agreed that it contained nothing which could in any way be construed as unethical due to my connection with the Air Corps, and that I was fully within my rights as an American citizen," Lindbergh wrote.

The question then arose as to whether Harry Woodring should see the speech. Lindbergh was reluctant. The secretary of war was a political appointee who served at the pleasure of the president. "I said I preferred not to have him see it, as I had very little confidence in him or in the politics of the Roosevelt administration of which he is a part. I told Arnold frankly that I had great confidence in him and in General Marshall, but not in Secretary Woodring." George Marshall was the army chief of staff. Arnold appeared to understand. "During these conversations, I could tell from Arnold's eyes that he was on my side."

In recounting this meeting for his journal, Lindbergh added something he didn't say to Arnold. "As a matter of fact, I am far from being sure that Roosevelt would not sacrifice this country in war if it were to his own personal interests." Lindbergh thought Roosevelt might put politics above patriotism. "He would persuade himself that it was also the best interests of the country."

Lindbergh learned soon enough how Roosevelt operated—or so Lindbergh concluded. That afternoon he returned to Arnold's office with a report for the general's signature. Arnold said he had told Woodring that Lindbergh was leaving the air corps. "He also told Woodring I was planning on speaking on the radio tomorrow night against the United States entering a European war," Lindbergh recorded. "Woodring was very much displeased, Arnold said. He asked Arnold if he (Arnold) couldn't find some way of stopping me. Arnold replied that he did not think so. Woodring then said he was very sorry because he had hoped to make use of me in the future, but didn't see how he could do so if I followed out my plans! (There was obviously something behind that statement.)"

The next day Lindbergh received a visit from Truman Smith. "He told me he had a message which he must deliver, although he knew in advance what my answer would be. He said the Administration was very much worried by my intention of speaking over the radio and opposing actively this country's entry into a European war. Smith said that if I would not do this, a secretaryship of air would be created in the Cabinet and given to me!" Smith added, "So you see, they're worried."

Lindbergh reflected, "This offer on Roosevelt's part does not surprise me after what I have learned about his Administration. It does surprise me, though, that he still thinks I might be influenced by such an offer. It is a great mistake for him to let the Army know he deals in such a way. Apparently the offer came through Woodring to General Arnold, and through General Arnold to Truman Smith. Smith told me that Arnold, like himself, felt they must pass the message on since it came from the Secretary of War's office. Smith said he asked Arnold if he (Arnold) thought for a minute that I would accept. Arnold replied, 'Of course not.'"

WHILE ROOSEVELT'S MEN were trying to keep Lindbergh off the air, the radio networks were doing the opposite. NBC and Columbia wanted a piece of the Lindbergh action, and they cut a deal with Mutual. "That means complete national coverage," Lindbergh remarked, with understandable pride. Originally the broadcast was to have been from a Mutual studio, but the addition of NBC and Columbia prompted a shift to a neutral location: Washington's Carlton Hotel.

Lindbergh had been on the air before, but he'd never seen anything like this. The engineers and their assistants, a squadron of around twenty, had filled a room at the Carlton with radio gear. On the desk where Lindbergh was to sit were six microphones, two for each network. He said he'd rather stand, and so they moved the microphones away from the desk and raised them to his standing height. Meanwhile a cadre of photographers circled about taking pictures.

The sound men asked Lindbergh to read the first part of his speech so they could adjust the volume. He declined, saying he didn't want to lose the freshness that came from a first reading. They responded professionally. "They were very considerate about this and said that they could adjust during the first word or two after I started," Lindbergh wrote.

He went on the air at quarter to ten in the East, quarter to seven on the West Coast. "In times of great emergency, men of the same belief must gather together for mutual counsel and action," he began. "If they fail to do this, all that they stand for will be lost. I speak tonight to those people in the United States of America who feel that the destiny of this country does not call for our involvement in European wars."

America's past entailed separation from Europe; America's future must do the same. "This country was colonized by men and women from Europe," Lindbergh said. "The hatreds, the persecutions, the intrigues they left behind, gave them courage to cross the Atlantic Ocean to a new land. They preferred the wilderness and the Indians to the problems of Europe." Crossing the ocean involved risk and invited danger; the immigrants weighed the hazards and went ahead. In doing so they were transformed. "In this country, they eventually found a means of living peacefully together—the same nationalities that are fighting abroad today. The quarrels of Europe faded out from American life as generations passed. Instead of wars between the English, French and Germans, it became a struggle of the new world for freedom from the old—a struggle for the right of America to find her own destiny."

Like Roosevelt, Lindbergh invoked George Washington. "He solemnly warned the people of America against becoming entangled in European alliances." Americans had wisely heeded the great founder. "For over one hundred years his advice was followed. We established the Monroe Doctrine for America. We let other nations fight among themselves."

Once America had erred. "In 1917 we entered a European war," Lindbergh said. "We were on England's side, and so were France and Russia." Germany was on the other side. By luck America had emerged relatively unscathed; the war ended before American forces were fully engaged. "We escaped with the loss of relatively few soldiers. We measured our dead in thousands. Europe measured hers in millions." No lasting good had come from the war, which was followed by two decades of turmoil.

Americans had a chance to show that they had learned from their mistake, or that they had not. "Now that war has broken out again, we in America have a decision to make on which the destiny of our nation depends. We must decide whether or not we intend to become forever involved in this age-old struggle between the nations of Europe." Lindbergh had chosen his adverb—*forever*—with care. There would be no backing out of a commitment to Europe this time. "Let us not delude ourselves. If we enter the quarrels of Europe during war, we must stay in them in time of peace as well. It is madness to send our soldiers to be killed as we did in the last war if we turn the course of peace over to the greed, the fear and the intrigue of European nations. We must either keep out of European wars entirely or stay in European affairs permanently."

Some asserted that the frontiers of American defense were across the seas. Lindbergh wondered if these people had ever looked seriously at a map. "What more could we ask than the Atlantic Ocean on the east and the Pacific on the west?" he said. Europe meant nothing to America's defense. "Our own natural frontiers are enough for that. If we extend them at all, we might as well extend them around the earth. An ocean is a formidable barrier, even for modern aircraft."

America's safety did not lie in fighting Europe's wars. "It lies in our own internal strength, in the character of the American people and of American institutions. As long as we maintain an Army, a Navy and an Air Force worthy of the name, as long as America does not decay within, we need fear no invasion of this country."

Lindbergh didn't expect to convince those who had already decided on a European—or global—future for America. Instead he spoke to the ordinary men and women who shared his view of an American foreign policy for Americans. "Our future and our children's future depend upon the action we take," he said. Americans had been misled into the World War by British propagandists and profit-seeking bankers and arms manufacturers. Americans must not be misled again. "We will be deluged with propaganda, both foreign and domestic—some obvious, some insidious. Much of our news is already colored. Every incident and every accident will be seized upon to influence us." Americans must become sophisticated consumers of news and opinion. "We must learn to look behind every article we read in every speech we hear. We must not only inquire about the writer and the speaker—about his personal interest and his nationality—but we must ask who owns and who influences the newspaper, the news picture and the radio station."

America's future, Lindbergh reiterated, lay at home—and within. "Let us look to our own defense and our own character. If we attend to them, we have no need to fear what happens elsewhere. If we do not attend to them, nothing can save us. If war brings more dark ages to Europe, we can better preserve those things which we love and which we mourn the passing of in Europe today by preserving them here, by strengthening them here, rather than by hurling ourselves thoughtlessly to their defense over there and thus destroying all in the conflagration."

17

LINDBERGH UNDERSTOOD WHY people tuned in to hear him. They wanted to hear the voice of the reclusive airman, the survivor of the horrible kidnapping and murder. He realized that his credentials were thin in the realm of foreign policy. He knew aviation, and he had seen more of the latest airplanes than anyone else. But he was no student of government or diplomacy. Yet neither were the vast majority of Americans. To them he spoke; *for* them he would speak, if they would let him.

They seemed so inclined. "I was not well satisfied with my delivery," he wrote immediately afterward. "I think it could have been much better. However, everyone else seemed to feel it was all right." Responses the next day encouraged him the more. He and Anne returned to their Long Island home. "About forty telegrams had arrived in regard to my address. Only one was unfavorable. The press reaction seems to be good—talk carried in full by both *Times* and *Tribune*." Distant responses reached him later. "The papers from the West arrived this afternoon, and I read the editorials about my radio talk," he recorded four days afterward. "They are about ninety per cent favorable. This country is at present, at least, definitely opposed to entering a European war."

The positive reaction inspired opponents of war and of Roosevelt to seek Lindbergh out. Herbert Hoover invited him to his New York apartment. "We talked for about forty minutes about the war and the policy of the United States," Lindbergh wrote. "He is definitely opposed to the United States entering this war." The administration was trying to repeal the embargo of arms to belligerents required by the current neutrality law. Hoover thought it would be a mistake for anti-interventionists to get bogged down in a fight in Congress; the real threat to American safety was the president. "He feels that Roosevelt definitely desires to get us into this conflict."

The structural problem behind the war, said Hoover, was the inability of the British and French to enforce the unrealistic treaty they had imposed on Germany at the end of the first war. "Hoover feels, as I do, that the British Empire has been on the decline for some time—he says since the last war," Lindbergh recorded. "He said it was inevitable that Germany would expand either peacefully or by fighting if necessary. He said he told Halifax"—the British foreign secretary who would become British ambassador in Washington—"some time ago that the only way to avoid a European war was to permit a German economic expansion in Eastern Europe."

The former president encouraged Lindbergh to play a role, when the time was right, in restraining Roosevelt. "Hoover suggested that after the embargo controversy was over, an organization should be gotten together to keep this country out of the war—nonpolitical, of course. He suggested that I take part in it."

Lindbergh was flattered by the suggestion. "I told him I would be much interested and would like to learn more about it." Yet in his journal he wrote parenthetically, "Hoover's favorite solution for any problem seems to be the construction of a committee. Personally, I am very skeptical about the effectiveness of most committees."

He received an invitation to meet with Harry Byrd. Lindbergh took the midnight train from Penn Station to Washington; the anti-Roosevelt Virginia Democrat came to Lindbergh's hotel for breakfast. "We discussed the war, American neutrality, the question of repealing the embargo act, what requirements to substitute for the act if repealed, Dick Byrd's expedition to the South Pole, etc., etc." Richard Byrd was Harry Byrd's brother; he had flown over—or perhaps only near—the North Pole and was about to embark on his third expedition to Antarctica. "We agree practically one hundred per cent on the necessity of keeping the United States out of war." The senator proposed to introduce Lindbergh around. "Byrd asked me if I would care to meet some of his friends in the Senate, and I accepted his invitation gladly."

Lindbergh met with Byrd again a few days later. The senator sought to engage Lindbergh in the fight over revising the neutrality law. "He brought the latest draft of the neutrality bill, and we discussed the entire question: what authority Roosevelt could be trusted with (we both agreed that it should be as little as possible), what restrictions on shipping and credit would be advisable, what would be acceptable to the different factions, etc. I brought up the danger to neutral shipping of an air blockade of England—the difficulty of recognizing the nationality of a ship by the bomber in a plane flying in poor weather or at high altitude."

Byrd took Lindbergh to the Senate. "We walked through the tunnel to the Capitol. We stopped for a moment in Byrd's office, then went on to another room where we had lunch with Senators Bailey (North Carolina), Burke (Nebraska), George (Georgia), Johnson (California), and Gerry (Rhode Island)—all Democrats." They discussed the war and its implications for America. "I believe all of them, except Burke, favored our keeping out of the war regardless of who wins. Burke felt the United States should go to war rather than let England and France lose."

THIS WAS HEADY brew for a political novice. The attention only increased. William Borah was a Washington presence in more ways than one. The "Lion of Idaho" had been a senator since the first decade of the century, a stirring orator during all that time, a lady's man even longer. He was married but not contentedly so; his paramours included Alice Roosevelt Longworth. The headstrong elder daughter of Theodore Roosevelt had married Nicholas Longworth, a liquor-loving womanizer, to spite her father, and she took up with Borah to spite her husband. The affair produced whispers and louder expressions of disapproval around Washington; it also produced a child, Paulina. Nick Longworth raised the child as his own, though knowing she wasn't. Alice referenced Paulina's paternity in the nickname she gave the child: Aurora Borah Alice.

Borah had split the capital and the country politically by his ferocious attack against Woodrow Wilson, the Treaty of Versailles and the League of Nations. Borah led the band of Senate "irreconcilables," the minority that prevented ratification of the treaty, and in the process nearly killed Wilson, who suffered an incapacitating stroke brought on by his desperate effort to win the country to the side of the treaty and the League. Twenty years later, Borah remained utterly opposed to American responsibility for any part of the world outside America's own hemisphere. He staunchly resisted repealing the arms embargo in the existing neutrality law.

"I liked him instantly," Lindbergh wrote after a meeting with Borah. "He is a true son of the West, and his face and eyes have strength in every line and glance." The senator treated Lindbergh like a peer. "Borah spoke frankly to me. I believe we both gained confidence in each other at first glance." He conducted Lindbergh to his office via the underground monorail from the Capitol. They shared lunch. "No one else was present, and we talked freely for about an hour." Borah distrusted Roosevelt as an internationalist reincarnation of Wilson, regardless of what Roosevelt might say to the contrary. Yet the senator respected—and feared—Roosevelt's political savvy. "Borah feels the debate on this embargo act will last in the vicinity of a month. He believes it is essential to demonstrate that there is a strong opposition, even though it may be necessary to compromise eventually."

Lindbergh's presence on Capitol Hill became known in the House of Representatives. Republican congressman George Tinkham of Massachusetts asked for an interview. Crossed signals delayed the session until that evening at the home of Truman Smith. "He stood up to greet me as I arrived—a strange-looking man of about sixty years—a high, bald head with a huge hooked nose curving down to a long heavy beard which still showed how black it had once been," Lindbergh wrote of Tinkham. "It was a face you could never forget— one you would recognize as long as life lay within it, regardless of the molding of intervening years."

Tinkham's conversations were as distinctive as his visage. "His vanity, which at first was the most obvious thing about his words, was soon subdued by a wisdom in observation and a richness of experience seldom encountered in any man," Lindbergh remarked. "He told me in length of his travels; twenty-seven trips to Europe, he said, and several of them extending beyond—Africa, China, Japan, scarcely a country in which he had not been. He talked of Europe in the past, in the present, in the future, and the hours of the night merged into this narrative of human life, until midnight came and went without our noticing it pass."

Contemporary issues weren't ignored. "In between, we talked of the arms embargo and of the policy America should follow," Lindbergh wrote. "He is definitely opposed to repeal—feels it would be a great step toward war, which he thinks would be disastrous for this country."

18

ROOSEVELT KICKED OFF the campaign for repeal of the arms embargo with an address to Congress, which he had summoned to an emergency session on account of the war. The president expressed hope debate on appropriate measures would be high-minded. "Because I am wholly willing to ascribe an honorable desire for peace to those who hold different views from my own as to what those measures should be, I trust that these gentlemen will be sufficiently generous to ascribe equally lofty purposes to those with whom they disagree," he said. All sought the best interests of their common country, including preservation from war. "Let no group assume the exclusive label of the 'peace bloc.' We all belong to it."

Roosevelt recounted the unfortunate trends of the last several years, during which the peace established at Paris after the World War unraveled. He emphasized American efforts to resist this trend. "The United States has constantly, consistently and conscientiously done all in its power to encourage peaceful settlements," he said. America had acted in its own interests, but also in recognition of the larger principle that war anywhere threatened civilization everywhere. Summarizing what had been American policy, and what remained American policy, Roosevelt declared, "The primary purpose of our foreign policy has been that this nation and this government should strive to the utmost to aid in avoiding war among nations. But if and when war unhappily comes, the government and the nation must exert every possible effort to avoid being drawn into the war." War had come, despite America's efforts; priority shifted to the second goal. "This government must lose no time or effort to keep our nation from being drawn into the war."

The question was: How to stay out of war? Some urged sticking to the approach established by the 1935 neutrality act in embargoing arms sales to belligerents. That policy was out of date, Roosevelt said. In fact, he now thought it had been unwise from the start. "I regret that the Congress passed that act. I regret equally that I signed that act." Roosevelt rarely admitted mistakes. Fortunately, there was time to rectify this one.

The problem with the arms embargo was that it denied victims of aggression the means to defend themselves. Roosevelt again didn't identify particular countries by name, but none of his listeners missed his meaning when he said of the effects of the existing law: "A land power which threatened war could thus feel assured in advance that any prospective sea-power antagonist would be weakened through denial of its ancient right to buy anything anywhere. This, four years ago, began to give a definite advantage to one belligerent as against another, not through his own strength or geographical position, but through an affirmative act on the part of the United States." Put starkly, if obliquely, America's existing policy played into the hands of Nazi Germany.

Prudence and fair play required repeal of the arms embargo. Some feared that such a measure would carry the United States closer to war. Not so, said Roosevelt. "I give to you my deep and unalterable conviction, based on years of experience as a worker in the field of international peace, that by the repeal of the embargo the United States will more probably remain at peace than if the law remains as it stands today."

To ease the concerns of Americans who feared a repetition of the events that led to American involvement in the World War, Roosevelt recommended modifications of the rest of the neutrality law to accompany repeal of the arms embargo. First, American merchant vessels should be forbidden to enter war zones. The sinking of American ships by German submarines had been a precipitant to American entry into the war. Second, American citizens should not be allowed to travel on belligerent vessels. The death of Americans on the British liner *Lusitania* in 1915 had been another spur to involvement in the war. Third, when foreigners purchased American goods, they must pay for them up front and carry them away in their own vessels. This cash-and-carry policy would prevent the financial entanglements with Britain and France that had helped draw the United States into the war.

"To those who say that this program would involve a step toward war on our part, I reply that it offers far greater safeguards than we now possess or have ever possessed, to protect American lives and property from danger," Roosevelt said. "It is a positive program for giving safety. This means less likelihood of incidents and controversies which tend to draw us into conflict, as they unhappily did in the last world war. There lies the road to peace!" The president hoped the members of Congress would put the country's interest before all others. "These perilous days demand cooperation among us without trace of partisanship," he said. "Our acts must be guided by one single hard-headed thought—keeping America out of this war."

19

C ONGRESS OVERWHELMINGLY SHARED Roosevelt's thought about the importance of staying out of the war. Yet members disagreed—vehemently—as to whether repeal of the arms embargo would make staying out easier or harder.

William Borah launched the counteroffensive against Roosevelt. The old irreconcilable told the Senate in public what he had told Lindbergh in private: that he didn't trust the president, that Roosevelt professed attachment to neutrality while actively undermining it. Borah blasted the administration for trying to delude the American people into thinking Europe had somehow moved next door to America. "We are met on the threshold of all debate, of all consideration, of this subject of neutrality with the statement often delivered and with an air of finality that we cannot be neutral, that Europe is now so near to the United States, owing to modern inventions and the mingling of business affairs, that neutrality is impracticable if not impossible," he said. The premise was bad geography, the conclusion ignoble policy. "This seems to me a spineless doctrine. It is not the doctrine inherited from our forebears. If true, we would be the most ill-fated nation on the earth instead of being, as we had long supposed, the most favorably circumstanced." George Washington had known better in declaring neutrality for the fledgling nation during the European war of his day. "Had he not so declared and made good, does anyone doubt the devastating effect upon freedom, upon liberty, upon this republic?"

What had been true for Washington remained true. "These wars are not our wars," Borah said. Roosevelt and the interventionists tortured truth to make it seem they were. Borah paraphrased their argument: "Although our people have sought peace and now seek peace, still we must make war because European governments maintain an eternal saturnalia of human sacrifices. Though the law of our land banishes racial and religious persecution from our common country, still, because Europe is 'near,' we must join in the racial and religious conflicts, and sacrifice our people over conditions which our forebears long since rejected. Though we seek no people's territory, nevertheless, because Europe is 'near,' we must sacrifice the savings of our people and the sons of our mothers in this endless imperialistic strife." Borah reverted to his own voice, no less sarcastic: "Though we would take no part of the loot which was divided up at the close of the World War, we are now called upon to make sure the title to a vast amount of this loot. What a fateful doctrine to propose!"

Borah demanded that the advocates of repealing the arms embargo level with the American people. "Is not your main purpose in securing repeal to enable us to furnish arms, munitions and implements of war to one group of nations and to deny them to another group of nations, which groups are now in mortal combat?" Was this not intervention in the war? "Is it not your purpose to take sides through the authority which will be available when the embargo law is repealed?" And what would be the result? "If the purpose of repeal is to do these things, and we do them, is not neutrality broken down, destroyed, and are we not thenceforth by every rule of international law, by every dictate of common sense and common honesty, parties to a European conflict?"

Roosevelt's request for repeal was much more than it seemed. "We are really considering in this debate the broad question of whether we are justified as a people in intervening in this conflict," Borah said. "We cannot escape that destination if we move along the lines now proposed."

Gerald Nye thought Roosevelt's reasoning dishonest; he agreed with Borah that the president wanted war, not peace. The North Dakota Republican assumed Roosevelt would be playing the patriotism card. "From here on the administration will be contending that every voice raised in opposition to administration wishes is at once a pro-Hitler voice." Nye wouldn't be silenced, though, and neither would other defenders of American neutrality and the American Constitution. "Voices will be raised, and there will be complete demonstration to the American people of what the president's wishes will certainly lead America into. Americans had better talk now before the gags of a declared emergency are placed." During the World War, critics of the Wilson administration had been imprisoned for sedition; Nye saw little reason to expect greater tolerance from Roosevelt.

Bennett Champ Clark was of the president's own party but not of the president's mind on revising the neutrality law to repeal the embargo. The Missouri senator recounted the steps by which America had been drawn into the World War, and said, "We are now to determine whether or not we have learned anything from that awful experience." Clark noted that some of the president's supporters didn't bother to deny their larger agenda. "My friend, Senator Elbert Thomas of Utah, one of the leading revisionists, let the cat out of the bag the other night as to the real position of the neutrality revisionists when he boldly declared: 'Let us give up this dream of impartiality, therefore of neutrality. It is better to take sides and fight.'"

Clark didn't like the pejorative connotations around the label of "isolationist," but the label existed and it wouldn't go away. So he made the most of it. He quoted Roosevelt from 1936, when amid his campaign for reelection the president defended the arms embargo against allegations of isolationism by saying, "We are not isolationists except in so far as we seek to isolate ourselves completely from war." Where was that Roosevelt now? demanded Clark. Speaking for himself and for those like him who put America's interests before the interests of other countries, he said, "We are but humble followers of the leaders whose teaching made this country great. According to some current definitions George Washington was an isolationist. Jefferson was an isolationist. The Adamses and Madison and Jackson and Lincoln were all isolationists. We are proud to be their followers."

Arthur Vandenberg, a Michigan Republican, echoed Clark in reminding Americans of their country's tragic waste of lives and money in the World War. "We did not 'make the world safe for democracy,'" Vandenberg said, quoting Wilson. "We did not win a war 'to end all wars.' These vivid invitations, then as now were persuasive but tragically futile. We have no right to forget these experiences, nor the sinister fact that Europe's power politics are beyond our ken." The world was large and wicked; better for Americans to keep to their own part of the planet. "We cannot escape tremendous interest in what happens in other sectors of the globe, but we have learned that we cannot control alien destiny," Vandenberg said. "Our supreme obligation to democracy and to civilization is here in our own United States of America and in this western world."

ROOSEVELT DIDN'T LACK defenders in Congress. Key Pittman held the crucial post of chairman of the Senate foreign relations committee, and he summarized the case for repeal of the arms embargo. "No such grave situation has threatened the world in all history," Pittman said. "The rapidly multiplying tragic events in the world today are appalling and arouse a feeling of fear and distrust in the minds of all people. The inconceivable developments in the European controversy strike with palsying force on the minds of even the most astute statesmen, confusing reason and delaying action."

The European conflict remained far from American shores and American life. "There is not cause for fear now that we will be drawn into the brutal and widening conflict," Pittman continued. But the future was unknowable, and unlikely events had to be allowed for. "We, as the representatives of a peace-loving, democratic people have no right to refuse to take into consideration that such a war, or a war that develops out of it, may not someday be brought to the gateway of our own country." Pittman was unpersuaded by the analogies to the previous war; times changed. Many Americans thought an arms embargo would keep them from being accomplices to the killing. This belief wasn't merely wrong, Pittman said; it was counterproductive. He stated this part of the case for repeal more dramatically than Roosevelt had. "We are participating in mass murder by the Japanese in China today," Pittman declared. Japan imported American raw materials, allowed under current law, and converted those materials into weapons that China, the victim of Japanese aggression, was prohibited by the embargo from purchasing.

Repeal of the embargo would give President Roosevelt the discretion to allow arms sales where they would help *preserve* neutrality, Pittman said. Some critics considered such unbridled executive discretion all the more reason to oppose repeal, but not Pittman. "I have every confidence in the President of the United States. I have confidence in the declaration that he intends to do everything in his power to keep us out of war."

20

L INDBERGH CONTINUED TO circulate in corridors of power new to him. His knowledge of aviation made him a military expert in the minds of the president's opponents. "Herbert Hoover phoned and asked me if I thought he would be safe in saying that France and England could be successful in a defensive policy built around the Maginot Line," he wrote in his journal in early October. "He said it seemed to him that while airplanes could cause great damage behind that line, they could not win a war by doing so. He said he thought England could maintain control of the surface of the sea in spite of German air attacks. He said he planned on making a statement at this time because he felt there was a wave of hysteria sweeping the United States—arising from the rather sudden realization that England and France might lose the war—and that he regarded it as essential to counteract this hysteria on the grounds that it would create, and be used to create, the desire for this country to enter the war. Hoover said he felt Germany could not win the war because of the Maginot Line and British fleet."

Lindbergh understood airplanes but no more about soldiers and ships than other well-informed people. Yet because the Roosevelt administration had first call on America's military professionals, and an effective monopoly on the latest military intelligence, Hoover and Roosevelt's other foes looked to him.

"I replied that I agreed the best policy for Britain and France to pursue would be a defensive one built on the Maginot Line and the British fleet, but that I thought Hoover should consider the possibility of a German thrust toward the Suez and North Africa, with the assistance of Italy and Russia and possibly that of Turkey," Lindbergh wrote. "I told him I thought it improbable that the Germans would attempt to cross the Western front. I also told him I felt he should be careful in saying what the result would be of a conflict between the British fleet and the German air force. I said that was something we knew very little about—that aviation people tended to be overenthusiastic and naval people too conservative."

Hoover stuck with his view that the Germans were being overrated. "Hoover replied that he did not think a German thrust toward the eastern Mediterranean would be practicable. He said he did not think the German air force could overcome the great supremacy of the British fleet."

POLITICAL TYPES LIKE Hoover and Borah weren't the only ones interested in Lindbergh's opinion. The ears of American financiers were still burning from the claims that they had lured the United States into the World War to protect the loans they had made to the Allied governments. But life went on, and new dangers and opportunities had to be weighed. Lindbergh was an obvious person to consult, having married into the House of Morgan—Anne's father was a partner there—besides conducting reconnaissance of Europe. He visited the firm's Wall Street headquarters.

"When I arrived in the office of the Morgan partners, old Mr. Morgan"—J. P. Morgan Jr.—"invited me to have lunch with him in the firm's big dining room. Mr. Morgan is really a fine character. I have liked him ever since I first met him years ago. He is now well on in life—not far from seventy, I suppose; I am not even sure on which side. He is a large, kindly faced man, with an air of pleasant hospitality. His handshake carries a feeling of personal warmth and integrity that persists as long as you are with him."

The Morgan bank had survived the depression much as it had survived financial crises dating back to its founding after the Civil War: unflustered and exuding solidity. "The entire place leaves the impression of mahogany and of oak-paneled walls, of heaviness, conservatism, and integrity—a proper impression for a great banking firm, I suppose, but rather depressing to me," Lindbergh wrote.

He was happy to visit but had never wished to enter his father-in-law's line of work. "I long for sunlight as soon as I get inside the doors, and feel that the people there mustn't know the wonders of the outdoor world, that they are, in a sense, like a blind man who has either never seen the sky or who has been blind so long that he has become inured to the loss of its beauty. Yet these men do get out to see the sky; they live on Long Island and in other outskirts of New York; they sometimes take long trips through the West. How they can spend most of their lives in that dark oppressive atmosphere of 23 Wall Street, I am unable to understand. I would rather a thousand times over live my life on a farm than in that building, regardless of the amount of money I could make."

Lunch came and the conversation began. "The talk turned to the war in Europe and the arms embargo. Mr. Morgan asked me if I planned on making any more radio speeches. I told him I was not certain, but that I probably would, and that it would depend largely on developments." Partners who had joined the lunch asked Lindbergh's view of the prospects of the opposing sides. "I expressed the opinion that France and England would lose the war if they tried to attack Germany across the Western front."

Thomas Lamont, one of the senior partners, said he thought the British and the French would wait for Germany to attack them. Germany couldn't withstand a long blockade and would have no choice.

"I told him that if Germany attacked, I did not think it would be in the West, but in the East—except that Germany might attempt an air blockade of England."

Lamont discounted the likelihood of a German attack in the east, meaning the eastern Mediterranean, as impractical. He also dismissed as improbable—"ten to one"—that Italy would join the war on Germany's side.

Talk turned to America's role. Lindbergh was asked if he had taken a position on the arms embargo.

"I said I had not, but that I doubted the advisability of complete repeal, either from Europe's standpoint or our own. That statement started a very warm discussion in which Tom Lamont took the lead. As far as I could tell, I was the only one in the room who was not in favor of unqualified repeal. Obviously, my stand was extremely unpopular."

Lindbergh wasn't surprised. Morgan & Co. would surely finance the arms sales the repeal of the embargo would allow. But he left this unsaid.

"We all parted in a courteous (no personal feelings, you know) but tense atmosphere," he recorded.

LINDBERGH DID GIVE another radio speech. Roosevelt had counted likely votes before calling the emergency session, and his tally made him think repeal of the arms embargo would pass. The one thing that might overturn the calculation was a strong response from the public. This was precisely what Lindbergh hoped to elicit.

"I speak again to the people of this country who are opposed to the United States entering the war which is now going on in Europe," he said to another national audience on October 13. "We are faced with the need of deciding on a policy of American neutrality. The future of our nation and of our civilization rests upon the wisdom and foresight we use."

Some opponents of intervention were simply pacificists; Lindbergh made clear he wasn't one of those. Pacificism was not a policy for a great power. "Let us give no one the impression that America's love for peace means that she is afraid of war," he said. "National life and influence depend upon national strength, both in character and in arms." But effective strength required marking a line between what could be defended at reasonable cost and what could not. "Let us make clear to all countries where this line lies. It must be both within our intent and our capabilities."

Lindbergh proposed to put the line at the boundary of the American hemisphere. No country outside the hemisphere should be allowed to cross the line in a hostile manner. "From Alaska to Labrador, from the Hawaiian Islands to Bermuda, from Canada to South America, we must allow no invading army to set foot," he said. "These are the outposts of the United States. They form the essential outline of our geographical defense. We must be ready to wage war with all the resources of our nation if they are ever seriously threatened." America's army, navy and air corps should be designed and maintained to crush any intruder.

America would defend the hemisphere, Lindbergh reiterated;

in exchange, countries of the hemisphere ought to behave circum-
spectly. "They should not place us in the position of having to defend
them in America while they engage in wars abroad." He was referring to Canada, which had joined the war on Britain's side. "Can we
rightfully permit any country in America to give bases to foreign
warships"—meaning British warships—"or to send its army abroad
to fight while it remains secure in our protection at home?" Lindbergh thought not. "We desire the utmost friendship with the people
of Canada. If their country is ever attacked, our navy will be defending their seas, our soldiers will fight on their battlefields, our fliers
will die in their skies. But have they the right to draw this hemisphere into a European war simply because they prefer the Crown of
England to American independence?" Again he thought not.

America was powerful but finitely so. Defense of the hemisphere
required not squandering American resources beyond it, Lindbergh
said. Involvement in the wars of Europe or Asia risked exactly such
squandering. The current neutrality law had the commendable goal
of keeping the United States out of European and Asian wars; great
care should be taken before altering it.

Lindbergh rejected the argument that repeal would aid democracy. "I do not believe that repealing the arms embargo would
assist democracy in Europe, because I do not believe this is a war
for democracy," he said. "This is a war over the balance of power
in Europe, a war brought about by the desire for strength on the
part of Germany and the fear of strength on the part of England
and France." Britain and France were democratic at home, but their
strength rested on their empires abroad, which were anything but
democratic. A victory for Britain and France would be a victory for
imperialism rather than for democracy.

Wars always damaged democracy, encouraging authoritarian ten-
dencies in the most liberal states, Lindbergh said. He didn't mention
his father's experience with the printing plate smashers during the
World War, but he must have been thinking of it. Repealing the arms
embargo would extend the European war and increase the damage
to democracy. "The more munitions the armies obtain, the longer
the war goes on; and the more devastated Europe becomes, the less
hope there is for democracy."

Some repealers said, often quietly, that selling arms to the European belligerents would benefit American industry. Lindbergh deemed this rationale beneath America's dignity. "We in America have not yet reached a point where we wish to capitalize on the destruction and death of war. I do not believe that the material welfare of this country needs, or that our spiritual welfare could withstand, such a policy. If our industry depends upon a commerce of arms for its strength, then our industrial system should be changed."

Lindbergh judged it tragic that Europe had gone to war again; he thought it would be more tragic if the United States joined the conflict again. The enduring rift in the world was not ideological, not between democracy and fascism, he said, but civilizational and racial, between Europeans and their descendants, on one hand, and the rest of the world, on the other. Europeans should stick together, for the good of Western civilization. They definitely should not try to slaughter one another, and Americans should not aid the slaughter. "Our bond with Europe is a bond of race and not of political ideology," he said. "It is the European race we must preserve; political progress will follow." In a war of civilizations, America might send arms and even troops to Europe, but not till then. "If the white race is ever seriously threatened, it may then be time for us to take our part in its protection, to fight side by side with the English, French, and Germans, but not with one against the other for our mutual destruction."

Speaking into a microphone to an invisible audience far away, Lindbergh couldn't gauge its reaction to this detour into racial theory. He might not have cared, taking pride in his willingness to say what others, especially politicians, wouldn't say. He might have considered his comments unremarkable. Theories of race underpinned imperialism abroad, including the British imperialism Americans were being asked to rescue. Race was written into American law, since the Supreme Court in the 1890s had approved segregation, and into American custom, as any visitor to any city in the country could see.

But to a degree Lindbergh, the willful political innocent, didn't anticipate, his injection of race into his arguments against Roosevelt and repeal of the arms embargo put him in bad company. This was the way the Nazis talked. The conclusion was easily drawn that Lindbergh was doing the Nazis' work. Lindbergh's allies in the neutrality camp struggled to keep the focus of their arguments on America and its graces, while their intervention-minded foes sought to make the fight about Germany and its sins. Lindbergh unwittingly did the interventionists' work for them.

The consequences would come later. Lindbergh pushed to the end of his address. The best policy for Western civilization, he said, was also the best policy for the United States: continued American neutrality. Roosevelt had claimed that repeal of the arms embargo would facilitate neutrality. Lindbergh thought Roosevelt was wrong. He also suspected Roosevelt was insincere, but he wasn't ready to say so in public.

Roosevelt was leading America down the same path that had led the country to war in 1917, Lindbergh said. Only the American people could stop him. They must act quickly to do so. "The United States of America is a democracy. The policy of our country is still controlled by our people. It is time for us to take action."

21

H AROLD NICOLSON KNEW Lindbergh from the latter's sojourn in England. He had opened his home to the aviator and his family. Nicolson had been a British diplomat; he was a man of letters and currently held a seat in Parliament. "Colonel Charles Lindbergh has again been broadcasting to the American people," Nicolson wrote in *The Spectator*, a venerable London weekly. "He urged them (as he had every right to do) not to repeal the Neutrality Acts."

Nicolson had liked Lindbergh; he suspected he still did, after a fashion. But most of his British compatriots did not. And their Canadian cousins definitely did not. The Canadians were outraged at Lindbergh's presumption in telling them what their foreign policy should be. As for the British, they accounted him ungrateful. They and their press had respected Lindbergh's privacy while he was in England; they thought he should have reciprocated by keeping his thoughts to himself while Britain was in danger. "I do not agree with this criticism," Nicolson rejoined. "I have myself enjoyed much hospitality in Germany and in Italy, but do not feel precluded thereby from expressing my views upon the foreign policy of Herr Hitler or Count Ciano. I see no need to excuse Colonel Lindbergh; I want to explain him."

Nicolson gave his British readers background on Lindbergh. "His grandfather emigrated from Sweden, and on reaching the United States changed his name from Manson to Lindbergh," he wrote. "His father was a gentle, conscientious, almost fanatical democrat. He

represented Minnesota in Congress, and belonged to a small group
of insurgents who fought the governing classes and Wall Street with
might and main. As a child in Washington young Lindbergh spent
much time listening to Victor Murdock and other fiery radicals
from the Middle West denouncing the whole political system of the
United States and the 'decadent Europeanism' of the Atlantic seaboard. Congressman Lindbergh died, and young Charles returned
with his mother to the bleak farm in Minnesota and to the rigours
of an impoverished boyhood."

Lindbergh escaped to the University of Wisconsin briefly, and
then to the air. "He entered the flying corps and became a pilot upon
the St. Louis–Chicago route. At 10 p.m. on May 21st, 1927, he landed
at Le Bourget, having flown the Atlantic alone."

Lindbergh's life was transformed by his feat, and he became a
symbol of far more in popular hopes and dreams than he or anyone could sustain. "He returned to the United States in a blaze of
glory," Nicolson wrote. "The American public had been deeply disappointed that the war had produced no romantic figure, and they
seized upon their 'lone eagle' as the embodiment of all that American
youth should be. His charm, his boyishness and his modesty were
everywhere acclaimed. He drove in triumph through New York; he
was the guest of the President at the White House; he visited every
State in the Union and was accorded the freedom of seventy-eight
cities. He found himself a national, even a world, hero, at the age of
twenty-five."

Lindbergh himself was changed by the experience, said Nicolson.
Anyone would have been. But the change in Lindbergh was peculiar.
"His head was not turned by this apotheosis; it merely became completely stiff. He remained from then onwards the lad from Minnesota,
the slim pilot upon the Chicago–St. Louis trail. The ideas which he
had acquired from his father, or at the University of Wisconsin, were
no whit changed by contact with men of great experience of or wide
outlook upon world affairs; when wealth came to him, and with it
the contact with gentler and more sensitive minds, he retained unal-
tered his simple habits of life; he never drank or smoked; his life was
completely ascetic; he continued to prefer corned beef to terrapin; he
continued to believe that virility was the highest human virtue and
that anything which might sap that virility (such as art, literature

or music) must be something un-American, some 'poisonous honey stolen from France.' To this day he remains the fine boy from the Middle West."

Yet the world wanted more from Lindbergh. "The strain was terrific," Nicolson wrote. "How was this young man to maintain his own simplicity, his own few clear-cut convictions, against the adulation of a whole continent? It was almost with ferocity that he struggled to remain himself. And in the process of that arduous struggle his simplicity became muscle-bound; his virility-ideal became, not merely inflexible, but actually rigid; his self-confidence thickened into arrogance; and his convictions hardened into granite. He became impervious to anything outside his own legend—the legend of the lad from Minnesota whose head could not be turned."

And then his burden grew immeasurably worse: his child was murdered. "The suffering which that dreadful crime entailed upon himself and those he loved did pierce the armour and enforce a change," Nicolson said. "He emerged from that ordeal with a loathing of publicity which was almost pathological. He identified the outrage to his private life, first with the popular press, and then, by inevitable associations, with freedom of speech and then, almost, with freedom. He began to loathe democracy."

Nicolson felt for Lindbergh. "We cannot blame him," he wrote. "The life which he and his were forced to lead became abnormal. He is not possessed of any sense of humour and was unable to add that lovely lubricant to the harsh grating of his machine. He could not buy a stick of chocolate without being mobbed in the drug-store; when he visited a theatre both he and Mrs. Lindbergh were forced to assume disguise."

Nicolson related an episode that explained Lindbergh's aversion to the press. "He told me that when his child had been kidnapped he received a clue which seemed at the time hopeful. He leapt into his car to follow it up. As he left Princeton he found four press cars following in his wake. He stopped and addressed the leading car. 'Yes, boys,' he said, 'I have got a clue. But unless I am left alone to follow it up, there is no chance of success. I beg you as human beings not to follow me.' The younger newspaper men were embarrassed by this appeal. An older member of the group was unmoved. 'Sorry, Colonel,' he said, 'but business is business.' Lindbergh turned his car back to Princeton and drove home in white anger. 'So you see,' he said to me, 'I have cause to hate the press.'"

Lindbergh's view of military power showed his personal predilections, Nicolson said. "Like most aviators, Colonel Lindbergh is certain that any modern war will be settled in the air. He was shown all the more modern types of German aeroplanes and given full facilities to observe their pilots practising. He became convinced that both in men and pilots the Germans possessed the mightiest air-force in the world."

Nor did his admiration stop there. "He liked their grim efficiency, he liked the mechanisation of the state, he was not at all deterred by the suppression of free thought and free discussion; he admired the conditioning of a whole generation to the ideals of harsh self-sacrifice; the rush and rattle of it all impressed him immensely."

By contrast, he found little to admire in England. "He would return to the little Kentish village where he lived. Slowly the smoke of burning weeds would rise against the autumn woods, and lazily the apples would drop in the orchard. His mind had been sharpened by fame and tragedy until it had become as hard, as metallic, and as narrow as a chisel. The slow, organic will-power of Britain eluded his observation; he regarded our indifference to the mechanical as a proof that we, as they say in Minnesota, were 'incurably effete.' He liked England; he had no desire to see her murdered; he hoped that we should run away before Marshal Goering could catch us."

People shouldn't be too hard on Lindbergh, Nicolson concluded. "Let us not allow this incident to blind us to the great qualities of Charles Lindbergh; he is, and always will be, not merely a school-boy hero, but also a school boy."

22

Roosevelt's allies were less forgiving of Lindbergh. Key Pittman said Lindbergh knew a lot about airplanes but little about affairs among nations. He was dangerously naïve in assessing the intentions of dictators. "The most unfortunate part of Colonel Lindbergh's statement is that it encourages the ideology of the totalitarian governments and is subject to the construction that he approves of their brutal conquest of democratic countries through war or threat of destruction through war."

Prentiss Brown, a Democratic senator from Michigan, concurred that Lindbergh's attitude facilitated conquest. "I condemn his remarks because they lend encouragement to the spirit of nationalistic imperialism that has cursed the world for centuries and which is the potent poison that has killed the peace." Brown added, "I would have the world know that he did not speak for America."

Various columnists castigated Lindbergh. Dorothy Thompson, a regular for the *New York Herald Tribune*, declared that sentiment played no part in Lindbergh's worldview. "He has a passion for mechanics and a tendency to judge the world and society purely from a technical and mechanical standpoint. The humanities, which are at the very center and core of the democratic idea, do not interest him, and he is completely indifferent to political philosophy." A brave man himself, he scorned those not equally bold. "He has the utmost contempt for physical weakness." America loved him, but he didn't love America back. "His are not the predilections of the majority of Americans or of democracies anywhere."

Eleanor Roosevelt, the wife of the president and herself a syndicated columnist, sideswiped Lindbergh through Thompson. To the readers of her "My Day" column, Mrs. Roosevelt recommended Thompson's piece by saying, "She sensed in Col. Lindbergh's speech a sympathy with Nazi ideals which I thought existed but could not bring myself to believe was really there."

ROOSEVELT HIMSELF GAVE Lindbergh the back of his hand. Speaking by radio, Roosevelt emphasized the need for honest reporting and commentary. He flattered his audience: "Radio listeners have learned to discriminate over the air between the honest advocate who relies on truth and logic and the more dramatic speaker who is clever in appealing to the passions and prejudices of his listeners." He praised reporters generally. "I should like to throw bouquets to the majority of the press and the radio. Through a period of grave anxiety, both have tried to discriminate between fact and propaganda and unfounded rumor, and to give to their readers and listeners an unbiased and factual chronicle of developments."

Yet the challenge persisted. "In and out of Congress we have heard orators and commentators and others beating their breasts and proclaiming against sending the boys of American mothers to fight on the battlefields of Europe. That I do not hesitate to label as one of the worst fakes in current history. It is a deliberate setting up of an imaginary bogey man. The simple truth is that no person in any responsible place in the national administration in Washington, or in any state government, or in any city government, or in any county government, has ever suggested in any shape, manner or form the remotest possibility of sending the boys of American mothers to fight on the battlefields of Europe. That is why I label that argument a shameless and dishonest fake."

Yet Roosevelt wasn't worried. He didn't name Lindbergh, but his meaning was clear when he said, "I have not the slightest objection to make against those amateurs who, to the reading and the listening public, discourse on the inner meanings of the military and naval events of the war in Europe." Ordinary Americans would have no difficulty seeing through the amateurs' arguments, Roosevelt said. "They do no harm because the average citizen is acquiring rapidly the gift of discrimination—and the more all of these subjects are talked about by amateur armchair strategists the more the public will make up its own mind in the long run. The public will acquire the ability to think things through for themselves."

Roosevelt repeated that the eventuality against which Lindbergh and the other opponents of intervention warned was nowhere on the horizon. "The fact of the international situation—the simple fact, without any bogey in it, without any appeals to prejudice—is that the United States of America, as I have said before, is neutral and does not intend to get involved in war." Claims that America would get involved in the war were simply lies, which honest Americans would reject. "We Americans begin to know the difference between the truth on the one side and the falsehood on the other, no matter how often the falsehood is iterated and reiterated," Roosevelt said. "Repetition does not transform a lie into a truth."

ROOSEVELT WAS SPEAKING for effect, at this point. His vote-counting had proved accurate, and the neutrality revisions he wanted moved inexorably to adoption. Some supporters presumably took Roosevelt and his supporters at their word that American arms would help preserve American neutrality. Others were motivated by the prospect of profits and jobs from an expanded arms trade. A few, most eager to get into the war against the Nazis, hoped the reasoning of Lindbergh and the opponents of repeal was right: that American arms would be followed by American troops. Senators and representatives aren't asked their reasons when the roll is called; they simply answer yea or nay.

Repeal prevailed by comfortable margins: two to one in the Senate, four to three in the House. It was accompanied by a cash-and-carry restriction on American trade with belligerents. The president was authorized to forbid American nationals and American ships from traveling in war zones.

23

LINDBERGH WASN'T SURPRISED by the outcome. Nor by the reaction to his opposition to the president. "Opened some of the letters from a sack of mail that had been sent over from the Mutual studios earlier in the day," he wrote after his second radio address. "There were many intelligent letters and telegrams, and nearly ninety per cent of those opened were favorable. Of course, the people who like what you say are more likely to write than those who don't—at least that is true in the intelligent classes. The unintelligent group is more likely to write when they don't like what you say. A neatly typewritten or handwritten sheet is usually favorable, while you can be almost certain that a dirty, scrawly, penciled sheet, or one written in red ink, is unfavorable."

He was disappointed by Harold Nicolson. "Morning papers carry a rather silly article by Harold Nicolson about my radio addresses—reprinted from some English publication," Lindbergh wrote. "Like so many others (I expected something better from him), he attacks me personally rather than the things I advocate with which he disagrees. Naturally, the English did not like my addresses, but I expected a somewhat more objective criticism from them than from my opponents in the United States. However, the country is at war, and one should be prepared to overlook and excuse many acts from the citizens of a country at war—even the things Nicolson wrote while claiming at the same time to be a friend."

Parts of the mail revived bad memories. "Threatening letters are beginning to come in, with the problems they always bring for us,"

Lindbergh wrote. "Where should we spend the winter, and where will the children be reasonably safe from this sort of thing? This house"—on Long Island—"is a little isolated to make me feel comfortable when I am away. Of course, safety for my family lies in my keeping out of the public eye and the attention of the press. That is hard enough in normal times, but in a period of crisis in which one's country may become involved in war, one must take part in the affairs of his country and exercise his influence in the direction he thinks right. I feel I must do this, even if we have to put an armed guard in the house." The experience reminded him why he had taken his family away from America. "It is a fine state of affairs in a country which feels it is civilized; people dislike what you do, so they threaten to kill your children."

LINDBERGH HAD ENTERED the political arena, but he refused to consider himself political. "Of course, I am rapidly being lined up as a Republican, although actually I have no special interest in that party," he wrote in his journal. "My primary interest lies in the character of a man, and not in whether he is a Republican or a Democrat. I would as soon vote for one as the other. The issues between them are quite superficial at this time." He didn't think the perception of him as a Republican would persist. "I have too little interest in either politics or popularity." He cherished his independence. "One of the dearest of rights to me is being able to say what I think and act as I wish. I intend to do this, and I know it will cause trouble. As soon as it does, the politicians will disown me quickly enough."

But he wasn't being disowned yet. Lindbergh had lunch with William Borah at the senator's office. "Borah and I discussed the coming presidential election and the possible candidates," Lindbergh recorded. "Neither of us are Roosevelt men, of course. Borah made the startling statement that he thought I might make a good candidate! This idea has been discussed in the press in isolated instances and in a few of the letters that arrive in the mail, but it is the first time anyone in an important political position has mentioned it to me."

The earlier mentions, combined with the fact that his father had been in politics, had caused Lindbergh to consider the fit of his temperament for politics. "Many years ago, about 1927 or '28,

Henry Breckinridge"—a Democrat who served in Woodrow Wilson's administration alongside Franklin Roosevelt, and who provided legal counsel to Lindbergh during the 1930s—"suggested that I lay my course toward the White House," he now recalled. It hadn't taken him long to conclude against it. "I enjoy too much the ability to do and say what I wish to ever be a successful candidate for President. I prefer intellectual and personal freedom to the honors and accomplishments of political office—even that of President."

He summarized his thinking to Borah in response to the senator's sounding him out. "I told Borah I felt his suggestion was a great honor but did not believe I was well suited for political office and that I would probably be very unhappy if I ever held one."

THE END OF the debate over the arms embargo coincided with a quieting of events in Europe. Following the partition of Poland by German and Soviet forces, the conflict settled into a wait-and-see mode. Britain and France were formally at war with Germany, but their armies couldn't figure out how to get at Germany, and Hitler appeared in no hurry to have his armies get at them. Observers who credited Hitler's claim that he was interested in territory only to the east hoped for a negotiated end to the war before fighting really began in the west. As a phrase of the day put it, blitzkrieg had given way to sitzkrieg.

"Anne and I went for a short walk, talking of the winter, and of building a permanent home somewhere in this country," Lindbergh wrote in early December. The couple discussed "the same old problem we have tried so unsuccessfully to solve all these years—how to obtain safety, normalcy, beauty, and a balance between seclusion for work and contact for inspiration. Of course, we cannot obtain everything we want in a home, but it is essential to weigh every element with the utmost care. Nothing is more important than one's home and all it represents." They had been on the move for most of a decade, and the experience had taken a toll. "The satisfaction of living, the effectiveness of thinking and acting, spiritual depth and appreciation, all are intertwined to a large extent with the home one lives in—not that these elements are *impossible* without a home, but they are lacking in balance. One needs roots, and those roots must have real soil to grow in and come back to. We have wanted for years a permanent home that we loved, and now I must find one."

The war complicated matters. "Stability will be hard to find from now on for an indefinite period. War and social upheavals are likely to upset all plans. But one must try; we may never see stability again in our lifetimes as we have known it in the past." One did what one could. "If we cannot build on a home, then we must build on life and the living of it, even though it be from day to day."

During the Christmas holidays Lindbergh and his family visited his mother in Detroit. He dropped in on Henry Ford in nearby Dearborn. "I talked to Ford about the war, the industrial situation in America, about his ideas of decentralization, etc. He is a combination of genius and impracticability, with the genius definitely on top." The mechanic in Lindbergh sat in awe of the most successful mechanic of the age. "Ford is a great man and a constructive influence in this country. One cannot talk to him without gaining new ideas and receiving much mental stimulation."

Yet there was that quirkiness. "His impracticability is demonstrated by his 'Peace Ship' at the time of the last war." In 1915 Ford had taken it upon himself to end the war by chartering an ocean liner and inviting peace activists to join him on a cruise to Europe, where they would shame the belligerents into stopping the conflict. Before the boat got there, the emissaries of peace were battling among themselves, and the affair proved a fiasco. Lindbergh knew the story and wondered what Ford had been thinking. "It seems utterly silly to me," he noted. But his respect for Ford deterred him from being too harsh. "Possibly I am not well enough acquainted with the circumstances that surrounded the project. It is unfair to judge without more information than I have."

Nor did Ford know much about aviation. He had tried to build a big plane to carry a hundred passengers yet wound up with "an abortion designed for thirty-six passengers, which taxied across the field at Dearborn but never took the air," Lindbergh remarked. "The plane was too far ahead of its time, and much too far ahead of the aeronautical engineers in the Ford organization." Here too, though, Lindbergh suspended judgment. "Even though it was a failure, it showed real vision. Ford simply tried to take too big a step for that period of aviation."

The aging industrialist and the young aviator apparently didn't discuss Lindbergh's latest musings on race and civilization. Lindbergh would have mentioned it in his journal. Ford had long promoted conspiracy theories involving Jews, but now he pressed his current enthusiasm on his guest. "At lunch we were introduced to a new drink—carrot juice. It was very good, I thought. Ford said it was made by crushing carrots and collecting the juice."

PART THREE

A Special Relationship

24

AMID THE FIGHT over the arms embargo, Roosevelt struck up a dialogue with a person whose patent aim was to make a liar out of him and a prophet out of Lindbergh. Winston Churchill and Roosevelt had met once before, in London in 1918, while Roosevelt was assistant secretary of the navy. Churchill had been Britain's first lord of the admiralty but been sacked after the disastrous Gallipoli campaign. The meeting made little impression on either man; Churchill forgot that it had even occurred.

Roosevelt's career had prospered better than Churchill's since then. Churchill wandered in the wilderness of British politics, seeking the cause that would convince his compatriots that they needed him. From a distance he watched Roosevelt win the governorship of New York and then the presidency of the United States. Suppressing his Tory skepticism of bigger government, Churchill sent Roosevelt a copy of the first volume of his biography of the first duke of Marlborough, a Churchill ancestor, and on the title page he inscribed an endorsement of the New Deal: "With earnest best wishes for the success of the greatest crusade of modern times."

Churchill remained outside the circles of power during most of the 1930s. He warned against Hitler before assailing Neville Chamberlain for appeasing the Nazi dictator. Most Tories considered him a crank, while Labour thought him a lunatic. But after Hitler did what Churchill had said he would do, Chamberlain decided that prudence required bringing Churchill into the cabinet, where his voice might be tempered by responsibility for government policy. Chamberlain made Churchill again first admiralty lord on the day Britain declared war on Germany.

This time Roosevelt took the initiative. "My dear Churchill," he wrote. "It is because you and I occupied similar positions in the World War that I want you to know how glad I am that you are back again in the Admiralty." The circumstances were different, Roosevelt acknowledged. Hitler wasn't Kaiser Wilhelm. "But the essential is not very different." Germany remained the foe. Roosevelt sensed that Churchill was destined for greater things; his star was clearly rising while that of Chamberlain was falling. In any event Roosevelt sought another perspective on British policy. "What I want you and the Prime Minister to know is that I shall at all times welcome it if you will keep me in touch personally with anything you want me to know about. You can always send sealed letters through your pouch or my pouch." The sealed British diplomatic pouch to the British embassy in Washington, and the American pouch to the American embassy in London, would keep the correspondence from prying eyes even within their own governments. Roosevelt closed with a belated response to Churchill's earlier gift and good wishes. "I am glad you did the Marlboro volumes before this thing started," he said. There were three more volumes after the first. "I much enjoyed reading them."

CHURCHILL WAS DELIGHTED to hear from Roosevelt. As soon as the letter arrived he placed a telephone call to the president. His purpose was to encourage further communications, but he also took the occasion to warn Roosevelt about a dastardly plot the Germans had devised. The American naval attaché in Berlin had reported being told by a German admiral that the British navy was going to sink an American merchant ship, the *Iroquois*, bound from Queenstown, Ireland, for America, and blame the Germans, with the goal of bringing the United States into the war on the British side. American officials inquired of the British; Churchill, as head of the navy, responded to Roosevelt.

Churchill accused the Germans of baleful disinformation; if anyone was intending to sink the *Iroquois*, he told Roosevelt, it was the Germans. At this point the ship was a thousand miles west of Ireland. "There remains about a thousand miles in which the outrage might be committed," Churchill said. The danger from German submarines in that stretch of the ocean was small. "The only method can be a time-bomb planted at Queenstown. We think this not impossible." Churchill urged Roosevelt to reveal the German plot. "I am convinced full exposure of all the facts known to the United States government, including the sources of information, especially if official, is the only way of frustrating the plot. Action seems urgent." Churchill added as an afterthought: "I presume you have warned the *Iroquois* to search the ship."

The ship had been searched. No bomb was found. None went off, nor was the *Iroquois* harmed. Roosevelt followed Churchill's advice, up to a point. The White House revealed the German warning about the British, even as Roosevelt's press secretary, Stephen Early, conveyed the president's skepticism. "We don't believe many people believe this report is true or could be true," Early said. "Certainly we don't believe any British or French or other ship would do such a thing."

Roosevelt was playing a subtle game. He didn't quite trust Churchill, whose reputation remained checkered. One thing Roosevelt did know about Churchill was that he was an unrepentant imperialist, who considered India an inalienable part of the British realm. Roosevelt might be willing for America to fight to defend Britain, if things came to that, but he didn't welcome the thought of defending the British hold on India.

He might not have a choice. Roosevelt was a realist when it came to foreign policy. Countries took allies where they could find them. If America went to war against Germany, Britain would be a necessary ally. And if Britain carried imperial baggage, so be it.

Meanwhile it suited Roosevelt's purposes to put into American minds the possibility that Germany might do something so heinous as sink an American ship and kill its crew. He wasn't looking for a *Lusitania* moment yet. But the time might come.

CHURCHILL CONTINUED TO cultivate Roosevelt. About the time Lindbergh was arguing for a militarized Monroe Doctrine, a policy that would employ American naval and air power to keep European forces out of the Western Hemisphere, a meeting in Panama of delegates from the American republics declared the Atlantic Ocean within a thousand miles of American shores off-limits to the navies of the European belligerents. Exception was made for Canada, a belligerent itself. Roosevelt's administration had sponsored the meeting and the declaration, with no reference or credit to Lindbergh.

Churchill applauded the idea of the prohibited zone but demurred on details. "We quite understand the natural desire of the United States to keep belligerents out of their waters," he wrote to Roosevelt. But a thousand miles was a bit much; three hundred miles would be better. On principle, Britain was loath to relinquish its rights on any part of the high seas. Yet its navy was currently stretched trying to chase German U-boats across the whole Atlantic. The question for Britain was who would enforce the American ban. "We should have great difficulty in accepting a zone which was only policed by some weak neutral," Churchill said. "But of course if the American navy takes care of it, that is all right." He concluded his letter reassuringly: "We wish to help you in every way in keeping the war out of the Americas."

ROOSEVELT DIDN'T BELIEVE him, if only because he knew he would have said the same thing in Churchill's place. In fact the British *wanted* the conflict to come to the Americas. They were pleased for American ships to patrol the western Atlantic; this would ease the strain on British ships. More important, it would put Americans in the German line of fire. Roosevelt might be willing to postpone a *Lusitania* moment; for Churchill it couldn't come too soon.

Churchill took Roosevelt into his confidence, relaying information whose sharing chafed British intelligence officials. "We have been hitting the U-boats hard with our new apparatus," Churchill wrote. The apparatus was an early version of sonar the British were calling ASDIC. "We should be quite ready to tell you about our asdic methods whenever you feel they would be of use to the United States Navy and are sure the secret will go no farther. They certainly are very remarkable in results and enable two destroyers to do the work that could not have been done by ten last time." Churchill added, in a comment Lindbergh would have found most interesting had the Roosevelt-Churchill correspondence not been closely held: "We have not been at all impressed by the accuracy of the Germans air bombing of our warships. They seem to have no effective bomb sights."

Churchill soothed Roosevelt when the needs of British security overrode American objections. After accepting the idea of a belligerent-free zone around the Americas, Churchill directed a British navy squadron to chase the German heavy cruiser *Admiral Graf Spee* almost onto the beach of Argentina. The German ship had roamed the oceans since the start of the war, sinking merchant vessels vital to the British war effort. Churchill gave the order to find the *Graf Spee* at all costs and do the ship in. The British tracked the *Graf Spee* to the estuary Rio de la Plata, or River Plate, between Argentina and Uruguay. A furious battle ensued, in which the *Graf Spee* crippled one British warship and damaged two others, and was damaged in turn. When the commander of the *Graf Spee* took refuge at Montevideo, the British pinned him there. Believing there was no escape, the commander scuttled the *Graf Spee* and killed himself.

The victory did wonders for British morale. It vindicated Britain's historic emphasis on naval power, and at a time—December 1939—when British ground forces couldn't yet reach Germany, it put substance into the British pledge to defend Poland, or at least punish Poland's invader.

But it defeated Roosevelt's attempt to keep the war out of American waters. Churchill apologized, unconvincingly. "I am very sorry there seems to be trouble about recent incidents," he cabled to the president after the battle. The British ships had had no choice but to follow the *Graf Spee* when the German cruiser violated the neutral zone. Yet the end had justified the means. "As a result of action off Plate whole South Atlantic is now clear and may perhaps continue clear of warlike operations. This must be a blessing to South American Republics whose trade was hampered by activities of raider and whose ports were used for his supply ships and information centers. In fact we have rescued all this vast area from war disturbances." Churchill remarked that the Argentine government had not protested. Nor should it, or the neighboring governments. "South American States should see in Plate action their deliverance perhaps indefinitely from all animosity."

Churchill emphasized that the British navy was serving the interests of global peace. "Much of world duty is being thrown on admiralty," he wrote. "Hope burden will not be made too heavy for us to bear. Even a single raider loose in North Atlantic requires employment half our battle fleet to give sure protection." On the topic of the North Atlantic, Churchill promised to consider American sensibilities even while he declined to accept the American desire for a broad neutral zone. "We cannot always refrain from stopping enemy ships outside international three-mile limit"—let alone a three-hundred- or one-thousand-mile limit—"when these may well be supply ships for U-boats or surface raiders," Churchill said, "but instructions have been given only to arrest or fire upon them out of sight of United States shores." American civilians wouldn't have to witness Britain's policing of international law.

Churchill went on to explain the challenges his navy faced. "We are at very full extension till the new wartime construction of anti-submarine craft begins to flow from May onwards. If we should break under load South American Republics would soon have worse worries than the sound of one day's distant seaward cannonade." The American people and their president should take note. "And you also, Sir, in quite a short time would have more direct cares. I ask that full consideration should be given to strain upon us at this crucial period and best construction put upon action indispensable to end war shortly in right way."

ROOSEVELT IGNORED THE *Graf Spee* incident when he addressed Congress and the nation at the start of 1940. "As the Congress reassembles, the impact of war abroad makes it natural to approach 'the state of the union' through a discussion of foreign affairs," he said. Yet foreign affairs were of a piece with domestic affairs in the modern age, and his administration would approach the former as it had the latter during the previous seven years, emphasizing the freedom and security of ordinary Americans. "In previous messages to the Congress I have repeatedly warned that, whether we like it or not, the daily lives of American citizens will, of necessity, feel the shock of events on other continents. This is no longer mere theory, because it has been definitely proved to us by the facts of yesterday and today."

Not everyone saw things this way, Roosevelt acknowledged. "There are those who wishfully insist, in innocence or ignorance or both, that the United States of America as a self-contained unit can live happily and prosperously, its future secure, inside a high wall of isolation while, outside, the rest of civilization and the commerce and culture of mankind are shattered." He didn't disparage the emotions that gave rise to this view. "I can understand the feelings of those who warn the nation that they will never again consent to the sending of American youth to fight on the soil of Europe."

But the warning was based on a misapprehension. "Nobody has asked them to consent, for nobody expects such an undertaking. The overwhelming majority of our fellow citizens do not abandon in the slightest their hope and their expectation that the United States will not become involved in military participation in these wars." Roosevelt counted himself in this large majority.

Yet hope and expectation mustn't exclude all else. "There is a vast difference between keeping out of war and pretending that this war is none of our business." The war existed, and wishing wouldn't make it go away. The question was how to secure American liberty and interest in a world at war. "We do not have to go to war with other nations, but at least we can strive with other nations to encourage the kind of peace that will lighten the troubles of the world, and by so doing help our own nation as well."

Roosevelt rejected the claim of the anti-interventionists to be the advocates of peace. "The time is long past when any political party or any particular group can curry or capture public favor by labeling itself the 'peace party' or the 'peace bloc.' That label belongs to the whole United States and to every right thinking man, woman and child within it." Again, Roosevelt included himself in this group.

And yet, again, peace wasn't simply the absence of war. True peace must rest on principles that were being flouted before the eyes of the world. Americans must hold to a vision of a peace that would endure. "We must look ahead and see the possibilities for our children if the rest of the world comes to be dominated by concentrated force alone, even though today we are a very great and a very powerful nation. We must look ahead and see the effect on our own future if all the small nations of the world have their independence snatched from them or become mere appendages to relatively vast and powerful military systems. We must look ahead and see the kind of lives our children would have to lead if a large part of the rest of the world were compelled to worship a god imposed by a military ruler, or were forbidden to worship God at all; if the rest of the world were forbidden to read and hear the facts—the daily news of their own and other nations—if they were deprived of the truth that makes men free."

Again, a small group of Americans lacked this vision. He urged their more far-seeing compatriots to bring them around, for their own sake as well as that of the country. "I hope that we shall have fewer American ostriches in our midst. It is not good for the ultimate health of ostriches to bury their heads in the sand."

Roosevelt's listeners in the House chamber chuckled, but he wasn't laughing. Ostriches were merely stupid; the purveyors of isolation were malign. "This is the danger to which we in America must begin to be more alert," Roosevelt said. "For the apologists for foreign aggressors, and equally those selfish and partisan groups at home who wrap themselves in a false mantle of Americanism to promote their own economic, financial or political advantage, are now trying European tricks upon us, seeking to muddy the stream of our national thinking, weakening us in the face of danger, by trying to set our own people to fighting among themselves." Americans must resist the message of the isolationists, and they must fight the isolationists themselves. "We must combat them, as we would the plague, if American integrity and American security are to be preserved."

THIS WASN'T THE first time Roosevelt had attacked his opponents as enemies of the American people. During his reelection campaign in 1936 he railed against "economic royalists"; in his acceptance speech to the Democratic convention that year he characterized opponents of the New Deal as "the resolute enemy within our gates."

Yet the language of treason cut deeper in the context of war. Lindbergh and other Roosevelt critics judged it outrageous. Some of them thought they knew why Roosevelt was speaking so intemperately. The president's distrusters believed he would employ the excuse of the war to try to break the oldest taboo in American politics: on third terms for presidents. Roosevelt was a political creature, they judged, who couldn't live without politics. He hadn't let polio force his retirement from politics, and he wasn't going to let an unwritten rule do so. His first term had been filled with legislative accomplishment, but his second term had been a mess. After the botched attempt to pack the Supreme Court, he had tried to purge Democratic conservatives in 1938, and failed miserably. If he left the White House on schedule, he might be judged by history as mediocre or worse—especially if a Republican succeeded him and started to dismantle the New Deal. Roosevelt saw the war as his ticket to longevity in office, said the skeptics. He would talk about preserving freedom, but what he really intended to preserve was himself from oblivion.

"Lunch with Harry Byrd in his office in the Capitol Building,"

Lindbergh wrote after a visit to Washington. "We discussed the war in Europe, the American gold policy, dangers of propaganda, and many other subjects. Byrd has no more confidence in Roosevelt than I have and thinks he may easily run for a third term. Byrd said Roosevelt had promised Farley"—James Farley, postmaster general and political confidant of the president—"that he would not run. Farley said later that Roosevelt could easily change his mind. Most people who know the President do not seem to regard his promises very highly." Roosevelt's divisive language had helped him win in 1936; apparently he thought such language would do the same in 1940.

ON THIS VISIT Lindbergh strolled around the Capitol. "I arrived a few minutes early so walked through the grounds where I played as a boy," he wrote in his journal. "For the first time I noticed what seems to be neglect and indifference in the care of the grounds. Footpaths were worn across the grass in many places—deep and yellow—giving more the impression of cow paths in a farm pasture than I like to see on the lawns of the national Capitol. Almost every tree on the grounds is badly in need of surgery, and there seems to be an unnecessary quantity of bits of paper lying about." People tramped through the flower beds. The season being winter, the trespassers did no particular damage, but the mere idea struck Lindbergh as wrong. "Worst of all, dozens of initials and names now adorn the outer pillars and walls of the Capitol building itself—some in crayon and others actually carved in the stone." As was his habit, Lindbergh read much into what he observed. "I felt depressed by the walk and could not avoid wondering if I was seeing the signs of the beginning of an American decline, and what could be done to stop such a trend. This nation is too young to decline, but there are alarming signs, and sometimes the smaller ones are most significant."

Harry Byrd introduced Lindbergh to Vice President Garner. "We talked for about five minutes, during which time I told Garner of the time in 1924 when I landed an old 'Canuck' in the center square of his home town of Uvalde, Texas. I was flying west and had lost my way. Fuel was running low when I reached Uvalde and finally located my position. There was an open square in the center of the town large enough to land in. I got down all right and refueled; but the square was not large enough to take off from, as it was surrounded by buildings. I decided to attempt a takeoff from the street that passed along one side of the square. To do this it was necessary to pass between two telephone poles that were only two or three feet farther apart than the wingspread of the plane. The road was rather badly rutted, and I missed by six inches. The plane was whipped around by the pole, and the nose hit the side of a hardware store, knocking down pots and pans that were hanging on the inside wall. Fortunately, neither the plane nor the wall was very badly damaged—a broken propeller and a few smashed boards being the major consequences of the accident. The store owner was not at all unpleasant about it. In fact, he seemed to enjoy the excitement and demonstrated true Texas hospitality rather than the complaint and objection one would expect under such circumstances. I had the plane patched up and flying again within a few days."

Lindbergh dropped in on Ernest Lundeen, a senator from Minnesota. "Lundeen knew my father well, and we spent the largest part of the next hour and a half talking about my father and various memories Lundeen had of him," Lindbergh wrote. Lindbergh knew that Lundeen had voted against American entry into the World War in 1917. The senator hadn't changed his mind. "Lundeen is greatly concerned lest we be pushed into this war, eventually drifting imperceptibly closer, as we did in the last war, until it is too late to stop."

WHAT LINDBERGH DID *not* know was that Lundeen's opposition to war against Germany was being financed by the German government. George Sylvester Viereck had emigrated from Germany to America as a boy, arriving with his family in the late 1890s. He pursued a literary life, publishing poetry, novels and plays and winning a reputation as a *wunderkind*. During the World War he defended Germany in a weekly magazine he edited called *The Fatherland*. An angry mob threatened to lynch him and drove him from his home. He was reported to have received support for his journal from the German government, but the American government took no official notice.

He remained a supporter of Germany after the war. He endorsed the works of authors who blamed American belligerence on bankers and munition-makers. He spotted Hitler early and pinned his hopes for a German revival on the National Socialist party. In 1934 he addressed a pro-Nazi rally of twenty thousand people at Madison Square Garden at which hundreds of uniformed men with Nazi armbands protected the participants against a greater number of self-identifying communists outside the hall shouting "Down with Hitler!"

Viereck claimed to speak for the thirty-five million Americans of German descent. He said it was possible to sympathize with the Nazi project without being anti-Semitic. "Whatever our attitude toward Hitler may be, there is no doubt that there was no alternative for Germany except Hitler—or chaos. Hitler saved not only Germany but all Europe from being inundated by the red sea of Bolshevism. Hitler emancipated Germany from the bondage of Versailles and unified the German people for the first time in a long history. Germany was the last of all great nations to achieve national unity. This unity is not complete even today." This was before the annexation of the Sudetenland and Austria.

Viereck, and the organization sponsoring the rally, complained about a boycott of Germany and German goods organized by American Jews since the Nazis took power in Berlin. Viereck said he was not a member of the sponsoring group; he had come to the rally on his own. "But I am completely in sympathy with its defensive measure against the reign of terror foisted upon the United States and especially the City of New York by certain professional Jews and their Bolshevist confederates." He went on, "I am opposed to all boycotts. I was opposed to the boycott of the Jews by the Germans. I am equally opposed to the boycott of the Germans by the Jews."

He reiterated that dramatic change had been necessary in Germany, and he praised how it had come about. "Germany has passed through the throes of a revolution which completely changed her social, financial, political and economic structure. It was the most civilized, the most bloodless revolution in history."

He repeated that anti-Semitism was not intrinsic to Nazism. "I hope and trust that the last word on the Jewish question has not been said. I hope and trust that when complete stability is established, the German people will differentiate Jews who are international plotters and Jews who are Germans before they are Jews. I hope that eventually a concordat will be established that will grant to the Jews in Germany the largest measure of justice possible in this imperfect world."

That was in 1934. Six years later—after Kristallnacht and numerous other anti-Jewish actions and laws—Viereck couldn't have said anything similar and been taken at all seriously. So he enlisted others to make the case. He worked quietly, providing talking points and drafts of editorials for opponents of American intervention in the war. There was less praise of Hitler and Germany and more criticism of Britain and Bolshevism. Viereck's activities received financial support from the German government; some of that money found its way to anti-interventionists, including Ernest Lundeen. At this point the criminality involved was minor. Foreign agents were supposed to register with the American government, and Viereck did not. If and when the United States went to war against Germany, he might be charged with sedition or espionage.

As for Lundeen and others who received funding, they probably hadn't broken any law. Yet there was a reason they kept their German connection quiet: it would destroy their credibility and likely their careers.

26

IN CHURCHILL'S LETTER defending British actions leading to the demise of the *Graf Spee*, the navy minister had promised to send Roosevelt details of the engagement. Churchill knew that Roosevelt, a former admiralty man himself, liked stories of war at sea, and the version Churchill had his aides write was filled with fire, smoke and British fortitude. Even the Germans came off well. The *Graf Spee* was a doughty foe. "A large hole was made on the port side of the fore messdeck, and other small holes elsewhere. It was also reported that the vessel was holed twice below the water line, but this cannot be vouched for. In all she was hit between 50 and 60 times." And still she did not sink.

"Ever so many thanks for that tremendously interesting account of the extraordinarily well fought action of your three cruisers," Roosevelt replied. "I am inclined to think that when we know more about the facts, it will turn out that the damage to the *Admiral Graf Spee* was greater than reported."

There were new issues to deal with. In the absence of a ground campaign, Britain's principal source of pressure on Germany was a naval blockade. Such blockades had been central to Britain's success as a maritime power for centuries, and they had caused problems for the United States almost as long. The British interdicted American trade during the Revolutionary War, the wars of the French Revolution and the Napoleonic wars. Britain's seizure of American ships helped trigger the War of 1812. British seizures prior to American entry into the World War prompted protests from Washington. In all those instances, the American government took the position that neutrals had the right to trade with belligerents during wartime, with exceptions made for weapons, conceded to be contraband.

As long as America had protested Britain's blockade policies, the British government had defended them. Sometimes London adduced legal theory and precedent, sometimes simple necessity. The two instances when the shoe had been on the other foot—when the United States during the Civil War had defined the rights of blockade broadly against the Confederacy, and after America's entry into the World War, when the American government expanded the definition of contraband to include almost anything bound for a hostile port—were afterward cited against American protests of British blockades.

The blockade question resurfaced as soon as the second war against Germany began. It was partly blunted by America's neutrality law, which required Roosevelt to declare a war zone from which American vessels were barred. American warships didn't police the war zone; rather, the law was enforced by insurance companies, which refused to cover losses incurred in violation of the law. Yet the neutrality law didn't solve the problem. The British built on the American precedent during the World War to claim a right to stop any ship bound for Europe, whether it would enter the American-defined war zone or not, and search it for contraband, which they now defined as nearly anything. American and other neutral vessels could avoid the sometimes risky process of interception at sea by stopping in a British-controlled port for certification that they weren't bound for Germany.

The process was time-consuming and therefore expensive in fuel and labor costs for the submitting ships. It also signified a surrender of American neutral rights. Shippers protested, and the protests echoed among the many Americans who disliked or distrusted the British. Irish-Americans, as always, and German-Americans, of late, were two large constituencies of Anglophobia; anti-interventionists were another.

Roosevelt and Churchill, still corresponding in secret, attempted to find a modus vivendi. Churchill proposed to his colleagues in the British government to exempt American ships from some of the restrictions enforced against ships of other neutrals. But

Churchill's colleagues were less sensitive to American opinion than he. Churchill's paternal line ran deep in the British aristocracy, but his mother was an American, a fact that some of the Churchill skeptics deemed worrisome.

Roosevelt himself could have lived with the British procedure. Though he had been a naval man, he had never depended on the merchant trade to meet a payroll or turn a profit. His concern for the capitalist class didn't keep him awake nights. Yet he didn't wish to give the anti-interventionists any more cause for complaint than they already had, and he didn't want to provide them grounds for saying he was in Britain's pocket. "At the time of dictating this, I think our conversation in regard to search and detention of American ships is working out satisfactorily," Roosevelt wrote to Churchill in February 1940. "But I would not be frank unless I told you that there has been much public criticism here. The general feeling is that the net benefit to your people and to France is hardly worth the definite annoyance caused to us. That is always found to be so in a nation which is 3,000 miles away from the fact of war. I wish much that I could talk things over with you in person—but I am grateful to you for keeping me in touch, as you do."

27

LINDBERGH FOLLOWED THE news from Europe with a
jaundiced eye toward what he saw in the papers. "Even the
most important and major events are shrouded in contradic-
tion," he wrote in his journal. "One can read almost anything about
the fighting, depending upon what newspaper he buys. It is obvious
that the press has no idea whatever of what is actually taking place."

Yet he watched, as well, as one keenly interested in a particular
aspect of modern war. "A great naval battle is reported under way in
the Skagerrak"—the strait between Denmark and Norway. In April
1940 Britain sought a foothold in Norway from which to harass
German naval operations in the North Sea. Germany contested the
effort, and the battle Lindbergh read about ensued. The conflicting
reports left much unclear. "Reading between the lines, however, it
seems to me that the Germans are meeting with amazing success in
taking over Norway in the face of the British fleet. If so, it is a victory
for air power and a turning point in military history."

The confusion persisted. "Our papers give the impression that
England and France have control of the sea, but this seems to be
more of a wish than a fact, if one can judge by the little information
that does seep through," Lindbergh wrote. "The Germans are carrying on an extremely daring project. It seems they have great confidence in the power of their aviation to cope with the British fleet. If
the British do bring their main fleet within reach of the German air
force, there is the possibility of one of the decisive battles of world
history—and a decisive battle could not be won by the fleet under

these circumstances." This was why he distrusted the news. "I doubt that the British would fully expose their main fleet."

Lindbergh labored, as before, to keep America out of the war. "Drove to New York for lunch at the Engineers Club; then to 505 Fifth Avenue for a conference with a Mr. Hart"—Merwin Hart, president of the New York State Economic Council—"who desires to bring together a number of men who are opposed to this country entering the war." Lindbergh was asked to speak at a dinner two weeks hence, where means to counter prowar agitation would be discussed. He agreed. "I believe this country is still solidly against entering the war, but as German success continues (as I believe it will), more and more pressure will be brought upon us by the Allies and their supporters. I would feel less disturbed about this if I had the slightest confidence in Roosevelt."

He met with Alanson Houghton, who had been the American ambassador to Britain when Lindbergh flew the Atlantic. "We discussed the war and trends in America and Europe. Later, Houghton asked me if I had forgiven him for sending me back home on the *Memphis* in 1927. It recalled the time clearly to my mind, and we both laughed." Lindbergh had flown to London after the historic flight to Paris; Houghton invited him to the embassy. He told Lindbergh that President Coolidge had sent a warship to fetch the country's new hero and bring him home in style. "I had no wish to leave Europe so soon and had hoped to fly to a number of countries in Europe," Lindbergh recalled. "I had then been to only three—France, Belgium, and England. I had even considered the possibility of continuing my flights eastward and eventually circling the world. I would much prefer to have flown back to America. But Houghton insisted I return home on a battleship"—cruiser, actually—"with the *Spirit of St. Louis* in a crate on board. He eventually won the argument by saying that it was an order from the President of the United States."

Lindbergh lately had arranged with Pan American Airways to act as a consultant; in this capacity he hoped to travel to Europe to investigate possible air routes from America. The war complicated matters, but it also provided additional reason to go: to see how the air forces of the belligerents were holding up. During a visit to Washington he called on Hap Arnold. "Took a taxi to the Munitions Building for a conference with him in regard to my projected trip to

Europe," Lindberg wrote in late April. Arnold summoned an army attaché who had just returned from Italy. "We talked for half an hour about conditions in that country." Lindbergh proceeded to another meeting. "I talked to Magruder"—General John Magruder, chief of intelligence for the War Department—"about the code telegrams which are to be sent to the military attaches in Europe in advance of my arrival."

He met again with opponents of intervention and of the apparent direction of Roosevelt's policies. The dinner he had agreed to attend took place. "There were fifteen or twenty men in all—invited by Mr. Hart to discuss the danger of our being drawn into the war, and means of counteracting the present propaganda for that purpose."

At the same time, he offered advice to American manufacturers of airplanes and other armaments. "I was very pleasantly surprised by the characteristics of the P-40," he wrote after a visit to Wright Field in Dayton, Ohio. "It is a type that was rushed through design and construction by the Curtiss-Wright Corporation after the Air Corps had suddenly woken up to find European pursuit planes far ahead of ours. This P-40 is really a P-36 with the nose changed sufficiently to incorporate an Allison liquid-cooled, in-line engine in place of the radial, air-cooled type used in the P-36. The wing is the same as the P-36 wing, and the fuselage back of the engine is the same, although the gross weight is about 1,000 pounds heavier. The speed of the P-40 is approximately 370 m.p.h., or a little over 60 m.p.h. faster than the P-36."

Lindbergh liked nothing more than to think about airplanes, talk about airplanes with other experts, and fly the airplanes the best designers and manufacturers were building. The experts, designers and manufacturers were eager to get the reactions of one who understood the theory and practice of flight as well as anyone in the world. And who, moreover, knew more than almost anyone about the planes these planes would be pitted against.

"Usually when a standard-type plane is changed to incorporate a radically different engine, the handling characteristics suffer," he remarked. "But the P-40 seems to be an exception, for it seemed to take off, control, and land just as well as the P-36. The forward vision is, of course, much better with the inverted, in-line engine. Everything considered, it seems to be an excellent single-engine pursuit plane, and a definite step forward from the P-36. I cannot help wondering, however, what the Germans are bringing out about this time. The P-40 is probably a little better than the Messerschmitt they have had in service during the last few months, but it is about time for them to produce something new, too."

The exhilaration of flight had lost none of its appeal. "I spent forty-five minutes in the P-40. (The XP-40, to be exact. It is the first one built and preceded the line production by some months.) Even at low altitude, the plane cruised at nearly 300 miles an hour. It gave me the greatest feeling of speed in flying I have yet experienced."

Altitude afforded relief from the cares of the earth, from the hash humans made of affairs below. "How interesting and enlightening it is to compare the streamline of an airplane to the awkward, complicated, and conflicting chapters of a law book. The success of one is clearly measured by nature, while the value of the other is estimated by partisan men. How beautiful and simple life really is, and how complicated man tries to make it. He worships God on the one hand; tries to improve upon Him on the other. The fallacy is rarely seen."

Whenever possible he traveled by air, in his own plane or one he was testing. He could avoid reporters and travel on his own schedule, subject to weather. The element of risk was as seductive as ever. "After lunch I drove to Patterson Field and took off for St. Louis in the Lambert. The engine started cutting out on take-off, just as I was about ten feet above the ground and headed for trees at the edge of the field. (One can always trust this plane to do something wrong at the most inopportune moment.) I banked quickly to follow the edge of the field and pulled out the altitude adjustment for a second or two. After the first few coughs the engine ran smoothly again and continued to do so as I climbed and circled the field. I set my course for St. Louis, detouring just enough to avoid the airways."

Nor did his flights ever fail to transport him back to the simpler times before he was famous. "A few minutes before reaching the Mississippi River I glanced at my map and noticed I was passing over the town of Sorento, where I had barnstormed on more than one occasion in the years preceding 1927. I circled, but could recognize none of the buildings or fields where I used to land. It was typical of the towns where I used to barnstorm when I first started flying, and it brought back old memories. I used to fly there from Lambert Field in the old 'Jenny,' which belonged to a man named Lingle. The plane did not fly too well, and most of the pilots around the field did not like to take it out on barnstorming trips. It had been somewhat rebuilt, and the original OX-5 engine had been replaced by a more powerful Hispano-Suiza. But the added weight of the engine more than made up for its power. The take-off was slow and the controls loggy. I seldom carried more than one passenger at a time when I flew it. Lingle usually went with me when I took this plane barnstorming, and we got along well together. He loved to fly, although I do not remember whether he ever soloed himself, and never lost an opportunity to go barnstorming with the plane.

"We would pick out some small town in Missouri or Illinois and attempt to find a farmer's field, not too far away, where we could land. After my first few months of barnstorming I could tell exactly what a field was like after I had circled it once or twice—whether it was level, how soft the ground was, whether there were any bumps or holes, in fact almost everything I could have learned by walking over it on the ground. As soon as we had landed, Lingle would go to look for the farmer who owned or rented the property to obtain permission for us to carry passengers. Meanwhile, I would walk over the field to confirm the impression I had gained of it from the air and to acquaint myself with the best directions for landing and taking off. By the time Lingle returned there was usually a small crowd gathered around the plane. Our price was standard for those days: $5.00 for a flight of between five and ten minutes. Lingle would stay on the ground and try to persuade people to fly, while I made flights over the nearby countryside."

28

THE GERMANS WON the battle for Norway, putting the world on notice of the importance of airpower in modern war. But before the world could absorb the lesson, Hitler launched a much larger offensive. In early May 1940 he sent three million German soldiers and airmen, five thousand warplanes and ten divisions of tanks into action against the Netherlands, Belgium and France.

Louis Lochner was one of three American reporters invited by Hitler to accompany the Wehrmacht on its invasion of Belgium. Hitler doubtless expected that Lochner, who worked for the Associated Press, and the others would be impressed by the prowess of the German military. It was hard for them not to be. "After crossing over from the last German border town in the dusk, in which morning mists mingled with smoke clouds from roaring planes, it took us but a short time to realize how completely war has been revolutionized by air force," Lochner wrote in his notebook. He later cabled his account to the AP office in New York. "This is how Germany operates in this decisive area: first, air scouters determine just how enemy troops are moving. They learn the exact strength of enemy forces, equipment, types of weapons used, etc. With this knowledge reinforced by photos, Germany's terrorizing Stukas, followed by heavy bombers, dash madly down upon the enemy, smashing towns if necessary through which moving troops are pushing, demolishing railway tracks, telephone lines, industrial plants, and annihilating marching columns. Meanwhile the air information service informs

the speedy mechanized units where the bombing has been successful. Quick as lightning these dart forward and face the enemy
with death-disdaining courage, while the foe is in utter confusion.
The suddenness of attack has usually proven successful. After these
mobile advance guards have thus routed the enemy, the main army
is ready to move in."

Belgian civilians did their best to get out of the way. Lochner
described the refugees: "Babies fastened onto baskets on bicycles on
which papa also loaded bedding and other necessities. Entire fami-
lies from aged grandmother to nursing infant miserably perched on
top of a springless cart drawn by a mangy horse. Interminable wan-
derers on foot, each weighed down with as much as he could carry."

The column Lochner traveled with encountered elements of the
Belgian, French and British armies, which were compelled to retreat
before the blitzkrieg. "Cannons boomed, shrapnel rent the air, German scouters roared overhead directing artillery, and ugly clouds of
yellow, white, or grey smoke indicated when deadly loads had been
deposited on the road whereon the Allied troops were withdrawing,"
Lochner wrote. "Invisible to us because hidden by trees was German infantry which relentlessly pushed after the enemy. Where we
stood, English artillery observers had been only the day before. Thus
quickly do the fortunes of war change in this area."

Belgium and the Netherlands were overrun. The Maginot Line,
on which France rested its defense strategy, trembled before the
onslaught.

"THE SCENE HAS darkened swiftly," Churchill wrote to Roosevelt, in a message marked "Most secret and personal." He went on:
"Although I have changed my office, I am sure you would not wish
me to discontinue our intimate, private correspondence." Neville
Chamberlain had been damaged politically by the outbreak of the
war in September but had clung to office through the quiet winter,
hoping to avert an all-out war. The offensive against France shred-
ded the last of the prime minister's credibility. He resigned in favor
of Churchill, who had warned most loudly against Hitler.

Churchill explained how dire the situation was. "The enemy have
a marked preponderance in the air, and their new technique is mak-

ing a deep impression upon the French. I think myself the battle on land has only just begun, and I should like to see masses engaged. Up to the present, Hitler is working with specialized units in tanks and air." The Germans had encountered no resistance to speak of. "The small countries are simply smashed up, one by one, like matchwood." The Germans most likely would receive Italian reinforcement. "We must expect, though it is not yet certain, that Mussolini will hurry in to share the loot of civilization."

Hitler wouldn't halt at the English Channel. "We expect to be attacked here ourselves, both from the air and by parachute and air borne troops in the near future, and are getting ready for them," Churchill told Roosevelt. "If necessary, we shall continue the war alone and we are not afraid of that."

Churchill got to the part of his message that involved America. He appreciated what he considered America's—or at least Roosevelt's—moral support. But more was needed. "I trust you realize, Mr. President, that the voice and force of the United States may count for nothing if they are withheld too long. You may have a completely subjugated, Nazified Europe established with astonishing swiftness, and the weight may be more than we can bear." Churchill wasn't requesting an alliance or a declaration of war yet. "All I ask now is that you should proclaim nonbelligerency, which would mean that you would help us with everything short of actually engaging armed forces."

The prime minister supplied a list. First: "The loan of forty or fifty of your older destroyers to bridge the gap between what we have now and the large new construction we put in hand at the beginning of the war. This time next year we shall have plenty. But if in the interval Italy comes in against us with another one hundred submarines, we may be strained to breaking point."

Second: "We want several hundred of the latest types of aircraft, of which you are now getting delivery. These can be repaid by those now being constructed in the United States for us."

Third: "Anti-aircraft equipment and ammunition, of which again there will be plenty next year, if we are alive to see it."

Fourth: "The fact that our ore supply is being compromised from Sweden, from North Africa, and perhaps from northern Spain, makes it necessary to purchase steel in the United States. This also applies to other materials. We shall go on paying dollars for as long as we can, but I should like to feel reasonably sure that when we can pay no more, you will give us the stuff all the same."

Fifth: "We have many reports of possible German parachute or air borne descents in Ireland. The visit of a United States squadron to Irish ports, which might well be prolonged, would be invaluable."

Sixth: "I am looking to you to keep that Japanese dog quiet in the Pacific, using Singapore in any way convenient."

ROOSEVELT WASN'T SURPRISED to receive Churchill's request, but its extent was more than he had expected. To this point Churchill had trod softly in American politics, acknowledging the sensitivity of the war question and the problems it raised for Roosevelt. But now the prime minister threw caution aside, asking for an alliance in all but name. If Churchill got what he wanted, America would become Britain's armorer, its financier, the source of its raw materials, the protector of its coast, and the guarantor of its Asian empire.

Churchill realized there was no way Roosevelt would deliver all this at once. But it couldn't hurt to ask, if only to plant a seed for future sprouting. And to put the president's conscience on the defensive in the matter of future requests.

"I have just received your message," Roosevelt replied. "And I am sure it is unnecessary for me to say that I am most happy to continue our private correspondence as we have in the past." The president said he was giving Churchill's requests the most careful consideration. Unfortunately, there were complications, especially with the destroyers. "A step of that kind could not be taken except with the specific authorization of the Congress, and I am not certain that it would be wise for that suggestion to be made to the Congress at this moment." Besides, America might need the ships for its own defense. And the vessels would require several weeks to be ready for handover.

As for the aircraft Churchill wanted: "We are now doing everything within our power to make it possible for the Allied Governments to obtain the latest types of aircraft in the United States."

Regarding the antiaircraft artillery: "The most favorable consideration will be given to the request made, in the light of our own defense needs and requirements."

On steel and other materials, Roosevelt was pleased to report that he was ahead of Churchill. "Satisfactory arrangements have been made."

On Ireland: "I shall give further consideration to your suggestion."

As for Japan and the Pacific: "The American fleet is now concentrated at Hawaii where it will remain at least for the time being."

Roosevelt left the door open. He would continue to ponder the suggestions he hadn't accepted. "I shall communicate with you again as soon as I feel able to make a final decision," he said. He encouraged further candid correspondence. "I hope you will feel free to communicate with me in this way at any time. The best of luck to you."

IF THE NEED hadn't been so pressing, Churchill must have been pleased at Roosevelt's response. The president had approved one request outright and conditionally approved two others. On the crucial request, regarding the destroyers, his negative sounded open to revision. Roosevelt said Congress would have to approve the transfer, which might or might not be true. Churchill knew enough of American politics to understand that presidents had more maneuvering room than a strict reading of the Constitution indicated. In any case, Roosevelt had persuaded Congress to repeal the arms embargo; he might persuade Congress to approve the loan of ships to Britain. Roosevelt had said America might need the ships for its own defense; Churchill hoped to convince Roosevelt that the defense of Britain *was* America's defense. And Roosevelt's objection that the ships couldn't be ready for six weeks wasn't really an objection at all. On the contrary, it sounded like encouragement. He could have said six months but didn't.

Yet Britain's need *was* pressing, and so Churchill was *not* pleased with Roosevelt's response, especially on the destroyers. He answered Roosevelt at once. "Many thanks for your message, for which I am grateful," he said. But conditions continued to worsen, and time was of the essence. "I do not need to tell you about the gravity of what has happened. We are determined to persevere to the very end whatever the result of the great battle raging in France may be. We must expect in any case to be attacked here on the Dutch model before long." The Netherlands had been assaulted by German bombers, by paratroops and gliders, and finally by sea-borne infantry and armor. Churchill and the British general staff thought the Dutch attack a warm-up for a cross-Channel operation. "We hope to give a good account of ourselves. But if American assistance is to play any part it must be available soon."

Churchill directed the British ambassador in Washington, Lord Lothian, to make the case to Roosevelt personally. Lothian did so and reported that Roosevelt hadn't moved. He didn't veto the destroyers, but neither did he suggest they could be released. He repeated that they would take time to deliver.

"I understand your difficulties but I am very sorry about the destroyers," Churchill wrote to the president. "If they were here in six weeks they would play an invaluable part." The fighting on the Continent approached a moment of truth. "The battle of France is full of danger to both sides," Churchill said.

He hoped the American planes would be coming soon, to replace British planes lost in the defense of France. "Though we have taken heavy toll of enemy in the air and are clawing down two or three to one of their planes, they have still a formidable numerical superiority," Churchill said. "Our most vital need is therefore the delivery at the earliest possible date of the largest possible number of Curtiss P-40 fighters now in course of delivery to your army."

In the gravest tone he could summon, Churchill delineated the stakes in the developing battle. "Our intention is, whatever happens, to fight on to the end in this Island and, provided we can get the help for which we ask, we hope to run them very close in the air battles in view of individual superiority." But victory was by no means guaranteed. "Members of the present administration would likely go down during this process should it result adversely." They would never give in. "In no conceivable circumstances will we consent to surrender."

America must ponder the consequences. "If members of the present administration were finished and others came in to parley amid the ruins, you must not be blind to the fact that the sole remaining bargaining counter with Germany would be the fleet, and if this country was left by the United States to its fate no one would have the right to blame those then responsible if they made the best terms they could for the surviving inhabitants." America would face the power of Nazi Germany suddenly augmented by that of the British navy.

"Excuse me, Mr. President, putting this nightmare bluntly," Churchill wrote. "I could not answer for my successors who in utter despair and helplessness might well have to accommodate themselves to the German will."

29

O N MAY 16, Roosevelt went before Congress. He had asked to address the two houses to explain the meaning of the events in Europe and what America's response must be. "These are ominous days, days whose swift and shocking developments force every neutral nation to look to its defenses in the light of new factors," Roosevelt said. "The brutal force of modern offensive war has been loosed in all its horror. New powers of destruction, incredibly swift and deadly, have been developed; and those who wield them are ruthless and daring. No old defense is so strong that it requires no further strengthening, and no attack is so unlikely or impossible that it may be ignored."

Roosevelt described the nature of war as practiced by the Germans. "Motorized armies can now sweep through enemy territories at the rate of two hundred miles a day. Parachute troops are dropped from airplanes in large numbers behind enemy lines. Troops are landed from planes in open fields, on wide highways, and at local civil airports." The blitzkrieg really was like lightning: immediate and deadly. "The element of surprise, which has ever been an important tactic in warfare, has become the more dangerous because of the amazing speed with which modern equipment can reach and attack the enemy's country."

The new technologies put the United States itself at risk as never before. "The Atlantic and Pacific Oceans were reasonably adequate defensive barriers when fleets under sail could move at an average speed of five miles an hour," Roosevelt said. "Even in those days by a sudden foray it was possible for an opponent actually to burn our national Capitol." This had happened during the War of 1812 against Britain. "Later, the oceans still gave strength to our defense when fleets and convoys propelled by steam could sail the oceans at fifteen or twenty miles an hour.

"But the new element—air navigation—steps up the speed of possible attack to two hundred, to three hundred miles an hour. Furthermore, it brings the new possibilities of the use of nearer bases from which an attack or attacks on the American continents could be made. From the fiords of Greenland it is four hours by air to Newfoundland; five hours to Nova Scotia, New Brunswick and to the Province of Quebec; and only six hours to New England. The Azores are only 2,000 miles from parts of our eastern seaboard and if Bermuda fell into hostile hands it would be a matter of less than three hours for modern bombers to reach our shores. From a base in the outer West Indies, the coast of Florida could be reached in two hundred minutes."

All this required Americans to reconsider their approach to national defense, Roosevelt said. In the first place, they must think hemispherically. The United States could not allow an enemy to gain those air bases from which its planes could reach American shores.

Second, the historic American policy of awaiting war before mobilizing was outmoded in the age of the blitzkrieg. "Surely, the developments of the past few weeks have made it clear to all of our citizens that the possibility of attack on vital American zones ought to make it essential that we have the physical, the ready ability to meet those attacks," Roosevelt said. A modern war could begin and end before a country mobilized. "This means military implements— not on paper—which are ready and available to meet any lightning offensive against our American interest. It means also that facilities for production must be ready to turn out munitions and equipment at top speed."

Roosevelt couldn't stress too much the need to prepare. "We have had the lesson before us over and over again: nations that were not ready and were unable to get ready found themselves overrun by the enemy. So-called impregnable fortifications no longer exist." Each week brought new lessons, especially regarding air power. "Where naval ships have operated without adequate protection by defending aircraft, their vulnerability to air attack has of course increased," Roosevelt told the lawmakers. "With the amazing progress in the design of planes and engines, the airplane of a year ago is out-of-date now. It is too slow, it is improperly protected, it is too weak in gun power."

America had increased its production of warplanes, but it must do more. "I should like to see this nation geared up to the ability to turn out at least 50,000 planes a year."

The army and the navy needed more, too. Roosevelt put a price tag on necessity: $896 million appropriated at once, and authorization for another $286 million.

Some would call him a warmonger merely for urging preparations, Roosevelt acknowledged. Better to pray for peace, the critics said. He rejected the criticism even as he embraced the spirit behind it. "I, too, pray for peace, that the ways of aggression and force may be banished from the earth. But I am determined to face the fact realistically that this nation requires also a toughness of moral and physical fiber."

America's task was plain. "Our defenses must be invulnerable, our security absolute. But our defense as it was yesterday, or even as it is today, does not provide security against potential developments and dangers of the future." America's defense must change with the times. "Defense must be dynamic and flexible, an expression of the vital forces of the nation and of its resolute will to meet whatever challenge the future may hold."

30

LINDBERGH READ ROOSEVELT's remarks in the paper the next morning. That same day he arranged to speak on the radio two days later, to deliver his riposte.

The bad news from Europe grew worse. "Antwerp has fallen, and the French armies seem on the verge of collapse," Lindbergh wrote in his journal. "The Germans are reported to be forty miles from Paris." He traveled to Washington to speak with Hap Arnold. "We discussed the situation in Europe, and I outlined to Arnold what I intended to cover in my talk tomorrow night. While I was in his office, a young officer came in to mark a new German advance into France. The Maginot Line west of Montmedy has been broken along a wide front. They went through the Maginot Line extension along the Belgian border as though it had been sand instead of concrete and steel. French and British air activity has dropped greatly during the last several days. They have fallen back on night bombardment, while the German air force flies freely during the day and German troops march along the roads in Belgium unmolested."

Arnold relayed a request from the Roosevelt administration, via War Secretary Woodring. The president had learned that Lindbergh would be speaking on the radio again. "The Secretary had asked Arnold whether he could get me to include several items in my speech about the percentage of Army appropriations used for maintenance of the services, the percentage left for new equipment, etc., etc."

Lindbergh was unsurprised and unimpressed. "It was obviously a clumsy effort to dull the edge of my talk and turn it to the Administration's advantage. I feel quite certain that Arnold did not wish me to follow Woodring's suggestions, but he passed them on like a good soldier. I did not impose upon him to ask his own opinion. I told Arnold that my speech was too far along to permit incorporating the Secretary of War's suggestions—that to do so would require complete rewriting (and that is true)."

The next day brought no respite from the bleak tidings. "The German advance continues," Lindberg wrote. He heard from his radio producer. "Miss Gillis of Columbia Broadcasting called and told me the Movietone organizations wanted me to read part of my speech for them. They offered to select one man and one camera to take the picture and to divide it equally among all the newsreel companies. Their offer was so reasonable and considerate that I told Miss Gillis I would think about it and call her back within the hour."

Lindbergh remained suspicious of the news-movie companies. "I can never quite get over the times their men tried to sneak up behind us with a microphone hidden under their coats. I do not believe they were ever successful in getting a conversation in this way, but they did succeed in leaving us with a feeling of disgust for newsreels in general. And then there was the time when Anne and I were on the *Mouette* during our honeymoon and anchored in an island bay off the Maine coast. Some motion-picture news photographers came in a speedboat and demanded that we come on deck and have our pictures taken. We made no reply, so for over six hours they circled the *Mouette* in the speedboat, just fast enough for the waves to keep our boat rocking unpleasantly from side to side, while they shouted at us loudly. I finally left the harbor and headed out to open ocean. They followed for a time and then turned back—without the pictures they wanted."

Nonetheless, he weighed the Movietone offer carefully. "This present situation concerns the welfare of the country and should not be decided on personal feelings. But what advantages and disadvantages are there in speaking for the sound pictures at this time? The advantage is that additional millions of people will be reached. The disadvantages include the fact that only a small portion of my speech would be carried and that I would not be able to control its setting. The news companies could sandwich my picture and talk between the sack of cities and the mangled bodies of refugees. Once they have such a film, they can cut it and use it in any way they like."

Lindbergh's distrust won out. "I decided against speaking for the sound films, but asked Miss Gillis to thank them very much for their offer."

HE SPOKE IN the studio of Columbia Broadcasting on Sunday evening; the Mutual system shared the broadcasting rights. Movietone buttonholed him in the studio; he again declined the newsreel company's request to speak for the camera.

His topic was the air defense of America, and he provided listeners a primer in what modern warplanes could and could not do. "The power of aviation has been greatly underrated in the past," he said. "Now, we must be careful not to overrate this power in the excitement of reaction." Newspapers carried frightening reports of German military strength; newsreels showed grim scenes of the destruction the Germans had done. Ordinary Americans couldn't help being alarmed—and confused. "It is difficult to think clearly amidst the conflict of facts and headlines, the contradictory advice of columnists, the claims and counter claims of propaganda, and the blind selfishness of party politics. The conservative who scoffed at aviation yesterday has become the radical who says that tomorrow we will be invaded by European aircraft."

Lindbergh urged his compatriots to take a breath. "Let us reexamine the position of America in the air." New discoveries affected different nations differently. "One nation may have a psychology and topography which promotes the development of aviation, while another finds itself entirely unadjusted to the tempo of the air." America was blessed. "Judged by aeronautical standards, we in the United States are in a singularly fortunate position. Our people have natural ability in the design, construction, and operation of aircraft. Our highly organized industry, our widely separated centers of population, our elimination of formalities in the interstate travel, all contribute to the development of American aviation. From the standpoint of defense, we still have two great oceans between us and the warring armies of Europe and Asia. In fact there is hardly a natural element contributing to air strength and impregnability that we do not now possess."

Yet to exploit this advantage, Americans must devise a sound air-defense policy. Lindbergh didn't directly reference Roosevelt's request for fifty thousand planes. But his listeners understood when he said, "Air strength depends more upon the establishment of intelligent and consistent policies than upon the sudden construction of huge numbers of airplanes." Before building the planes, Americans must decide what the planes were expected to do. "The speed and range of our fighting planes depend upon the bases available for their use. If we are to defend the United States alone, then we must construct numerous air bases along the Mexican and Canadian borders. Such a plan would require large numbers of small bombers and pursuit planes, and eventually it would leave us as vulnerable to air attack as the nations of Europe are today." That is, if an enemy could establish air bases in Mexico or Canada, mere borders drawn on a map couldn't prevent its planes from penetrating American airspace. This was the lesson France was being taught by the German air force.

"On the other hand, if we are to defend the entire western hemisphere, we need long range bombers capable of attacking a hostile fleet a thousand miles or more at sea." The bombers would keep the enemy at a distance, preventing its ships from approaching American shores. This was the policy Lindbergh proposed.

But it raised a related issue. "An adequate air defense of the western hemisphere necessitates the cooperation of the other nations of this hemisphere. Our military aircraft must have access to their bases. Their foreign policy must have some relationship to ours. We cannot hold this hemisphere free from foreign war if nations which lie within it declare war on foreign powers." This was why Lindbergh had chided Canada earlier. And it was why American diplomats must work overtime to forge a hemispheric alliance—whether formal or informal—against encroachment or invasion from outside the hemisphere.

Lindbergh ridiculed claims by alarmists—he let his listeners include Roosevelt in this category—that modern aircraft made America newly vulnerable to invasion. "It is true that bombing planes can be built with sufficient range to cross the Atlantic and return. They can be built either in America or Europe. Aeronautical engineers have known this for many years. But the cost is high, the target large, and the military effectiveness small. Such planes do not exist today in any air force. A foreign power could not conquer us by dropping bombs in this country unless the bombing were accompanied by an invading army." The army would have to be transported by a navy. "And no foreign navy will dare to approach within bombing range of our coasts."

Such peril as confronted America came not from abroad but from within, Lindbergh said. "We are in danger of war today not because European people have attempted to interfere with the internal affairs of America, but because American people have attempted to interfere with the internal affairs of Europe." If Americans desired peace, they needed merely to stop treating Europe's problems as their own. "No one wishes to attack us, and no one is in a position to do so. The only reason that we are in danger of becoming involved in this war is because there are powerful elements in America who desire us to take part. They represent a small minority of the American people, but they control much of the machinery of influence and propaganda. They seize every opportunity to push us closer to the edge."

Lindbergh asked Americans to be true to their heritage. "Let us guard America today as our forefathers guarded it in the past. They won this country from Europe with a handful of revolutionary soldiers. We certainly can hold it now with a population of one hundred and thirty million people. If we cannot, we are unworthy to have it." The wisdom of the fathers was wisdom still. "We decided to stay out of foreign wars. We based our military policy on that decision. We must not waver now that the crisis is at hand."

31

M R. PRESIDENT, THE other night Colonel Lindbergh said this country was in no danger of being invaded," a reporter commented at Roosevelt's next press conference, two days later. "And he had some other things to say about our foreign policy. At the same time it seems there are quite a few jitters about this war news. Is there anything you can say to reassure us?"

"I can tell you off the record," Roosevelt replied, "the fact is that I have been so busy since Sunday night that I have not read Colonel Lindbergh's speech, so I don't know."

Roosevelt's answer was as complete a dodge as the president ever made: an off-the-record no-comment. Quite possibly Roosevelt himself hadn't read Lindbergh's speech. But members of his staff certainly had, and they must have apprised him of its content and tone. Roosevelt probably realized Lindbergh had put him in a corner. If Roosevelt said he agreed with Lindbergh, that the United States was not at risk of invasion, his agreement would enhance Lindbergh's credibility. He didn't want that. If Roosevelt said he disagreed, judging instead that an invasion was in fact a danger, his warning would make him seem one of the alarmists Lindbergh warned of. He didn't want that either.

Roosevelt's problem was that on the central part of Lindbergh's argument—that America was in no direct peril—Lindbergh was right. The other part of Lindbergh's case—that any danger to America from Europe would be of America's own making—was more contestable, but Roosevelt didn't want to engage Lindbergh on the point. He preferred not to engage Lindbergh at all.

He really *was* busy, trying to manage America's reaction to the bad news from Europe. The news itself was making his case that Hitler was a very bad man. But Roosevelt thought the reporters could use a reminder. "I think the country, on the whole, is pretty well united in understanding the needs of the present situation, and the faster the news comes in from the other side, the more united they are," he said. "I won't tell you, but you are probably getting the story from others, of those three to five million women and children and a few old men who are fleeing southward on any available road on the front of about 250 miles, with roads blocked, nearly everybody, either on foot or in a bullock cart; and at the same time enemy planes are swooping down those roads with their machine guns wide open, and the toll of death of those women and children and old men is something probably the world has never seen before. I think the country realizes some of the implications of that disaster and of that method of warfare."

Two days later Roosevelt reemphasized the unity theme. He had convened his business advisory council, a group of leaders from industry and commerce who presented him with a resolution recognizing the "unprecedented gravity" of the current situation, "in which our very lives and liberties may be involved"; asserting "the need for complete unity in the cooperation of all of our country's vital forces"; and pledging their "full aid to this end."

Roosevelt thanked the council for its support. He proceeded to elaborate on his understanding of national unity in the present moment. He acknowledged that not everyone saw things the way he and the council did. "A good many people—I wish you could see it; it is one of the things we have to face—after last Thursday's message I got about five hundred telegrams, of which about four hundred were entirely favorable to increasing the national defenses, and about a hundred of them were very bitterly opposed. They said it was excessive, that it would bust the country, that it was a process of getting us into the war of our own volition. Then there was the usual percentage of telegrams: 'I want my boys to get jobs here rather than graves in France'—that kind of thing. There is, of course, in the country, a very large element that is opposed to improving the defenses. We have to recognize that."

On the other hand were those who thought he wasn't doing enough. "There were a lot of people that said that the amount asked for was altogether too small," Roosevelt said. Balancing competing views was what presidents did, and what he had done in devising his defense budget request. "Between these different schools of thought, I took the line which I considered to be the maximum that we could profitably spend or contract for in the next four or five months." Beyond that time, he didn't presume to predict. "No human being can guess about the future."

Yet Roosevelt claimed to have foreseen the present from the past. "I was sort of—who was the fellow? John the Baptist?—the voice crying in the wilderness all last summer. I was perfectly sure that there would be a war, and well over a year ago I had told the Senate military affairs committee, in here, in a famous session, not that our frontier was on the Rhine, but that the continued existence of, for example, Finland, or the Baltic states, or the Balkan states, or the Scandinavian nations, as independent nations did have a pretty definite relationship to the defense of the United States. And there was a most awful howl of protest all over the country, as you know, at that time. I was accused of being an alarmist, accused of wanting to send troops to the other side, and things of that sort. I am quite accustomed to that sort of thing. And, after all, today we are faced with a complete fulfillment of that, because practically the whole of Europe is falling into the hands of a combination headed by the Nazi school of thought and school of government, with a pretty close association and affiliation with the Communist school of thought and school of government, and a third school, which is balancing very carefully on the edge of a knife, at the present time, the Fascist school of thought and school of government."

As president, he had to weigh certain possibilities, even as he had to watch his language. "If I had said this out loud in a fireside talk, again people would have said that I was perfectly crazy. The domination of Europe, as we all know, by Nazism, including also the domination of France and England, takes what might be called the buffer out of what has existed all these years between those new schools of government and the United States." America had been protected from the dictators not merely by the Atlantic but by France and Britain—in particular, by the French army and the British fleet. "If those two are removed, there is nothing between the Americas and those new forces in Europe." Roosevelt had written off the Atlantic as protection. "And so we have to think in terms of the Americas, more and more and infinitely faster."

Roosevelt had to deal with the armchair admirals and generals in the press. "We have had lately, for example, a number of columnists on a chain of papers in this country, with a very large circulation, which has been advocating certain things," he said. "One of the things they are advocating is a separate air force. Well, of course, anybody who knows anything about it knows that the one essential in time of war is unity of command." The "self-appointed omniscient people" posed as experts on all manner of issues. "Of course, they don't know a damn thing."

Roosevelt had to consider what the increase in military production would do to the economy. The slack in employment from the depression was just about taken up; the worry now was prices, which had shot higher. And high prices caused workers, especially unionized ones, to demand higher wages. If they didn't get what they wanted, they'd strike, throwing production still farther behind.

Roosevelt explained that he had to find a path that suited both capital and labor. "We want a profit for capital, but I would like to see no new war millionaires created out of this program." Profiteering by industry had been a problem in the World War. "At the same time I don't want any labor profiteers." These were the small groups of critically placed craftsmen who could strike and shut down whole factories. "We don't want to see any little key trade union in a factory, that employs not more than three or four percent of the employees in that factory, like the pattern makers or the drafting force, hold up and stop the works for the other ninety-six or ninety-seven percent of the employees by going on strike just because of the power they have."

Roosevelt's audience this day, the members of the business advisory council, didn't like regulations on management; doubtless some had hoped to become new war millionaires themselves. But they were inclined to give him the benefit of the doubt in the current situation. If they hadn't been, they wouldn't have been on his council. They seemed impressed with his presentation of the factors he had to consider in responding to the events in Europe. At the end of the meeting their spokesman thanked the president for his candor and offered their support. "You give us the command and we will march behind you," he said.

ROOSEVELT TOOK HIS case to the American people in a fireside chat. He warned against complacency and the siren call of self-interested troublemakers. "There are many among us who in the past closed their eyes to events abroad—because they believed in utter good faith what some of their fellow Americans told them—that what was taking place in Europe was none of our business; that no matter what happened over there, the United States could always pursue its peaceful and unique course in the world," Roosevelt said. "There are many among us who closed their eyes, from lack of interest or lack of knowledge, honestly and sincerely thinking that the many hundreds of miles of salt water made the American Hemisphere so remote that the people of North and Central and South America could go on living in the midst of their vast resources without reference to, or danger from, other continents of the world." These people were wrong and they were trying to lead America astray. They were abetted by political troublemakers. "There are a few among us who have deliberately and consciously closed their eyes because they were determined to be opposed to their government, its foreign policy and every other policy, to be partisan, and to believe that anything that the government did was wholly wrong."

The threat to America from violence abroad was great, but it was no greater than the threat from within. "Today's threat to our national security is not a matter of military weapons alone," Roosevelt told the millions of Americans listening. "We know of new methods of attack: the Trojan horse, the fifth column that betrays a nation unprepared for treachery." The term "fifth column" was of recent coinage, an artifact of the civil war in Spain. A Nationalist general directed four armed columns closing in on Madrid; he boasted that a "fifth column" of sympathizers inside the city would assist the attackers. Roosevelt employed the term to describe secret Nazi sympathizers in America. He promised that the government, with the aid of loyal Americans, would deal sternly with these inner enemies.

"There is an added technique for weakening a nation at its very roots, for disrupting the entire pattern of life of a people," he went on. "It is important that we understand it. The method is simple. It is, first, a dissemination of discord. A group—not too large, a group that may be sectional or racial or political—is encouraged to exploit its prejudices through false slogans and emotional appeals. The aim of those who deliberately egg on these groups is to create confusion of counsel, public indecision, political paralysis and, eventually, a state of panic. Sound national policies come to be viewed with a new and unreasoning skepticism, not through the wholesome political debates of honest and free men, but through the clever schemes of foreign agents."

These subtle saboteurs would block needed legislation. "Armament programs may be dangerously delayed. Singleness of national purpose may be undermined. Men can lose confidence in each other, and therefore lose confidence in the efficacy of their own united action. Faith and courage can yield to doubt and fear. The unity of the state can be so sapped that its strength is destroyed."

Roosevelt had confidence that most Americans would see through these insidious techniques. Yet they must never let down their guard. "New forces are being unleashed, deliberately planned propagandas to divide and weaken us in the face of danger as other nations have been weakened before. These dividing forces are undiluted poison. They must not be allowed to spread in the New World as they have in the Old. Our morale and our mental defenses must be raised as never before against those who would cast a smoke screen across our vision."

32

WHILE ROOSEVELT WAS warning the American people against saboteurs and fifth columnists, the German army was trapping the expeditionary force Britain had sent across the Channel to defend France. Churchill and British commanders had to decide what to do with the three hundred thousand troops: order them to stand and fight, or try to get them out. They chose the latter. Thus began an epic evacuation, from the French port of Dunkirk.

Edward R. Murrow covered the story from London. Murrow had joined CBS in New York in 1935; two years later he relocated to Europe to head CBS operations there. He helped pioneer international radio news, and early in the war he commenced regular broadcasts from England. With his matter-of-fact tone, resonant timbre and knack for painting audio pictures, he became the authoritative voice of the war for tens of millions of Americans.

"We are told tonight that the Allied forces are holding out around Dunkerque and that bad weather has decreased German air activities," Murrow related on May 31. "The evacuation of Allied troops from the area around Dunkerque continues. Barges, lifeboats, paddle steamers, anything that will float, are being used to take them off. This evacuation is being carried out from open beaches. No figures can be given concerning the total number saved, but there is reason to believe that more men will be taken off than appeared possible two days ago."

Murrow introduced America to ordinary English men and women. He told their stories and, in some cases, let them tell the stories themselves.

"Here beside me is a British soldier, a private. He drove the first British car that rolled across the frontier into Belgium. Since then he's done a great deal of traveling and some fighting, but that's his story and here he is to tell it."

"We were retreating with the remnants of the Belgian division, which had seen very heavy fighting the previous day," said the soldier, unnamed on orders of the British censors. "We had been bombed and machine-gunned from the air continuously since dawn. As many as thirty or forty planes were over us at the time. About six o'clock in the evening we were being bombed by sixteen Dorniers when suddenly four Spitfires appeared. The first ones we had seen. Within six minutes they had brought down four Dorniers, the others broke and dispersed. Further Dorniers fell within a few yards of our column."

The soldier told of his escape from France. "Coming over in our little ship, I was walking around what we call the sharp end of the ship when I heard a swishing noise. I half turned and saw a motor torpedo boat about twenty yards away. It let go the first torpedo and then another one, but they both missed. I fired my rifle when I realized it wasn't one of ours and the second mate rushed out shouting about it. The captain came running with a gun and we kept on firing away as fast as we could at the Germans. When he realized he hadn't sunk us he came around again and ordered us to stop, but we didn't stop. He then circled at a wider distance. Actually in this spot he was about thirty-five or forty yards away, running around us. As he went around we crossed over sides and kept rattling bullets at him as fast as we could."

The battle continued for twenty minutes. "The Germans were using machine guns. We could see the tracer marks flying over the deck like fireworks. He got some of us but he wasn't much good. We finally silenced him and when he finally drifted across our stem he was only five or six yards away and there was no sign of life at all. First we thought of towing him, but we wanted to get away as quickly as we could, so we just left him there. We were lucky to get him because, if we hadn't, he would have probably fetched his pals and had another go. That's how we got back to England."

The next day Murrow provided an update. "The evacuation of British and French troops in the area around Dunkerque has continued throughout the day," he said. "It is stated here that the withdrawal is proceeding satisfactorily." Murrow ventured out of London. "During the day I've driven one hundred and fifty miles in southern and southeast England. Most of that part of the country is soft, green, and rolling, interlaced with winding, hard-surfaced roads. The road signs are all gone; signs giving the names of towns and villages have been removed." This was to frustrate German invaders. "Working parties of soldiers are putting up barricades; gun emplacements are being prepared at strategic crossroads. Driving along through hop fields or between high hedges, I often noticed old trucks, tractors, and farm carts parked in the bushes, ready to be pushed out into the road. A dozen times I was stopped by sentries with fixed bayonets, who asked very politely to see my credentials. It was like crossing the frontiers of a dozen states on the Continent in peacetime. The complete absence of road signs and place names is confusing. The only thing to tell the traveler that Canterbury is Canterbury is the big cathedral rising out of the plain. There are no signs—there are no signs pointing to London, Cambridge, Wells, Seven Oaks, or anywhere else."

The war was across the Channel, but its evidence was all around. "Occasionally a squad of big British bombers, possibly coming back from Dunkerque, growled overhead. At other times sleek, fast fighters whined away toward the coast in search of German bombers, probably to be found not more than ten minutes' flying distance away. Occasionally, at towns and villages on the railroad leading up from the south coast, crowds of people gathered around the railway station, watching ambulances pick up their loads from the troop trains."

He reached the southeast coast. "I spent several hours at what may be tonight or next week Britain's first line of defense, an airfield on the southeast coast," Murrow reported on June 2. "The German bases weren't more than ten minutes' flying time away—across that ditch that has protected Britain and conditioned the thinking of Britishers for centuries. I talked with pilots as they came back from Dunkerque. They stripped off their light jackets, glanced at a few bullet holes in wings or fuselage, and as their ground crews swarmed over the aircraft, refueling motors and guns, we sat on the ground and talked. Out in the middle of the field the wreckage of a plane was being cleared up. It had crashed the night before. The pilot had been shot in the head, but managed to get back to his field. The Royal Air Force prides itself on never walking out of a plane until it falls apart."

Murrow admired the RAF pilots, and he made his listeners admire them too. "They were the cream of the youth of Britain. As we sat there, they were waiting to take off again. They talked of their own work, discussed the German air force with all the casualness of Sunday-morning quarterbacks discussing yesterday's football game. There were no nerves, no profanity, and no heroics. There was no swagger about those boys in wrinkled and stained uniforms. The movies do that sort of thing much more dramatically than it is in real life. They told me of the patrol from which they'd just returned. 'Six Germans downed. We lost two.' 'What happened to Eric?' said one. 'Oh, I saw him come down right alongside one of our destroyers,' replied another. 'The Germans fight well in a crowd. They know how to use the sun, and if they surprise you, it's uncomfortable. If twenty or so of them catch five of us, we stay and fight,' they said. 'Maybe that's why we get so many of them,' added one boy, with a grin. They all told the same story about numbers. 'Six of us go over,' they said, 'and we meet twelve Germans.' 'If ten of us go, there's twenty Germans.' But they were all anxious to go again."

On the morning of June 3 Murrow delivered welcome news. "We are told today that most of the British Expeditionary Force is home from Flanders. There are no official figures of the number saved, but the unofficial estimates claim that as much as two thirds or perhaps four fifths of the force has been saved. It is claimed here that not more than one British division remains in the Dunkerque area. It may be that these estimates are unduly optimistic, but it's certainly true that a week ago few people believed that the evacuation could have been carried out so successfully."

Murrow drove to Westminster to gauge the government's reaction. "I sat in the House of Commons this afternoon and heard Winston Churchill, Britain's tired old man of the sea, sum up the recent operations," Murrow reported on June 4. "He tried again, as he has tried for nearly ten years, to warn this country of the threat that impends. He told of the 335,000 troops, British and French, brought back from Dunkerque. British losses exceed 30,000—killed, wounded, and missing. Enormous material losses were sustained. He described how the eight or nine German armored divisions swept like a sharp scythe to the right and rear of the northern armies. But the thrust did not reach Dunkerque, because of the resistance put up at Boulogne and Calais. Only thirty unwounded survivors were taken off from the port of Calais. A grave situation was made worse by the capitulation of the King of the Belgians, a pitiful episode, said Mr. Churchill.

"He then paid his tribute to the Royal Air Force. It decisively defeated the main strength of the German air force, inflicting losses of at least four to one. As he talked of those young fliers, greater than knights of the round table, crusaders of old, Mr. Churchill needed only wings and an engine to take off. But wars, he said, are not won by evacuations. Nearly a thousand guns had been lost. All transport and all armored vehicles with the northern armies had been lost. A colossal military disaster had occurred, and another blow must be expected almost immediately. Home defense must be built up. And there will be a secret session on that subject next week.

"Mr. Churchill believed that these islands could be successfully defended, could ride out the storm of war and outlive the menace of tyranny, if necessary for years—if necessary, alone.

"There was a prophetic quality about that speech. We shall go on to the end, he said; we shall fight in France, we shall fight on the seas and oceans, we shall fight on the beaches, in the fields, in the streets, in the hills; we shall never surrender. If this island or a large part of it were subjugated and starving, then the Empire beyond the seas, armed and guarded by the British fleet, would carry on the struggle until, in God's good time, the New World with all its power and might sets forth to the rescue and liberation of the Old.

"With those words, the Prime Minister sat down. I have heard Mr. Churchill in the House of Commons at intervals over the last ten years. I heard his speech on the Norwegian campaign, and I have some knowledge of his writings. Today, he was different. There was little oratory; he wasn't interested in being a showman. He spoke the language of Shakespeare with a direct urgency such as I have never before heard in that House. There were no frills and no tricks. Winston Churchill's speeches have been prophetic. He has talked and written of the German danger for years. He has gone into the political wilderness in defense of his ideas. Today, as Prime Minister, he gave the House of Commons a report remarkable for its honesty, inspiration, and gravity."

33

T HE MIRACLE OF Dunkirk, as it was called in Britain, didn't seem so miraculous in France, for it left the French alone to fight the Germans. Some of the French determined to do just that; others concluded that if the British were giving up, so should they. Churchill did what he could to persuade the French to keep fighting, but the Dunkirk decision had diminished his credibility with those he left behind.

He looked to Roosevelt for assistance. The demands of the evacuation had kept him from writing to the president as frequently as before, but he found time to renew his request for arms. Churchill had hoped his warning of an imminent British defeat would move Roosevelt further on the arms question, but the president discounted for melodrama. He continued to put Churchill off. The success of the Dunkirk evacuation indeed made Churchill's alarm appear overdrawn.

Churchill persisted nonetheless. "I understand your position regarding additional aircraft priorities," he wrote to Roosevelt even as the evacuation continued. "Nevertheless, I feel justified in asking for the release to us of 200 Curtiss P-40 fighters now being delivered to your Army. The courage and success of our pilots against numerical superiority are a guarantee that they will be well used. At the present rate of comparative losses, they would account for something like 800 German machines. I also understand your difficulties, legal, political and financial, regarding destroyers. But the need is extreme."

Roosevelt answered Churchill in a speech to the gradu-
ating class of the University of Virginia in Charlottesville. "Every
generation of young men and women in America has questions to
ask the world," Roosevelt said. "Most of the time they are the simple
but nevertheless difficult questions, questions of work to do, opportunities to find, ambitions to satisfy. But every now and again in the
history of the republic a different kind of question presents itself—a
question that asks, not about the future of an individual or even of
a generation, but about the future of the country, the future of the
American people."

The generation of the American Revolution had grappled with
this question. Likewise the generation of the Civil War. "There is
such a time again today," Roosevelt said. "Again today the young men
and the young women of America ask themselves with earnestness
and with deep concern this same question: 'What is to become of the
country we know?'"

They had reason to ask, and reason for their concern. Each day
the young people read news revealing that democracy was under
assault. "They read the words of those who are telling them that
the ideal of individual liberty, the ideal of free franchise, the ideal of
peace through justice, are decadent ideals. They read the words and
hear the boast of those who say that a belief in force—force directed
by self-chosen leaders—is the new and vigorous system which will
overrun the earth. They have seen the ascendancy of this philosophy
of force in nation after nation where free institutions and individual
liberties were once maintained."

Young Americans naturally asked what these words spoken in distant countries meant for them. What would the triumph overseas of
rule by force imply for America?

Roosevelt acknowledged that in ages past, Americans ignored the
world across the oceans, and prospered. But the world lived in a new
age—the age of the machine. The machine age had brought progress
and plenty to mankind in countries that practiced the rule of law.
Elsewhere, in countries that lived by the rule of force, it brought
oppression and destruction. "In this new system of force the mastery
of the machine is not in the hands of mankind. It is in the control of

infinitely small groups of individuals who rule without a single one of the democratic sanctions that we have known. The machine in the hands of irresponsible conquerors becomes the master; mankind is not only the servant; it is the victim, too."

The conquerors paid no respect to democracy or to national borders. Americans were waking to the threat this posed to their own democracy and borders. "Perception of danger to our institutions may come slowly or it may come with a rush and a shock, as it has to the people of the United States in the past few months. This perception of danger has come to us clearly and overwhelmingly; and we perceive the peril in a world-wide arena—an arena that may become so narrowed that only the Americas will retain the ancient faiths."

Not all Americans had yet awakened. "Some indeed still hold to the now somewhat obvious delusion that we of the United States can safely permit the United States to become a lone island, a lone island in a world dominated by the philosophy of force. Such an island may be the dream of those who still talk and vote as isolationists. Such an island represents to me and to the overwhelming majority of Americans today a helpless nightmare of a people without freedom—the nightmare of a people lodged in prison, handcuffed, hungry, and fed through the bars from day to day by the contemptuous, unpitying masters of other continents."

Roosevelt proposed to speak for that majority, and for others besides. "Let us not hesitate—all of us—to proclaim certain truths. Overwhelmingly we, as a nation—and this applies to all the other American nations—are convinced that military and naval victory for the gods of force and hate would endanger the institutions of democracy in the western world, and that equally, therefore, the whole of our sympathies lies with those nations that are giving their life blood in combat against these forces."

Italy had that day declared war on Britain and France. Roosevelt expressed his disappointment and disapproval. "The hand that held the dagger has struck it into the back of its neighbor," he said.

The Italian declaration confirmed America in its decision to defend democracy. "On this tenth day of June, 1940, in this university founded by the first great American teacher of democracy, we send forth our prayers and our hopes to those beyond the seas who are maintaining with magnificent valor their battle for freedom." America would do more. Here Roosevelt gave Churchill his answer. "We will extend to the opponents of force the material resources of this nation," he said.

He hadn't forgotten Lindbergh and the Americans-for-the-Americas crowd. Lest they accuse him of neglecting the hemispheric home front, Roosevelt added, "At the same time, we will harness and speed up the use of those resources in order that we ourselves in the Americas may have equipment and training equal to the task of any emergency and every defense."

34

CHURCHILL COULDN'T HAVE been happier. "We all listened to you last night and were fortified by the grand scope
of your declaration," he wrote to Roosevelt. "Your statement
that the material aid of the United States will be given to the Allies
in their struggle is a strong encouragement in a dark but not unhope-
ful hour."

British troops were no longer fighting in France, but the French
remained crucial to Britain's defense, Churchill explained to Roosevelt. "Everything must be done to keep France in the fight and to
prevent any idea of the fall of Paris, should it occur, becoming the
occasion of any kind of parley. The hope with which you inspire
them may give them the strength to persevere. They should continue
to defend every yard of their soil and use the full fighting force of
their army."

In the same vein, Britain remained crucial to the defense of democracy, of which Roosevelt had just spoken so eloquently. "Hitler thus
baffled of quick results"—should the French continue to fight—"will
turn upon us, and we are preparing ourselves to resist his fury and
defend our Island." Success wasn't guaranteed, but Roosevelt's words
allowed Churchill to look beyond Britain. "As soon as divisions can
be equipped on the much higher scale needed for Continental service they will be despatched to France. Our intention is to have a
strong army fighting in France for the campaign of 1941."

The United States could do its part, as the president had just promised it would. "I have already cabled you about airplanes, including

flying boats"—seaplanes—"which are so needful to us in the impending struggle for the life of Great Britain. But even more pressing is the need for destroyers. The Italian outrage makes it necessary for us to cope with a much larger number of submarines which may come out into the Atlantic and perhaps be based on Spanish ports. To this the only counter is destroyers."

Churchill specified: "Nothing is so important as for us to have the thirty or forty old destroyers you have already had reconditioned. We can fit them very rapidly with our ASDICS and they will bridge the gap of six months before our war-time new construction comes into play. We will return them or their equivalents to you without fail at six months notice if at any time you need them."

He reiterated that timing was everything. "The next six months are vital. If while we have to guard the East Coast against invasion a new heavy German-Italian submarine attack is launched against our commerce, the strain may be beyond our resources; and the ocean traffic by which we live may be strangled. Not a day should be lost."

PART FOUR

Dissent or Disloyalty?

35

ROOSEVELT HAD A gift for orchestrating inevitability. James Farley had noticed it appreciatively during Roosevelt's rise from the governorship of New York to the presidency, which he facilitated as campaign manager and political fixer. Farley had benefited by being made postmaster general, which put his finger on the pulse of the nation through the thousands of postmasters across the country. Farley was less appreciative of Roosevelt's gift now, when its exercise came at his expense.

"I had lunch with Garner on May 28, two days before my fifty-second birthday," Farley recalled later, referring to the vice president. With the 1940 election barely five months away, both men wondered whether Roosevelt would run again.

"Jim, what's the Boss going to do?" asked Garner.

"Your guess is as good as mine," said Farley. "I've given up guessing."

Garner tried to read Farley, who was supposed to know everything about Roosevelt. "I guess he's going to run," Garner said.

"It begins to look that way."

"Hell, he's fixed it so nobody else can run now." Garner had thought that after eight loyal years as vice president, during which he had often bitten his tongue on matters where he disagreed with the president, it would be his turn to try for the top spot. Roosevelt had encouraged this thinking.

Farley, even more loyal than Garner and with a connection of longer standing, had cherished his own hopes for the presidency. Roosevelt had encouraged Farley's hopes too. Cordell Hull, the secretary of state, had a story like Garner's and Farley's.

"I wouldn't have gotten in myself, or I would have handled myself . . . ," said Garner, letting the reflection hang. "Ah, well, there's no use watering spilt milk."

"I went along with the assurances he gave me that he wouldn't run," said Farley. "So did you and so did Cordell. And we are all left high and dry."

Farley insisted on hearing the president's decision on a third term from the president directly. He drove to Hyde Park on a Sunday when Roosevelt was home for the weekend. Farley and a few other Roosevelt intimates sat down for lunch. The talk briefly touched on the war, then wandered to other subjects. After lunch the guests dispersed, with Roosevelt going to his study. A short while later he summoned Farley.

"For a half hour or more the conversation was about everything and nothing," Farley recalled. "It was apparent to me the President was having difficulty in approaching the subject, and frankly, I was not disposed to help him. I made up my mind that I would not open the discussion of his candidacy." Roosevelt would have to raise the issue.

He took the hint. "Jim, last July when we canvassed the political situation, I indicated definitely that I would not run for a third term," he said, smiling as he always did when trying to persuade. "I believe we decided that on or about February 1, I would write a letter to one of the states which has an early primary, stating I would not be a candidate for reelection."

"It was the North Dakota chairman you were going to write to," Farley said. He had taken note and remembered.

"Well, after that conversation of ours, the war started," Roosevelt continued. "And when it got along to February 1, I could not issue that statement. It would have destroyed my effectiveness as the leader of the nation in the efforts of this country to cope with the terrible catastrophe raging in Europe. To have issued such a statement would have nullified my position in the world and would have handicapped the efforts of this country to be of constructive service in the war crisis."

Roosevelt paused, thinking back. "I must say that I am disappointed that my efforts have not accomplished what I hoped. In all probability it would have been just as well if I had made the announcement as planned. We bullied Mussolini in every way possible and tried to get the influence of the Pope to keep Italy from getting into war, but Italy went in."

Roosevelt lit another cigarette. The smoke wafted around his face. He was still smiling. Farley let him talk.

"So I would probably have been better off if I had said I didn't want to run. I still don't want to run for the presidency. I want to come up here." Roosevelt gestured with his hand to indicate the study and the homeplace in general.

"Jim, I don't want to run and I'm going to tell the convention so." His voice and expression would have conveyed sincerity to most people.

Not to Farley. "If you make it specific, the convention will not nominate you," he said, challenging the president.

"Well, there could be several ways of doing it," Roosevelt said. "I could write a letter to someone like Senator Norris and decline." George Norris of Nebraska had been a Republican but switched to independent in 1936. "Two, I could broadcast it. Three, I could issue a statement. And four, I could write a letter to be read by you at the convention."

Roosevelt seemed to want a reaction. Farley didn't oblige.

"You know, Jim, I want to fully explain my position in order to be honest with myself about the situation, because I am definitely opposed to seeking a third term. In justice to my conscience I want that thoroughly understood by the delegates and the country."

Farley said if that was really the way he felt, he could issue a statement freeing the delegates to back other candidates. Farley went on to say he thought a third term was a bad idea. The two-term principle had served the nation well. If another Democrat couldn't win by running on the record of the last seven and a half years, the party deserved to lose. No man was indispensable.

Roosevelt had stopped smiling.

Farley returned to what Roosevelt should say if he didn't want a third term. "You're not going to like it or pay any attention to it," he said. "In your position I would do exactly what General Sherman did many years ago—issue a statement saying I would refuse to run if nominated and would not serve if elected."

Roosevelt shook his head. "Jim, if nominated and elected, I could not in these times refuse to take the inaugural oath, even if I knew I would be dead within thirty days," he said.

Farley was taken aback. "This statement made a powerful impression on me," he wrote in his memoirs. "And it has been etched deeper into my mind by what happened less than five years later. I can see him now, with his right hand clasping the arm of his chair as he leaned back, his left bent at the elbow to hold his cigarette, and his face and eyes deadly earnest. This picture has often been in my mind since his death"—in 1945, of a cerebral hemorrhage. "I cannot help wondering whether during that year he pondered the remark made to me and whether he knew he was under the shadow of the dark angel's wings."

The premonition, if such it was, broke the mood of the moment. "From this point on, the conference lost what pattern of order it had. He had made his speech and I had made mine. Now he reverted to his customary restless, rambling consideration of a problem, which so often reminded me of a pup worrying a slipper. He talked on aimlessly about the third term, saying that Grant, who had served for eight years, could not push it aside; that Theodore Roosevelt, who had served a few months less, could not forego an attempt to break tradition"—by seeking a third term in 1912 after stepping aside in 1908—"and that Coolidge debated long before he issued what he described as a 'yes-no' statement. I did not press this phase of the discussion, because it was more than evident he had his mind made up and he was trying to justify his position to me, and also seeking to justify his failure to tell me he had changed his mind since our last discussion."

Farley left the meeting feeling disillusioned and angry. Roosevelt had used him for all he was worth and tossed him aside. "Al Smith warned me never to rely on Roosevelt's word," Farley told Garner. Smith was a former governor of New York and an early mentor to Roosevelt; Roosevelt had pushed past Smith when ambition called. "I laughed at him," Farley said to Garner of Smith. "Now he's laughing at me."

America discovered a new hero when Charles Lindbergh flew across the Atlantic in 1927. The unprecedented feat won the twenty-five-year-old mid-westerner a large cash prize and the admiring affection of his compatriots.

The historic flight, in a plane Lindbergh called the *Spirit of St. Louis*, put the world on notice of American technical know-how, even as it appeared to shrink the oceans that had long distanced the United States from Europe and Asia.

The political classes, starting with President Calvin Coolidge, capitalized on Lindbergh's popularity.

Lindbergh's face could be found everywhere. The Lone Eagle, as he was called, didn't say much, but he seemed to see far into the future.

Lindbergh's fame had a grim accompaniment. His son Charles Jr. was kidnapped from the family home in New Jersey and subsequently found dead. The media frenzy that ensued caused Lindbergh, shown here on the witness stand at the trial, to move his family to Europe.

When Americans could tear themselves from the Lindbergh saga, they read of the rise of fascism in Europe. Benito Mussolini of Italy, left, and Adolf Hitler of Germany appeared bent on starting another war, less than twenty years after the World War.

Senator Gerald Nye of North Dakota was determined that any new war not enmesh the United States. He led an investigation into the causes of American participation in the World War, and his findings spurred Congress to write a series of neutrality laws, to ensure American isolation from another war.

Franklin Roosevelt was no isolationist, but he signed the neutrality laws. He awaited a more promising moment to move America toward international reengagement, which he deemed essential to American interests and world peace.

In Europe, Lindbergh learned a great deal about the air forces of the countries there. Upon his return to America in early 1939, Roosevelt summoned him to share what he knew. Photographers, delighted to see Lindbergh back, ambushed his cab to the White House.

The meeting went badly. Lindbergh thought Roosevelt was using him as a political prop. And he hated the cameras as much as ever.

Hitler's war talk produced actual hostilities in September 1939, when German troops invaded Poland. Britain and France responded by declaring war on Germany. Roosevelt took the occasion to call for a repeal of the arms embargo dictated by the neutrality laws.

Lindbergh, appalled by the idea of another American war, overcame his aversion to publicity and took to radio to oppose repeal of the arms embargo. He predicted that where American arms went, American soldiers would inevitably follow.

Key Pittman (left), chairman of the Senate Foreign Relations Committee, rebuked Lindbergh on behalf of Roosevelt. The president knew what he was doing, Pittman said. Americans should trust him. Lindbergh should stick to flying.

Burton Wheeler defended Lindbergh against Pittman and Roosevelt. For decades the senator from Montana had opposed American involvement in the affairs of Europe; he did so now more strongly than ever.

Roosevelt won repeal of the arms embargo, but the change in American policy didn't prevent German forces from smashing French opposition in the spring of 1940. By late June, Paris was at Hitler's feet.

Hitler thereupon unleashed his warplanes against Britain. Starting in the summer of 1940, the Luftwaffe pounded British military installations and cities by day and night, killing thousands of civilians.

Roosevelt convinced himself that the war crisis permitted a breaking of the venerable taboo against third terms for presidents, and he persuaded American voters to elect him a third time. His margin was smaller than before, but he took the fact of his victory as endorsement of his handling of the war.

Roosevelt soon proposed a sweeping departure from existing policy. America would provide weapons to countries fighting the fascists, regardless of their ability to pay. He asserted that sending American weapons abroad, under the terms of what came to be called Lend-Lease, would reduce the chances of having to send American soldiers abroad.

Lindbergh again rejected Roosevelt's reasoning. Lend-Lease would simply add to the momentum toward war, he told a committee of Congress. Full American participation would become irresistible.

Roosevelt found Lindbergh increasingly irksome. He challenged Lindbergh's loyalty to America, and he encouraged attacks on Lindbergh's motives and character. Harold Ickes, the interior secretary, pictured here on the right, drew the most blood.

Lindbergh initially declined to join the America First Committee, the leading antiwar group, lest it inhibit his freedom of action. But as war drew closer, Lindbergh concluded that solidarity among the antiwar forces was essential. He addressed this America First rally at Madison Square Garden in May 1941.

Since the start of the war, Roosevelt had maintained a secret correspondence with Winston Churchill. The two men decided to meet in person, still in secret, off the coast of Newfoundland in the summer of 1941. What Roosevelt told Churchill made the British prime minister believe the Americans would be joining the war soon.

Miscues by Lindbergh and the antiwar movement, combined with Roosevelt's political savvy, made full-scale American intervention almost inevitable by the autumn of 1941. Japan erased all doubt by attacking American ships and personnel at Pearl Harbor.

36

L INDBERGH WASN'T PRIVY to what Churchill and Roosevelt wrote to each other. The existence of the correspondence, let alone its content, was a closely held secret. Yet Lindbergh had no difficulty guessing what was on Churchill's mind, and he feared the prime minister would succeed in frightening Roosevelt into making America the armorer of the British Empire.

"The German Army is reported thirty-five miles from Paris and advancing rapidly," Lindbergh wrote in his journal on the day Roosevelt gave his Charlottesville address. "It was announced that Mussolini would speak in Rome at 1:00 EST. We brought the radio down to the dining room to hear him. It was, as we expected, a declaration of war against France and England. Mussolini shouted until it must have been impossible even for an Italian to understand him. Every few words were punctuated by great howls from the crowds—howls for blood. It was like a pack of animals ready for the kill, howling over the division of the body—the already half-dead body, the mortally wounded body of France. I shall never forget that broadcast as long as I live. Mussolini's voice was incapable of the pitch and volume he attempted. But the mob carried on for him, and it was all in keeping—the leader and the pack."

That evening Lindbergh listened to Roosevelt. He wasn't sure he liked the president's style of rhetoric much better than Mussolini's. "His speeches never seem to me to be those of a quite normal man. I seldom listen to him and always trust him less after I do. Tonight, as his voice came over the radio, I felt he would like to declare war, and was held back only by his knowledge that the country would not stand for it. He was dramatic and demagogic as usual."

Lindbergh consulted other opponents of Roosevelt's increasingly interventionist policy. Bennett Champ Clark invited Lindbergh to the Senate for a chat. "We discussed the war, the Administration, and the pressure being brought to bear to involve the United States in the war," Lindbergh wrote. "We both agree that conditions are critical and that the trend toward war must be stopped." Clark brought in several other senators and representatives. "We discussed plans for counteracting war agitation and propaganda. Everyone is very much worried about Roosevelt and feels he is leading the country to war as rapidly as he can."

The lawmakers encouraged Lindbergh to continue his campaign of countering the president. On returning to his hotel, he called the NBC studios. "They told me they would be glad to give me time," he noted.

"I HAVE ASKED to speak to you again tonight because I believe that we in America are drifting toward a position of far greater serious-ness to our future than even this present war," Lindbergh told the country on June 15. He accused the president and the interventionists of conflating two issues: the defense of America and the defense of Europe. Lindbergh fully favored the first, as did most Americans. "Our people are solidly behind an adequate military preparedness, and no one believes in it more than I." Defending America was quite in keeping with the country's traditions. "Arming for the defense of America is compatible with normal life, commerce, and culture. It is an integral part of the destiny of our nation."

The second half of the president's equation was what didn't add up. "Arming to attack the continent of Europe would necessitate that the lives and thoughts of every man, woman, and child in this coun-try be directed toward war for the next generation, probably for the next several generations," Lindbergh said. His listeners mustn't be fooled by the president's fine phrases in defense of democracy. For Americans, a war to defend democracy in Europe would be an *offen-sive* war. Americans would not be fighting on their own soil; they would be fighting on foreign soil, thousands of miles from American shores. They would have to invade France and then Germany.

This was where the president's policy would surely lead. "We cannot continue for long to follow the course our government has taken without becoming involved in war with Germany," Lindbergh said. Americans were deluding themselves if they thought otherwise. "There are many perfectly sincere men and women who believe that we can send weapons to kill people in Europe without becoming involved in war with those people. Still others believe that by gestures and applause we can assist France and England to win without danger to our own country." Lindbergh didn't criticize these people, whose opinions were honestly, if myopically, held.

His condemnation was for those who led them on. "There are men among us of less honesty who advocate stepping closer and closer to war, knowing well that a point exists beyond which there can be no turning back. They have baited the trap of war with requests for modest assistance." This group was winning the debate at present.

Lindbergh drew on American history. "There is a saying that grew up in the old West to the effect that a man who enjoys life should never touch his gun unless he means business; that he should never draw unless he is ready to shoot, and that he should never shoot unless he is ready to kill. Those old pioneers of ours knew from long experience that there can be no successful dabbling with death." The wisdom of the old West had been forgotten. "Our present danger results from making gestures with an empty gun after we have already lost the draw."

The policy of the president and the administration was not simply dangerous; it was feckless. "Our leaders have lost the influence we could have exerted as the world's greatest neutral nation," Lindbergh said. "The driblets of munitions we have sold to England and France have had a negligible effect on the trend of the war, and we have not sufficient military strength available to change that trend. We demand that foreign nations refrain from interfering in our hemisphere, yet we constantly interfere in theirs. And while we have been taking an ineffective part in the war abroad, we have inexcusably neglected our defenses at home."

While there was still time, Americans should think seriously about what a European war would mean for the United States. "People visualize the war that is now going on in Europe," Lindbergh said. "They think of sending more arms, and possibly some soldiers. There is still very little understanding of what our entrance into European war would mean." A regional war would become a global war, upon America's entrance. "We must realize that we are considering the greatest struggle the world has yet known—a conflict between hemispheres, one half of the white race against the other half."

Moreover, America would enter the war under inauspicious circumstances. "Before we can take effective action in a European war the German armies may have brought all Europe under their control," Lindbergh said. "In that case, Europe will be dominated by the strongest military nation the world has ever known, controlling a population far larger than our own. If we decide to enter war, we must be prepared to attack that nation. We must prepare to invade a continent which it controls."

The decision to enter the war would be made by the present generation but would have consequences for generations to come. "We hold our children's future in our hands as we deliberate, for if we turn to war the battles will be hard fought and the outcome is not likely to be decided in our lifetime. This is a question of mortgaging the lives of our children and our grandchildren. Every family in the land would have its wounded and its dead."

Such a conflict would not play to America's strengths, certainly not at first. "We start at a disadvantage because we are not a military nation. Our is not a land of guns and marching men. If we decide to fight, then the United States must prepare for war for many years to come, and on a scale unprecedented in all history." America would become a garrison state. "We should start to build an army of several million men. We will need several hundred thousand airplanes before the battling is over. And we must have a navy large enough to transport this force across the sea."

Americans understandably compared another war in Europe to the last one. They were wrong to do so, Lindbergh said. This next war would not be like the last. "It would be more comparable to the struggle which took place between Athens and Sparta, or Rome and Carthage. It would involve the destiny of America and of Western civilization as far into the future as we can see."

This did not have to be America's future. Americans didn't have to cross the oceans to build their defenses. They should do so closer to home, within their own hemisphere. "With an adequate defense, no foreign army can invade us. Our advantage in defending America is as great as our disadvantage would be in attacking Europe. From a military geographical standpoint, we are the most fortunate country in the world. There is no other nation in this hemisphere strong enough even to consider attacking us, and the Atlantic and Pacific Oceans separate us from the warring armies of Europe and Asia." Recent events underlined the impregnability of the Americas. "If the British navy could not support an invasion of Norway against the German air force, there is little reason for us to worry about an invasion of America as long as our own air force is adequately maintained."

Lindbergh asked his listeners to ponder carefully. The danger to their country had grown with each step the administration had taken toward belligerence. America was near the point of no return, as the president intended it be. But Americans could still reclaim the country's fate. The choice was theirs. "Shall we throw away the independent American destiny which our forefathers gave their lives to win? Shall we submerge our future in the endless wars of the old world? Or shall we build our own defenses and leave European war to European countries?" American democracy was endangered by the war-mongering of the president and his allies, but it wasn't dead yet. "Some of your representatives in Washington are already considering a declaration of war, but they are responsible to you for the action they take. Let them know how you feel about this. Speak to your friends and organize in your community. Nothing but a determined effort on the part of every one of us will prevent the disaster toward which our nation is now heading."

37

I T APPEARS THAT Colonel Lindbergh, who has resided long in Great Britain as its guest, through fear of incensing Hitler would deprive the people of Great Britain and France of the weapons necessary to protect their lives," Key Pittman declared the next night in a radio address of his own.

The White House had indicated that President Roosevelt had more pressing business than answering the criticisms of the aviator. It left the rebuttal to Pittman, its point man in Congress on the war and related issues. The foreign relations chairman taxed Lindbergh for inconsistency as well as ingratitude. He had made no complaint against sales of American weapons to Germany in the years before the war, but he wanted to keep Britain and France from leveling the field with American weapons now.

Lindbergh said he feared that the present course would lead the United States into the war. "Well, suppose it does," said Pittman. "Who would institute and conduct the war? Not the United States, but Germany." Lindbergh had cited the spirit of the Americans who settled the old West. "He evidently was not informed entirely as to the courage and spirit of those early pioneers." Nor was he aware of their attitude toward guns. "They never refused to give a gun even to a stranger whose life was threatened by a bandit. Selfishness and cowardice were not so marked with the early pioneers."

Pittman said that Lindbergh grossly exaggerated what American belligerence would entail. In doing so, he badly misled the American people. "He tells them with the authority of a Pershing that if they get into a war with Germany they have to undertake the impossible task of transporting millions of men from the United States to fight in Germany." This was ludicrous. "The United States has no desire to conquer Germany. We simply intend to prevent Hitler from conquering any country in the Western Hemisphere. Instead of the United States undertaking the practically impossible feat of conveying an invading army to Germany, that necessity will be placed upon Hitler, if and when he ever attempts to invade the Western Hemisphere."

Pittman challenged Lindbergh's good faith. "It is strange the motives that actuate men," he said. Instead of opposing Hitler, as any reasonable person would, Lindbergh had taken aim at his own government. Was he merely foolish in doing so? "Has Colonel Lindbergh unwittingly been led into an attack on the President of the United States?" Or was he sly? "Has the cunning incitement of his ambition blinded him as to the safety of his country?"

Pittman concluded condescendingly. "Colonel Lindbergh is a young man, subject to flattery, as all of us are, and through flattery are often deceived. Colonel Lindbergh is a courageous man. No one doubts his patriotism. But he is a young man inexperienced and totally unfamiliar with our country, its statesmanship and its military matters."

AROUND THIS TIME a letter arrived at the White House, addressed to "Mr. President Roosevelt." The handwritten text said, "Your Excellence, Isn't Col. Lindbergh a pro-Nazi? Doesn't he belong to the 'Fifth Column'? Isn't it rather dangerous to put aviation plans and secrets into his hands?" The letter was signed "A good citizen."

Roosevelt received other letters on the subject of Lindbergh as a fifth columnist; he passed them on to J. Edgar Hoover, director of the Federal Bureau of Investigation at the Department of Justice. Hoover commenced a file on Lindbergh. Some letters came directly to the FBI. "I don't understand why your Department don't bind and gag that man Charles A. Lindbergh," one said. "He is the most dangerous man in the country today. He is a *German* and is doing his utmost to spread disunion in the U.S. You are after Fifth Columnists and traitors, so why let him escape?" This letter was signed "Real American."

A typewritten letter included a news photo of Lindbergh captioned "Col. Charles A. Lindbergh, as he arrived in Chicago yesterday to make a speech advocating U.S. cooperation with Germany." The unsigned letter warned, "If you don't get rid of this traitor and all his kind, you will not have to go to Europe to get a war. We will wake up some day and find we have a war right on our doorstep and then it will be too bad for all concerned."

Another unsigned letter berated the government for laxness in dealing with Lindbergh. "You talk of 5th Columnists," the writer said. "Why don't you get Chas. Lindbergh who is masquerading as a Colonel. He I think is one of the leaders of Nazis 5th Column in this Country since Germany bought him off with a medal that does not worth 2 cents." This was a reference to the decoration Hermann Goering had given Lindbergh. "Watch him. Listen to him."

A writer from New York urged the FBI to keep watch. "For the protection of the United States, every step that Col. Charles Lindberg makes should be investigated thoroughly. He is the worst enemy that the United States can have, since he is on Germany's side. Most of his property is in Germany. He translates all plans of defense made by the United States in German and then they are sent to Germany. This is according to what I heared from a German man."

The FBI office in Detroit forwarded to headquarters testimony from a man named Snyder about Lindbergh and his time in Germany. According to the Detroit agent in charge, Snyder stated "that on one occasion he saw Charles A. Lindbergh ride through the streets of Berlin while a storm troop raid was in progress and that Lindbergh was riding in an open car with a parade of these soldiers and that people were being beaten in the streets and houses set fire to and indescribable tortures taking place, and during the entire episode, Lindbergh, whom he, Snyder, described as grinning jackanapes, rode through the streets in the open car waving to people on the sidewalks."

A letter addressed to Roosevelt, forwarded from the White House to the FBI, insisted that the president take action against Lindbergh. "While the Department of Justice is hot on everybody's trail these days, why don't they delve into the REAL REASONS for 'Lindy's' obviously pro-German Nazi leanings?" Lindbergh was nothing less than a German agent. "He hasn't been the same since he was entertained and impressed by Nazi Germany. They were pretty foxy, weren't they, when they cunningly captured the loyalty and affection of the young American aviator, whose words were literally soaked up by the youth of the U.S., and whose opinions are, in spite of his years, respected by sane citizenry. Verily, Berlin could have no more astute Ambassador than Colonel Lindbergh. Thus far, he has obeyed his instructions to the letter. What's more, he is defiant and disdainful of anybody to stop him." It was high time somebody *did* stop him. "Why does not the FBI 'tail' the Colonel and ascertain truly what the bird is up to? There must be some reason for his leanings— was he promised a realm of his own over here, or more iron crosses and decorations from the most brutal, fiendish, treacherous race of people whom God in one of his dishmop moods had the misfortune to create?"

Several of the letters contained clippings from newspapers. One from an apparently paid notice in the *Shreveport Times* of Louisiana included a cartoon showing Hitler pinning a swastika on Lindbergh, who is giving the Nazi salute. The two are standing on a hilltop from which a burning city can be seen. The caption reads "Heil Lindbergh. A Nazi Decoration Well Deserved." Additional text, referring to Lindbergh's recent speech, says, "He insists that the United States has nothing to worry about in the murderous rape of the small countries of Europe; that we do wrong to meddle with the mad Nazi drive for world domination; that we refrain from hysteria just because of a few million women and children have been killed, crippled and driven away from their homes to starve in the Nazi-made wilderness. Can the so-called Lone Eagle believe that his Goebbels-inspired suggestions will be accepted in this country that has read with sickened heart of his decoration by the blood-thirsty, democracy-hating Hitler? ... Is it possible that he is so little an American he would forsake the United States if trouble should come? Does he forget that with only a sandwich he made the Atlantic the path for a horde of bombers without a sandwich."

A card addressed "To whom it may concern" found its way into Hoover's Lindbergh file. "As an American citizen I protest Lindbergh's political speeches on the air," the writer declared. "And I suggest you investigate his connections in this country. He doesn't sound like an American to me—more like a Nazi."

A writer from Los Angeles sent a typed note to the FBI. "Gentlemen: It seems very strange to me, to my friends, to thousands upon thousands of Americans, that when every effort is being made to suppress and stamp out Bundists, Communists, and all who would impede and obstruct the war-like preparations of our country, that Col. Charles Lindbergh should be permitted to come on the air and give aid and advice to such un-American activity."

From South Portland, Maine—per the printed stationery—a writer recommended investigating the radio networks that broadcast Lindbergh's speeches. As for the speaker himself: "Mr. Lindbergh could have done no better for Herr Hitler and coincided with his methods had he been a son of Germany."

A letter to Roosevelt from New York likened Lindbergh's approach to that of Hitler. "In 'Mein Kampf' Hitler declared that through the process of repetition he could foist any sort of propaganda on the mass of people," the writer said. "Here in our country an alarming number of people have fallen for the 'Lindbergh Line.' The time has come for spokesmen of true Americanism and Democracy to tell the truth about Mr. Lindbergh; to REPEAT IT, REPEAT IT, and REPEAT IT until all America has learned and accepted it."

Another writer from New York said he had recently been informed that the German consulate in the city was "a hot-bed of espionage—fifth-column activities and sabotage to take place." Lindbergh was identified as "a protégé of Adolf Hitler." The writer implored Hoover: "Please investigate these claims, with a view to check and oust these subversive elements in this our country—our true and real Democracy—in fact the only Democracy in this world."

When the FBI released the Lindbergh files many years later, it blacked out the names and street addresses of the letter writers. Occasionally the redactors slipped. Hoover sent a reply to a letter from New York; the name of the recipient was blacked out at the head of Hoover's reply. But in the unredacted body of the reply, Hoover wrote, "I wish to acknowledge receipt of your posted card dated June 16, 1940, and signed by you and Mrs. Meyer." Hoover went on to say, "It was indeed kind of you to bring this information to my attention, and your courtesy and interest in doing so are sincerely appreciated. Should you obtain any further information which you believe to be of interest to this Bureau, please feel free to communicate directly with Mr. B. F. Sackett, Special Agent in Charge." Agent Sackett's office address in New York was appended.

38

FOR THE TIME being Roosevelt left Lindbergh to Hoover. If the FBI director had Lindbergh followed or otherwise watched, nothing came of the surveillance.

Roosevelt had bigger problems, starting with how to keep France fighting. On June 10 he received a plea for help from Paul Reynaud, the French premier. "For six days and six nights our divisions have been fighting without one hour of rest against an army which has a crushing superiority in numbers and material," Reynaud wrote. "Today the enemy is almost at the gates of Paris." French forces would continue to resist, he vowed. "We shall fight in front of Paris; we shall fight behind Paris; we shall close ourselves in one of our provinces to fight and if we should be driven out of it we shall establish ourselves in North Africa to continue the fight and if necessary in our American possessions."

Reynaud wished Roosevelt to get this message out. "May I ask you, Mr. President, to explain all this yourself to your people, to all the citizens of the United States, saying to them that we are determined to sacrifice ourselves in the struggle that we are carrying on for all free men." He hoped Roosevelt would add a message of his own. "At the same time that you explain this situation to the men and women of America, I beseech you to declare publicly that the United States will give the Allies aid and material support by all means short of an expeditionary force." Reynaud understood he was asking a lot. "I know the gravity of such a gesture." But it was needed. And it must come soon. "I beseech you to do this before it is too late."

Roosevelt answered Reynaud, in part, with his speech at Charlottesville. But his promise in that speech of "material resources" to be sent to the "opponents of force" was vague and not timely enough to be helpful. Roosevelt knew it, and intended it so. He applauded Reynaud's statement of French resolve, but he had no confidence in the French government's ability to back it up. He wasn't willing to go out on a limb that might snap at any moment.

WINSTON CHURCHILL WISHED he would. The British prime minister, having a more immediate stake in the developments across the Channel, urged Roosevelt to heed Reynaud's warnings and act. "The practical point is what will happen when and if the French front breaks, Paris is taken and General Weygand reports formally to his government that France can no longer continue what he calls 'coordinated war,'" Churchill wrote to Roosevelt. "The aged Marshal Petain, who was none too good in April and July 1918 is, I fear, ready to lend his name and prestige to a treaty of peace for France. Reynaud on the other hand is for fighting on and he has a young general de Gaulle who believes much can be done. Admiral Darlan declares he will send the French fleet to Canada"—to place it beyond German control. Churchill, still a navy man at heart, considered this point crucial. "It would be disastrous if the two big modern ships fell into bad hands," he said, referring to the pride of the French fleet. "It seems to me that there must be many elements in France who will wish to continue the struggle either in France or in the French colonies or in both. This, therefore, is the moment for you to strengthen Reynaud the utmost you can and try to tip the balance in favor of the best and longest possible French resistance."

Churchill didn't want Roosevelt to think any French defeatism had or would cross the Channel. "Of course I made it clear to the French that we shall continue, whatever happened, and that we thought Hitler could not win the war or the mastery of the world until he had disposed of us, which has not been found easy in the past and which perhaps will not be found easy now. I made it clear to the French that we had good hopes of victory and anyhow had no doubts whatever of what our duty was."

Nonetheless, France and Britain looked to America. "If there is anything you can say publicly or privately to the French, now is the time," Churchill closed.

Roosevelt replied to Reynaud and sent a copy to Churchill. "Your message of June 10 has moved me very deeply," Roosevelt told the French leader. "As I have already stated to you and to Mr. Churchill, this government is doing everything in its power to make available to the Allied governments the material they so urgently require, and our efforts to do still more are being redoubled. This is so because of our faith in and our support of the ideals for which the Allies are fighting. The magnificent resistance of the French and British armies has profoundly impressed the American people. I am personally particularly impressed by your declaration that France will continue to fight on behalf of democracy even if it means slow withdrawal, even to North Africa and the Atlantic."

Roosevelt understood that Reynaud and Churchill would be disappointed by this response, which added nothing to the generalities he had already stated. Nor could Reynaud have been heartened by the postscript the president included in his cover cablegram to the American embassy secretary who would deliver the letter: "When this message is delivered it must be made entirely clear that the message is personal and private and not for publication."

CHURCHILL DIDN'T GIVE up. "Ambassador Kennedy will have told you about the British meeting today with the French at Tours of which I showed him our record," he wrote to Roosevelt on June 14. "I cannot exaggerate its critical character. They were very nearly gone. Weygand had advocated an armistice while he still had enough troops to prevent France from lapsing into anarchy. Reynaud asked us whether in view of the sacrifice and sufferings of France we would release her from the obligation about not making a separate peace. Although the fact that we have unavoidably been largely out of this terrible battle weighed with us, I did not hesitate in the name of the British government to refuse consent to an armistice or separate peace."

Churchill had offered Reynaud advice. "I urged that this issue should not be discussed until a further appeal had been made by Reynaud to you and the United States, which I undertook to second," he told Roosevelt. Reynaud had been heartened by this suggestion, perhaps thinking Churchill knew something more from Roosevelt. "Reynaud felt strongly that it would be beyond his power to encourage his people to fight on without hope of ultimate victory, and that that hope could only be kindled by American intervention up to the extreme limit open to you. As he put it, they wanted to see light at the end of the tunnel."

Churchill recommended in the strongest terms that Roosevelt at least allow the publication of his letter to Reynaud. "Mr. President, I must tell you that it seems to me absolutely vital that this message should be published tomorrow, June 14, in order that it may play the decisive part in turning the course of world history. It will I am sure decide the French to deny Hitler a patched-up peace with France. He needs this peace in order to destroy us and take a long step forward to world mastery. All the far-reaching plans strategic, economic, political and moral which your message expounds may be still-born if the French cut out now. Therefore I urge that the message should be published now."

Churchill granted that publication would make Britain's immediate lot harder. "We realize fully that the moment Hitler finds he cannot dictate a Nazi peace in Paris he will turn his fury on to us. We shall do our best to withstand it, and if we succeed, wide new doors are opened upon the future and all will come out even at the end of the day."

Roosevelt received from Reynaud the letter Churchill had encouraged him to write. "Four days of bloody fighting have gone by," Reynaud said, referring to the interval since his previous message. "Our army is now cut into several parts. Our divisions are decimated. Generals are commanding battalions. The Reichswehr has just entered Paris. We are going to attempt to withdraw our exhausted forces in order to fight new battles. It is doubtful, since they are at grips with an enemy which is constantly throwing in fresh troops, that this can be accomplished. At the most tragic hour of its history, France must choose. Will she continue to sacrifice her youth in a hopeless struggle? Will her government leave the national territory so as not to give itself up to the enemy and in order to be able to continue the struggle on the sea and in North Africa? Will the whole country then live abandoned, abating itself under the shadow of Nazi domination with all that that means for its body and its soul? Or will France ask Hitler for conditions of an armistice?"

The choice depended crucially on America, Reynaud said. "We can choose the first way, that of resistance, only if a chance of victory appears in the distance and if a light shines at the end of the tunnel." He specified the light France needed. "The only chance of saving the French nation, vanguard of democracies, and through her to save England, by whose side France could then remain with her powerful navy, is to throw into the balance, this very day, the weight of American power."

Reynaud knew that an American president could not declare war by himself. But this American president could do a great deal toward that end. The alternative was almost too grim to imagine. "If you cannot give France, in the hours to come, the certainty that the United States will come into the war within a very short time, the fate of the world will change. Then you will see France go under like a drowning man and disappear, after having cast a last look towards the land of liberty from which she awaited salvation."

ROOSEVELT RESPONDED TO Churchill first. "I am very much impressed by your message and I am grateful to you for giving me so frankly the account of the meeting at Tours yesterday," he said. "The magnificent courage and determination shown by the British and French governments and by the British and French soldiers have never been exceeded."

Churchill realized by this point of the letter that Roosevelt wasn't going to give him what he wanted. "You realize, as I hope Prime Minister Reynaud realizes, that we are doing our utmost in the United States to furnish all of the material and supplies which can possibly be released to the Allied governments," Roosevelt continued. "At the same time I believe you will likewise realize that while our efforts will be exerted towards making available an ever increasing amount of material and supplies a certain amount of time must pass before our efforts in this sense can be successful to the extent desired."

Roosevelt appeared to take back some of what he had given. "My message of yesterday's date addressed to the French Prime Minister was in no sense intended to commit and did not commit the government to military participation in support of Allied governments. You will know that there is of course no authority under our Constitution except in the Congress to make any commitment of this nature." And he explicitly rejected Churchill's plea about publishing the earlier letter to Reynaud. "I regret that I am unable to agree to your request that my message be published since I believe it to be imperative that there be avoided any possible misunderstanding."

Roosevelt disappointed Reynaud directly. "I am sending you this reply to your message of yesterday which I am sure you will realize has received the most earnest, as well as the most friendly, study on our part," he told Reynaud. "First of all, let me reiterate the ever-increasing admiration with which the American people and their government are viewing the resplendent courage with which the French armies are resisting the invaders on French soil."

He went on: "I wish also to reiterate in the most emphatic terms that, making every possible effort under present conditions, the government of the United States has made it possible for the Allied armies to obtain during the weeks that have just passed airplanes, artillery and munitions of many kinds, and that this government, so long as the Allied governments continue to resist, will redouble its efforts in this direction. I believe it is possible to say that every week that goes by will see additional materiel on its way to the Allied nations."

In words likely written to encourage Reynaud, but which might have had the opposite effect, Roosevelt explained how America would respond to a French defeat. "In accordance with its policy not to recognize the results of conquest of territory acquired through military aggression, the government of the United States will not consider as valid any attempts to infringe by force the independence and territorial integrity of France."

Roosevelt offered further moral support. "In these hours which are so heart-rending for the French people and yourself, I send you the assurances of my utmost sympathy." But France would receive nothing material beyond what had been previously announced. And even the moral support was hedged. "I know that you will understand that these statements carry with them no implication of military commitments," Roosevelt reminded Reynaud. "Only the Congress can make such commitments."

CHURCHILL REFUSED TO accept Roosevelt's answer. "I understand all your difficulties with American public opinion and Congress, but events are moving downward at a pace where they will
pass beyond the control of American public opinion when at last it
is ripened," he wrote to Roosevelt. "Have you considered what offers
Hitler may choose to make to France? He may say, 'Surrender the
fleet intact and I will leave you Alsace Lorraine,' or alternatively,
'If you do not give me your ships I will destroy your towns.' I am
personally convinced that America will in the end go to all lengths
but this moment is supremely critical for France. A declaration that
the United States will, if necessary, enter the war might save France.
Failing that, in a few days French resistance may have crumbled and
we shall be left alone."

But if America wouldn't rescue France, it still might save Britain,
Churchill said. This was the main point of his message. The prime
minister renewed his warning of the government that might follow
his own. "Although the present government and I personally would
never fail to send the fleet across the Atlantic if resistance was beaten
down here, a point may be reached in the struggle where the present ministers no longer have control of affairs and when very easy
terms could be obtained for the British islands by their becoming a
vassal state of the Hitler empire. A pro-German government would
certainly be called into being to make peace and might present to a
shattered or a starving nation an almost irresistible case for entire
submission to the Nazi will."

Churchill reiterated what this might mean for America. "The
fate of the British fleet, as I have already mentioned to you, would
be decisive on the future of the United States, because if it were
joined to the fleets of Japan, France, and Italy and the great resources
of German industry, overwhelming sea power would be in Hitler's
hands." Japan had not formally allied with Germany and Italy, but
it was on the verge of doing so. "This revolution in sea power might
happen very quickly and certainly long before the United States
would be able to prepare against it. If we go down you may have a
United States of Europe under the Nazi command far more numerous, far stronger, far better armed than the new world."

Churchill returned to his argument for lending Britain some American destroyers, augmented by the new threat from Italy. "I am sending you through Ambassador Kennedy a paper on destroyer strength prepared by the naval staff for your information. If we have to keep, as we shall, the bulk of our destroyers on the east coast to guard against invasion, how shall we be able to cope with a German-Italian attack on the food and trade by which we live? The sending of the 35 destroyers as I have already described will bridge the gap until our new construction comes in at the end of the year. Here is a definite practical and possible decisive step which can be taken at once and I urge most earnestly that you will weigh my words."

Churchill cited statistics on the losses of British warships in the last several months. Sobering in themselves, the numbers would get worse with the consequences of recent and unfolding events. "We are now faced with the imminent collapse of French resistance, and if this occurs, the successful defence of this island will be the only hope of averting the collapse of civilization as we define it. We must ask therefore as a matter of life or death to be reinforced with these destroyers."

39

ERMAN TANKS TODAY clanked across the Seine bridges,
past the Arc de Triomphe and down the tree-lined Champs
Elysees into the heart of Paris," the United Press reported
in a dispatch that appeared in hundreds of American papers on
June 15. "Flanked by armored cars, the dust-stained tanks swung tri-
umphantly into Paris from the northwest at the head of Nazi units
occupying the 'City of Light,' German accounts of the event said."
The American news syndicate had to rely on the German accounts
because German advance units had severed independent communications with the outside world. "One of the first acts of the Germans
in Paris was to take over the radio stations, over which the playing of
German music began immediately."

The censorship, which under other circumstances might have cast
doubt on the German conquest, instead underlined its complete-
ness. "The tanks rumbled between thin lines of tense and silent Pari-
sians," the UP dispatch continued. "Reports from the French capital
estimated that probably a third of the city's normal population of
2,800,000 had remained in Paris." The other two-thirds had fled the
city by car, train, bicycle and foot, mostly to the south, away from the
invading army.

The Reynaud government had made a decision not to defend
Paris, lest the city be destroyed. After French armies failed to stem
the German offensive from the north, the government had decamped
for Tours, 150 miles to the southwest. The German forces took the
capital unopposed. "Nazi officers at the head of the procession set

their course for the headquarters of French officials still in the city, it was said, and formally took it over. The French police, fire department and other city departments were said to have placed themselves at the disposal of the Germans. They offered to maintain order and discipline during the occupation of the capital." They didn't have much work. "The city was like a city of the dead—shops closed, iron shutters in windows, those people who remained mourning in their homes and wondering what was coming. Police and civil guards patrolled the streets slowly, almost alone. They had handed in their rifles and pistols. They were now a completely civilian force."

LINDBERGH'S INCREASINGLY VISIBLE opposition to Roosevelt had put a political target on his back. And it was putting a target of a more literal sort on the backs of his loved ones, if the threats against them were to be taken seriously. "An hour or so after supper Mrs. Morrow phoned from Englewood to tell me she had just received a phone call from some unknown person, telling her that her daughter (Anne) was in danger," Lindbergh wrote in his journal. "Again, that same old feeling of unknown danger. I would rather live in the front-line trenches than have the constant worry of safeguarding my family against criminal stealth."

He asked his mother-in-law about the call. "Some woman 'with a calm and steady voice' had telephoned her at Next Day Hill"—the Morrow home—"saying that she (the woman) was a friend of the Lindleys (old Englewood people), and that she wanted to tell Mrs. Morrow her daughter was in danger," he wrote.

"Which daughter?" she asked.

"The famous one."

The woman hung up. Mrs. Morrow called the Lindleys, who didn't answer. Lindbergh told his mother-in-law it was probably a crank call and shouldn't be taken seriously. "Nevertheless, it brings back the same uncomfortable feeling we had before going to Europe to live in 1935," he wrote. "We used to get threatening letters every week then. Government officials made more than a dozen arrests because of threatening letters we received during the previous two years. One of the worst parts about these threats is the effect they have on one's home. They create an atmosphere in which it is impossible to bring up a family normally. Anne is wonderful about it, but I realize what is going through her mind when I hear her say, as she did this evening, 'I told you to stay upstairs, Thor.'" Thor was the German shepherd Lindbergh had acquired after the kidnapping and murder of Charles Jr. Thor spent each night near the children.

LINDBERGH'S ASSOCIATES FACED harassment of a different order. "I have decided not to see any of my friends in the Air Corps on this trip," he wrote on the way to Washington, "as I know that the politicians of this administration make as much trouble as possible for anyone I have contact with. Since I do not want to make life difficult for my friends, it is best not to see them—except where they are already known opponents of the Administration."

Fulton Lewis was one of those opponents. A print journalist who had switched to radio, Lewis aired news and commentary five nights a week over the Mutual system. Lindbergh joined Lewis for lunch at the Chevy Chase Club. "We discussed politics and the war. He told me that someone had started the rumor that he had taken part in writing my radio addresses and that two of his sponsorships in New York City had been canceled as a result. Lewis had been forced to state over the radio that he had nothing whatever to do with writing my addresses."

Lindbergh heard from supporters as well as critics. Immediately after his latest speech he was approached by a Yale student who said he wanted to organize college men against American entry into the war. Lindbergh spoke to the fellow for half an hour. Lindbergh was leaving the studio when he was handed a batch of some thirty telegrams that had already come in. "All but three were in support of my stand."

Two days later more bad news from Europe arrived. "The radio announces that France has asked for peace terms," Lindbergh wrote. Without their capital—and without a promise from Roosevelt of American intervention—the French had concluded they couldn't continue the fight against Hitler.

Lindbergh knew no more than anyone else what this meant. "Now that Germany has about conquered the continent of Europe, what will England do? And what will our reaction be in America?"

Roosevelt's opponents wanted to learn Lindbergh's reaction to the events abroad. "A phone call came from someone connected with the Republican convention arrangements in Philadelphia, asking me if I would attend the convention." He didn't have to think twice. "I replied that I felt I would have more influence in my stand on the war if I did not go to Philadelphia." Yet he didn't spurn the Republicans entirely. That evening he and Anne had dinner at the home of John Foster Dulles, an international lawyer and sometime diplomat who was being touted as a likely secretary of state in the next Republican administration.

LINDBERGH RETREATED TO Long Island with Anne and the children. The beach bore the signs of encroaching civilization. "The shore is becoming littered with tin cans, bottles, oranges, paper, and other refuse from the myriad boats that appear on Long Island Sound during the summer months," he wrote. "I long for real wilderness with its cleanness and solitude, away from the crowded litter of cities. When this crisis has passed—whenever that may be—Anne and I will go far into the north or into the desert until the space and solitude have washed all this feeling of crowded city life away."

He had taken his stand, but he didn't know where it had left him. "I went for a walk after lunch through the woods and along the beach. It seems I spend most of my time these days thinking. My mind is not on the trees and birds and clouded sky as I would wish it to be, but on the war and chaos of these turbulent days. I wish I could be either wholeheartedly in the war and fighting for true beliefs and ideals, or else far enough away from it mentally and physically to be able to see the forest when I walk through it, and to feel the beauty of wind-rippled water without having part of my mind thinking of politics and bombing planes and plans. Here, at this moment, I feel in contact neither with the world of men nor with the world of God. What can be done to bring this country back? What has happened to America? To the character of the pioneer? To the courage of the Revolutionary Army? To the American destiny that we once had?"

He looked to his political model for counsel. "Spent the evening reading Father's *Why Is Your Country at War?*"

BENNETT CHAMP CLARK called to tell of an antiwar rally to be held in Chicago. The Missouri Democrat hoped Lindbergh would speak. "I think I will accept, but want to learn a little more about it," Lindbergh wrote. He was satisfied with what he learned, and told Clark he accepted the invitation.

He visited his mother in Detroit and dropped in on Henry Ford. The old carmaker had been asking again how he could oppose American intervention; Lindbergh said a donation to the American Legion, which was taking a strong antiwar stance, would be useful. "He agreed completely."

Lindbergh recalled when he had given Ford his first ride in an airplane. Lindbergh was touring with the *Spirit of St. Louis* and had landed at the airport in Dearborn where the Ford company tested its own airplanes. "I showed Ford the plane and then asked him if he would like to go up in it. Ford had always refused to go up in his own tri-motored ships, and the *Spirit of St. Louis* had only one engine and one cockpit. But, to my surprise, Ford accepted my invitation. He had to sit crouched up on the arm of my seat in anything but a comfortable position. I took off and flew around the field at Dearborn, probably five or ten minutes in the air. Ford apparently enjoyed the trip greatly. Later on, I took him up in one of his own tri-motored planes together with a number of officers of the company."

Lindbergh and Anne hosted Truman Smith, the army attaché, and his wife for dinner and the night. "We discussed the war and Roosevelt's recent actions. Will he try to take over the French islands in the West Indies? What will his policy be in South America? Does he or does he not wish to draw this country into the war?" The uncertainty left everything in limbo. "All life seems to revolve around the war, and I suppose it must revolve around all major wars. But how I wish I could put my mind on other things."

Lindbergh and Anne drove to Maine for a holiday. They took a room at an inn where they had stayed several years earlier. Their hopes for privacy evaporated almost at once. "A large number of people were visiting the inn—many tourists. We were not bothered during dinner, but found we could not go walking through the grounds afterward. As soon as I stepped out the door, I was met with demands for autographs." The demands continued as they walked to a small church nearby. "Two carloads of people followed us over and shouted at us: 'Hey Lindy! We know ya. Why dontcha say something? Come over and talk to us!' And as we walked back to the inn one of the cars followed less than ten feet behind us, its lights turned on us, and its occupants still excited and shouting."

THE CHICAGO EVENT approached, but Lindbergh wasn't hearing details. He called Champ Clark but couldn't reach him. He called again. No luck. "Something is wrong, and I am not yet sure what it is," he wrote. "Possibly he now thinks the Chicago meeting is dangerous politically. His secretary always says the Senator will be in within an hour or two, but he is never there when I call, and does not call back."

In New York, Lindbergh met with Roy Howard, head of Scripps-Howard Newspapers, at Howard's office in the Grand Central Building. Together they drove to the dock where Howard's diesel yacht was moored. With Howard's wife and another couple, they ate dinner while cruising on Long Island Sound in the direction of Lloyd Neck, where Lindbergh's home was. Howard wanted Lindbergh to write an article in favor of a unified air force—as opposed to the separate air corps of the army and the navy.

"I told Howard that while I was with his policy in general in regard to a unified Air Force, an article would require careful study, and that in making such a study I would want to discuss the matter with various Army and Navy officers," Lindbergh recorded. "It would be difficult to do this, I told him, because of the stand I have taken in regard to the country's involvement in war, not from the standpoint of the officers I wished to talk to, but because such conversations might place them in difficulty with the Administration."

Howard said that talking to senior officers of the army and navy would be a waste of time. Naturally they would defend their existing bailiwicks.

"I said the value to me would lie in hearing the best opposition arguments and that without a comprehensive knowledge of those arguments one could not take an intelligent stand. I told Howard I would also want to talk to the younger officers in both services."

They neared Lloyd Neck. Lindbergh thanked Howard for the lift home. "I had planned on swimming ashore at Lloyd Neck, and had brought bathing trunks and an oilskin in which to wrap my clothes for towing through the water. However, since the yacht carried a dinghy, I went ashore in it instead."

40

THE CHICAGO RALLY was set for Sunday, August 4. Lindbergh still hadn't heard from Champ Clark. Finally his suspicions were confirmed. "Senator Clark's secretary called to tell me the Senator was in a St. Louis hospital with an infected foot and would not be able to attend the Chicago meeting!"

On Friday, August 2, Lindbergh finished drafting his speech. "It will not be popular but, I think, covers subjects which must be brought out and discussed," he wrote in his journal.

He flew to Chicago and stayed at the home of Robert McCormick, publisher of the *Chicago Tribune*. McCormick had served with distinction during the World War, and he still enjoyed being called Colonel McCormick. He was staunchly conservative and considered Roosevelt a socialist or worse. He was certain Roosevelt was trying to maneuver America into the European war. He was delighted to host Lindbergh.

A crowd of forty thousand gathered at Soldier Field that hot Sunday afternoon. The organizers called themselves the Citizens Committee to Keep America Out of War. The stage was crowded with uniformed veterans of the World War. The organizers and some local political figures spoke first. Avery Brundage, a Chicago engineer and developer, a former Olympic athlete and the current president of the American Olympic committee, introduced Lindbergh.

"Several weeks have passed since I received the honor of your invitation to speak," Lindbergh said to the organizing committee. At the time of the invitation, trends indicated that America might be swept into war at any moment. "The agitation for our entry in the war was increasing with alarming rapidity. Hysteria had mounted to the point where anti-parachute corps were being formed to defend American cities against air attacks from Europe. Greenland, with its Arctic climate, its mountainous terrain, and its ice-filled seas was called an easy stepping-stone for German bombing planes invading America. Cartoons showed the Atlantic Ocean reduced to the width of the English Channel. American safety was said to depend upon the success of European armies. Foreign propaganda was in full swing, and it seemed in many ways that we were approaching the greatest crisis in the history of our country."

The American people had known better. Their common sense had prevailed. "The underlying tradition of American independence arose, and in recent weeks its voice has thundered through the weaker cries for war." The crowd this day was testament to the popular prudence.

Yet peril persisted, Lindbergh warned. "We have by no means escaped the foreign entanglements and favoritisms that Washington warned us against when he passed the guidance of our nation's destiny to the hands of future generations. We have participated deeply in the intrigues of Europe, and not always in an open democratic way. There are still interests in this country and abroad who will do their utmost to draw us into the war." Against these interests true patriots must remain on guard.

Lindbergh retained hope. Polls revealed broad opposition to war. "People are beginning to realize that the problems of Europe cannot be solved by the interference of America. We have at last started to build and to plan for the defense of our own continent." Americans were taking their defense into their own hands, not leaving it to the whims of others. "Our eyes are turned once more in the direction of security and peace, for if our own military forces are strong, no foreign nation can invade us, and, if we do not interfere with their affairs, none will desire to."

Lindbergh asked his audience to look ahead. "Since we have decided against entering the war in Europe, it is time for us to consider the relationship we will have with Europe after this war is over." The same clear view that had kept America out of war so far must be maintained.

Lindbergh knew he was venturing onto treacherous ground. "I have a different outlook toward Europe than most people in America. In consequence, I am advised to speak guardedly on the subject of the war. I am told that one must not stand too strongly against the trend of the times, and that, to be effective, what one says must meet with general approval." He didn't deny the sincerity or insight of those who proposed this course to him. Yet he couldn't heed their caution. "It is contrary to the values that I hold highest in life. I prefer to say what I believe, or not to speak at all."

He shared what his travels had taught him. "I found conditions in Europe to be very different from our concept of them here in the United States. Anyone who takes the trouble to read through back issues of our newspapers cannot fail to realize what a false impression we had of the belligerent nations. We were told that Germany was ripe for revolution, that her rearmament was a bluff, that she lacked officers, that she flew her airplanes from one field to another so they would be counted again and again by foreign observers. We were informed that Russia had the most powerful air fleet in the world, that the French army was superior to any in Europe, that the British navy was more than a match for the German air force, that Germany lacked enough food, fuel, and raw material to wage war, that the Maginot Line was impregnable, that Italy would never enter a war against England. Statements of this sort have issued forth in an endless stream from Europe, and anyone who questioned their accuracy was called a Nazi agent."

Lindbergh didn't mention that he himself had challenged much of the conventional wisdom, and been called a Nazi agent for doing so. He let recent events, which had proven these assertions wrong, one after the other, speak for themselves.

Lindbergh said he had seen something deeper while in Europe. He had hoped the last war had taught the world that change must come by agreement, by diplomacy. What he saw abroad shook that hope. "Living in Europe made me fear that it would come only through war," he said. "When I saw the wealth of the British Empire, I felt that the rich had become too rich. When I saw the poverty of Central Europe, I felt that the poor had become too poor." The disparity of the status quo couldn't last.

He had seen how it would be challenged. "From 1936 to 1939, as I travelled through European countries, I saw the phenomenal military strength of Germany growing like a giant at the side of an aged and complacent England. France was awake to her danger, but far too occupied with personal ambitions, industrial troubles, and internal politics to make more than a feeble effort to rearm. In England there was organization without spirit. In France there was spirit without organization. In Germany there were both." He realized that the last war had never ended. "The sons of victory and the sons of defeat were about to meet on the battlefields of their fathers."

Recently much had been said of the need to defend democracy. Lindbergh asked where the defenders of democracy were when it was struggling for its life in Germany in the decade after the war. Interventionists demanded that America defend small nations against aggression. Where were they when Japan swallowed Manchuria and Italy bludgeoned Abyssinia?

The struggle in Europe wasn't about democracy, he said. It was about territory and wealth. It wasn't new. "It has caused conflict in Europe since European history began." It wasn't to be resolved by America or any other non-European country. "The longer I lived in Europe, the more I felt that no outside influence could solve the problems of European nations, or bring them lasting peace. They must work out their destiny, as we must work out ours."

Lindbergh came to the hard part of his counsel. "In the past, we have dealt with a Europe dominated by England and France. In the future we may have to deal with a Europe dominated by Germany." Many of his listeners would find this difficult to accept. "We are often told that if Germany wins this war, cooperation will be impossible, and treaties no more than scraps of paper."

Lindbergh differed. "I reply that cooperation is never impossible when there is sufficient gain on both sides; and that treaties are seldom torn apart when they do not cover a weak nation." America was no such weak nation. As ever, its defense must rest on American arms, not on treaties. "I would be among the last to advocate depending upon treaties for our national safety. I believe that we should rearm fully for the defense of America, and that we should never make the type of treaty that would lay us open to invasion if it were broken."

Some Americans liked to lecture other countries and governments. This led nowhere, Lindbergh said. "Nothing is to be gained by shouting names and pointing the finger of blame across the ocean. Our grandstand advice to England, and our criticism of her campaigns, have been neither wanted nor helpful. Our accusations of aggression and barbarism on the part of Germany simply bring back echoes of hypocrisy and Versailles. Our hasty condemnation of a French government, struggling desperately to save a defeated nation from complete collapse, can do nothing but add to famine, hatred, and chaos."

Americans must look to themselves in conceiving any plan for lasting security. "That plan should be based upon the welfare of America. It should be backed by an impregnable system of defense. It should incorporate terms of mutual advantage. But it should not involve the internal affairs of Europe. They never were, and never will be, carried on according to our desires."

41

L INDBERGH WAS RIGHT in thinking his message wouldn't improve his popularity. Claude Pepper, a Democratic senator from Florida, told his colleagues in the upper chamber that Lindbergh's admiration for Germany made him "the chief of the fifth column in this country." Of course Lindbergh wasn't worried about a German victory in Europe—or in America, Pepper said. "I don't think he would be so terribly frightened if news came that the Germans had landed in this country, because Colonel Lindbergh would know that at least Colonel Lindbergh wouldn't be harmed under the Fuehrer of Germany."

Scott Lucas, a Democratic senator from Illinois, went on radio to rebut Lindbergh. "I was not only amazed but somewhat shocked by Colonel Lindbergh's attitude of complacency toward Adolf Hitler," Lucas said. Lindbergh was within his rights in speaking his mind, but it would behoove him to remember that American rights required defending. "It is freedom of expression, freedom of thought, and freedom of action that are always denied by the totalitarian governments once they conquer a country." Lindbergh dismissed a German invasion of America as impossible. "I hope he is right, but I remind the American people that the apparent impossible in the last few months in Europe has become accomplished fact."

Lucas sneered at Lindbergh's presumption in advising Americans on weighty matters of state. "If the American people are looking for guidance and counsel in this hour of American uncertainty, I say, with all due deference to Colonel Lindbergh, that you should stop, look and listen before you follow this youthful man who has blossomed overnight into an oracle who instructs the world and his country on such momentous problems as war, statesmanship and diplomacy." Lucas damned Lindbergh with ironic praise: "Colonel Lindbergh is a great American flier."

L. M. Birkhead was the national director of a group calling itself the Friends of Democracy; he sent a telegram to Henry Stimson, the newly installed secretary of war. "There is widespread alarm over the character of Colonel Charles A. Lindbergh's public and radio addresses," declared Birkhead on behalf of his group. "The American people want to know what Colonel Lindbergh's position is with the United States Army." Whatever that position was, it ought to be terminated at once. "These times are so critical that every citizen must stand up and be counted. Why spend billions for military defense and at the same time permit the morale of the American people to be destroyed by apologists for Hitler?"

Walter Lippmann responded more thoughtfully. The syndicated columnist suggested that Lindbergh's critics attacked him selectively, picking out parts of his speech that seemed to favor Germany while ignoring others that didn't. Summarizing his own reading of the speech, Lippmann wrote, "Colonel Lindbergh thinks the United States could live in the same world with a Nazi-dominated Europe providing the defense of the United States were 'impregnable.'"

Lippmann didn't challenge Lindbergh's logic. Rather he questioned the proviso. "The defenses of the United States are very far from being impregnable." Nor, on current appropriation trends, could they be made impregnable for several years. Until then, the British fleet would be essential to American security.

John Pershing, the American military commander from the World War, had recently recommended the transfer of fifty American destroyers to Britain, to give America time to strengthen its own defenses. Lippmann thought Lindbergh should heed the old soldier's recommendation, if Lindbergh were to be consistent. "Since Colonel Lindbergh himself declared that we can make dependable treaties with a Nazi-dominated Europe only if our defenses are impregnable, no disinterested and patriotic follower of Colonel Lindbergh can afford to disregard the warning and plea made by General Pershing. If we need an impregnable defense, then we need the time to construct it, and we cannot be sure that the time will be granted us if the British fleet is sunk, or worse still, captured."

PERSHING'S PROPOSAL AND Lippman's endorsement brought the question of the destroyers into the public arena. Probably Roosevelt had a hand in causing it to come up. The president never courted controversy without testing the waters. He waited nine days after Pershing's recommendation and a week after Lippmann's column. Neither provoked an uproar.

Roosevelt thereupon sent Churchill the message the prime minister had been desperate to hear. "It may be possible to furnish to the British Government as immediate assistance at least 50 destroyers," the president said. These could be accompanied by torpedo boats and some fighter planes.

Yet the presentation of the transfer mattered greatly. "Such assistance, as I am sure you will understand, would only be furnished if the American people and the Congress frankly recognized that in return therefor the national defense and security of the United States would be enhanced."

Roosevelt proposed conditions for the aid. "1. Assurance on the part of the Prime Minister that in the event that the waters of Great Britain become untenable for British ships of war, the latter would not be turned over to the Germans or sunk, but would be sent to other parts of the Empire for continued defense of the Empire. 2. An agreement on the part of Great Britain that the British Government would authorize the use of Newfoundland, Bermuda, the Bahamas, Jamaica, St. Lucia, Trinidad and British Guiana as naval and air bases by the United States in the event of an attack on the American hemisphere by any non-American nation."

Roosevelt's first condition was simply a request that Churchill confirm what he had already said about never surrendering. The second condition allowed the president to treat the provision of destroyers as part of a shrewd bargain he had wrung from the British. The details of the agreement on the bases could be worked out; the point was to show the American people that the president had their interests, and not those of Britain, most at heart.

CHURCHILL WAS ECSTATIC. "I need not tell you how cheered I am by your message or how grateful I feel for your untiring efforts to give us all possible help," he replied to Roosevelt. "The worth of every destroyer that you can spare to us is measured in rubies."

Yet Churchill didn't waste time on gratitude. Having broken through Roosevelt's reserve, he pressed for more. "We also need the motor torpedo boats which you mentioned and as many flying boats and rifles as you can let us have. We have a million men waiting for rifles. The moral value of this fresh aid from your government and people at this critical time will be very great and widely felt."

Meeting Roosevelt's conditions would not be a problem, Churchill said. "But I am sure that you will not misunderstand me if I say that our willingness to do so must be conditional on our being assured that there will be no delay in letting us have the ships and flying boats."

Churchill added that he hoped Roosevelt wouldn't publicize Britain's agreement not to let the destroyers fall into German hands via surrender. "We intend to fight this out here to the end and none of us would ever buy peace by surrendering or scuttling the fleet. But in any use you may make of this repeated assurance you will please bear in mind the disastrous effect from our point of view and perhaps also from yours of allowing any impression to grow that we regard the conquest of the British Islands and its naval bases as any other than an impossible contingency."

WORD GOT OUT that Roosevelt and Churchill had been discussing destroyers for Britain and bases for America. Roosevelt deflected questions at press conferences.

"Could you tell us your view, Mr. President, on the suggestion of General Pershing that we sell fifty destroyers to the British?" a reporter asked.

"There is no news on that at the present time," Roosevelt said.

Roosevelt had dispatched William Donovan, called Wild Bill for his exploits during the World War, to London to talk with Churchill and other British officials.

"Can you give us any indication of the nature of Donovan's mission abroad?" a reporter queried.

"I cannot and he won't tell you."

The stories persisted. Roosevelt felt obliged to say something. He decided to treat the destroyers and the bases as two separate questions, and to lead with the latter. "This has nothing to do with destroyers in the sense that a quid pro quo is under discussion, but I am initiating, holding conversations with the British government for the acquisition of naval bases and air bases for the defense of the Americas and particularly with relationship to the Panama Canal," he told reporters on August 19. "If you want to put that in quotes, you can put it this way: that the United States government is holding conversations with the government of the British Empire in regard to the acquisition of naval and air bases by the United States for American hemispheric defense, with special reference to the Panama Canal—end of quote."

A reporter wanted to make sure he had the president's position regarding the bases just right. "Did I understand you to say, Mr. President, that they had no relation to destroyers?"

Roosevelt hesitated to deny categorically something so patently true. "I would not use it on destroyers," he said vaguely. "That is just a little private tip."

A follow-up question elicited a firmer denial. "It is not a matter of destroyers. That is exactly the point."

"Destroyers are out?"

Roosevelt waffled. "I do not know. I do not know what the quid pro quo is going to be." He thought some more. "The emphasis is on the acquisition of the bases. That is the main point, for the protection of this hemisphere. And I think that is all there is to say."

Yet that wasn't all he said. "To make it perfectly clear, there are two items, entirely separate from each other." Again he stressed the bases. "What I am trying to do is to acquire American bases. Let us make that clear."

Finally, on September 3, he issued a public statement in the form of a message to Congress. The charade of no quid pro quo had been abandoned. Roosevelt transmitted a series of notes by which the United States acquired the right to lease naval and air bases in Newfoundland, Bermuda and the British West Indies. "The right to bases in Newfoundland and Bermuda are gifts, generously given and gladly received," Roosevelt said. "The other bases mentioned have been acquired in exchange for 50 of our over-age destroyers." Churchill had political reasons for handling Newfoundland and Bermuda differently than the West Indies.

The president treated the bases as the central part of the exchange. And he characterized the deal in terms designed to keep the isolationists from erupting. "This is not inconsistent in any sense with our status of peace. Still less is it a threat against any nation. It is an epochal and far-reaching act of preparation for continental defense in the face of grave danger." No foreign government could take it amiss. "Preparation for defense is an inalienable prerogative of a sovereign state. Under present circumstances this exercise of sovereign right is essential to the maintenance of our peace and safety."

Roosevelt touted the bargain effusively. "This is the most important action in the reinforcement of our national defense that has been taken since the Louisiana Purchase. Then as now, considerations of safety from overseas attack were fundamental. The value to the Western Hemisphere of these outposts of security is beyond calculation. Their need has long been recognized by our country, and especially by those primarily charged with the duty of charting and organizing our own naval and military defense."

So *there*, Lindbergh, Roosevelt seemed to be saying about the bases. "They are essential to the protection of the Panama Canal, Central America, the northern portion of South America, the Antilles, Canada, Mexico, and our own eastern and Gulf seaboards. Their consequent importance in hemispheric defense is obvious."

Yet Roosevelt claimed the credit for himself. "For these reasons I have taken advantage of the present opportunity to acquire them."

42

WILLIAM DONOVAN, ROOSEVELT's envoy to Churchill, was more than a message boy. He was, in fact, the president's liaison to a secret British operation that would have shattered Roosevelt's credibility and jeopardized his entire approach to the war had it become known.

The operation began in the spring of 1940, when William Stephenson, a British intelligence operative, traveled to Washington. "Ostensibly private business was the purpose of the journey," explained the official—and for decades highly confidential—history of British intelligence activities in America during World War II. "In fact, he travelled at the request of CSS." CSS was the director of the British Secret Intelligence Service, or SIS. The mission of Stephenson—"WS" in the official history—was to establish a working relationship with J. Edgar Hoover of the FBI.

Hoover greeted Stephenson cordially but explained that orders from the State Department prevented him from working with the British in any way that might compromise American neutrality. The only way around this injunction was special dispensation from the president. "Accordingly," the official history continued, "WS arranged for a mutual friend to put the matter before the President, and Mr. Roosevelt, upon hearing the arguments in favour of the proposed liaison, endorsed them enthusiastically. 'There should be the closest possible marriage,' the President said, 'between the FBI and British Intelligence.'"

The wedding vows were exchanged behind closed doors—closed even to the State Department—and the union was consummated. Stephenson established an intelligence operation in New York in an office labeled Passport Control. Stephenson's assignment subsumed three tasks: "to investigate enemy activities, to institute adequate security measures against the threat of sabotage to British property, and to organize American public opinion in favour of aid to Britain." The FBI, at the direction of Roosevelt, assisted Stephenson and his men in pursuing their goals. "Hoover could hardly have been more cooperative," the British history said. "Clearly WS's organization, employing as it did not only its own intelligence agents but what amounted to its own police force, represented an obvious threat to United States neutrality and could not have existed at all without the FBI's sanction. But Hoover was more than its licensor. He was, in a very real sense, its patron." Hoover set up a secure radio channel by which Stephenson could communicate with his superiors in London. He kept Stephenson's secrets from the State Department and other American offices. "On a personal basis he worked very closely with WS to further the wholly unneutral purpose of protecting British interests, and he instructed his officers to assist BSC"—British Security Coordination, the name by which Stephenson's operation was known in London—"in every way open to them. In short, he led his Bureau into a full-fledged alliance with British Intelligence, as the President had urged."

The FBI and Stephenson's group shared tricks of the craft. A Stephenson operative showed the FBI how to open and reseal correspondence previously thought impervious to tampering. The FBI assisted in a British disinformation campaign designed to shake the confidence of Germany in its nonaggression pact with the Soviet Union.

Stephenson facilitated a secret trip to London by William Donovan. "US Embassy not being informed of visit," Stephenson cabled ahead of Donovan. Donovan returned to America to serve as a powerful pro-British voice at the highest levels of the American government. Among other activities he wrote a series of articles on German "fifth-column" activities and published them in American newspapers. The articles gained credence from Donovan's military reputation and from his not revealing that he got most of his information from Stephenson and the British. Donovan's heft in Washington made him a favorite among the British. As one British intelligence officer explained, "Donovan exercises controlling influence over Knox, strong influence over Stimson, friendly advisory influence over President and Hull." Frank Knox was secretary of the navy. Stephenson, in communication to London, referred to Donovan as "our man."

Donovan wasn't the only useful American. Robert Sherwood was a playwright who became a speechwriter for Roosevelt. He was as determined as Donovan to aid the British cause. Whenever Roosevelt was scheduled to deliver a speech on the war, Sherwood would show a draft to Stephenson, who would suggest changes. "He did this with the President's knowledge and approval," the secret history explained.

While directing British propaganda to Roosevelt through Donovan and Sherwood, Stephenson obstructed the communications of persons opposed to aid to Britain. He cultivated informants among employees of antiwar newspapers, including the personal assistant of Roy Howard of the Scripps-Howard chain. He hatched a scheme to blackmail the Hearst news syndicate, by buying callable loans owed by the company and demanding repayment. The British treasury, itself strapped at the time, decided against the scheme, concluding that the required funds were needed elsewhere.

Stephenson developed covert contacts at important newspapers, including the *New York Times*, the *New York Herald Tribune* and the *Baltimore Sun*. To these it fed information favorable to the British cause. According to the secret history, Stephenson's office insisted, "as a matter of policy from which only occasional divergence was allowed, on restricting its output to accurate information which had genuine news value." This minimized the potential for embarrassment to the friendly papers. And the stories, once broken, perpetuated themselves.

A crucial Stephenson connection was with the Overseas News Agency, a recent creation of the Jewish Telegraph Agency, an international news service established in 1917. Both organizations were strongly opposed to Germany. Through Stephenson the British government became an underwriter of the ONA. "After a series of secret negotiations, BSC agreed to give the ONA a monthly sub-sidy in return for promise of cooperation in certain specific ways," the secret history explained. The cooperation included distributing stories written by Stephenson's men. In time dozens of American newspapers picked up and published the stories on a regular basis, unaware of their origin.

43

AFTER THE DEFEAT of France, the Germans had commenced an air campaign against Britain, to neutralize the Royal Air Force ahead of a possible invasion of Britain. The first objective was to destroy British planes and air support facilities; in time it broadened to weaken the will of the British people at large.

Edward Murrow continued to broadcast the war into the homes of American radio listeners. "During the last three days, I have driven more than five hundred miles in the south of England," he reported over the CBS network. "Many times the sirens sounded and a few times we saw the bombs fall. There is something unreal about this air war over Britain. Much of it you can't see, but the aircraft are up in the clouds, out of sight. Even when the Germans come down to dive-bomb an airfield, it's all over in an incredibly short time. You just see a bomber slanting down toward his target; three or four little things that look like marbles fall out, and it seems to take a long time for those bombs to hit the ground.

"The other day we drove for twenty-five miles through rural country while an air-raid alarm was on. Coasting down the smooth white road between tall green hedges, we would slide through a little village tucked away at the bottom of a hill beside a stream. There would be one greystone church, an arched bridge over the stream, perhaps a couple of dozen little brick cottages with red-tiled roofs, and a public house, generally the Farmers' Arms, the Bull & Bush, or something of the kind. That village would be dead, the streets as empty and silent as they were at two in the morning in peacetime. Even the air was quiet and heavy as it is just before a thunderstorm, but standing on the bridge near the church or at the crossroads would be one small middle-aged man, generally with a mustache, generally smoking a pipe, and always wearing a tin hat. He was the air-raid warden in complete command of the village until the 'all-clear' sounded—the sole protection against the German bombers, except for the boys in Hurricanes and Spitfires high overhead and the men manning the antiaircraft batteries. In some of the cities and larger towns people stand about in the streets, but the small villages take cover."

German planes at this point were targeting military sites. "Yesterday afternoon I stood at a hotel window and watched the Germans bomb the naval base at Portland, two or three miles away. In the morning I had been through that naval base and dockyard and satisfied myself that the Admiralty communique reporting earlier bombings had been accurate. The naval officers, including the admiral, had been kind and courteous, but as I stood and watched huge columns of smoke and fire leap into the air I thought some of those officers and men would no longer be of this world. As soon as the 'all-clear' sounded we jumped into the car and drove to the naval dockyard again. The workers who had been underground were just leaving. We secured permission to go into the dockyard for the second time that day and for the second time talked with the admiral. We asked him for evidence. He said: 'Look around for yourselves. They missed us again.' And they had—he was right. As we left, a big sergeant of marines at the gate asked us if we had seen the Germans bailing out. It was, he said, a lovely sight."

Civilians were still getting used to the bombing. "From what I could see, the people down along the coast had been badly shaken. Many of them don't like the sound of the sirens. It's loud, penetrating, and can't very well be ignored. The sirens seem to be about as disturbing and upsetting as the distant crump of bombs. Coming home today we were stopped by a constable in a little village. The street was lined with children and civilians. I pulled over to the side of the road beside a horse-drawn fireman's cart. We didn't know what was happening, thought maybe bombs had fallen. Suddenly from behind us we heard a police car with a loudspeaker: 'Clear the street for His Majesty, the King. Hold that horse's head.'

"The police car was followed by a big maroon car carrying the

King and a couple of staff officers. Behind that another car and a lone policeman riding a motorcycle. That was all. The local constable waved us ahead and for fifty miles I drove a little ten-horsepowered car just behind the policeman who was just behind the King. We made good time. There was a policeman at each crossroad to keep the main road clear. I saw those country folk as the King saw them and he must have been encouraged. They were a calm-looking, smiling lot of people and most of them know the hum of German planes overhead and the sound of exploding bombs. As I followed that small royal cavalcade over the rolling country (I gained on them going downhill), I wondered in what other country in this mad world can a king, a dictator, or a head of state travel with as little protection. The policeman on the motorcycle didn't even have a pistol."

City dwellers had a new routine. "Just as I reached London this afternoon, the air-raid sirens were sounding again, the people were heading for the shelters in orderly fashion. Only a few of them running. I saw no signs of panic. I did see a woman drive through a red light at about sixty miles an hour but that may have had nothing to do with the excitement or preoccupation created by the sirens. A few minutes after the 'all-clear' had sounded people were sitting patiently on little canvas stools on the sidewalk outside Queen's Hall, queuing up for tonight's concert. I have come to the conclusion that bombs that fall some distance away seem very unreal. Queen's Hall is only about half an hour from Croydon, which in the British vernacular caught a pocket last night, but from the attitude of those people on the sidewalk it might have been hundreds of miles away. One thing I do know—that is, that the bombs that drop close to you are real enough."

In early September, Hitler ordered the raids against London intensified. They took place at night, when the incoming bombers were harder to spot and hit. "I've spent the day visiting the bombed areas," Murrow reported on September 9. "The King did the same thing. These people may have been putting on a bold front for the King, but I saw them just as they were—men shoveling mounds of broken glass into trucks, hundreds of people being evacuated from the East End, all of them calm and quiet. In one street where eight or ten houses had been smashed a policeman stopped a motorist who had driven through a red light. The policeman's patience was obviously exhausted. As he made out the ticket and lectured the driver, everyone in the street gathered around to listen, paying no attention at all to the damaged houses; they were much more interested in the policeman. These people are exceedingly brave, tough, and prudent. The East End, where disaster is always just around the corner, seems to take it better than the more fashionable districts in the West End."

The bombing produced quite a show, with brilliant flashes of light and thudding concussions of sound. Murrow wondered how long the show would last. "This night bombing is serious and sensational. It makes headlines, kills people, and smashes property; but it doesn't win wars. It may be safely presumed that the Germans know that, know that several days of terror bombing will not cause this country to collapse. Where then does this new phase of the air war fit? What happens next?"

The bombing went on. "This is London at three-thirty in the morning," Murrow announced on September 13. "This has been what might be called a 'routine night'—air-raid alarm at about nine o'clock and intermittent bombing ever since. I had the impression that more high explosives and few incendiaries have been used tonight. Only two small fires can be seen on the horizon. Again the Germans have been sending their bombers in singly or in pairs. The antiaircraft barrage has been fierce but sometimes there have been periods of twenty minutes when London has been silent. Then the big red buses would start up and move on till the guns started working again. That silence is almost hard to bear. One becomes accustomed to rattling windows and the distant sound of bombs and then there comes a silence that can be felt. You know the sound will return—you wait, and then it starts again. That waiting is bad. It gives you a chance to imagine things. I have been walking tonight—there is a full moon, and the dirty-gray buildings appear white. The stars, the empty windows, are hidden. It's a beautiful and lonesome city where men and women and children are trying to snatch a few hours' sleep underground."

Murrow elaborated on what life in London felt like to the people who lived there. "We've told you about the bombs, the fires, the smashed houses, and the courage of the people. We've read you the communiques and tried to give you an honest estimate of the wounds inflicted upon this, the best bombing target in the world. But the business of living and working in this city is very personal—the little incidents, the things the mind retains, are in themselves unimportant, but they somehow weld together to form the hard core of memories that will remain when the last 'all-clear' has sounded. That's why I want to talk for just three or four minutes about the things we haven't talked about before; for many of these impressions it is necessary to reach back through only one long week. There was a rainbow bending over the battered and smoking East End of London just when the 'all-clear' sounded one afternoon. One night I stood in front of a smashed grocery store and heard a dripping inside. It was the only sound in all London. Two cans of peaches had been drilled clean through by flying glass and the juice was dripping down onto the floor.

"There was a flower shop in the East End. Nearly every other building in the block had been smashed. There was a funeral wreath in the window of the shop—price: three shillings and six pence, less than a dollar. In front of Buckingham Palace there's a bed of red and white flowers—untouched—the reddest flowers I've ever seen.

"Last night, or rather early this morning, I met a distinguished member of Parliament in a bar. He had been dining with Anthony Eden and had told the Secretary for War that he wouldn't walk through the streets with all that shrapnel falling about and as a good host Eden should send him home in a tank. Another man came in and reported, on good authority, that the Prime Minister had a siren suit, one of those blue woolen coverall affairs with a zipper. Someone said the Prime Minister must resemble a barrage balloon when attired in his siren suit. Things of that sort can still be said in this country. The fact that the noise—just the sound, not the blast—of bombs and guns can cause one to stagger while walking down the street came as a surprise. When I entered my office today, after bombs had fallen two blocks away, and was asked by my English secretary if I'd care for a cup of tea, that didn't come as much of a surprise.

"Talking from a studio with a few bodies lying about on the floor, sleeping on mattresses, still produces a strange feeling but we'll probably get used to that. Today I went to buy a hat—my favorite shop had gone, blown to bits. The windows of my shoe store were blown out. I decided to have a haircut; the windows of the barbershop were gone, but the Italian barber was still doing business. Someday, he said, we smile again, but the food it doesn't taste so good since being bombed. I went on to another shop to buy flashlight batteries. I bought three. The clerk said: 'You needn't buy so many. We'll have enough for the whole winter.' But I said: 'What if you aren't here?' There were buildings down in that street, and he replied: 'Of course, we'll be here. We've been in business here for a hundred and fifty years.'

"But the sundown scene in London can never be forgotten—the time when people pick up their beds and walk to the shelter."

44

THE GERMAN AIR campaign against Britain coincided with the American presidential campaign of 1940. Unusually—but unsurprisingly, given the concurrent events—the campaign emphasized foreign affairs. At the Republican national convention in Philadelphia, the delegates avowed their anti-interventionist faith. "The Republican Party is firmly opposed to involving this Nation in foreign war," their platform said. One European war had been more than enough. "We are still suffering from the ill effects of the last World War: a war which cost us a twenty-four billion dollar increase in our national debt, billions of uncollectible foreign debts, and the complete upset of our economic system, in addition to the loss of human life and irreparable damage to the health of thousands of our boys."

The Republicans weren't hard-hearted, they said of themselves. "Our sympathies have been profoundly stirred by invasion of unoffending countries and by disaster to nations whose ideals most closely resemble our own." Nor at this late hour would they insist on strict neutrality. "We favor the extension to all peoples fighting for liberty, or whose liberty is threatened, of such aid as shall not be in violation of international law or inconsistent with the requirements of our own national defense."

But that national defense must be America's priority. "The Republican Party stands for Americanism, preparedness and peace." The party insisted on leadership that put America first, and that obeyed the Constitution. "We deplore explosive utterances by the President directed at other governments which serve to imperil our peace; and we condemn all executive acts and proceedings which might lead to war without the authorization of the Congress of the United States."

The Republican nominee for president was Wendell Willkie. A midwesterner by birth, Willkie made his name as a New York lawyer and corporate president. He was a late convert to Republicanism, switching from the Democrats only in 1939. More than a few Republicans questioned his sincerity, but the party lacked credible challengers to Roosevelt, who had dominated national political life for nearly eight years. Some of its biggest names—men like Robert Taft of Ohio, son of William Howard Taft—were isolationists, whose appeal diminished with each success of Roosevelt in moving the country from neutrality to pro-British nonbelligerence. Willkie's position on the war differed little from the position Roosevelt espoused in public, and to the Republican delegates he appeared the least unsatisfactory of the men willing to accept the nomination.

THE DEMOCRATIC CONVENTION attracted greater interest. Roosevelt had conspicuously declined to make any such Shermanesque statement of withdrawal as Jim Farley desired, and the president's silence continued to paralyze potential opposition. Yet though his renomination appeared increasingly inevitable, it would be historic, and the nation wanted to hear how he would explain his defiance of George Washington and a century and a half of hallowed tradition.

He began by ghostwriting a party platform that stole themes from Lindbergh. "The American people are determined that war, raging in Europe, Asia and Africa, shall not come to America," the party's manifesto declared. "We will not participate in foreign wars, and we will not send our army, naval or air forces to fight in foreign lands outside of the Americas, except in case of attack. We favor and shall rigorously enforce and defend the Monroe Doctrine. The direction and aim of our foreign policy has been, and will continue to be, the security and defense of our own land and the maintenance of its peace."

No more than the Republicans would the Democrats overlook the affronts to democracy abroad. "The world's greatest democracy cannot afford heartlessly or in a spirit of appeasement to ignore the peace-loving and liberty-loving peoples wantonly attacked by ruthless aggressors. We pledge to extend to these peoples all the material aid at our command, consistent with law and not inconsistent with the interests of our own national self-defense."

But self-defense was the touchstone by which all proposals would be measured. And America's defense must be the stoutest possible. Roosevelt might have made Lindbergh secretary of war, to judge by the platform's prescription: "We must be so strong that no possible combination of powers would dare to attack us. We propose to provide America with an invincible air force, a navy strong enough to protect all our seacoasts and our national interests, and a fully-equipped and mechanized army."

Roosevelt accepted the nomination in a radio address, which repeated and expanded upon what he had told Farley. He started with the expected note of humility. "I find myself, as almost everyone does sooner or later in his lifetime, in a conflict between deep personal desire for retirement on the one hand, and that quiet, invisible thing called conscience on the other." He had not sought a third term, he said. "When, in 1936, I was chosen by the voters for a second time as president, it was my firm intention to turn over the responsibilities of government to other hands at the end of my term. That conviction remained with me. Eight years in the presidency, following a period of bleak depression, and covering one world crisis after another, would normally entitle any man to the relaxation that comes from honorable retirement."

But such retirement was not meant to be. "During the spring of 1939, world events made it clear to all but the blind or the partisan that a great war in Europe had become not merely a possibility but a probability, and that such a war would of necessity deeply affect the future of this nation." Yet still he had hoped to hand the presidency to a successor. He had planned to make a public statement to that effect.

"It soon became evident, however, that such a public statement on my part would be unwise from the point of view of sheer public duty. As President of the United States, it was my clear duty, with the aid of the Congress, to preserve our neutrality, to shape our program of defense, to meet rapid changes, to keep our domestic affairs adjusted to shifting world conditions, and to sustain the policy of the Good

Neighbor"—being nice to the other countries of the Americas. "It was also my obvious duty to maintain to the utmost the influence of this mighty nation in our effort to prevent the spread of war, and to sustain by all legal means those governments threatened by other governments which had rejected the principles of democracy."

And so he had made no declaration on retirement. "Thinking solely of the national good and of the international scene, I came to the reluctant conclusion that such declaration should not be made before the national convention." Roosevelt didn't mention that his silence left the convention no alternative to him.

"Like any other man, I am complimented by the honor you have done me," Roosevelt said. But the final decision rested with the people and the country. "Lying awake, as I have, on many nights, I have asked myself whether I have the right, as Commander-in-Chief of the Army and Navy, to call on men and women to serve their country or to train themselves to serve and, at the same time, decline to serve my country in my own personal capacity, if I am called upon to do so by the people of my country." If the people summoned him to service again, he would answer again. He couldn't do otherwise. "Only the people themselves can draft a president. If such a draft should be made upon me, I say to you, in the utmost simplicity, I will, with God's help, continue to serve with the best of my ability and with the fullness of my strength."

Looking to the campaign ahead, he said he would not run as a regular candidate. The demands upon the president at this moment were too many and large. "I shall not have the time or the inclination to engage in purely political debate." Yet he would speak out on issues essential to American security and welfare. Democracy was endangered as never before. "In Europe, many nations, through dictatorships or invasions, have been compelled to abandon normal democratic processes." He was pleased to report that the American government had resisted this evil trend. "The government of the United States for the past seven years has had the courage openly to oppose by every peaceful means the spread of the dictator form of government." It must continue to do so, under present management or new. "If our government should pass to other hands next January—untried hands, inexperienced hands—we can merely hope and pray that they will not substitute appeasement and compromise with those who seek to destroy all democracies everywhere, including here."

Yes, there were appeasers here at home—"fifth columnists who charged me with hysteria and war-mongering." They must be exposed and guarded against. He himself had warned against them. "I felt it my duty, my simple, plain, inescapable duty, to arouse my countrymen to the danger of the new forces let loose in the world." He would continue to do so.

And he would, of course, abide by the verdict of the ballot box. "All that I have done to maintain the peace of this country and to prepare it morally, as well as physically, for whatever contingencies may be in store, I submit to the judgment of my countrymen."

The nation and the world were at a turning point. "We face one of the great choices of history," Roosevelt said. "It is not alone a choice of government by the people versus dictatorship. It is not alone a choice of freedom versus slavery. It is not alone a choice between moving forward or falling back. It is all of these rolled into one. It is the continuance of civilization as we know it versus the ultimate destruction of all that we have held dear—religion against godlessness; the ideal of justice against the practice of force; moral decency versus the firing squad; courage to speak out, and to act, versus the false lullaby of appeasement."

45

THE CAMPAIGN KICKED off, as campaigns then did, in early September, which happened to be when Roosevelt announced the destroyers-for-bases deal with Britain. The timing was awkward for Willkie, as Roosevelt knew it would be. The challenger didn't disagree with the substance of the deal, so he was left to dispute the process. "The country will undoubtedly approve of the program to add to our naval and air bases and assistance given to Great Britain," Willkie declared. "It is regrettable, however, that the president did not deem it necessary in connection with this proposal to secure the approval of Congress or permit public discussion prior to adoption. The people have a right to know of such important commitments prior to and not after being made." The president claimed to be supporting democracy abroad. He should do so at home. "We must be extremely careful in these times when the struggle in the world is between democracy and totalitarianism not to eliminate or destroy the democratic processes while seeking to preserve democracy. It is the contention of the totalitarian rulers that democracy is not effective. We must prove that it is effective by making full use of its processes. Congress has constitutional functions as important and sacred as those of the chief executive."

Other Republicans were less restrained. Samuel Pryor, the vice chairman of the Republican national committee, assailed Roosevelt's negotiating skills. "You must remember that Great Britain owes us a great deal of money," Pryor said, referring to debt from the World

War. But the worst of the deal was what it said about Roosevelt's disdain for the checks and balances of the Constitution. "The great issue involved is that it is the first step toward taking us into this war, without consulting the representatives of the people. It is the act of a dictator."

Willkie caught on to what was expected of him. He amended his genteel chiding of Roosevelt to something harsher. "This trade is the most dictatorial action ever taken by any president," he said. "It does us no good to solve the problems of democracy if we solve them with the methods of dictators."

Willkie promised he would keep America out of war. "If I am president, I shall never lead this country into war. When I say that, I mean it." Listeners were to infer that Roosevelt, in saying the same thing, did *not* mean it. Willkie drew a sharp line between helping Britain against Germany and joining Britain. "I believe that the United States should give all possible help to Great Britain, short of war. And when I say short of war, I mean short of war."

He tried to put Roosevelt on the spot. "I want to ask the president, and I demand an answer: Are there any international understandings to put America into the war that we citizens do not know about?" To an audience at Theodore Roosevelt High School in the Bronx, he said, "Is there anyone here who really thinks that the president is sincerely trying to keep us out of war?" Unlike the Rough Rider, Franklin Roosevelt played fast with facts; especially now, this was intolerable. "An administration that is not telling the truth is not qualified to head the country in time of crisis, or at any other time."

The unreliability of Roosevelt's word became a Willkie theme. "If his promise to keep our boys out of foreign wars is no better than his promise to balance the budget, they're already almost on the transports," he said.

His own promise was good, Willkie said, and said again. "I promise, as I have promised many times before, not to send your husbands and sons and brothers to death on a European or Asiatic battlefield." He would refuse to let America be maneuvered into the conflict, as Roosevelt was letting America be maneuvered. "I will avoid bringing about the condition of affairs that will make war necessary."

ROOSEVELT RECONSIDERED HIS promise not to campaign like a regular candidate. He felt obliged to answer the charges or implications that he was going to lead America into war, despite his assurances to the contrary. Sounding quite like a candidate, he told a convention of Teamsters in Washington, "I hate war, now more than ever. I have one supreme determination—to do all that I can to keep war away from these shores for all time." He recited the Democratic platform: "We will not participate in foreign wars, and we will not send our army, naval or air forces to fight in foreign lands outside of the Americas, except in case of attack."

He elaborated on this theme to a crowd in Philadelphia. Lamenting the libels that had been leveled against him by the Republicans, he added, "There is one more false charge—one outrageously false charge—that has been made to strike terror into the hearts of our citizens. It is a charge that offends every political and religious conviction that I hold dear. It is the charge that this administration wishes to lead this country into war." The charge was utterly without foundation, as any honest examination of the previous eight years revealed. "My every act and thought have been directed to the end of preserving the peace of the world, and more particularly, the peace of the United States—the peace of the Western Hemisphere."

This remained the goal, and it would be the goal as long as he was president. "To Republicans and Democrats, to every man, woman and child in the nation I say this: Your President and your Secretary of State are following the road to peace. We are arming ourselves not for any foreign war. We are arming ourselves not for any purpose of conquest or intervention in foreign disputes." He repeated again the platform, and he concluded, "It is for peace that I have labored; and it is for peace that I shall labor all the days of my life."

In repeating the platform plank, with its closing qualifier "except in case of attack," Roosevelt reserved some room for maneuver on the war question. But during the last week of the campaign he threw aside the disclaimer. "While I am talking to you mothers and fathers, I give you one more assurance," he told a rally in Boston. "I have said this before, but I shall say it again and again and again: Your boys are not going to be sent into any foreign wars."

JAMES ROOSEVELT, THE president's eldest son, listened to the Boston speech with misgivings. James had grown up in politics; he would later be elected to Congress from California. During the Roosevelt presidency he often served as his father's secretary and strong right arm. The latter was almost literal: when Roosevelt stood in public, with his legs locked in heavy steel braces, one arm held a cane and the other often the arm of James.

James thought he knew where Roosevelt's policies were taking the country, and he thought his father did too. After events proved him right, he raised the issue. "I had a conversation with Father, in which I discussed the dishonesty of his stand on war," James recalled. "Father said, 'Jimmy, I knew we were going to war. I was sure there was no way out of it. I had to delay until there was no way out of it. I knew we were woefully unprepared for war, and I had to begin to build up for what was coming. But I couldn't come out and say a war was coming, because the people would have panicked and turned from me. I had to educate people to the inevitable, gradually, step by step, laying the groundwork for programs which would allow us to prepare for the war that was drawing us into it.

"'If I don't say, I hate war, then people are going to think I don't hate war. If I say we're going to get into this war, people will think I want us in it. If I don't say, I won't send our sons to fight on foreign battlefields, then people will think I want to send them. I do hate war. I don't want to send our men to war. I tried to say these things in such a way as to say we won't go to war until we have to go to war. Sometimes you have to deny your political opposition the paint they need to present the public picture of you they want to show. You can't feed your enemies ammunition.'

"I remember Father saying, 'Jimmy, I would have loved to have said that, as president, I was in a position to know what was happening in the world, much more than was the public, or even the members of Congress, and that I can see we are going to have to go to war sooner or later with the fascist forces, and we better build up for it fast, and perhaps even attack before we are attacked. But I couldn't say that because the public and congressmen didn't want to hear it, and so they wouldn't have believed it, and would have turned on me. There were those who saw that this was true, and helped me, but I couldn't take every congressman into my confidence because he'd have run off the Hill, hollering that FDR is a war monger.'"

Roosevelt hadn't written the rules of American politics, but he understood them. "You play the game the way it has been played over the years, and you play to win," he told James.

The younger man reflected on this. "I think Father believed he really was needed in 1940, when a new election was at hand. After all, he knew what was happening in the world as no one else did. But I also think he loved the power of the presidency and enjoyed the privileges and prestige of the office enormously, and really didn't want to walk away from it. He couldn't walk away from it, of course. He would roll away in his wheelchair to a life as a cripple, without an active part to play, and he didn't want that."

And so he did what he did. "In the end, Father, as usual, piloted his own ship. 'I think I'm needed,' he said to me one day. 'And maybe I need it.'"

46

A MID THE PRESIDENTIAL campaign a meeting was held in Chicago of individuals opposed to the trend they saw in Roosevelt's foreign policy. Like Lindbergh, they believed the United States was being drawn into the European conflict, and they sought to avert that outcome. They decided to pool their efforts and they formed the America First Committee.

The committee required time to distill its principles into four that would fit neatly into a newspaper advertisement. In that form they were posted in papers across the country. "1. The United States must build an impregnable defense for America. 2. No foreign power, or group of powers, can successfully attack a PREPARED America. 3. American democracy can be preserved only by keeping out of the European war. 4. The cash-and-carry provisions of the existing Neutrality Act are essential to American peace and security. Aid to a belligerent beyond the limitations of the act weakens us in war abroad. Any change in the law to permit American vessels to enter the combat zone would inevitably plunge the country into Europe's war."

Robert E. Wood, a West Point graduate, a general during the World War, and currently the chairman of Chicago-based Sears, Roebuck and Company, headed the America First Committee. Other Chicago business, professional and civic leaders filled out the charter membership.

The committee attracted attention at once. Days after the announcement of the Chicago meeting, Charles A. Beard, the most widely read historian in America, issued a statement in New York endorsing the committee's principles, in particular defending it against charges already surfacing that it was doing the work of the Nazis. "The party of non-intervention represented by the America First Committee includes no 'appeasers,' no 'ostrich isolationists,' no foreigners of any nationality in letter or spirit, and no pacificists," Beard wrote. "It believes that the foreign policy of the United States should be directed to the preservation of the peace and security of this nation in its continental zone of interests; that the United States should not resort to any more measures verging in the direction of war outside its continental zone of interests; that measures should be adopted for the adequate defense of this continental zone of interests."

The America First Committee welcomed distinguished volunteers like Beard; it also conducted recruiting efforts. Lindbergh was one of its initial targets. James Van Zandt, a Republican congressman from Pennsylvania, invited Lindbergh to his office, saying a young man from Chicago wished to speak with him. The young man was R. Douglas Stuart, a Yale law student who had been organizing his fellow students against the war. During the summer of 1940 he carried the message to Chicago, where his father, a vice president at the Quaker Oats Company, introduced him around. The result was the America First Committee. "We discussed the Chicago organization and plans for an antiwar campaign," Lindbergh wrote in his journal. Lindbergh asked Stuart to lunch. "He seems a fine type of young fellow." Lindbergh wasn't ready to enlist in the committee, still wishing to retain his freedom of action. But he encouraged Stuart and the others in the Chicago group.

Stuart, who would become the national director of the committee, took Lindbergh's counsel to heart. He arranged a meeting between Robert Wood and Henry Ford, and, knowing of Lindbergh's connection to Ford, he asked Lindbergh to join them. Lindbergh drove to Detroit—he had a car he wanted to donate to Ford's collection, and driving it himself was the simplest way to get it there. Besides, he liked road trips almost as much as flying.

The meeting was set for nine in the morning at the Ford River Rouge plant. "I arrived ten minutes early," Lindbergh recalled. "Ford arrived promptly at nine. Before there was time to say more than good morning, General Wood and R. D. Stuart came in through the door. We discussed the America First Committee, its policies and organization. Ford was cautious at first and reluctant to become a member—said he would have to look into it very carefully." Ford recalled his experience with the Peace Ship in the World War and said he didn't want to repeat that. Lindbergh and the others let him talk. "As the discussion developed, Ford became more interested and indicated he would probably take an active part on the committee. As we shook hands good-bye, Ford told me he had had a hard week—out five nights straight at his grandchildren's parties, he said."

Lindbergh liked what he had seen and heard. "General Robert Wood is an able man and carried on the conversation intelligently and with great discretion. Stuart is alert, enthusiastic, and a hard worker." Lindbergh drove the two from the Rouge plant to the Detroit airport, where they caught a plane back to Chicago.

Harry Bennett was Ford's assistant and chief of security, infamous around Detroit for his union-busting activities. On this day he was simply a facilitator. "Immediately after lunch, Bennett phoned and said that both Mr. and Mrs. Ford were willing to go on the committee and were anxious to help in any possible way," Lindbergh wrote. "Half an hour later Ford telephoned and said he wanted to do everything possible for us. He asked if a donation would be in order. I told him that accepting membership was the most important aid he could give and that if the committee needed more money they could get in touch with him about that later on. Ford said he and Mrs. Ford had signed a letter for the committee, which they had left at Bennett's office for me. I told him I would get it personally."

Lindbergh called Wood to convey the welcome news. Wood was delighted. Lindbergh drove back to the Rouge plant to pick up Ford's letter, which he dropped in the mail.

Lindbergh continued to work as a liaison for the America First Committee. He alerted Wood and Stuart to promising prospects, and he directed interested parties to Chicago. He suggested links between America First and the American Legion and other groups opposing the war.

Stuart consulted Lindbergh for help dealing with the radio networks. "Stuart says he is having trouble buying radio time for the America First Committee," Lindbergh noted. "Some of the radio stations have taken the stand that the committee has to do with a 'controversial issue' and therefore comes under the code they have formed against selling time for controversial issues. It is a fine state of affairs if the question of war and peace cannot be debated before the American people because it is a 'controversial issue'!"

Lindbergh knew more was involved. The radio networks made money from advertisements, the rates for which were based on audience size. If the networks lost listeners by airing unpopular messages, they would feel the effect in their bottom lines. One didn't have to conjure conspiracy—though some people did—or assume political favoritism on the part of network owners—though owners certainly had political opinions—to realize that certain views would be favored over others.

Lindbergh escorted Stuart around New York. In early October they met at the Engineers Club. "We discussed the America First Committee and the advertisement they have in this morning's *Times*," Lindbergh wrote. "I think it is very good, but a little confused in layout. After talking over America First Committee plans and its relationship to eastern antiwar groups, we went to Chester Bowles's office for a half hour's discussion about the committee. Bowles is one of its members, and he took a major part in laying out the advertising campaign." Bowles was co-founder of Benton & Bowles, one of New York's and therefore America's leading advertising agencies.

Lindbergh and Stuart met with a group of anti-interventionists at the University Club. Some there suggested forming a New York counterpart to the America First Committee of Chicago. Lindbergh was dubious. "We don't need a committee," he wrote to himself. "What we need is a man of ability to take over and direct an eastern organization, as General Wood is directing the America First Committee in Chicago. In lieu of such a man, the best thing for us to do is to throw our support behind the Chicago group. I think I can bring this about, but it will take a little time."

They went to see Herbert Hoover at the former president's residence at the Waldorf-Astoria. "I asked his advice about men who might take part in an eastern antiwar organization," Lindbergh wrote. "It is obvious that they will be difficult to find in New York City."

The difficulty reflected the geographic gradient in American attitudes toward the war. Similar differences had long affected American thinking about the world. People living on the East Coast felt closer to Europe than people in the center of the country. Proximity in space was part of the perception; during the World War, German U-boats had sunk American ships within sight of observers on the beach. It wasn't difficult for East Coasters to imagine German submarines doing the same again.

Proximity in time influenced the feeling as well. Where immigrants to America before the industrial revolution settled mostly in farming regions, those who arrived in the late nineteenth and early twentieth centuries clustered in cities, notably in the East. When Europe went to war, in the 1910s and now in the late 1930s and early 1940s, those immigrants and their children felt a deeper emotional investment in the outcome of the fighting than did the midwestern children of the earlier immigrants. A Minnesotan like Lindbergh might have distant cousins in the old country; a New Yorker had siblings and parents.

Jewish Americans had a particular stake in the current conflict, given the anti-Jewish policies of Hitler and the German government. The Nazi policies had followed German armies into the countries they occupied, especially Poland, where Jews were deprived of property and forced into ghettos. In Warsaw four hundred thousand Jewish men, women and children were jammed into hardly more than a square mile. Jews were forced to wear badges identifying them as Jews and singling them out for scorn. Many were herded into forced-labor camps where conditions were often lethal. When Hitler had talked of *Lebensraum* to Germany's east, he didn't intend to share that territory with the Poles. Most would be driven out, murdered or enslaved. Polish Jews were the first to feel the effects of the campaign.

Some Jewish Americans were themselves refugees from Hitler's pogroms; many more knew people who were; nearly all had family experience of anti-Semitism in one part of Europe or another. Jews in America tended to live in cities, especially those of the East, and in a democracy their hopes and fears shaped the politics of eastern cities and states. An elected official from the Midwest who said that the troubles of Europe weren't America's problem could expect to anger relatively few constituents; an elected official from New York who said the same thing could count on angering many.

47

FOR THESE REASONS, the anti-interventionists struggled to find eastern audiences comparable to those they engaged farther west. Not that Lindbergh didn't try. He prepared another radio address and made arrangements to broadcast it.

In the drafting he looked back through his journal for the previous two years. His radio speech would include predictions, if only implicit, about events to come; he thought he owed it to himself and his radio audience to revisit past predictions and see what he'd got right and what wrong.

"As I read through my daily entries in 1939, I am struck by the fact that I applied a little too much logic to the peoples and the politicians in Europe," Lindbergh wrote. "It is not that I thought people were logical; I cannot remember ever entertaining such a fallacy. I do not even believe it is desirable for people to be completely logical in their viewpoint. Logic must be based on knowledge; and since knowledge is limited in man, so must be his logic. I never trust logical conclusions unless they combine with an inner intuitive feeling, which I find to be really much more reliable. Unless I have this feeling I know with almost complete certainty that my logical reasoning is wrong."

He had been wrong about the Europeans. "Until war was actually declared by England and France, I felt, although without much confidence, that a major European conflict would not take place in 1939," he said. "Until the movement of armies began, I kept hoping for a peaceful settlement, or at least a postponement of hostilities. I had seen the strength of Germany, and I knew the weakness of England and France. I felt certain that Germany would expand eastward, even at the cost of a major war, but I did not believe she wished to throw herself against England and France—at least at that time. As far as England and France were concerned, I could not believe that in their weakened and unprepared condition they would throw their forces against the German Western Wall, or that they would open their cities to the attack of the vastly superior German Air Force."

But the war did come in 1939. "Germany moved her armies into Poland; that I expected. Poland resisted; that did not surprise me in view of the encouragement given by England and France. England and France declared war on Germany; this did surprise me, for it was obvious they could not help Poland, and just as obvious that they could not invade Germany through the Western Wall and against the German Air Force. Russia entered the Polish war on the German side; nothing that Russia did would surprise me, for that country is completely unpredictable."

Why had he gotten things wrong? "As I read through my diaries, I realize that the element I foresaw least clearly was the vacillation of the 'democracies' and their complete inability to follow a consistent policy. I could not believe that the nations which let Germany rearm, march into the Rhineland, take over Austria, build the Western Wall, and disarm the Czechoslovakian Army, would declare war over Poland under conditions which made it impossible to give her effective aid."

Lindbergh confessed to having been unconcerned about Germany's policies in the direction of Russia. "I felt the welfare of our Western civilization necessitated a strong Germany as a buffer to Asia, just as it necessitated a strong British Empire. I felt that peace in Europe, and throughout the world, for that matter, could be maintained only by co-operation between England and Germany. In view of my 'reasoning' I thought up to the last days that 1939 might pass without a major European war, and here my judgment was probably somewhat affected by my hope. I had seen war avoided at the time of 'Munich,' and there seemed even more reason to avoid it at the time of 'Poland.'"

War was declared over Poland, although heavy fighting between Britain and France, on the one side, and Germany, on the other, didn't start at once. "France moved her armies up to the Western Wall, and there they stopped. England chased all German commerce from the oceans and then could do no more." Americans watched, increasingly upset. "The United States became ineffectively hysterical about the whole situation."

Lindbergh concluded that he had been right in substance but wrong on timing. "All the logic I used in concluding that war would probably not come before 1940 turned out to be correct. I thought Germany would expand eastward—she did. I thought the French Army could not break through the West Wall—they failed. I felt there was no way to give effective aid to Poland—none was given. . . . I knew the German Air Force was vastly superior to all other air forces in Europe combined—that is now a well-established fact. In every technical estimate I was right; in fact, my estimates turned out to be conservative. Nevertheless, war was declared—declared by the weak and not the strong, by those who would lose, not by those who would win. The declaration was brought about by something that lies completely outside of logic—by emotion, by blindness, by vanity, by courage, by indifference, by pride, by many and infinitely complicated elements, by elements which are intangible, unpredictable, and unforeseen."

Lindbergh prided himself on his logical reasoning; he had assumed—much as people often do—that other people were like him. The discovery that they were not, and on such a crucial matter as the fate of Western civilization, required a recalibration of his thinking.

He owned his other errors. "I did not realize the weakness of the Maginot Line along the Belgian border. I did not expect the Germans to break that line during the early stages of the war. I expected Germany to strike at France and England by air bombing, and by submarine blockade. I thought both sides would take up their positions in the Maginot–Western Wall lines and remain in them until at least a partial decision had been reached in Eastern Europe. . . . I did not foresee the ease with which the German armies would march through Belgium, break the Maginot Line, rout the British expeditionary force in Flanders, and defeat France."

Yet he was in good company in his errors. "I know of no one who accurately estimated either the weakness of the Maginot Line extension west of Sedan, or the irresistible strength of the German mechanized divisions. Our military estimates were wrong in each of these instances—more wrong about the Maginot Line than about the German strength. But between the overestimate on one hand and underestimate on the other, the breaking of the Maginot Line was a shock to everyone; I think the ease with which it was done must have been something of a shock to the Germans themselves."

Lindbergh acknowledged that he, like most others, had overestimated the morale and effectiveness of the French army. "I knew that France was in a weakened condition, that her politics were corrupt, her financial situation serious, her people divided, her workmen dissatisfied. This had been the case for some years. Looking back now, it seems obvious that a country with such internal conditions could not have a large, efficient, and well-disciplined army." Lindbergh proposed a generalization: "In this modern, mechanized age the condition of an army can be closely estimated from the condition of the country in which it is raised. A prosperous country *may not* have a good army, but a demoralized country *cannot* have a good army today."

Notwithstanding his miss on France, the war played out much as Lindbergh had anticipated. "The German Army and Air Force was a little stronger than I thought; the French Army was considerably weaker than I realized; the British have bungled about as much as I expected them to; Germany has been successful in most of her actions and seems to be in a better position than ever to win the war."

So much for the past; what about the future? "Will America enter the war? It seems to me that logical reasoning says she should not. Our interference will do no good in Europe; we should have acted five years ago if we intended to fight; we are not prepared for a foreign war; it seems improbable that we could win a war in Europe under present circumstances (we would have to land and maintain an expeditionary force on the continent of Europe against the opposition of the German Army, Navy, and Air Force); polls of the country show over eighty per cent of our people opposed to entering the war; before we could take an effective part the chances are that England will be defeated; in which case we would have to attack Europe unaided to be successful; Japan is in a position to cause trouble in the Pacific if we turn all of our effort toward Europe."

Logic said America shouldn't enter the war. "But here again I am using logic at an emotional and illogical time," he conceded. "Will we in America allow ourselves to be enticed into war, as were the people of England and France, under conditions that make success impossible, even though by some miracle we were able to defeat the armies of the Axis? Will our vanity, our blindness, and our airy idealism throw us, too, into the conflict, heedless of the future? Must we fly mothlike into the flame of a war that burns an entire ocean away?

"I am not sure. I know what we should do, but no one knows what we will do. Our thinking is confused; our direction is undecided; our leadership uncertain. I shall work against war, but lay plans for one."

48

Lindbergh's radio broadcast was scheduled for the evening of Monday, Oct. 14. He lunched that day with Champ Clark and E. Eugene Cox, a Georgia congressman, as well as Fulton Lewis and William Dolph of the Mutual Broadcasting System. Lewis drove him to the Mutual studio in Washington for final arrangements. "The newsreels again requested that I read part of my address for them after I had broadcast," Lindbergh wrote. "In the past I have refused their requests; first, because of the difficulty they have often caused for me; second, and much more important, because of the Jewish influence in the newsreels and the antagonism I know exists toward me. To speak for the newsreels on a political subject is dangerous, because one has no control over the way they cut the picture or over the setting in which they place it. They can pick either the best or the worst sentences from your talk, as they wish; and they can control the emotional attitude of the audience to a large extent by the type of picture they place before yours. By speaking for the newsreels, I take the chance that they will cut my talk badly and sandwich it in between scenes of homeless refugees and bombed cathedrals. However, this is a critical period, and I think it is worth the chance."

Another request came from the radio company. "The Mutual Broadcasting Company headquarters in New York had telephoned Dolph to ask me to remove the sentences at the end of my address which referred directly to the election. Dolph said it would be a great favor to him if I could do this, but that if I felt I could not do so, he would not insist. Copies of my address had already gone to the papers, but Dolph said that made no difference as long as I made the change in reading it over the radio. The changes he asked for were unimportant from my standpoint, so I gladly made them." Lindbergh reflected on the rules governing radio broadcasts. "It seems the broadcasting companies have agreed on a code which requires them to prevent political speeches from being made over their system unless the speeches are paid for at the regular commercial rates. Since my radio time is not paid for, I come under this code. Although it is not strictly enforced, the broadcasting companies are expected to make a reasonable effort toward its enforcement."

He returned to the studio that evening in time to broadcast at 8:45. "Then spent about an hour reading portions of it for the newsreels in an adjoining room—very bright and hot lights." As Lindbergh mopped his face on leaving, he recalled that this was another reason to dislike reading for the newsreel cameras.

"I COME BEFORE you tonight to enter a plea for American independence," Lindbergh began. "It is amazing that one should have to plead for American independence in a nation with a heritage such as ours; in a nation which, in its infancy, revolted against foreign control, and whose people have fought time and time again against the armies and interference of the old world. Yet the independence and the destiny of America were never more in jeopardy than they are today."

He reminded his listeners that Americans spent the first century and a quarter of their nation's existence beating back the powers of Europe: Britain, France and Spain. "We won our independence from England when we were a nation of less than four million people. We numbered only ten million when the Monroe Doctrine was established. With the population of thirty-five million, even though we had just emerged from four years of the Civil War, we made France remove her invading army from Mexico. Later in the century, with a population of seventy-five million, we forced Spain to withdraw entirely from the New World.

"Why, then, with one hundred thirty million people, are we being told that we must give up our independent position, that our frontiers lie in Europe, and that our destiny will be decided by European armies fighting upon European soil? What has happened to this nation that it fears in maturity the forces that it conquered in its youth? What change has come over us; what foreign influence has sprung up among us? Where is the blood of such leaders as Washington, Jefferson, and Lincoln; blood that stood firm on American soil against the threats, the armies and the navies of the greatest empires on earth?"

America's leadership at present fell woefully short of the standard of the past. "No one doubts that we are in the midst of a world crisis. No one denies that our defenses are weak, that our debt is great, that dissatisfaction is rising among us. We do not question the need for rearmament, for reform, for a better economic system. What we do question is the leadership that has brought these conditions upon us. We question that the men who were unable to foresee these conditions in time to avoid them, who could not foresee the war in time to prepare for it, who refused to believe reports of rearming abroad, when there was still time to take action, are now competent to carry this nation successfully through a period of great crisis. Under their leadership we have alienated the most powerful military nations of both Europe and Asia, at a time when we ourselves are unprepared for action, and while the people of our nation are overwhelmingly opposed to war."

Americans were as brave and patriotic as ever. "There is no question about the fundamental courage and solidarity of Americans, when our national welfare is at stake. There is no division among us about the defense of our own country. We have always been ready to fight against the interference of foreign powers in our affairs. If need be, we are ready to die for the independence of America, as our forefathers have died before us when necessity arose. On a clearly American issue, we stand a united nation. It is only when we are asked to take part in the quarrels of foreign countries that we divide; only when we are asked to merge our destiny with that of other lands; only when an attempt is made to transfer loyalty for America to loyalty for some other nation."

The fact was that Americans were now divided; for this Lindbergh blamed America's leaders. "Instead of a Washington warning us against the wiles of foreign influence and excessive partiality for any nation, we are told that our frontiers lie in Europe. Instead of a Lincoln telling us that if danger ever reaches us, it must spring up amongst us, and that it cannot come from abroad, we are informed that we may be invaded from the icebound mountains of Greenland, and by fleets of non-existent transatlantic bombers. We find the same men who have led us to the greatest national debt in our history, now telling us that as a nation we are weak and unprepared; that we must appropriate more billions of dollars, and devote more years of time, to building up our military. These same leaders who have failed to solve even our peacetime problems, who have a consistent record of promise followed by failure, now ask us to put ourselves in their hands again as they lead us steadily toward that climax of all political failure—war."

The leaders proceeded by deception. "They do not tell us openly what their intentions are. They say we should leave our decisions and our destiny to specialists—to their particular specialists—to the same specialists who have made us a weakened nation in the center of an antagonistic world. They harangue us about 'democracy,' yet they leave us with less knowledge of the direction which we are headed than if we were citizens of a totalitarian state. We are told that we are being prepared to defend America at the same time that orders are placed for the type and quantity of armament that would be used for a war in Europe."

Lindbergh spoke from his own expertise. "We do not need untold thousands of military aircraft, unless we intend to wage a war abroad. What we do need is a thoroughly modern and efficient air corps, trained, equipped, and maintained for the specific mission of American defense." Money and time had been wasted preparing for the wrong war. "With intelligent leadership, we could have built an impregnable defense for America without disturbing seriously our national life and industry. We have already spent more than enough money to have done this. With an army, a navy and an air corps of high-quality and reasonable size, we could have maintained our position with safety at home and respect abroad. But today, while we listen to talk of aircraft, guns and battleships, couched in figures so astronomical that they compare only to our national debt, we find ourselves in confusion at home, and under ridicule abroad."

Americans must demand better of those they chose for office. "We must select leaders whose promises we can trust, who know where they are taking us, and who tell us where we are going. The entire future of America, and of our system of life hangs upon the action we take and the judgment we show. It does not depend upon the outcome of the war in Europe, but upon men, regardless of their party, who will lead us to strength and peace rather than to weakness and to war."

The decision was in the hands of American voters. "Our vote next month can either bring or avoid a disastrous war for our country. We can either throw the world into chaos, or lead it to new heights of civilization. The future of America and of our system of life hangs upon the action we take at that time. It does not depend upon the outcome of the war in Europe, but upon the quality and wisdom of the leadership that we choose for our nation in November—upon our Congress, upon our Senate, and upon our president; upon men, regardless of their party, who will lead us to strength and peace, rather than to weakness and to war."

VOTERS HEEDED ROOSEVELT rather than Lindbergh. Roosevelt won his race, with a margin of victory smaller than in either of his previous campaigns but still large enough for him to claim a mandate for his leadership.

Yet the mandate was ambiguous. Had voters responded to his support for Britain? His rhetorical defense of democracy? Or his promise not to send American boys to fight in foreign wars?

Roosevelt was shrewd enough not to parse the matter too finely. The important thing was that he'd won. He wouldn't have to face the voters for another four years, if at all. In four years the whole world could change. His job now was to see that it didn't change irretrievably for the worse.

PART FIVE

Executive Unbound

49

CHURCHILL WAS QUICK with congratulations. "I did not think it right for me as a foreigner to express any opinion upon American policies while the election was on, but now I feel you will not mind my saying that I prayed for your success and that I am truly thankful for it," the prime minister wrote to Roosevelt. Churchill had taken pains to stay out of the American conversation entirely while the election's outcome pended, knowing that Roosevelt's critics—starting with Lindbergh but extending across the political spectrum—suspected the president of excessive Anglophilia when they didn't condemn him for it outright.

Churchill allowed Roosevelt time to savor his victory. Then, in early December, the prime minister proposed an audacious collaboration between the countries the two men headed. "As we reach the end of this year I feel that you will expect me to lay before you the prospects for 1941," Churchill wrote. "I do so strongly and confidently because it seems to me that the vast majority of American citizens have recorded their conviction that the safety of the United States as well as the future of our two democracies and the kind of civilisation for which they stand are bound up with the survival and independence of the British Commonwealth of Nations." This was a generous—to Britain and Churchill—interpretation of the American vote, as the prime minister knew. But he had a case to make.

"Only thus can those bastions of sea-power, upon which the control of the Atlantic and the Indian Oceans depends, be preserved in faithful and friendly hands," Churchill continued. He suggested a division of responsibilities. "The control of the Pacific by the United States Navy and of the Atlantic by the British Navy is indispensable to the security of the trade routes of both our countries . . ." He might have stopped here in the sentence, but he understood American sensitivities and Roosevelt's political needs, so he went on: "and the surest means to preventing the war from reaching the shores of the United States."

At present, Britain was bearing most of the burden. It would continue to do so until the United States could convert its industrial capacity to war production. "It is our British duty in the common interest, as also for our own survival, to hold the front and grapple with Nazi power until the preparations of the United States are complete," Churchill said. This might take as long as two years. "Victory may come before the two years are out; but we have no right to count upon it to the extent of relaxing any effort that is humanly possible. Therefore I submit with very great respect for your good and friendly consideration that there is a solid identity of interest between the British Empire and the United States while these conditions last."

Churchill had followed the American election campaign closely enough to know that Roosevelt's critics accused him of aiming to send American armies to Europe, and that Roosevelt had seemingly promised not to do so. Churchill now said an American army wouldn't be necessary. "Even if the United States was our ally instead of our friend and indispensable partner, we should not ask for a large American expeditionary army." Britain had soldiers; what it needed was ships. "Shipping, not men, is the limiting factor."

Churchill was pleased to say that Britain had withstood Germany's air assault. The RAF had fought the Luftwaffe to a draw in the aerial Battle of Britain, denying Hitler the air superiority over the English Channel he required for a successful invasion. German bombing raids on British cities continued, and wouldn't cease until the middle of 1941, by which time forty thousand British civilians had been killed and millions of homes, offices, churches, hospitals and schools destroyed. But Britain's will to fight survived the Blitz, and among many was stronger than ever.

"The danger of Great Britain being destroyed by a swift overwhelming blow has for the time being very greatly receded,"

Churchill wrote in his letter to Roosevelt. Peril persisted but in a different form. "The decision for 1941 lies upon the seas; unless we can establish our ability to feed this Island, to import munitions of all kinds which we need, unless we can move our armies to the various theatres where Hitler and his confederate Mussolini must be met, and maintain them there and do all this with the assurance of being able to carry it on till the spirit of the continental dictators is broken, we may fall by the way and the time needed by the United States to complete her defensive preparations may not be forthcoming."

The seaborne danger to Britain came chiefly from German submarines, which were sinking by the hundreds the merchant vessels Britain required to provision itself and conduct war operations. The U-boat threat had increased dramatically upon the surrender of France and the loss to the anti-Axis cause of that country's naval bases and fleet. Roosevelt's decision to send destroyers to Britain helped with the campaign against the submarines, but the danger continued to grow.

Churchill said that Roosevelt could ease the pressure by taking responsibility for safe travel on part of the Atlantic. "Could not United States naval forces extend their sea control over the American side of the Atlantic, so as to prevent molestation by enemy vessels of the approaches to the new line of naval and air bases which the United States is establishing in British islands in the Western Hemisphere?" he asked. After all, what were those bases for if not control of the sea lanes?

Churchill suggested that America do something about Japan. The fall of France to Germany had prompted Japan, which had failed to deliver a knockout blow against China, to occupy French Indochina. Churchill feared Japan might keep going. "The Japanese are thrusting southward through Indo China to Saigon and other naval and air bases, thus bringing them within a comparatively short distance of Singapore and the Dutch East Indies," he said. From there they would threaten British India. Britain's navy had its hands full with the Germans; America, to which Churchill had assigned primacy in the Pacific, should take responsibility for containing Japan.

"Last of all I come to the question of finance," Churchill said after several more suggestions. Britain would run out of money before it ran out of need for American arms. "The more rapid and abundant the flow of munitions and ships which you are able to send us, the sooner will our dollar credits be exhausted." Neither Britain nor America would benefit from letting the former's illiquidity crimp the flow of war matériel that would keep Britain in the war. Britain could transfer assets to America, as it had swapped bases for destroyers. But there were limits to what was possible or desirable. Churchill hoped America would finance what Britain could not.

Britain would continue to do its part for freedom and democracy, he assured Roosevelt. "The rest we leave with confidence to you and to your people, being sure that ways and means will be found which future generations on both sides of the Atlantic will approve and admire," Churchill told Roosevelt. "If, as I believe, you are convinced, Mr. President, that the defeat of the Nazi and Fascist tyranny is a matter of high consequence to the people of the United States and to the Western Hemisphere, you will regard this letter not as an appeal for aid, but as a statement of the minimum action necessary to the achievement of our common purpose."

50

ROOSEVELT ANSWERED CHURCHILL in the final days of
1940. On December 29, the president delivered only his second fireside chat of the year. "This is not a fireside chat on
war," he said. "It is a talk on national security; because the nub of the
whole purpose of your President is to keep you, now, and your children later, and your grandchildren much later, out of a last-ditch war
for the preservation of American independence and all the things
that American independence means to you and to me and to ours."

The peril to America was very great. "Never before since James-
town and Plymouth Rock has our American civilization been in such
danger as now," Roosevelt said. He cited the Tripartite Pact of three
months earlier, expanding the Germany-Italy Axis to include Japan,
as evidence of the growing threat. Germany was the ringleader. "The
Nazi masters of Germany have made it clear that they intend not
only to dominate all life and thought in their own country, but also
to enslave the whole of Europe, and then to use the resources of
Europe to dominate the rest of the world." Hitler himself was on
record as asserting the incompatibility of fascism and democracy.
"There are two worlds that stand opposed to each other," Roosevelt
quoted Hitler as saying. The president translated: "In other words,
the Axis not merely admits, but the Axis proclaims that there can be
no ultimate peace between their philosophy of government and our
philosophy of government."

Americans must give up any hope of imminent peace. "The
United States has no right or reason to encourage talk of peace until

the day shall come when there is a clear intention on the part of the aggressor nations to abandon all thought of dominating or conquering the world."

Anyone who suggested otherwise—as usual, Roosevelt declined to give names, but Lindbergh would have occurred to many listeners—was reckless or worse. "Some of our people like to believe that wars in Europe and in Asia are of no concern to us." Lindbergh had said as much. "But it is a matter of most vital concern to us that European and Asiatic war-makers should not gain control of the oceans which lead to this hemisphere." At present the British navy stood guard in the Atlantic. "Does anyone seriously believe that we need to fear attack anywhere in the Americas while a free Britain remains our most powerful naval neighbor in the Atlantic? Does anyone seriously believe, on the other hand, that we could rest easy if the Axis powers were our neighbors there?"

Roosevelt delineated the grim alternative. "If Great Britain goes down, the Axis powers will control the continents of Europe, Asia, Africa, Australasia, and the high seas, and they will be in a position to bring enormous military and naval resources against this hemisphere. It is no exaggeration to say that all of us, in all the Americas, would be living at the point of a gun—a gun loaded with explosive bullets, economic as well as military. We should enter upon a new and terrible era in which the whole world, our hemisphere included, would be run by threats of brute force. To survive in such a world, we would have to convert ourselves permanently into a militaristic power on the basis of war economy."

Roosevelt disputed Lindbergh's claim that the oceans would still protect America. "The width of those oceans is not what it was in the days of clipper ships. At one point between Africa and Brazil the distance is less from Washington than it is from Washington to Denver, Colorado—five hours for the latest type of bomber. And at the north end of the Pacific Ocean, America and Asia almost touch each other. Why, even today we have planes that could fly from the British Isles to New England and back again without refueling. And remember that the range of the modern bomber is ever being increased."

The appetite of the dictators was insatiable, Roosevelt said. "The Nazis have proclaimed, time and again, that all other races are their inferiors and therefore subject to their orders. And most important of all, the vast resources and wealth of this American Hemisphere constitute the most tempting loot in all the round world." Any who thought America could be safe while Nazism existed were deluding themselves and endangering their country.

The enemy had already infiltrated America. "Let us no longer blind ourselves to the undeniable fact that the evil forces which have crushed and undermined and corrupted so many others are already within our own gates. Your government knows much about them and every day is ferreting them out." On Roosevelt's orders, the FBI since the mid-1930s had been monitoring groups sympathetic to the Nazis for evidence of espionage; within months of Roosevelt's fireside chat the bureau would break a ring of nearly three dozen individuals who would be convicted of spying for Germany. Meanwhile the FBI created a Special Intelligence Service that attached undercover agents to American embassies in Latin America, where they worked to detect and neutralize German agents in that region.

"They seek to stir up suspicion and dissension to cause internal strife," Roosevelt continued of the German agents. "They try to turn capital against labor, and vice versa. They try to reawaken long slumbering racial and religious enmities which should have no place in this country. They are active in every group that promotes intolerance. They exploit for their own ends our own natural abhorrence of war. These trouble-breeders have but one purpose. It is to divide our people; to divide them into hostile groups and to destroy our unity and shatter our will to defend ourselves."

Some of the enemy were less obvious. "There are also American citizens, many of them in high places, who, unwittingly in most cases, are aiding and abetting the work of these agents. I do not charge these American citizens with being foreign agents. But I do charge them with doing exactly the kind of work that the dictators want done in the United States. These people not only believe that we can save our own skins by shutting our eyes to the fate of other nations; some of them go much further than that. They say that we can and should become the friends and even the partners of the Axis powers."

They couldn't be more wrong. "The experience of the past two years has proven beyond doubt that no nation can appease the Nazis. No man can tame a tiger into a kitten by stroking it. There can be no appeasement with ruthlessness. There can be no reasoning with an incendiary bomb. We know now that a nation can have peace with the Nazis only at the price of total surrender."

American defeatists—"the American appeasers"—said the United States should prepare to make the best bargain it could with the tyrants. "They tell you that the Axis powers are going to win anyway; that all of this bloodshed in the world could be saved; that the United States might just as well throw its influence into the scale of a dictated peace, and get the best out of it that we can. They call it a 'negotiated peace.'"

"Nonsense!" said Roosevelt. "Is it a negotiated peace if a gang of outlaws surrounds your community and on threat of extermination makes you pay tribute to save your own skins? Such a dictated peace would be no peace at all. It would be only another armistice, leading to the most gigantic armament race and the most devastating trade wars in all history."

What should America do? Simply this: everything it could to keep the British fighting. "The British people and their allies today are conducting an active war against this unholy alliance. Our own future security is greatly dependent on the outcome of that fight. Our ability to keep out of war is going to be affected by that outcome."

In the most serious tone he could muster, Roosevelt declared, "I make the direct statement to the American people that there is far less chance of the United States getting into war if we do all we can now to support the nations defending themselves against attack by the Axis than if we acquiesce in their defeat, submit tamely to an Axis victory, and wait our turn to be the object of attack in another war later on."

There were no guarantees in life, Roosevelt said. "If we are to be completely honest with ourselves, we must admit that there is risk in any course we may take. But I deeply believe that the great majority of our people agree that the course that I advocate involves the least risk now and the greatest hope for world peace in the future."

He detailed what he had in mind. "The people of Europe who are defending themselves do not ask us to do their fighting. They ask us for the implements of war, the planes, the tanks, the guns, the freighters which will enable them to fight for their liberty and for our security. Emphatically we must get these weapons to them; get them to them in sufficient volume and quickly enough, so that we and our children will be saved the agony and suffering of war which others have had to endure."

"Let not the defeatists tell us that it is too late," Roosevelt said, taking dead aim at Lindbergh. "It will never be earlier. Tomorrow will be later than today."

It was not too late to aid the British. "Great Britain and the British Empire are today the spearhead of resistance to world conquest. And they are putting up a fight which will live forever in the story of human gallantry."

He repeated that the British weren't asking for troops. "There is no demand for sending an American Expeditionary Force outside our own borders. There is no intention by any member of your government to send such a force. You can, therefore, nail, nail any talk about sending armies to Europe as deliberate untruth."

Instead, America would send weapons, Roosevelt said. "We must be the great arsenal of democracy."

American factories and American workers were already churning out weapons. "But all our present efforts are not enough. We must have more ships, more guns, more planes—more of everything." No effort should be spared, no expense begrudged. "For us this is an emergency as serious as war itself. We must apply ourselves to our task with the same resolution, the same sense of urgency, the same spirit of patriotism and sacrifice as we would show were we at war."

Roosevelt lashed again at Lindbergh and his ilk. "We have no excuse for defeatism." Defeatism was un-American. And it was misguided. "We have every good reason for hope—hope for peace, yes, and hope for the defense of our civilization and for the building of a better civilization in the future."

Roosevelt was certain Americans would rise to the challenge. "I have the profound conviction that the American people are now determined to put forth a mightier effort than they have ever yet made to increase our production of all the implements of defense, to meet the threat to our democratic faith," he said. "I call upon our people with absolute confidence that our common cause will greatly succeed."

51

I FEEL IT MY duty on behalf of the British Government and indeed the whole British Empire to tell you, Mr. President, how lively is our sense of gratitude and admiration for the memorable declaration which you made to the American people and to the lovers of freedom in all continents," Churchill wrote to Roosevelt on January 1, 1941. The president's summons to America to be the "arsenal of democracy" sounded like salvation to the prime minister. "We cannot tell what lies before us, but with this trumpet-call we march forward heartened and fortified and with the confidence which you have expressed that in the end all will be well for the English speaking peoples and those who share their ideals."

LINDBERGH GREW MORE skeptical than ever. "Roosevelt demands more aid for Britain," he wrote in his journal the day after Roosevelt's broadcast. "Says Axis will lose war." Two days later Lindbergh and Anne went to see a newsreel Anne was in. The Friends Service Committee had organized a campaign to get food relief to children in Europe. Anne spoke on behalf of the committee and the children to a newsreel crew. On January 1, 1941, she and Lindbergh went to a theater to see how she had been edited. "She was thrown on the screen immediately after a picture of Roosevelt," Lindbergh recorded. Roosevelt was giving his fireside chat. "The caption was 'Shall We Feed Hitler's Europe?'! They never miss a chance to do something like that." The opponents of food aid said it would weaken the effect of the British blockade of the territory controlled by Germany. Anne Lindbergh and the supporters of aid contended that care was being taken to see that the food went to the children and not, for example, to German soldiers. The newsreel company seemed to be siding with the opponents.

So did the audience at the theater. "Anne's delivery could not have been better," Lindbergh wrote. "The audience showed no reaction whatever. In fact, during the entire newsreel the only time they cheered was when Roosevelt said the Axis would not win the war. And the only time they booed was when a picture of Mussolini was thrown on the screen. They almost snarled at Mussolini—reminded me more of animals than of people. To my surprise, there was not the slightest attempt at cheering when films of soldiers going to training camps were shown." Apparently the viewers liked warlike words better than warlike actions.

Lindbergh grew more discouraged. "The pall of the war seems to hang over us today," he wrote on January 6. "More and more people are simply giving in to it. Many say we are as good as in already. The attitude of the country wavers back and forth. First, it seems the antiwar forces are gaining, and then there is a swing in the other direction and one must always try to separate the headlines in the newspapers from the factual attitude of the country. But, on the whole, I think we who are against American intervention have been slowly losing ground, at least from a relative standpoint. Our greatest hope lies in the fact that eighty-five per cent of the people in the United States (according to the latest polls) are against intervention. On the other hand, about sixty-five per cent want to 'aid Great Britain, even at the risk of war.'" Lindbergh was referring to a recent Gallup survey of public opinion. "In other words, we seem to want to have Britain win without being willing to pay the price of war. We are indulging in a type of wishful thinking that must lead us, sooner or later, to an impossible position."

ROOSEVELT DISCOURAGED LINDBERGH the more when Congress convened on January 6. "I address you, the members of the Seventy-seventh Congress, at a moment unprecedented in the history of the Union," Roosevelt said at the start of his State of Union speech. "I use the word 'unprecedented' because at no previous time has American security been as seriously threatened from without as it is today."

As he and others had done during the last decade, Roosevelt looked to America's past for guidance as to its present. What he found was different from what some others had discovered. Where Lindbergh and the opponents of involvement pointed to the advice of George Washington against foreign entanglements, Roosevelt cited a history of American struggle for the rights of neutrals to trade and otherwise engage where they wished. "What I seek to convey," he said by summary, "is the historic truth that the United States as a nation has at all times maintained clear, definite opposition to any attempt to lock us in behind an ancient Chinese wall while the procession of civilization went past." This was a tradition worth preserving. "Today, thinking of our children and of their children, we oppose enforced isolation for ourselves or for any other part of the Americas."

Besides, isolation in the fifth decade of the twentieth century meant something different than isolation had in the eighteenth or nineteenth centuries, or even in the early part of the twentieth. "Except in the Maximilian interlude in Mexico, no foreign power sought to establish itself in this hemisphere," Roosevelt said. "Even when the World War broke out in 1914, it seemed to contain only small threat of danger to our own American future." Since the World War, Americans had come to see that isolation was no longer possible. The threat to America had changed. "As time went on, the American people began to visualize what the downfall of democratic nations"—even in once-distant Europe—"might mean to our own democracy."

Roosevelt didn't try to defend the peace settlement after the World War. Nor did he dwell on the failure of the democracies to deal with the challenges to that settlement. Yet he observed that what the world had seen recently was worse than what the Paris peace conference produced. "The peace of 1919 was far less unjust than the kind of 'pacification' which began even before Munich, and which is being carried on under the new order of tyranny that seeks to spread over every continent today."

It was this tyranny with which the world, and now America, had to deal. "Every realist knows that the democratic way of life is at this moment being directly assailed in every part of the world—assailed either by arms, or by secret spreading of poisonous propaganda by those who seek to destroy unity and promote discord in nations that are still at peace. During sixteen long months this assault has blotted out the whole pattern of democratic life in an appalling number of independent nations, great and small. The assailants are still on the march, threatening other nations, great and small."

Roosevelt had reached the part of the annual address where presidents acknowledged their constitutional obligation. "Therefore, as your President, performing my constitutional duty to 'give to the Congress information of the state of the Union,' I find it, unhappily, necessary to report that the future and the safety of our country and of our democracy are overwhelmingly involved in events far beyond our borders."

Democracy was fighting for its life, with the fate of the planet, including the Americas, in the balance. "Armed defense of democratic existence is now being gallantly waged in four continents. If that defense fails, all the population and all the resources of Europe, Asia, Africa and Australasia will be dominated by the conquerors. Let us remember that the total of those populations and their resources in those four continents greatly exceeds the sum total of the population and the resources of the whole of the Western Hemisphere— many times over."

Roosevelt gave the back of his hand to Lindbergh and others who thought like him, even as he misrepresented their case. "In times like these it is immature—and incidentally, untrue—for anybody to brag that an unprepared America, single-handed, and with one hand tied behind its back, can hold off the whole world. No realistic American can expect from a dictator's peace international generosity, or return of true independence, or world disarmament, or freedom of expression, or freedom of religion—or even good business. Such a peace would bring no security for us or for our neighbors."

Americans must close their ears to these foolish, fearful men. "As a nation, we may take pride in the fact that we are softhearted; but we cannot afford to be soft-headed. We must always be wary of those who with sounding brass and a tinkling cymbal preach the 'ism' of appeasement." Many listeners would have inferred a reference to Lindbergh's sobriquet "Lone Eagle" as Roosevelt warned, "We must especially beware of that small group of selfish men who would clip the wings of the American eagle in order to feather their own nests."

Roosevelt took on Lindbergh more directly, but still not by name. "There is much loose talk of our immunity from immediate and direct invasion from across the seas. Obviously, as long as the British Navy retains its power, no such danger exists. Even if there were no British Navy, it is not probable that any enemy would be stupid enough to attack us by landing troops in the United States from across thousands of miles of ocean, until it had acquired strategic bases from which to operate. But we learn much from the lessons of the past years in Europe—particularly the lesson of Norway, whose essential seaports were captured by treachery and surprise built up over a series of years."

Roosevelt didn't use the term "fifth columnist" in this address, but he conveyed the same idea. "The first phase of the invasion of this hemisphere would not be the landing of regular troops. The necessary strategic points would be occupied by secret agents and their dupes—and great numbers of them are already here, and in Latin America. As long as the aggressor nations maintain the offensive, they—not we—will choose the time and the place and the method of their attack. That is why the future of all the American republics is today in serious danger."

Roosevelt paused to let this sink in.

"That is why this annual message to the Congress is unique in our history," he continued. "That is why every member of the executive branch of the government and every member of the Congress faces great responsibility and great accountability. The need of the moment is that our actions and our policy should be devoted primarily—almost exclusively—to meeting this foreign peril."

Roosevelt's message was indeed unique. No president had ever delivered what amounted to a war message before the country had gone to war. But Roosevelt did just that now.

"Our national policy is this," he declared. "First, by an impressive expression of the public will and without regard to partisanship, we are committed to all-inclusive national defense. Second, by an impressive expression of the public will and without regard to partisanship, we are committed to full support of all those resolute peoples, everywhere, who are resisting aggression and are thereby keeping war away from our hemisphere. By this support, we express our determination that the democratic cause shall prevail; and we strengthen the defense and the security of our own nation. Third, by an impressive expression of the public will and without regard to partisanship, we are committed to the proposition that principles of morality and considerations for our own security will never permit us to acquiesce in a peace dictated by aggressors and sponsored by appeasers. We know that enduring peace cannot be bought at the cost of other people's freedom."

Roosevelt noted that Wendell Willkie had not disputed the administration's handling of the war in Europe. "In the recent national election there was no substantial difference between the two great parties in respect to that national policy. No issue was fought out on this line before the American electorate." Congress and the American people concurred on the need to rebuild American defenses.

Much had been done on that front, but more was required. "The immediate need is a swift and driving increase in our armament production." Roosevelt gave examples. "We are behind schedule in turning out finished airplanes; we are working day and night to solve the innumerable problems and to catch up. We are ahead of schedule in building warships but we are working to get even further ahead of that schedule." He conceded the magnitude of the challenge. "To change a whole nation from a basis of peacetime production of implements of peace to a basis of wartime production of implements of war is no small task."

Nor was it a task like any America had undertaken before. Roosevelt asked Congress for funds to build America's own arsenal. And he requested something more, something new. "I also ask this Congress for authority and for funds sufficient to manufacture additional munitions and war supplies of many kinds, to be turned over to those nations which are now in actual war with aggressor nations. Our most useful and immediate role is to act as an arsenal for them as well as for ourselves. They do not need man power, but they do need billions of dollars worth of the weapons of defense."

Financing should not be a consideration. "The time is near when they will not be able to pay for them all in ready cash. We cannot, and we will not, tell them that they must surrender, merely because of present inability to pay for the weapons which we know they must have." In the World War the United States had loaned money to foreign countries to pay for American arms. That approach had ended in recriminations and default. It would not be repeated. "I do not recommend that we make them a loan of dollars with which to pay for these weapons—a loan to be repaid in dollars. I recommend that we make it possible for those nations to continue to obtain war materials in the United States, fitting their orders into our own program." Most of the weapons would be of the same kind used by American forces. "Nearly all their materiel would, if the time ever came, be useful for our own defense."

Worrying about money would cloud the basic issue. "Let us say to the democracies: 'We Americans are vitally concerned in your defense of freedom. We are putting forth our energies, our resources and our organizing powers to give you the strength to regain and maintain a free world. We shall send you, in ever-increasing numbers, ships, planes, tanks, guns. This is our purpose and our pledge.'"

SAMUEL ROSENMAN HAD helped Roosevelt write speeches since Roosevelt was governor of New York. Rosenman's phrase "New Deal," introduced in Roosevelt's speech accepting the Democratic nomination in 1932, came to summarize his domestic policies as president. As war loomed larger in American politics, Rosenman spent more time on foreign policy. He naturally worked on the State of the Union address in which Roosevelt unveiled his proposal for aid to the democracies. Rosenman and the others who contributed to the effort were pleased with the body of the speech, but they had difficulty bringing it to a close.

"We were sitting in the President's study one night grouped around his desk as usual—Harry, Bob and I," Rosenman recalled. Harry was Harry Hopkins, Roosevelt's closest adviser; Bob was Robert Sherwood. Roosevelt was at his desk. "The President held the original of the third draft in his hand. Each of us had a carbon copy of the draft, and a yellow pad on his lap on which to make notes. Dorothy

Brady"—one of Roosevelt's secretaries—"was taking dictation this night; but by the time a speech had reached this stage, there was not much dictation to take, usually only those inserts by the President which were too long for him to write out longhand.

"The President announced as he came near the end of the draft that he had an idea for a peroration. We waited as he leaned far back in his swivel chair with his gaze on the ceiling. It was a long pause—so long that it began to become uncomfortable.

"Then he leaned forward again in his chair and said: 'Dorothy, take a law.'" This was a case of life imitating art imitating life. A Broadway musical had spoofed Roosevelt's handling of Congress during his first months in office, depicting him as dictating laws to his secretary rather than waiting for Congress to act. Roosevelt laughed and made "take a law" his standard summons to a secretary for dictation.

"He dictated the following," continued Rosenman. "'We must look forward to a world based on four essential human freedoms. The first is freedom of speech and expression—everywhere in the world. The second is the freedom of every person to worship God in his own way—everywhere in the world. The third is freedom from want—which, translated into international terms, means economic understandings which will secure to every nation everywhere a healthy peacetime life for its inhabitants. The fourth is freedom from fear—which, translated into international terms, means a world-wide reduction of armaments to such a point and in such a thorough fashion that no nation anywhere will be in a position to commit an act of physical aggression against any neighbor.'"

Rosenman had heard Roosevelt mention such freedoms earlier. Clearly he had been thinking about them of late. "The words seemed now to roll off his tongue as though he had rehearsed them many times to himself," Rosenman recalled. "He dictated them so slowly that on the yellow pad I had on my lap I was able to take them down myself in longhand as he spoke."

Roosevelt gazed around the group, as he did when inviting reactions. Hopkins questioned the president's emphasis on "everywhere in the world." "That covers an awful lot of territory, Mr. President," Hopkins said. "I don't know how interested Americans are going to be in the people of Java."

"I'm afraid they'll have to be, Harry," said Roosevelt. "The world is getting so small that even the people in Java are getting to be our neighbors now."

Roosevelt kept his thoughts about Java to himself. Otherwise his version of the "four freedoms," slightly edited, rounded off his State of the Union address.

52

LINDBERGH HAD EXPECTED no better. "Roosevelt has asked for 'all-out aid' to the democracies, but his message is not specific—as usual," Lindbergh wrote the next day. "Roosevelt seems to be holding back somewhat on the war. Is he afraid it is too late for us to enter it successfully?"

Roosevelt talked a good game, but what did he believe? "I think he has the ability to persuade himself that whatever he wants himself is also to the best interests of the country. I feel sure he would, consciously or unconsciously, like to take the center of the world stage away from Hitler. I think he would lead this country to war in a moment if he felt he could accomplish this object."

A war would be a huge gamble—for America and for Roosevelt. "If Roosevelt took this country into war and won, he might be one of the great figures of all history. But if we lost, he would be damned forever."

Lindbergh didn't know how things would turn out. "The cards are now stacked against us, and I think that is why he is wavering—temptation balanced against discretion." The president was a formidable foe, unfortunately. "Roosevelt is clever, even though I do not give him credit for being very wise."

ON JANUARY 10 the president's allies in the House offered a bill "to promote the defense of the United States," which they cleverly numbered H.R. 1776. Critics argued that the bill would undo what the founders had done in 1776; it would tie America's fate once more to Britain's. Supporters shifted to "Lend-Lease," the name that stuck.

The bill would deliver control of arms procurement and distribution to the president, declaring, "The President may, from time to time, when he deems it in the interest of national defense, authorize the Secretary of War, the Secretary of the Navy or the head of any other department or agency of the Government to manufacture in arsenals, factories, and shipyards ... any defense article for the government of any country whose defense the President deems vital to the defense of the United States" and "to sell, transfer title to, exchange, lease, lend, or otherwise dispose of, to any such government any defense article."

The introduction of the bill produced an uproar. Opponents split over which aspect of the bill posed the greater danger: the unprecedented power it gave to the president or the shotgun wedding of America to Britain. Herbert Hoover stressed the former peril. "The first thing Congress has to consider is the suggestion of enormous surrender of its responsibilities," the former president declared. "No such powers were granted in the last war." Hoover supported an acceleration of American war production. "But the practical surrender of power to take these steps that are possible under this legislation is something else."

Thomas Dewey, New York's district attorney and a recent and presumed future candidate for the Republican presidential nomination, put the matter more strongly. "The president's so-called defense bill would bring an end to free government in the United States and would abolish the Congress for all practical purposes."

Alf Landon, the Republican nominee from 1936, called the proposed law "the first step toward dictatorship by Mr. Roosevelt." Landon remarked the swift turnaround of the president. "It has not been sixty days since he spoke for peace and promised to keep this country out of war." Now Roosevelt was taking the country *into* war, whatever he might still say to the contrary. The Germans would interpret this bill as a war declaration and would act accordingly. The consequence was inescapable. "The minute an American ship is sunk and the American flag is fired upon and Americans are killed, we are then in the war." Landon predicted that Roosevelt wouldn't be content with a third term, but would insist on a fourth. He was following the antidemocratic playbook of the fascists. "In defeating totalitarianism abroad, we may strengthen its hold here at home," Landon said.

Burton Wheeler excoriated the bill and the president for proposing it. "Never before have the American people been asked or compelled to give so bounteously and so completely of their tax dollars to any foreign nation. Never before has the Congress of the United States been asked by any president to violate international law. Never before has this nation resorted to duplicity in the conduct of its foreign affairs. Never before has the United States given to one man the power to strip this nation of its defenses in time of war or peace. Never before has the Congress coldly and flatly been asked to abdicate." The Montana Democrat shuddered to think the bill might pass. "Is it possible that the American people are so gullible that they will permit their representatives in Congress to sit supinely by while an American president demands totalitarian powers in the name of saving democracy?" Wheeler said the administration's bill was more of the same bankrupt do-goodism the president had imposed on America for years. Alluding to the Agricultural Adjustment Administration, a Roosevelt agency that paid farmers to reduce production, Wheeler characterized the Lend-Lease program as a "New Deal triple A foreign policy—plow under every fourth American boy."

Gerald Nye called the measure a step "not *short* of war," but one that propelled the country "all but straight *into* war." He said Roosevelt's proposal was "the most brazen request ever made" of Congress. University of Chicago president Robert Hutchins warned that the American people were "about to commit suicide" by "drifting into war."

A group of Brooklyn clergymen condemned the bill as "machinery of a Fascist character which is novel in the history of our nation." America risked repeating the folly of Germany and Italy. "The Fascist government of other lands gained control by bills such as this being passed through their legislatures under the guise of a national emergency." America should stick with democracy. "We believe in the American form of government and that we can trust our representatives in Congress, elected by the people."

The American Youth Congress, an advocacy group heretofore favored by Eleanor Roosevelt, gathered three thousand members at the Mecca Temple in New York to oppose the bill. The young people cheered when Congressman Vito Marcantonio, a disillusioned New York Republican who had leapfrogged the Democrats to the American Labor party, denounced the bill as having been designed by "Wall Street and Downing Street imperialism."

53

COLONEL, WE SHALL be very glad to have you proceed at this time," said Sol Bloom, the New York Democrat who chaired the House committee on foreign affairs. Lindbergh had been summoned to a hearing on the Lend-Lease bill.

He began with a prepared statement. "I understand that I have been asked to appear before this committee to discuss the effect of aviation upon America's position in time of war," he said. "I believe that this effect can be summed up briefly by saying that our position is greatly strengthened for defense and greatly weakened for attack. I base this statement upon two facts. First, that an invading army and its supplies must still be transported by sea. Second, that aviation makes it more difficult than ever before for a navy to approach a hostile shore." The American continents were more impregnable than ever, assuming the United States kept up its guard. "I do not believe there is any danger of an invasion of this continent, either by sea or by air, as long as we maintain an army, navy and air force of reasonable size and in modern condition, and provided we establish the bases essential for defense."

How large should the American air force be? "We would be wise to construct as rapidly as possible a total air force of about 10,000 thoroughly modern fighting planes plus reserves. This number would, I believe, be adequate to ensure American security, regardless of the outcome of the present European war."

As for the bases: "Accompanying this expansion of our air force should be the construction of aviation bases in Newfoundland, Canada; the West Indies; parts of South America; Central America; the Galapagos islands; the Hawaiian islands and Alaska." Greenland could be useful for secondary bases.

Lindbergh drew an important distinction. "Since many people are discussing the possibility of an air invasion of America, I would like permission to bring a few points to your attention in this connection. It is first necessary to establish clearly the difference between an air invasion where troops are landed, and a bombing raid where there is no attempt to establish a base on enemy territory." The first was unprecedented and still improbable. "There has never been an invasion of enemy territory by air alone. The two outstanding examples of what might be called a partial air invasion were furnished by the German occupations of Norway and Holland. But in each of these instances, the landing of troops by air was carried on simultaneously with a ground army invasion on a major scale."

The fundamental reason air invasion had never been attempted was lack of carrying capacity. "The maximum number of troops that could have been transported and supplied by air would have been ineffective without the immediate support of a ground army. If air invasion alone could be successful, it would have been used by the Germans against England many months ago." An air invasion of America would be incomparably harder. "It is important to note that the transport of troops by air in Europe has been over a distance of a few hundred miles at most. An air invasion across the ocean is, I believe, absolutely impossible at this time or in any predictable future."

Air raids were a different matter. "It is, of course, perfectly possible today to build bombing planes that could cross the ocean, drop several tons of bombs, and return to their starting point," Lindbergh said. But their effect would be psychological at most. "Transoceanic bombing raids could do considerable damage on peacetime standards, but they would have very little effectiveness on wartime standards. The cost of transoceanic bombing would be extremely high, and the losses would be large, and the effect on our military position negligible. Such bombing could not begin to prepare the way for an invasion of this continent." Again Lindbergh pointed to Europe. "If England is able to live at all with bases of the German air force less than an hour's flight away, the United States is not in great danger across the Atlantic Ocean."

Lindbergh proceeded to note that the ocean's effect on aviation worked in both directions. "Almost every advantage we have in defense would be a disadvantage to us in attack. It would then be our problem to cross the ocean in ships and force a landing against the established air bases of our enemy." In effect, aviation made the oceans wider, not narrower. "Aviation has added to America's security against Europe and to Europe's security against America. One might sum up the matter by saying the aviation decreases the security of nations within a continent against each other, but increases the security of the continent as a whole against foreign invasion."

America was the big winner from the revolution in the technology of flight. "We have a country and climate well-suited to the development of aircraft. We have natural sources, great industries, and a national psychology ideally adapted to the tempo of the air. In conclusion, I would like to say that aviation is to us unquestionably an asset. It greatly strengthens our position and increases the security of this entire hemisphere from foreign attack."

THE QUESTIONS BEGAN. "Colonel Lindbergh, is it not a fact that more than a year ago—and you will probably know the exact date—you either made a statement or a radio address urging our government to acquire air bases in South and Latin America?" asked Hamilton Fish, a Republican from New York.

"I have been urging the acquisition of air bases in South America and elsewhere for a long time," Lindbergh responded. "I think that is vital to our national defense."

"What would be our position if foreign nations sought to acquire military or naval air bases in South America?"

"I believe without question we should go to war with all of our resources if there is any attempt to establish a foreign base in North or South America."

"In other words, Colonel Lindbergh, you are an upholder and defender of the Monroe Doctrine?"

"To that extent at least."

"Against invasion by any armed force or the establishment of military or air naval bases on this continent?"

"Right."

Lindbergh was asked about statements he had made regarding issues beyond air defense. "In the radio speeches which you made—I believe you made one on September 25, 1939, and another on October 13, 1939; that was, shortly after the outbreak of the present European war in September, at the time Congress was concerned with the question of whether or not the arms embargo provision of the neutrality law should be repealed—you expressed opposition to the proposal so to do, did you not?"

"Yes," said Lindbergh. "I think that"—repeal of the arms embargo—"was a mistake."

Other opponents of repeal had changed their minds subsequently, the questioner noted. "You still think you were right about that?"

"I believe it was a mistake; yes, sir."

"You also said in those speeches that the war that has broken out in Europe was a war over the balance of power in Europe. You used that expression?"

"I believe it is primarily; yes."

Had Lindbergh expressed an opinion about one side or the other being to blame?

"No, sir; I have not. I believe the fault of the war is about evenly divided in Europe, and the causes of it."

"Which side do you want to win?"

"I prefer to see neither side win. I would like to see a negotiated peace. I believe a complete victory on either side would result in prostration in Europe such as we have never seen."

"In every contest, we have a feeling for one side or the other, but you have none; you are absolutely neutral?"

"I feel it would be better for us, and for every nation in Europe, to have this war end without a conclusive victory."

"Do you think it would be to the best interests of the United States for Hitler to be defeated?"

"No. I think a negotiated peace would be to the best interests of this country, sir."

"You do not think that it is in the best interests of the United

States economically as well as in the matter of defense for England to win?"

"No, sir. I think that a complete victory, as I say, would mean prostration in Europe and would be one of the worst things that could happen there and here."

"Do you think the fall and destruction of the British Empire would menace the United States in her defense against attack?"

"Not seriously."

"Not seriously?"

"No, sir."

"It would be just a small matter?"

"I believe this nation is in itself impregnable, sir, if we maintain reasonable forces."

Another questioner asked Lindbergh's opinion of the bill before Congress.

"I am opposed to this bill for two reasons," Lindbergh said. "One, I think it is one more step away from democracy and the democratic system. And the other one is that I think it is one step closer to war. I do not know how many more steps we can take and still be short of war."

The questioner reverted to Lindbergh's desire for a negotiated peace. "We have the announcement of Mr. Hitler and his echoes in Japan and Italy that they propose to create a new world order—not a European order, but a world order—and that they propose to do that by force. And they propose, when they have crushed the world by force, to place one race—their race—in control of the rest of us, who will then be the producing slaves in the interests of our owners and superiors. Under those circumstances, how can we possibly begin negotiations for a peace, unless Mr. Hitler has a change of mind?"

"I believe, sir, that no matter what is desired in Europe and in Asia—and that I do not know—we are strong enough in this nation and in this hemisphere to maintain our own way of life regardless of what the attitude is on the other side. I do not believe we are strong enough to impose our way of life on Europe and on Asia. Therefore my belief is that the only success for our way of life and our system of government is to defend it here at home and not attempt to enter a war abroad."

QUESTIONING TURNED TO aircraft production. In his prepared statement Lindbergh had said America needed ten thousand airplanes. Hadn't he also said that Germany could produce twenty thousand? "Do you not think, Colonel Lindbergh, that this country should have at least the facilities to produce as many planes as any other country?"

"Not unless we intend to invade other countries, sir," Lindbergh replied.

"You differentiate, then, between the building of planes for invasion or aggression and building them for defense?"

"Yes, sir. And also taking into consideration our geographical position."

But was Lindbergh not worried about the large number of planes the Germans had built?

"Not the types that are being built there, sir. Those planes are being built for European attack. They are incapable of flying across to this country. They are not of a type that would be fit for an attempted invasion. I should say that ten thousand planes here would be very adequate to meet the present production of war planes in Europe."

What about airplane carriers—the ships also called aircraft carriers?

Lindbergh wasn't worried here either. "The total number of aircraft that can be carried by the airplane carriers in existence today would not be enough to affect our military position in this country." They could be used for raids but not for anything substantial. "I would like to state, in support of my argument, that the number of planes being used against England today is many times the number that could be carried on all the aircraft carriers in the world." And England, a much smaller country than the United States, survived.

Another questioner circled back to the matter of aid to Britain. Was Lindbergh in favor?

"Our people have taken a stand on that, sir, which I personally think was a mistake." But mistake or not, the pledge had been given. "And I do not believe we can reverse a stand that this country has taken or a promise that has been made." All the same, the American government should work to end the war as quickly as possible. "I say that, sir, to be perfectly frank, because I do not believe it is possible, aside from something completely unforeseen, for England to invade the continent of Europe and win the war."

But what about England and the United States together?

"I think it is improbable, sir, that England and the United States together could successfully invade the continent of Europe, unless a collapse came first and preceded the invasion."

A questioner referred to Lindbergh's assertion that the United States would have to come to terms with whichever country won the war. "If Hitler succeeds in establishing a new order in Europe, according to you, Colonel, we must prepare to make an agreement?" A trade agreement, perhaps?

"I think historically and also practically we will trade with Europe, regardless of what the situation there is, as we have with every nation in the world in the past."

"If he succeeds in establishing a new order, it would be necessary for us to come to a friendly agreement?"

"Somewhat the same as we have with Russia, sir."

Another questioner asked Lindbergh to elaborate on his statement that the war in Europe was not America's war.

"There are a great many reasons," Lindbergh said. "For one reason, we were given no part in the declaration of the war." Britain and France had declared war in defense of Poland. Lindbergh had thought this imprudent, given that Poland was indefensible under the circumstances at the time. "Another reason is that these European wars have gone on ever since there has been European history." The ancestors of most Americans had left Europe expecting to be rid of that continent's wars. This expectation had served America well and should still be honored. A third reason was the United States, by rejecting the Treaty of Versailles, had opted out of the peace structure created at the end of the previous war, making clear that it would not be responsible for European affairs. "Logically we took the stand that we would not enter another war." A fourth reason looked to the future. "If we are going to be in wars in Europe, we have to be in the peace that follows the war, and take part in European politics permanently."

In response to a subsequent question, Lindbergh gave another reason for staying out of Europe's wars. The debate over intervention distracted Americans from their first responsibility: protecting their homeland. "We are not moving as rapidly as we should in the defense of America," he said. "Our people have been divided on the question of foreign war." The distraction was dangerous and unnecessary. "We should never have had any question as to whether our preparation for war was for the defense of America or for participation in war abroad. And I believe if we were given the opportunity to concentrate on the defense of America, with no question of taking part in wars abroad, our rearmament program would go ahead very much faster."

A questioner pressed Lindbergh on his remark about America opting out of European security after the World War. Was that decision unwise? "Did we have a duty to support the League of Nations and rewrite the map of Europe?"

"I do not think we had the duty," Lindbergh said. "I think it was wise to withdraw. But I think it would be a mistake to withdraw and then go back as soon as another war starts."

Did Lindbergh believe that intervention now would commit the United States to European security permanently?

"I think that it is a step in that direction."

"And that anybody who is for this bill"—Lend-Lease—"must also be for the League of Nations?"

"I think it is a step in that direction."

"And the projection of America into European politics?"

"Yes, sir."

A REPORTER COVERING the hearing noted for his readers the effect of Lindbergh on the audience in the room. "Colonel Lindbergh's appearance before the committee had all the atmosphere of a gala occasion," the reporter wrote. "Long before the doors of the ways and means committee room in the new House office building, where the hearings were being held, were opened a few minutes before 10 o'clock this morning, long lines of prospective spectators were waiting to surge into the hall. The vast majority of them were admirers of the aviator and showed their admiration, repeatedly, by prolonged applause, in defiance of rules and of not very stern admonitions on the part of Representative Bloom of New York, chairman of the foreign affairs committee. Their admiration was expressed on one occasion by boos directed at Representative Courtney of Tennessee, who tried to pin the colonel down on the question of which side he wanted to win the war in case it went through to a decisive conclusion. The catcalls and derisive expressions of disapprobation drowned out the witness's reply, but it later developed that he had answered as usual, 'Neither side.'"

Chairman Bloom expressed his own admiration at the close of Lindbergh's testimony. "Colonel Lindbergh, you have been on the stand for nearly four hours and a half," he observed. "You have been examined by proponents of the bill and by opponents, and you have been asked a great many questions, and you have answered them." Bloom had not asked any questions till now, and at this late hour he chose not to extend things further. "But the Chair wishes to say this, Colonel Lindbergh: you have made one of the best witnesses that this committee could possibly ever hear. You have answered all the questions as only a Colonel Lindbergh could answer them; and I know that I am speaking for every member of the committee when I say we thank you. To add anything to that would be superfluous. It has been a very great pleasure to have you here, and we thank you very, very much."

The official transcript of the hearing added parenthetically at this point: "There was applause as Colonel Lindbergh left the stand, many members of the committee rising."

54

LINDBERGH WAS PLEASED at the response at the hearing. Another ovation was less welcome. The German foreign ministry called Lindbergh's testimony "courageous" and saluted him with "Hats off!"

Berlin's cue gave Roosevelt the opening the president desired. At a news conference the next day, he remarked that Americans should beware of how government-controlled papers in the fascist countries exploited the procedures of American politics, including congressional hearings. "Certain statements that are made on the Hill—never mind by whom; you can guess—the maker of those statements has become the hero—the front-page hero—of those nations, with the general intimation that those people represent the overwhelming mass of American public opinion," Roosevelt said. He repeated, "Everybody in this country should understand that those people are the heroes in Germany and Italy and Japan."

Roosevelt had other responses to his critics. Burton Wheeler's prediction that Lend-Lease would cause the plowing under of every fourth American boy provoked the president's wrath. "The most untruthful, the most dastardly, unpatriotic thing that has ever been said" was how he characterized the remark. "Quote me on that," he added. "That really is the rottenest thing that has been said in public life in my generation."

Some criticisms he simply brushed aside. A reporter asked Roosevelt to comment on an objection that the Lend-Lease bill was written so that if it seemed necessary the British navy could be purchased by the United States.

"Don't you think this is awfully—*awfully*—cow-jumped-over-the-moon business?" replied Roosevelt. "I do."

A subsequent question was about a meeting between the president and the Apostolic Delegate—the pope's representative. Had they talked about Lend-Lease?

"I should have discussed with him the possibility of acquiring the Vatican navy!" said Roosevelt, laughing.

LINDBERGH REPRISED HIS House testimony before the Senate foreign relations committee. "The Senate hearing was, on the whole, conducted with more dignity than the House hearing on the Lend-Lease bill," he wrote in his journal. "Senator Pepper of Florida took up almost half of the time I was on the stand and got himself into several rather amusing situations. He and two or three other Administration Senators were definitely antagonistic, but only during their questioning. When the committee adjourned for lunch, they were courteous and friendly. I have often noticed this in Washington: Congressmen and Senators will curse each other in debate and be, apparently at least, on the most friendly terms after it is over. Pepper has called me everything from a fifth columnist on down, but he was smiling and good-natured during the lunch hour. In a sense, it demonstrates a dangerous irresponsibility in the speech of public men. I think that more care about the accuracy and dignity of what is said would create a better and more stable government."

Lindbergh drafted an essay for the *Saturday Evening Post* titled "A Letter to Americans." He could tell the tide was against the opponents of Lend-Lease; Roosevelt's campaign of vilification of him was working, and the president's mastery of Congress was proving unstoppable once more. But Lindbergh wasn't willing to surrender; he'd try again to reach the American people.

A bout of chicken pox laid him low for a week. By the end of that period, the chances of blocking the aid bill were less than ever. The editor of the magazine phoned him. "He told me the *Post* had decided not to take my article. He said that while he 'agreed with practically every word of it,' he felt it was 'a little too late.'"

Upon Lindbergh's recuperation he took a walk. "I went to the bluff, but I could not see the lighthouse or the bay. They made an impression on my eyes but not within my mind and feeling. I could not see the trees, or the stones along the path, or the last year's leaves, or the frost crystals on the shady side of the banks. All these things were there, but only as flat, physical facts. Life and spark were gone from them, for my mind is on the war, on politics, on the things spread over the front pages of the morning newspapers." He needed to get away, to find solitude outside the cities where he was spending so much time. "Some say real solitude can be found in the midst of cities—in an empty room, or on a park bench, or along a darkened street in the hours past midnight. I think there *is* an element of solitude in these places—a ray that passes through a hole in deep clouds—but to me solitude means beauty and distance and uninhabited places. I feel a city around me, even though no one knows where I am within it. There seems to be an atmosphere of people and unhappiness and the uninspired drabness of everyday life. I feel it as I feel the smoke in my lungs and the concrete under my feet. I sometimes think I can feel the tension and turmoil of a city as I fly over it 5,000 feet in the air."

In New York he met with members of the America First Committee. Some urged the holding of a last-ditch rally against Lend-Lease. Lindbergh had kept his distance from the committee, but he agreed to speak at the rally.

He and Anne attended a dinner of opponents of the war. "The table consisted of Roy and Mrs. Howard, Mrs. Howard's sister, Colonel and Mrs. Theodore Roosevelt"—son and daughter-in-law of the Rough Rider—"and a Mr. Parker of the *World-Telegram*. We spent most of the evening discussing the war and its accompanying trends and policies. Howard is a quick, able, and cautious man, with an exceptional knack for illustrating his conversation with typically American expressions. Howard's general policy seems to be to stay close enough to center so he will not be caught out, whichever way events turn. In this way he has the double advantage of safety and great influence over the mass of people who stay close to center in thought and action.

"I think his policy is wise, but personally I prefer the adventure and freedom of going as far from center as my thoughts, ideals, and convictions lead me. I do not like to be held back by the question of influencing the mass of people or by the desire for the utmost security. I must admit, and I have no apology to make for the fact, that I prefer adventure to security, freedom to popularity, and conviction to influence. I like to be in contact with the 'center,' and to use it as a base from which to organize, so to speak, but I prefer to spend most of my life and thought on the frontier—or occasionally somewhat beyond."

From New York he monitored events in Washington during the last days of the Lend-Lease campaign. "Phoned Senator Byrd to talk to him about the Lend-Lease bill. I asked what he thought Roosevelt actually had in mind in regard to our participation in the war. Byrd replied that he did not think Roosevelt wanted to get the country into the war, at least at this time, and that he himself (Byrd) felt it would be disastrous for us to intervene, but that the trouble was no one could tell when the President would change his mind. Byrd said Senator George (Chairman, Senate Foreign Relations Committee) was definitely opposed to intervention, but that Roosevelt had persuaded him that he actually intended to keep this country out of the war, and that he wished the Lend-Lease bill passed in order to help England negotiate a better peace than she could otherwise obtain—'a sixty per cent peace instead of a forty per cent peace,' according to what Byrd said George said Roosevelt told him."

The America First Committee canceled plans for the Washington rally, effectively conceding defeat in the fight against Lend-Lease.

THE VOTE ON the measure was much as expected. After two months of hearings and debate, the House approved Lend-Lease by a margin of 260 to 165 and the Senate by 60 to 31.

Roosevelt took a victory lap at a dinner of the White House Correspondents' Association. To be sure, Americans had argued over the arms-for-democracy program, he said, but that's what democracies did. Then they voted, as democracies did, and they came to a decision. "The decisions of our democracy may be slowly arrived at. But when that decision is made, it is proclaimed not with the voice of any one man but with the voice of one hundred and thirty millions. It is binding on us all. And the world is no longer left in doubt." The reporters hosting the dinner always wanted a story; Roosevelt served it up to them. "The big news story of this week is this: The world has been told that we, as a united nation, realize the danger that confronts us, and that to meet that danger our democracy has gone into action."

The dictators underestimated democracy—its resourcefulness, its resilience, its determination. They thought they could eliminate democracy. They were wrong. "The enemies of democracy were wrong in their calculations for a very simple reason," Roosevelt said. "They were wrong because they believed that democracy could not adjust itself to the terrible reality of a world at war. They believed that democracy, because of its profound respect for the rights of man, would never arm itself to fight. They believed that democracy, because of its will to live at peace with its neighbors, could not mobilize its energies even in its own defense." The recent vote had revealed their fundamental mistake. "They know now that democracy can still remain democracy, and speak, and reach conclusions, and arm itself adequately for defense."

Roosevelt looked beyond the reporters to Americans at large. They had a big job before them. "I must tell you tonight in plain language what this undertaking means to you—to you in your daily life," he said. "Whether you are in the armed services, whether you are a steel worker or a stevedore, a machinist or a housewife, a farmer or a banker, a storekeeper or a manufacturer—to all of you it will mean sacrifice in behalf of your country and your liberties. Yes, you will feel the impact of this gigantic effort in your daily lives. You will feel it in a way that will cause, to you, many inconveniences. You will have to be content with lower profits, lower profits from business, because obviously your taxes will be higher. You will have to work longer at your bench, or your plow, or your machine, or your desk."

Roosevelt drew a distinction. "Let me make it clear that the nation is calling for the sacrifice of some privileges, not for the sacrifice of fundamental rights. And most of us will do it willingly. That kind of sacrifice is for the common national protection and welfare; for our defense against the most ruthless brutality in all history; for the ultimate victory of a way of life now so violently menaced."

Roosevelt asked for unity and loyalty. "There will be no divisions of party or section or race or nationality or religion," he said. The vote in Congress reflected the national will. "This will of the American people will not be frustrated, either by threats from powerful enemies abroad or by small, selfish groups or individuals at home."

The task ahead was great, yet it was necessary. And it would redound to America's glory. "Never in all our history have Americans faced a job so well worthwhile. May it be said of us in the days to come that our children and our children's children rise up and call us blessed."

55

I N T H E W A K E of the defeat on Lend-Lease, Lindbergh traveled
to Florida with Anne for a winter vacation. "Thank God we
have no newspapers to read and no radio to listen to," he wrote
in his journal. They just missed crossing paths with Roosevelt, who
took his own trip to Florida, to sit in the sun aboard the presidential
yacht *Potomac* and to bask in the glow of victory on the latest war
measure.

The holiday recharged Lindbergh. The train from Florida deposited the Lindberghs in New York. He took a cab to the garage where
he had left the car. "One of the men there recognized me and came
up to say he had read my 'Letter to Americans' in *Collier's*"—which
had published what the *Saturday Evening Post* declined—"and thoroughly agreed with my stand. Said a lot of other men around there
did also."

"Ed Webster came for lunch," Lindbergh recorded on March 30.
Webster represented the America First Committee. "He wants me to
take the national chairmanship of America First. Says I will receive a
letter from General Wood shortly, asking me to do this." Lindbergh
put Webster off. "I told Webster I would gladly work with America
First and assist the committee in any way possible, but that I felt it
would be a mistake for me to take the national chairmanship at this
time, if at all. I told him that if I took the national chairmanship,
I would have to give up the type of work I am now doing, that I
could not write and make addresses on the war and at the same time
carry on the executive duties that would be required. After I out-

lined my reasons Webster agreed and suggested I take the honorary chairmanship or some other office. I told him I would consider that, but I felt it would probably be enough for me to join the national committee—that I could do as much in that capacity as in any other."

The Wood letter arrived, and Lindbergh set it aside. Other letters arrived too. Lindbergh had lunch with two *Collier's* editors. "They said the mail they received in regard to my 'Letter to Americans' was possibly the largest they had ever received concerning a *Collier's* article. The mail addressed to *Collier's* was, they said, about two to one in support of their publishing the article; while the mail addressed directly to me was nearly twenty to one in support of the article itself."

He drove to New York to speak with General Wood. "We discussed America First and his letter asking me to replace him as chairman. I told him I thought it would weaken the organization greatly if he resigned as chairman, and I outlined my objections to taking the chairmanship myself." Yet Lindbergh did agree to add his name to the committee.

This had to be handled carefully. Squabbles over tactics had vexed the committee and were breaking into the open after the defeat on Lend-Lease. Lindbergh was reminded why he didn't like committees, though he didn't change his mind about joining. "It is essential not to have the announcement of my membership in the committee coincide with the outbreak of internal trouble," he noted. "Our opposition would be only too quick to make use of such a situation." He had his own reputation to consider as well. "I decided to feel my way slowly in regard to the America First connection—to burn no bridges unnecessarily."

Lindbergh agreed to address an America First rally in Chicago, still the center of antiwar sentiment. He swung south to Washington en route to the Midwest. He met with Harry Byrd. "We discussed the war and trends in this country," Lindbergh wrote. "Byrd thinks the trend is away from intervention; says the people are at last seeing the futility of our entering the war." Lindbergh hoped he was right.

Chicago seemed a different world than Washington and New York. "Arrived at auditorium at 8:00. Songs. Then General Wood introduced Mr. Pettengill"—Samuel Pettengill, former congressman from Indiana—"who made a forceful but slightly too long extemporaneous speech. General Hammond"—Thomas Hammond, business leader and head of the Chicago chapter of America First—"spoke next. Then General Wood introduced me, and I spoke for about twenty-five minutes. Well received; enthusiastic crowd. Had expected considerable opposition, but there was practically none. (In fact, I had thought there might be some fighting and was surprised by the orderliness of the crowd. Was also surprised by the amount of anti-British feeling in Chicago.) The hall was jammed—crowd estimated at 10,000 to 11,000 inside and about 4,000 outside."

56

THE DEFEAT OF Lindbergh and the opponents of war on the issue of arming Britain was a boon in one respect. It clarified the issue at the heart of the whole debate: whether the United States would join the European war. Roosevelt and the interventionists were still saying they aimed to keep America out of the war, but every time the president declared that Nazism could not allow democracy to survive, he strengthened the case for direct American involvement. No one thought Britain could invade the European continent and defeat Germany alone, and Roosevelt was ruling out a negotiated peace. Ergo, American involvement was nearly inevitable.

The success of the Chicago rally prompted the America First Committee to take their campaign to the heart of enemy territory: New York. Lindbergh agreed to headline a rally there.

The news that he would be speaking stirred passions in the great city. Supporters showed up early outside the Manhattan Center on Thirty-fourth Street to get a glimpse and give a cheer. Lindbergh's opponents appeared in comparable numbers, to denounce the fifth columnist friend of Hitler and show his backers that the city wasn't big enough for both views. Police struggled to keep the two groups apart. Observers wondered if the war wasn't already coming to America.

"There are many viewpoints from which the issues of this war can be argued," Lindbergh began. "Some are primarily idealistic. Some are primarily practical." A sound policy would balance the two. "But since the subjects that can be covered in a single address are limited, tonight I shall discuss the war from a viewpoint which is primarily practical. It is not that I believe ideals are unimportant, even among the realities of war; but if a nation is to survive in a hostile world, its ideals must be backed by the hard logic of military practicability."

Hard truths were unpopular, yet they had to be told. "I will be severely criticized by the interventionists in America when I say we should not enter a war unless we have a reasonable chance of winning," Lindbergh predicted. "That, they will claim, is far too materialistic a viewpoint." But the critics' argument was what had led to the defeat of France, which declared a war it wasn't ready to fight. America must not follow the French example. "I do not believe that our American ideals, and our way of life, will gain through an unsuccessful war. And I know that the United States is not prepared to wage war in Europe successfully at this time. We are no better prepared today than France was when the interventionists in Europe persuaded her to attack the Siegfried Line."

The idealists were preparing a cataclysm. "I have said before, and I will say again, that I believe it will be a tragedy to the entire world if the British Empire collapses. That is one of the main reasons why I opposed this war before it was declared, and why I have constantly advocated a negotiated peace. I did not feel that England and France had a reasonable chance of winning. France has now been defeated; and, despite the propaganda and confusion of recent months, it is now obvious that England is losing the war. I believe this is realized even by the British government. But they have one last desperate plan remaining. They hope that they may be able to persuade us to send another American Expeditionary Force to Europe."

Lindbergh didn't blame the British for hoping for an American rescue. He didn't even fault them for overstating their case in pleading for help. But America was not Britain, and Americans didn't have to believe everything the British said. "We in this country have a right to think of the welfare of America first, just as the people in England thought first of their own country when they encouraged the smaller nations of Europe to fight against hopeless odds. When England asks us to enter this war, she is considering her own future, and that of her empire. In making our reply, I believe we should consider the future of the United States and that of the Western Hemisphere."

Americans had the obligation to themselves and their children to weigh the practicality of involvement in Britain's war. "I have attempted to do this, especially from the standpoint of aviation," Lindbergh said. "And I have been forced to the conclusion that we cannot win this war for England, regardless of how much assistance we extend."

Lindbergh asked his listeners to imagine the map of Europe. "See if you can suggest any way in which we could win this war if we entered it. Suppose we had a large army in America, trained and equipped. Where would we send it to fight? The campaigns of the war show only too clearly how difficult it is to force a landing, or to maintain an army, on a hostile coast. Suppose we took our navy from the Pacific, and used it to convoy British shipping. That would not win the war for England. It would, at best, permit her to exist under the constant bombing of the German air fleet." The fundamental problem was geographic. "I do not see how we could invade the continent of Europe successfully as long as all of that continent and most of Asia is under Axis domination."

The war party complained that merely making this argument was intolerable. "The interventionists shout that we are defeatists, that we are undermining the principles of democracy, and that we are giving comfort to Germany by talking about our military weakness," Lindbergh said. But the Germans and the Japanese had intelligence officers who read American newspapers and monitored congressional hearings. "Our military position is well known to the governments of Europe and Asia. Why, then, should it not be brought to the attention of our own people?"

Lindbergh threw the charge of aiding the enemy back at the war party. "I say it is the interventionist in America, as it was in England and in France, who gives comfort to the enemy. I say it is they who are undermining the principles of democracy when they demand that we take a course to which more than eighty percent of our citizens are opposed. I charge them with being the real defeatists, for their policy has led to the defeat of every country that followed their advice since this war began." The interventionists would produce an American defeat if not resisted. "There is no shorter road to defeat than by entering a war with inadequate preparation." And war was surely at the end of the road down which the interventionists were taking the country.

The battle over intervention had merely started, Lindbergh said. America's fate had yet to be written. That fate lay with Lindbergh's listeners. "The time has come when those of us who believe in an independent American destiny must band together, and organize for strength. We have been led toward war by a minority of our people. This minority has power. It has influence. It has a loud voice. But it does not represent the American people."

Lindbergh shared some personal experience. "During the last several years, I have traveled over this country, from one end to the other. I have talked to many hundreds of men and women, and I have had letters from tens of thousands more, who feel the same way as you and I. Most of these people have no influence or power. Most of them have no means of expressing their convictions, except by their vote, which has always been against this war. They are the citizens who have had to work too hard at their daily jobs to organize political meetings." They voted, but the candidates they voted for forgot the promises they had made in the campaigns.

These honest, independent Americans must take back their country from the small groups who controlled the newspapers and radio stations and newsreels. Peril impended but disaster wasn't inevitable. Speaking to the ordinary people of the country, Lindbergh closed: "We ask you to share our faith in the ability of this nation to defend itself, to develop its own civilization, and to contribute to the progress of mankind in a more constructive and intelligent way than has yet been found by the warring nations of Europe. We need your support, and we need it now."

57

ROOSEVELT ONCE MORE refused to dignify Lindbergh's remarks with a direct response. But the next day the president's secretaries of war and navy—Henry Stimson and Frank Knox—gave major addresses rebutting Lindbergh's argument and affirming Lend-Lease.

Roosevelt himself held a press conference. "Mr. President, the newspapers this morning generally seem to regard these speeches as indicating that it may soon be necessary to resort to an extended use of the navy in protecting the 'bridge of ships,'" one reporter said. The term had come into use to describe the transport of goods to Europe under Lend-Lease. The issue was whether American warships would guard the civilian vessels in their passage. "Would you consider that a fair interpretation of the speeches?"

Roosevelt dodged the question. "I don't think that we had better talk about interpretations," he said. He filibustered. "I think we had better confine ourselves to facts, and I am sorry, but I have to make a liar out of a lot of people, some of them in this room. I will tell you how. In September 1939, about a year and a half ago, the whole subject of hemisphere defense came up, as we know. And at that time, because of the conditions surrounding the outbreak of the war—in other words, a complete failure to adhere to international law, a surprise invasion, which was followed by other surprise attacks on peaceful nations—at that time there was instituted by the Western Hemisphere what is known as a patrol, and that patrol extended on all sides of the hemisphere as necessary at the time. Of course, nobody here knows geography. People said it was 300 miles offshore. It wasn't. It was a patrol that was carried out partly by the American navy, partly by other American ships, off what was then considered a reasonable limit, depending on where it was. A lot of very careless people called it 300 miles. If you went over to the eastern shore of Maryland, you would have found for the past year and a half that that patrol was extended a thousand miles out to sea at that point. It was maintained as a patrol for such distances as seemed advisable, in view of the conditions at the time. That patrol has been extended from time to time in different places. Some places it has been pulled in, depending entirely on the conditions and the locations on any given duty. That was a patrol. It was not a convoy."

Finally Roosevelt had reached the question the reporter had asked. Would American warships convoy the cargo vessels across the Atlantic? The president appeared to be saying no.

Or maybe he was saying yes. "I think some of you know what a horse looks like," Roosevelt continued. "I think you also know what a cow looks like. If, by calling a cow a horse for a year and a half, you think that that makes the cow a horse, I don't think so. Now, that's pretty plain language. You can't turn a cow into a horse by calling it something else, calling it a horse; it is still a cow. Now this is a patrol, and has been a patrol for a year and a half, still is, and from time to time it has been extended, and is being extended, and will be extended—the patrol for the safety of the Western Hemisphere."

Lindbergh's emphasis on hemispheric defense had sunk in; Roosevelt was claiming that the navy would be guarding the hemisphere rather than the ships going to Britain.

The reporters were skeptical. "Could you tell us, sir, how far it may possibly go?" one asked, referring to the patrol.

"That is exactly the question I hoped you would ask. As far on the waters of the seven seas as may be necessary for the defense of the American hemisphere."

"Will there be any extension of its functions?"

"No, no."

"Could you define its functions?"

"Its function is protection of the American hemisphere."

"By belligerent means?" Would American warships fire on German vessels?

"Protection of the American hemisphere."

"Mr. President, does that include the protection of shipping, that is—"

"Protection of the American hemisphere."

"Mr. President, just what—"

"Just what? What do you mean, just what? The point of it is the protection of the American hemisphere, and it will be so used as it has been for the past year and a half. Now I can't tell you what is going to happen."

"Mr. President, can you tell us the difference between a patrol and a convoy?"

"You know the difference between a cow and a horse?"

"Yes, I know the difference."

"All right, there is just as much difference. Just exactly as much difference."

The reporters still weren't buying. Roosevelt offered another analogy. "I was talking to one of the senators over the telephone today. He happened to come from the West, and it's rather a good simile. In the old days a wagon train across the plains—of course it had its immediate guard around it, that was perfectly true—but it didn't go across the plains unless it got reports from a long ways—200 to 300 miles—off. It was not felt safe to wait until the Indians got two miles away before you saw them. It was advisable, if possible, to find out if the Indians were 200 miles away."

"Mr. President, if this patrol should discover some apparently aggressive ships headed toward the Western Hemisphere, what would it do about it?"

"Let me know."

The reporters laughed. Roosevelt smiled too, pleased to take some of the testiness out of the air.

But one reporter wouldn't let him off. "Mr. President, has this government any idea of escorting convoys?"

"No, no," Roosevelt said. He smiled again, sardonically this time. "That, I am afraid, will be awfully bad news to some of you." He knew the reporters wanted him to say there would be convoys; then they would have a story.

"Mr. President, are we doing anything special, with any—"

"Just an extension. After all, it's just what has been going on for a year and a half. Now, that will answer all your questions."

OF COURSE IT didn't. And Roosevelt in fact had something more to say. Without naming Lindbergh, he denounced "this mythical person in our midst who takes the attitude that dictatorships are going to win anyway," who said, "We have got to do the best we can. We have got to make our peace."

The reporters knew he was talking about Lindbergh. One asked, "Mr. President, how is it that the army, which needs now distinguished fliers, etc., has not asked Colonel Lindbergh to rejoin his rank as colonel? If I am not mistaken, I think he is still on the reserve list."

"I don't know," Roosevelt said. He recited more history. "If you go back to the roster of the army in the Civil War, we called on liberty-loving people on both sides—both the Confederates and the North—and from outside this country we had people fighting for us because they believed in it. On the other hand, the Confederacy and the North let certain people go. In other words, in both armies there were—what shall I call them?—there were Vallandighams"— referring to Clement Vallandigham of Ohio, a prominent Confederate sympathizer, or Copperhead. "Well, Vallandigham, as you know, was an appeaser. He wanted to make peace from 1863 on because the North 'couldn't win.'" Roosevelt reached deeper. "Once upon a time there was a place called Valley Forge and there were an awful lot of appeasers that pleaded with Washington to quit, because he 'couldn't win.' Just because he 'couldn't win.' See what Tom Paine said at that time in favor of Washington keeping on fighting! It's worth reading."

"Wasn't it 'These are the times that try men's souls'?"

"Yes, that particular paragraph."

Two questions later a reporter wanted to be clear about Roosevelt's reference to Vallandigham and the appeasers at Valley Forge. "Were you still talking about Mr. Lindbergh?"

"Yes."

58

"LYMAN PHONED IN the late afternoon to tell me that Roosevelt had attacked me personally in his press conference," Lindbergh wrote. "A few minutes later Webster phoned and said that, among other things, Roosevelt had implied treason in connection with my name. I sent for the afternoon papers. The President's attack was more than just a political attack, for he did so in connection with my commission in the Army. If it had been only a political attack, without any connection with my commission, I would pay little attention to it. As it is, a point of honor is at stake, and it may be necessary to tender my resignation." Despite his earlier offer to Hap Arnold to resign, Lindbergh remained in the air corps reserve. Once he had concluded that Arnold wasn't being blamed for his—Lindbergh's—criticism of administration policy, he decided not to sacrifice his commission to Roosevelt's deviousness. The president's attack in the press conference compelled another reconsideration. Now he might have to resign out of self-respect. But he wouldn't do so lightly. "My commission in the Air Corps has always meant a great deal to me, and I would prefer to hold it."

Lindbergh reflected on the position he'd gotten himself into. "What luck it is to find myself opposing my country's entrance into a war I *don't* believe in, when I would so much rather be fighting for my country in a war I *do* believe in. Here I am stumping the country with pacifists and considering resigning as a colonel in the Army Air Corps, when there is no philosophy I disagree with more than that of the pacifist, and nothing I would rather be doing than flying in the Air Corps. If only the United States could be on the *right* side of an intelligent war!"

He wondered if the campaign against the war was worth the effort he continued to put into it. "Sometimes I feel like saying, 'Well, let's get into the war if you are so anxious to. Then the responsibility will be yours.' In comparison to the work I am now doing the fighting would be fun. But my mind tells me that we'd better face our problems and let Europe face hers without getting messed up in this war. I have an interest in Western civilization, and I have an interest in my race, or culture, or whatever you want to call it, and I have an interest in the type of world my children are going to live in.

"That is why I will probably stay on the stump with the pacifists and why I will resign my commission if necessary and never regret my action in doing so. This war is a mistake; we will only bring disaster if we enter it; we will do no good either to Europe or ourselves, and therefore I am going to put everything I have behind staying out."

Europe's fate was the result of Europe's folly. "No one, not even Germany, was more responsible for the conditions which caused this war than England and France. They declared the war without consulting us. If it were possible to help them win, the result would probably be Versailles all over again. Europe must straighten out her own family affairs. Our interference would simply cause another postponement, as the last war did. Europe faces adjustments that must be made, and only she can work out what they are going to be."

Lindbergh traveled to Washington to discuss resignation with Truman Smith and other friends in the army. While there he visited Missouri's Champ Clark. "He is just back from a speaking tour through the Southwest. Says sentiment is rising against war, but 'no one knows what Roosevelt will do next.'"

He decided resignation was the only honorable option. "If I did not tender my resignation, I would lose something in my own character that means even more to me than my commission in the Air Corps. No one else might know it, but I would. And if I take this insult from Roosevelt, more, and worse, will probably be forthcoming."

"My dear Mr. President," wrote Lindbergh in a letter he released to the press. "Your remarks at the White House press conference on April 25 involving my reserve commission in the United States Army Air Corps have of course disturbed me greatly. I had hoped that I might exercise my right as an American citizen to place my viewpoint before the people of my country in time of peace without giving up the privilege of serving my country as an Air Corps officer in the event of war. But since you, in your capacity as President of the United States and Commander in Chief of the Army, have clearly implied that I am no longer of use to this country as a reserve officer, and in view of other implications that you, my President and superior officer, have made concerning my loyalty to my country, my character, and my motives, I can see no honorable alternative to tendering my resignation as colonel in the United States Army Air Corps Reserve. I am, therefore, forwarding my resignation to the Secretary of War.

"I take this action with the utmost regret, for my relationship with the Air Corps is one of the things that have meant most to me in life. I place it second only to my right as a citizen to speak freely to my fellow countrymen, and to discuss with them the issues of war and peace which confront our nation in this crisis.

"I will continue to serve my country to the best of my ability as a private citizen.

"Respectfully, Charles A. Lindbergh."

59

BURTON WHEELER CAME to Lindbergh's defense against Roosevelt. "To smear is beneath the dignity of the President of the United States," said the Montana Republican. "And for anyone to attack Colonel Charles A. Lindbergh as a Copperhead is shocking and appalling to every right-thinking American." Speaking to an America First meeting in Chicago, Wheeler said Roosevelt's rejection of the idea of a negotiated peace raised the specter of the "total annihilation of our magnificent modern civilization." He added, "The whole policy of Franklin D. Roosevelt has been to ignore and to destroy the neutrality of the United States, until today this nation is not neutral; it has become a nonbelligerent poised on the brink of war." Wheeler added, for good measure, "We are rushing down the road to war and dictatorship."

Gerald Nye echoed Wheeler's sentiments. "Col. Charles Lindbergh offers a direct and clean-cut appeal for some consideration for America in this hour when we are being marched to war by an organized minority of interventionists," the North Dakota senator said. "None undertake to answer the arguments of Col. Lindbergh, but columnists and the President proceed with an effort to tear him limb from limb as a rank 'Copperhead' for his brilliant exercise of his right as an American to freedom of speech."

Charles Tobey, a Republican senator from New Hampshire, likewise supported Lindbergh against Roosevelt. "Shame on any man—president, senator or rank and file—who tried to deny another man the right of free speech. Is this free America? We'd better sing 'God

Save America' instead of 'God Bless America' if the Constitution is to prevail."

"READ DOSTOEVSKY IN the evening," Lindbergh wrote in his journal. During the day he prepared for an antiwar rally in St. Louis; after hours he escaped into literature. "Certainly the Russian has a viewpoint on life far different from that of the Central and Western European. Possibly one should consider the Russian as midway between the European and the Oriental. We do not expect to understand the outlook of the Oriental, but the Russian is sufficiently European to mislead us. We always expect to understand him better than we do."

Yet he could escape only so long. "The pressure for war is high and mounting. The people are opposed to it, but the Administration seems to have 'the bit in its teeth' and hell-bent on its way to war. Most of the Jewish interests in the country are behind war, and they control a huge part of our press and radio and most of our motion pictures. There are also the 'intellectuals,' and the 'Anglophiles,' and the British agents who are allowed free rein, the international financial interests, and many others."

Lindbergh told his St. Louis audience how he had warned the British, years before the war, against the German peril they faced. "The prime minister"—Stanley Baldwin—"was very courteous, but he changed the subject immediately. Time and again, whenever the opportunity arose, I talked to members of the British government about military aviation in Europe. They were always courteous, but seldom impressed."

Now America was being asked to rescue Britain from its refusal to face reality. Lindbergh shook his head in dismay. "Why must our people be divided over this question of European war?" Americans had all they needed at home. "We have every geographical advantage for defense. We have unlimited natural resources. We have the most highly organized industry in the world."

He paused. "And we have another advantage in defending our country—the most important of all. It is unity of purpose. Every true American is ready to fight to preserve our nation. Every one of us is ready to lay down his life if necessary for the defense of America. On questions of defense, our strength is multiplied by the unity among us. It is only when we are told that our destiny lies in Europe, in Asia, in the Suez, in Singapore or in Dakar, that we divide."

Lindbergh said he would rather still be in the air corps, flying for his country, than giving lectures and radio addresses. "Those of us who are arguing against the war have nothing to gain except the welfare of our country. We speak only from the depths of our conviction. Most of us desire nothing more than to return to our private lives and occupations. But we know that this nation is being led into a major disaster and we would be poor Americans if we stood quietly by without even raising our voices in opposition."

Lindbergh was pleased by the St. Louis turnout. "There were about 15,000 people present, although the meeting had not been well advertised," he noted afterward. "We had a fine and enthusiastic crowd." What happened later was less agreeable. "Hundreds of people—all types. Shook hands until train time. There are few things I dislike more than shaking hands with an endless line of people. Your hand gets sore, and everybody says silly things because there isn't time to speak sensibly. You get hot and packed in with people who are also hot and tired." He supposed the flesh-pressing came with the cause. "Possibly it will bring money and support to the St. Louis America First chapter; if so, it was probably worth while attending. But if it weren't for the intensity of my feeling about this war, no amount of money, or persuasion, or anything else, could get me to attend such things."

HIS NEXT APPEARANCE was scheduled for Minneapolis. He took a midnight train to Chicago. He stayed in the suburbs of that city and had a chance for a walk at the edge of development. "I suddenly realized that the fields had a very familiar appearance. And then I remembered that these were the fields, or rather just like the fields outside of Detroit, that my grandfather took me to on Sundays when I was a child. It all came back so clearly it seemed he was there beside me, that if I turned my head he would be there, walking along with his paper bag for mushrooms in one hand and a bunch of wild flowers in the other. I imagined for a moment it was really thirty years ago and that all that had happened in between was just a dream. And it seemed I saw through childish eyes again. We were among the fields of Seven Mile Road (it is all built up now) on a Sunday morning, walking on the spring-green grass. Now we were passing through an open gate and into a tree-filled pasture. There were patches of wake-robins and dandelions, and here and there a few jack-in-the-pulpits. The roots of the oaks were lost in violets. Two wild ducks flew up from one of the pools left over from a recent rain. My feet sank into the damp dead leaves and mold as I crossed its edge. A turtle slipped into the water from a fallen branch, and a frightened rabbit hopped away into the wood."

His commercial flight to Minneapolis summoned a different nostalgia. "It is strange to me, this flying as a passenger in a modern transport—nothing to do and rather unpleasantly screened from the outside air and the ground below. It has none of the 'feel' of flying that I have always loved so much." Ah, for the old days. "It is the very contact it used to have with the elements that made flying in those early planes such an attraction for me." The present suffered badly by comparison. "Riding in a modern transport plane is strangely like riding the train in a subway. In an aisle seat you see and feel about as much in the one as in the other."

Members of the local America First chapter met him at the airport and took him to his hotel. "I was given the 'Nordic Suite'!" he wrote. "What a press story that could make!" But only if the reporters were from the East or someplace similarly distant. "'Nordic' out here doesn't mean what it does in the East. In Minnesota the word 'Nordic' has no anti-Semitic tint. And the situation is probably saved because, as I learned soon after arrival, Lord Halifax and his party stayed in this same suite and left only yesterday." The British ambassador had sought to preempt and neutralize Lindbergh's message.

The response at the rally made him think he was doing good work. Ten thousand people filled the hall and thousands more stood outside. "The people seemed to be one hundred percent behind our stand on the war," Lindbergh wrote. "As I go around to these meetings I feel that, without question, if this country is run by the people, we will not enter this war."

Yet the interests never rested. "I know that tomorrow, or the day after, as I read the misinformation and propaganda in our newspapers, I will begin to wonder whether the people can withstand such a barrage indefinitely. And even if they can withstand it, will popular opinion be enough to keep us out of the war? Which is stronger, the money and power and propaganda pushing us into war, or the will of the people to stay out?"

Minnesota was his boyhood home and the political home of his father; Lindbergh made the connection for his audience. "The greatest satisfaction I have had at any of these meetings lay in the applause I received when I spoke of my father tonight. People are beginning to appreciate his vision and his courage."

Some who had known his father saw a chip off the family block. "Mr. Appel took me over to a corner of the room and told me he hoped I would consider moving back to Minnesota and run for Senator!" Lindbergh declined, to little effect. "I tried to tell him I was not cut out to be a politician, that I was not suited for political work by training, experience, or inclination, and that I was appearing on public platforms now only because we were in a wartime emergency and because I felt so strongly we should not enter the war that I could not in justice to my own conscience remain inactive. But I could make no impression in the few minutes we had without interruption. Mr. Appel thought I was giving him nothing but a clever political 'front'! He replied that I was taking exactly the right attitude at this time and that it would be inadvisable to let people know I had my eye on political office until a later date!!"

Politics pursued him. Even his friends conspired against his peace of mind. "Some of my friends are already saying I must enter politics permanently and eventually run for office," Lindbergh wrote. "They say I cannot avoid it, that I will find myself pushed into it."

Lindbergh disagreed. "I *can* avoid it, and I can do it by making one address, or by writing one article, in which I discuss truthfully and openly the fundamental issues which face this country today."

IN NEW YORK, Lindbergh took part in the largest antiwar rally to date. Twenty-two thousand people filled Madison Square Garden to hear speeches by Lindbergh, Burton Wheeler and others. Wheeler lavished praise on Lindbergh. "No man has served the United States more intelligently, more courageously, and more effectively," he said. "Upon him the warmongers have turned their scorn and abuse. But he has continued the fight of peace and democracy. To Colonel Lindbergh I say: The greatest eventual glory comes not from wars won or lost but from wars prevented."

The Montanan aimed to assist the gallant quest. "I speak to you tonight not as a Democrat, not as a Republican, but as a plain ordinary citizen who is deeply interested in this country of ours. I am here to urge you to muster the courage to fight as you have never fought before—to fight to save your sons from the bloody battlefields of Europe, Asia and Africa—to fight against one-man government in the United States." The world had too many one-man governments already. "I hate one-man government. I was denouncing Mussolini when Churchill was saying in 1927, 'If I were an Italian I would be a Fascist.' I was denouncing Hitler when Lord Halifax was shooting wild boar with Goering in Germany."

Wheeler had recently been traveling across America. One sentiment stood out, he said. "The American people are firmly resolved to avoid this war." Polls might suggest that the American public would approve American convoys across the Atlantic. "But if I know anything of public sentiment or the temper of the American people, I fear the fate of those who would take them into the hell of war today."

Wheeler professed affection for the British. "No blood but English blood flows through the veins of any of my family," he said. "I greatly admire the English. Unlike us, they have never been guilty of being sentimental suckers. Lord Palmerston said, I quote: 'England has no eternal enmities and no eternal friendships. She has only interests.' An Englishman, my friends, wherever you may find him, loves England first. And I only wish there were more Americans in the United States of America that loved America first."

Wheeler derided the alarmists who said that Britain was America's last defense against Nazi conquest. "Our warmakers in frightened tones and with a tremor in their voice pose the question, 'What if Germany seized the British fleet?' They imply all would be lost. They suggest that we would suffer an immediate invasion—that Panzer divisions would roll down Broadway and that parachutists would be landing in Montana. How fantastic!" Had the fearmongers no faith in their own country? "We are no small, trembling nation. We are strong and growing stronger. We are mighty and becoming mightier." Who *were* these defeatists? "Those who parade as Americans but who tell us that we are dependent upon the British navy are unworthy of the name of American."

The fearmongers had a second lament, that America would be economically marooned in a Nazi world. This was equally absurd. "Have faith in American industry, in American labor, in American business and in American genius," Wheeler said. "Free American industry is superior to controlled Nazi industry, free American workers can produce more than Nazi slaves, and I know that American business men can compete anywhere in the world."

Wheeler confessed to one fear. "I am afraid that if President Roosevelt repudiates his election promise not to take us into a foreign war, the American people will lose faith not only in their president but in their form of government," he said. "I am afraid that if the president accepts the advice of that little coterie who surround him, most of whom have never faced an electorate or met a payroll or tried a lawsuit, and many of whom are impractical dreamers, he will wage an undeclared war. And then constitutional government in the United States will be at an end."

60

ROOSEVELT IGNORED WHAT Lindbergh, Wheeler and the America Firsters demanded. Far from seeking peace, he pushed the country closer to war.

His tone was serious, even stern, as he spoke from the White House by radio. America faced problems greater than almost any in its history, he said. "We cannot afford to approach them from the point of view of wishful thinkers or sentimentalists. What we face is cold, hard fact."

The first and most fundamental fact threatened America's very existence. "What started as a European war has developed, as the Nazis always intended it should develop, into a world war for world domination," Roosevelt said. "Adolf Hitler never considered the domination of Europe as an end in itself. European conquest was but a step toward ultimate goals in all the other continents. It is unmistakably apparent to all of us that, unless the advance of Hitlerism is forcibly checked now, the Western Hemisphere will be within range of the Nazi weapons of destruction."

Roosevelt described what his administration had done to deal with the Nazi threat. "First, we have joined in concluding a series of agreements with all the other American Republics. This further solidified our hemisphere against the common danger." In fact, Roosevelt was speaking in the presence of the governing board of the Pan American Union.

"And then a year ago we launched, and are successfully carrying out, the largest armament production program we have ever undertaken." The army and the navy were stronger than they had ever been, and they were getting stronger by the month.

"We instituted a policy of aid for the democracies, the nations which have fought for the continuation of human liberties." This began with the repeal of the arms embargo. It continued with the swap of American destroyers for British bases. It produced the Lend-Lease Act and the appropriations to fund that measure.

The necessary work went on. So it must, for there was no compromise with the Nazi war machine. "Your government knows what terms Hitler, if victorious, would impose," Roosevelt said. "Under those terms, Germany would literally parcel out the world—hoisting the swastika itself over vast territories and populations, and setting up puppet governments of its own choosing, wholly subject to the will and the policy of a conqueror."

Nazi troops wouldn't need to occupy all the subject countries. "Quislings would be found to subvert the governments in our republics; and the Nazis would back their fifth columns with invasion, if necessary." This was no theoretical peril, Roosevelt insisted. "I am not speculating about all this. I merely repeat what is already in the Nazi book of world conquest. They plan to treat the Latin American nations as they are now treating the Balkans." German troops, coordinating with Italian forces, had recently invaded and occupied Yugoslavia and Greece. "They plan then to strangle the United States of America and the Dominion of Canada."

Americans would be forced to bow to their new masters. "The American laborer would have to compete with slave labor in the rest of the world. Minimum wages, maximum hours? Nonsense! Wages and hours would be fixed by Hitler. The dignity and power and standard of living of the American worker and farmer would be gone. Trade unions would become historical relics, and collective bargaining a joke. Farm income? What happens to all farm surpluses without any foreign trade? The American farmer would get for his products exactly what Hitler wanted to give. The farmer would face obvious disaster and complete regimentation. Tariff walls—Chinese walls of isolation—would be futile. Freedom to trade is essential to our economic life. We do not eat all the food we can produce; and we do not burn all the oil we can pump; we do not use all the goods we can manufacture. It would not be an American wall to keep Nazi goods out; it would be a Nazi wall to keep us in."

Such would be America's fate if Hitler survived. Such would ensue were the admonitions of American appeasers followed. Such, Roosevelt said, was what he and his administration had vowed to prevent. "We do not accept, we will not permit, this Nazi 'shape of things to come.' It will never be forced upon us, if we act in this present crisis with the wisdom and the courage which have distinguished our country in all the crises of the past."

Roosevelt announced new measures to avert this grim destiny. "First, we shall actively resist wherever necessary, and with all our resources, every attempt by Hitler to extend his Nazi domination to the Western Hemisphere, or to threaten it. We shall actively resist his every attempt to gain control of the seas. We insist upon the vital importance of keeping Hitlerism away from any point in the world which could be used or would be used as a base of attack against the Americas.

"Second, from the point of view of strict naval and military necessity, we shall give every possible assistance to Britain and to all who, with Britain, are resisting Hitlerism or its equivalent with force of arms. Our patrols are helping now to insure delivery of the needed supplies to Britain. All additional measures necessary to deliver the goods will be taken. Any and all further methods or combination of methods, which can or should be utilized, are being devised by our military and naval technicians, who, with me, will work out and put into effect such new and additional safeguards as may be needed." Roosevelt was erasing any distinction, however strained or spurious, between patrols and convoys. America's navy would ensure the goods got through.

The American people must do their part. They must be constantly vigilant against "the enemies of democracy in our midst—the Bundists, the Fascists, and Communists, and every group devoted to bigotry and racial and religious intolerance," Roosevelt said. "It is no mere coincidence that all the arguments put forward by these enemies of democracy, all their attempts to confuse and divide our people and to destroy public confidence in our government, all their defeatist forebodings that Britain and democracy are already beaten, all their selfish promises that we can 'do business' with Hitler—all of these are but echoes of the words that have been poured out from the Axis bureaus of propaganda."

Loyalty was needed in this hour of danger. It would be the test of true Americans. "Your government has the right to expect of all citizens that they take part in the common work of our common defense—take loyal part from this moment forward," Roosevelt said. Loyal Americans would be given the tools to do their duty. "I have recently set up the machinery for civilian defense. It will rapidly organize, locality by locality. It will depend on the organized effort of men and women everywhere." Defense meant more than fighting by arms. "It means morale, civilian as well as military; it means using every available resource; it means enlarging every useful plant. It means the use of a greater American common sense in discarding rumor and distorted statement. It means recognizing, for what they are, racketeers and fifth columnists, who are the incendiary bombs in this country of the moment.

"Therefore," Roosevelt concluded, "with profound consciousness of my responsibilities to my countrymen and to my country's cause, I have tonight issued a proclamation that an unlimited national emergency exists and requires the strengthening of our defense to the extreme limit of our national power and authority."

61

ROOSEVELT'S SPEECH RIVETED America like nothing since his first fireside chat, amid the banking crisis of 1933. Baseball games on this May evening were halted so spectators could hear the president over the public address systems. Movie theaters announced that Roosevelt's message of war—as many expected—or peace or something between would be piped into the lobbies, causing the films to play to sparse crowds while the president spoke. At the Capitol Theater in Washington, actors paused mid-scene while a radio carried the address to the audience. Telephone companies reported that their wires fell silent during the forty-five minutes of Roosevelt's speech. The Associated Press operator in New York couldn't remember a time during his twenty-four years of service when his message board had been so quiet. Times Square was deserted, but walkers in the city could hear the speech coming from open doors and windows on the warm night.

Many of Roosevelt's listeners liked what he said. At the Capitol Theater the audience applauded the president's performance and burst into "God Bless America" at the end. A fireman in Washington told a roving reporter, "Boy, he's got the best ideas in the world, and ninety-five percent of the people will say the same." An electrician in the city agreed that it was a great speech. "I'll stick behind him," he said of Roosevelt.

Some had questions. "Does a national emergency mean anybody who says anything against the government will be thrown in jail?" asked a Washington cabdriver. "If so, I'm against it." But baker Myrtle Talbert wasn't concerned. "Everything he says is all right," she told the reporter.

The political classes were more discriminating. Most Democrats applauded the president. House Speaker Sam Rayburn of Texas praised Roosevelt's "very forceful and clear statement of the situation." "Superb," chimed Guy Gillette, senator from Iowa. But other Democrats worried. "The speech would be a good deal more reassuring to 130 million citizens of this country if he had left out that part about seeing that our supplies reached England," said Nevada's Senator Pat McCarran. "His statement that it is imperative to convoy is almost equal to a declaration of war, as far as the executive is concerned."

Republicans disliked what they heard. Hamilton Fish of New York said, "It was a typical Rooseveltian speech to promote further war hysteria and fear to break down the will of over 80 percent of the American people who are against involvement in European and Asiatic wars." Representative Melvin Maas of Minnesota said, "It sounds to me like an executive declaration of a war policy." Congressman William Lambertson of Kansas thought Roosevelt's remarks unworthy of America's highest official. "The president is surely scared to death of Hitler," Lambertson said.

"WE LISTENED TO Roosevelt's fireside chat in the evening," Lindbergh wrote. "His address was confusing and clever, as usual. He seemed somewhat held back—and, to me, he always sounds vindictive—but he ended by proclaiming a 'full national emergency.' What does a 'full national emergency' mean? What effect will it have on free speech and our America First meetings? I must find out exactly what is involved in this proclamation—and that requires specialized legal advice."

Lindbergh needed to know, for he was scheduled to speak in Philadelphia shortly. He consulted members of America First with legal and political experience. Philip La Follette was a former governor of Wisconsin and a son of Robert La Follette, an ardent opponent of American involvement in the World War. Amos Pinchot was a New York lawyer and longtime advocate of progressive causes. Neither man was unfamiliar with controversy or inclined to shy from it.

"It seems that Roosevelt's 'full national emergency' need not have much effect on our plans and meetings," Lindbergh wrote after speaking with La Follette and Pinchot. "Roosevelt's proclamation, as I thought, does not in any way limit our freedom of speech or our right to hold meetings. Of course, the interventionist groups will try to make people think it is unpatriotic for us to continue our opposition to war now that the President has said a full national emergency exists, and in view of the criticism he directed toward us in his speech. They will try to use this speech to silence us, while the prowar groups increase their propaganda with the encouragement of the administration."

Lindbergh sensed that the antiwar movement was approaching a moment of truth. "The next few days, during the formation of public attitude, will be critical for us. We must fight hard and intelligently. Much will depend on the reaction to my Philadelphia address, as it will be our first major America First meeting after Roosevelt's 'chat.' Much also depends on the reaction in Congress. Roosevelt seems hell-bent for war. If the country backs him in all of his 'steps' toward it, we may be shooting before many more weeks pass. If people have the courage to hold back, we may still be able to keep out. One of my greatest hopes is that the American public is slowly beginning to realize that a Roosevelt promise is not to be relied upon, and that what he says one month is often the reverse of what he says the next."

ROOSEVELT WAS INDEED difficult to pin down. Did the emergency declaration allow the convoying of supply ships to Europe? The president had said in his radio address that the convoy method of the previous war was outmoded. "Can you explain how the newer method is more effective?" a reporter asked.

"Well, I think probably that was explained last night," Roosevelt answered unhelpfully. He continued, "As you know, I mentioned other elements which came into the dangers of ocean shipping at the present time, not just the submarine but an improved submarine, and the raider and the aircraft. Understand, of course, the old convoy method didn't have those three things to contend with."

"You think it would be more than a patrol?"

"I don't think that it would be quite comparable in any way, as you know if you read last night's speech. It is a part of our policy to be quite certain, so far as we possibly can—for our patrols to know where any German submarine, plane or raider is on the ocean at any given time."

"Do you see any further need of extending the Atlantic patrol?"

"Well, that is like asking me where Destroyer 446 is at the present time. What is her latitude and longitude? I'm not going to tell you, even if I do know. I don't happen to know." Roosevelt laughed. The reporters did not join him. "In other words, that is purely a military and naval matter."

"Mr. President, could you tell us if naval patrol ships have been ordered to resort to any new measures, as yet, beyond signaling?"

"That is the one thing Hitler wants to know."

"Are we to assume from these answers that all of the steps you may take from now on of a naval and military character are secret?"

"There are some things that obviously I am not going to tell you about, and you will get accustomed to not asking them after a while."

LINDBERGH CONTENDED THAT the secrecy shrouding the administration's policy was both antidemocratic and a mark of the policy's bankruptcy. The scheduled Philadelphia rally against the war had to be moved after the proprietors of the meeting hall got nervous about Roosevelt's admonition to give no aid to appeasers. The undeterred attendees found their way to the new venue, which they filled to bursting. Lindbergh gave them what they came to hear.

Picking up on a Roosevelt statement that American defense required American control of the Cape Verde islands off the African coast, Lindbergh accused the president of doing precisely what he imputed to Hitler. "Suppose the Germans said that the safety of Europe lay in controlling the Fernando de Noronha Islands off the coast of South America. Obviously, this country would go to war. If we take the attitude that we must control the islands of the Eastern Hemisphere, Europe has just as much reason to demand control of the islands of the Western Hemisphere. If we say our frontier lies on the Rhine, they can say that theirs lies on the Mississippi. Such a policy means that one of the hemispheres must dominate the other before it can be satisfied or successful. Mr. Roosevelt claims that Hitler desires to dominate the world. But it is Mr. Roosevelt himself who advocates world domination when he says that it is our business to control the wars of Europe and Asia, and that we in America must dominate islands off the African coast."

Lindbergh charged Roosevelt with surrendering the direction of American policy to the British, with dismal results. "Always the same story: one defeat after another since this war began. And always the demand for more assistance from America. First they said, 'Sell us the arms and we will win.' Then it was, 'Lend us the arms and we will win.' Now it is, 'Bring us the arms and we will win.' Tomorrow it will be, 'Fight our war for us and we will win.'"

Americans didn't have to go abroad to fight for democracy, Lindbergh said. Democracy needed defending at home. "We are not the blind followers of a totalitarian regime. We are the citizens of a free country, a country governed by the people and for the people." Reform would start when the president stopped lying to the American people. "We demand the truth from our leaders. We demand that they tell us where they are leading us."

Lindbergh reiterated that the president was adopting the very policies he decried in the fascist countries. "They say that the only way we can defend democracy is by adopting the policies of a totalitarian state ourselves. They tell us it is undemocratic to question the type of leadership that has taken to defeat every nation in the world that followed it."

Far from obeying the administration, patriotic Americans should work on replacing it. "Their prophecies have been false, their policies have failed, and their promises have been worthless," Lindbergh said. "Yet now they demand that we too enter the greatest conflict in history, unprepared. I ask you, is our nation to follow them further? Is it not time for us to turn to new policies and to a new leadership?"

LINDBERGH LIKED THE response. "In some ways the audience was the most enthusiastic we have yet had," he noted in his journal. "They seemed to be one hundred per cent with us all of the time. I think it was partly a reaction to Roosevelt's address. This country is not ready for war, and the people who are against it do not intend to be intimidated into silence. Our meeting gave them the chance to express their attitude, and they took it."

Yet he sensed a chill descending upon the country. In Philadelphia he was introduced to various residents of the city. "Among them was an old man who had come to this country from Germany nearly sixty years ago. He was a contractor by trade, and told me he had already lost a number of contracts because of his nationality."

On returning to New York, Lindbergh met with Herbert Hoover. The former president had a stature in the Republican party and the country no other person in the antiwar movement could match; he also had sources of information different from those of Lindbergh and the rest. "Hoover thinks England may be considering a negotiated peace and that the terms may be under discussion at this moment," Lindbergh noted after the meeting. "There are strong rumors, according to Hoover, that Churchill will tell Roosevelt that either the United States enters the war in the near future or England will negotiate."

Yet Hoover could be slow on the uptake. "Hoover said this morning that the British 'cannot win' the war! That seemed obvious to me before they declared it. But why has it taken Hoover so long to come around to that conclusion? It is partly due to his underestimation of air power. But in addition to that, I do not believe he recognized the decadence in England or the virility in Germany. Hoover, like most other Americans—though in a much lesser degree—had never carefully analyzed the claim to greatness of the present generation of Englishmen. It was an inherited claim, and, like most things inherited, it had never stood the test of conflict."

Lindbergh recognized Hoover's importance to the antiwar cause. "He has opposed our entry into the war from the beginning, and his influence and effort in this respect has been of the utmost value," Lindbergh wrote. "His judgment is far ahead of that of most men in political office today." He was solid and honest, in both respects a comforting contrast to Roosevelt.

Yet he wasn't a great leader. "He lacks a certain spark; he lacks that intangible quality that makes men willing to follow a great leader even to death itself."

All the same, one used the tools at hand. "My primary object in going to see Hoover was to ask if he would consider making another antiwar address in the near future. He told me he was planning such an address and that he would probably speak in about a week—depending on when the time seemed opportune. He thinks it would be inadvisable for him to speak sooner—to which I agree."

62

IN EARLY JUNE 1941 American papers carried a report that an American merchant ship, the *Robin Moor*, had been sunk in the South Atlantic off the African coast. The report originated with the master of a Brazilian ship that had picked up eleven survivors in a lifeboat; they related that their vessel had been sunk on May 21 about midway between Natal, Brazil, and Dakar, French West Africa. Three other lifeboats had carried away the rest of the passengers and crew. The first reports didn't state who had sunk the *Robin Moor*. A German submarine was presumed to be responsible, but an accidental sinking by a British warship wasn't ruled out.

Additional reports confirmed the German responsibility for the sinking. Yet questions remained regarding the motives of the German submarine commander and his superiors. The *Robin Moor* was bound from New York for Mozambique via South Africa; its cargo was miscellaneous consumer goods.

Roosevelt kept still for several days, hoping for clarity. But on June 20 he sent a blistering message to Congress blaming Hitler and the Nazi war machine. "The sinking of this American ship by a German submarine flagrantly violated the right of United States vessels freely to navigate the seas," he said. "The passengers and crew of the *Robin Moor* were left afloat in small lifeboats for approximately two to three weeks, when they were accidentally discovered and rescued by friendly vessels. This chance rescue does not lessen the brutality of casting the boats adrift in mid-ocean." The sinking of the ship and the endangering of the passengers and crew marked Germany as an international outlaw, one that now targeted American nationals. "The government of the United States holds Germany responsible for the outrageous and indefensible sinking of the *Robin Moor*. Full reparation for the losses and damages suffered by American nationals will be expected from the German government."

A larger issue was at stake. "Our government believes that freedom from cruelty and inhuman treatment is a natural right. It is not a grace to be given or withheld at the will of those temporarily in a position to exert force over defenseless people." The government of Germany clearly had a different view. "The present leaders of the German Reich have not hesitated to engage in acts of cruelty and many other forms of terror against the innocent and the helpless in other countries, apparently in the belief that methods of terrorism will lead to a state of affairs permitting the German Reich to exact acquiescence from the nations victimized. This government can only assume that the government of the German Reich hopes through the commission of such infamous acts of cruelty to helpless and innocent men, women, and children to intimidate the United States and other nations into a course of non-resistance to German plans for universal conquest—a conquest based upon lawlessness and terror on land and piracy on the sea."

To fail to hold Germany to account would invite the direst consequences. "Heretofore, lawless acts of violence have been preludes to schemes of land conquest. This one appears to be a first step in assertion of the supreme purpose of the German Reich to seize control of the high seas, the conquest of Great Britain being an indispensable part of that seizure. Its general purpose would appear to be to drive American commerce from the ocean wherever such commerce was considered a disadvantage to German designs; and its specific purpose would appear to be interruption of our trade with all friendly countries."

Roosevelt waxed categorical. "We must take it that notice has now been served upon us that no American ship or cargo on any of the seven seas can consider itself immune from acts of piracy. Notice is served on us, in effect, that the German Reich proposes so to intimidate the United States that we would be dissuaded from carrying out our chosen policy of helping Britain to survive. In brief, we must take the sinking of the *Robin Moor* as a warning to the United States not to resist the Nazi movement of world conquest."

The stakes were higher than ever. "Were we to yield on this we would inevitably submit to world domination at the hands of the present leaders of the German Reich." America's determination was stronger than ever. "We are not yielding and we do not propose to yield."

LINDBERGH WAS ON the other side of the continent that night. America First had secured the Hollywood Bowl for an antiwar rally. "We arrived at 8:00," Lindbergh recorded. "The Bowl was already jammed, and there were several thousand people on the hills and standing outside the doors. It is the most beautiful and inspiring meeting place I have ever seen—open sky and stars above, and hills dimly outlined in the background, so that the rows of people merge into the hills themselves." The managers of the Hollywood Bowl reported the audience to be the largest in the amphitheater's history. "The crowd was enthusiastic, good-natured and attentive," Lindbergh noted.

63

TWO DAYS LATER Germany invaded the Soviet Union. Rumors of an impending double-cross of Stalin by Hitler had been circulating within the intelligence communities of America and Britain; Roosevelt and Churchill went so far as to warn Stalin of the invasion. Apparently Stalin suspected disinformation on the part of the capitalists, for he failed to act on the warnings and left his army unprepared. The first days and weeks of the German invasion went badly for the Red Army and well for the Wehrmacht. Recalling the speed with which the Germans had broken French and British forces the previous year, many observers expected a Russian collapse before long.

In America, the interventionists and the anti-interventionists had to assess what this new development meant for their causes. Lindbergh concluded that it made the arguments for staying out of the war all the stronger. Speaking before another packed house, at San Francisco's Civic Auditorium, he pointed out that entering the war against Hitler would now mean entering on the side of Stalin. If he had to pick between devils, he wouldn't choose the Bolshevik one. "I would a hundred times rather see my country ally herself with England or even with Germany, with all her faults, than with the cruelty, the godlessness and the barbarism that exist in Soviet Russia," Lindbergh said. "An alliance between the United States and Russia should be opposed by every American, by every Christian and by every humanitarian in this country."

Lindbergh pointed out that the America First Committee had

never accepted communists or fascists as members. This policy remained. "We accept no foreign way of life and no foreign ideologies. We reject them all. But the idealists who have been shouting about the horrors of Nazi Germany are now ready to welcome Soviet Russia as an ally. They are ready to join with a nation whose record of cruelty, bloodshed and barbarism is without parallel in modern history."

Lindbergh declined to point out that he had predicted that the war in Europe would lead to chaos. He simply recounted how the convoluted course of the conflict had tied the interventionist party in America in knots. "The longer this war in Europe continues, the more confused its issues become. When it started, Germany and Russia were lined up against England and France. Now, less than two years later, we find Russia and England fighting France"—Nazi-controlled France—"and Germany." It was hard to keep track. "The murderers and plunderers of yesterday are accepted as the valiant defenders of civilization today, and the valiant defenders of yesterday have become the wicked aggressors of today." China, fighting Japan, had been added to the list of Lend-Lease recipients. Russia was next. "We are now asked to defend the Russian way of life."

Was this what Americans really wanted? "I ask you, is the Russian way of life our way of life? Are we now to be responsible for the policies of Stalin as well as for those of Churchill and Chiang Kai-shek?" Chiang was the leader of the Chinese government.

What went around came around, Lindbergh said. "Two weeks ago the interventionists were accusing the America First Committee of associating with the subversive influence of communism. Now, I suppose, it is our turn to ask whose meetings the communists attend."

The ethical somersaults of the interventionists were the inevitable consequence of a policy tethered to Europe rather than one anchored in American interest. Worse was yet to come. "Judging from Europe's record, if we enter this war, we can't be sure whether we will have Russia or Germany for a partner by the time we finish it. We don't even know whether we will end up with France or England on our side. It is quite possible that we would find ourselves alone fighting the entire world before it was over."

The abrupt reversal in German-Russian relations, and the Roosevelt administration's reaction to it, made the case for the policy of

America first, Lindbergh said. "The only sensible thing for us to do is to build up an impregnable defense for America, and keep this hemisphere at peace."

HAROLD ICKES HAD been itching for a chance to go after Lindbergh and the isolationists. Roosevelt's secretary of the interior had been at the head of administration officials seeking ways to rescue Jews from the Nazi onslaught; he went so far as to suggest Alaska, then a territory, as a haven for Jewish immigrants who would be admitted to the United States beyond statutory limits. Ickes's plan generated only lukewarm support from Roosevelt, and an equally tepid response from American Jewish leaders, who worried that Alaska might become an American ghetto. But it marked Ickes as the one in the administration best placed to take on the isolationists. And Lindbergh's latest afforded an opening.

Ickes spoke at a Bastille Day rally hosted by the France Forever society in New York. He charged Lindbergh with taking orders from Berlin. An honest man would have responded at once to the German invasion of the Soviet Union, Ickes said; Lindbergh had hesitated. "It was clear that Lindbergh did not have his cue. Cautious man that he is, he did not want to say the wrong thing. So he posed as a heavy thinker, making an effort to concoct an effective apology for this latest flowering of Hitler gangsterism. Nine days passed, during which the Nazi party line was worked out and the official Nazi propaganda was handed out in Germany to Hitler mouthpieces and Nazi fellow-travelers all over the world. Then arose the Knight of the German Eagle"—a reference again to the decoration Lindbergh had received—"and offered this Nazi party line to the country."

Lindbergh was nothing but a tool of the Nazi regime, repackaging Nazi propaganda as his own interpretation of events, Ickes said. "Goebbels was undoubtedly chuckling at this shameless distortion of elementary truth, this pathological violation of the canons of decency. Undoubtedly he enjoyed it all the more because it fell from the lips of a man who had gained fame and fortune at the hands of the American people."

Lindbergh was more concerned with the feelings of the Germans than with those of the people the Germans brutalized. "No one has ever heard Lindbergh utter a word of horror at, or even aversion to, the bloody career that the Nazis are following, nor a word of pity for the innocent men, women and children who have been deliberately murdered by the Nazis in practically every country in Europe," Ickes said. "No, I have never heard Lindbergh utter a word of pity for Belgium, or Holland, or Norway, or England. I have never heard him express a word of pity for the Poles or the Jews who have been slaughtered by the hundreds of thousands by Hitler's savages. I have never heard Lindbergh say a word of encouragement to the English for the fight that they are so bravely making for Lindbergh's right to live his own life in his own way, as well as for their own right to do so. As a matter of fact, I have never heard Lindbergh say a word for democracy itself. Has any one of you?"

"No!" roared the audience.

In the crowd were many French nationals who were sensitive to the defeatism that had surrendered France to Germany; to them Ickes declared, "We have our own defeatists and appeasers, Hitler's conscious and unconscious tools, who would make us soft and malleable against the coming of Hitler's angels of hell." Lindbergh's sudden abhorrence of communism was a transparent ploy, Ickes said. "I denounce with all my heart the obvious trick that Lindbergh and others are helping the Nazis to play when they say that to help Britain defend herself from the Nazis while the latter are fighting Russia is to help communism."

The American people had not been fooled, Ickes said. They knew who the enemy of decency and civilization was. "That enemy is still Hitler." And Lindbergh was his friend.

CONSIDERING THE SOURCE, Lindbergh expected no better. "Secretary of the Interior Ickes has been attacking me and spreading misinformation about me for months in the cheapest and most inexcusable sort of way," he wrote in his journal. "My policy has been to say nothing in reply and to let him have all the rope he wants on the theory that he will eventually hang himself. In his latest utterances, however, I believe he has put both himself and the President in a position where I can attack with dignity and effectiveness."

Lindbergh decided to write another letter to Roosevelt, again with a copy to the newspapers. "In this way I think I can counteract Roosevelt's tactics, which are to put his Cabinet members out in front while he 'carries the ball.' Thus he lures his opposition into attacking his Cabinet officers instead of himself. I am trying to reverse that procedure and to strike through Roosevelt's interference by holding him personally responsible for his appointees. Nothing is to be gained by my entering a controversy with a man of Ickes's type. But if I can pin Ickes's actions on Roosevelt, it will have the utmost effect."

"My Dear Mr. President," began Lindbergh's published letter. "I address you, sir, as an American citizen to his President. I write concerning statements made by an officer of your Cabinet, the Secretary of the Interior. For many months, and on numerous occasions, your Secretary of the Interior has implied in public meetings that I am connected with the interests of a foreign government, and he has specifically criticized me for accepting a decoration from the German Government in 1938.

"Mr. President, is it too much to ask that you inform your Secretary of the Interior that I was decorated by the German Government while I was carrying out the request of your Ambassador to that government? Is it unfair of me to ask that you inform your Secretary that I received this decoration in the American Embassy, in the presence of your Ambassador, and that I was there at his request in order to assist in creating a better relationship between the American Embassy and the German Government, which your Ambassador desired at that time?

"Mr. President, if the statements of your Secretary of the Interior are true, and if I have any connection with a foreign government, the American people have a right to be fully acquainted with the facts. On the other hand, if his statements and implications are false, I believe that I, as an American citizen, have a right to an apology from your Secretary.

"Mr. President, I give you my word that I have no connection with any foreign government. I have had no communications, directly or indirectly, with any one in Germany or Italy since I was last in Europe, in the Spring of 1939. Prior to that time my activities were well known to your embassies in the countries where I lived and traveled. I always kept in close contact with your embassies and your military attaches, as the records in your State Department and War Department will reveal.

"Mr. President, I will willingly open my files to your investigation. I will willingly appear in person before any committee you appoint, and there is no question regarding my activities now, or any time in the past, that I will not be glad to answer.

"Mr. President, if there is a question in your mind, I ask that you give me the opportunity of answering any charges that may be made against me. But, Mr. President, unless charges are made and proved, I believe that the customs and traditions of our country give me, as an American citizen, the right to expect truth and justice from the members of your Cabinet.

"Respectfully, Charles A. Lindbergh"

64

LINDBERGH ASSUMED HE was already under investigation. He received a visit from a Captain Smith, associated with the America First Committee. "He had phoned to say he had an urgent message that he must deliver personally. The message is that the F.B.I. began tapping our telephone last Saturday and have a constant watch on it. The men in the F.B.I. are, according to Smith, on the whole, friendly; they are simply following out orders. Smith says the America First telephones are also tapped."

Lindbergh wasn't surprised, nor was he particularly upset. He definitely wasn't worried. "I told him to tell everyone in America First that there was nothing we wished to hide and that if our phones were tapped we should speak more plainly, rather than less plainly, in the future. I told him to tell his friends on the F.B.I. that if there was anything they didn't understand in my own phone conversations, I would be glad to give them additional information."

WHEN ROOSEVELT RECEIVED Lindbergh's challenge to investigate his activities, the president might already have known the FBI had nothing incriminating on him. Or he might have concluded that Lindbergh wouldn't have issued the challenge if he had anything to hide. For whatever reason, Roosevelt ignored the challenge. Yet neither did he chastise Ickes or ask the secretary to make an apology. Instead Roosevelt moved against Lindbergh by other means. In July 1941 the president named William Donovan to be "coordinator of information." The title sounded innocuous, but the job was weighty. And it hinted at the degree to which Roosevelt had linked his administration to the British cause before the connection became public.

Donovan continued to work closely, and in strictest confidence, with William Stephenson, the British spymaster in America. Stephenson continued to feed British propaganda to American newspapers, still concealing its source. In 1941 Stephenson took his covert campaign to the air. He subtly enlisted the services of a shortwave radio station, WRUL, whose fifty-thousand-watt transmitter made it one of the most powerful in the world. The station had run into funding difficulties that afforded Stephenson and his British Security Coordination group an opening. "Through cut-outs, BSC began to supply it with everything it needed to run a first-class international programme worthy of its transmitting power," the secret history of British intelligence operations said. "BSC subsidized it financially. It recruited foreign news editors, translators and announcers to serve on its staff. It furnished it with material for news bulletins, with specially prepared scripts for talks and commentaries and with transcribed programmes. By the middle of 1941, station WRUL was virtually, though quite unconsciously, a subsidiary of BSC, sending out covert British propaganda all over the world."

Stephenson wasn't satisfied. He asked for greater support from the British government, warning that the battle for American hearts and minds was far from won. Meanwhile he took fresh action on his own. "He instructed the recently created SOE"—Special Operations Executive—"division to declare a covert war against the mass of American groups which were organized throughout the country to spread isolationism and anti-British feeling."

At the head of the list was the America First Committee. In Stephenson's view, the committee was a worthy foe in the propaganda battle. "It appealed to pacifists, haters of Roosevelt, haters of Great Britain, anti-Communists, anti-Semites, admirers of Germany, American imperialists, devotees of big business, and to those who hated Europe, who regarded that continent as a corrupt and backward region which stood for all the things from which the Pilgrim Fathers and their successors had fled." Stephenson monitored the growth of the America First movement. "By the late spring of 1941, it had 700 chapters and nearly 1,000,000 members, with Charles Lindbergh emerging as its leader. The principal call on its energies was a campaign directed against the passing of the Lend-Lease Act and against the proposal for convoying ships across the Atlantic."

Stephenson moved to disrupt the activities of the America Firsters. "Agents were despatched to each part of the country to attend its meetings, to keep track of its new members and to ponder upon new and effective ways of instigating counter-propaganda." One prong of the counterattack involved exposing members' ties to organizations sympathetic to Germany. A second prong urged pro-British groups to plan their own attacks on America First. A third prong sought to cast the America Firsters as traitors to America.

Stephenson's unit printed handbills attacking Gerald Nye as an appeaser and Nazi-lover and passed them out at a rally where Nye spoke. When Hamilton Fish appeared in Minneapolis to argue against American intervention, a Stephenson operative approached him afterward and handed him a card conveying the message: "Der Fuehrer thanks you for your loyalty." A planted photographer captured the moment and the message. At a rally where Lindbergh was to speak, Stephenson's men printed counterfeit tickets and distributed them to opponents of America First, who filled the seats in the auditorium before the supporters could get there. Stephenson hoped fights would result. As things turned out, attendance by the latter was smaller than expected. Stephenson's ploy backfired, making the auditorium fuller than it would have been.

Stephenson sponsored bogus polls that seemed to show the anti-interventionists as weaker and less numerous than they actually were. "Great care was taken beforehand to make certain that the poll results would turn out as desired and that they would be given the fullest possible publicity," the secret history related. The poll reported that 96 percent of respondents thought defeating Hitler was more important than keeping America out of the war. The poll also asked about individuals. Lindbergh was voted "U.S. Fascist Number One" and Burton Wheeler "Fascist Number Two."

Stephenson went so far as to enlist an agent who pretended to be an astrologer. This fellow was instructed to show no interest in Britain or Britain's welfare; his sole job was to shake the confidence of Americans in the invincibility of Hitler, who was known to believe in astrology himself. The man posed as a Hungarian expert in the knowledge of the stars; Stephenson set up a press conference at which the faux guide to the cosmos explained that Hitler's fall was inevitable. Neptune was in the House of Death and Uranus was similarly inauspicious; the position of the two planets, which had special significance for Hitler, doomed the German leader.

By previous arrangement, a report came from Egypt that an Arab astrologer had delivered the same verdict. Likewise a cable from Nigeria. The coincidence arrested the attention of many who read about it. The final piece was a prophecy by the fake Hungarian that an ally of Hitler would go mad within ten days. A story planted by Stephenson said that an admiral in the pro-German Vichy government of France was raving uncontrollably.

Perhaps the success of the astrologer-agent went to his head. Perhaps the success went to *Stephenson*'s head. At a convention of American astrologers, the would-be wizard announced that Lindbergh had fallen victim to a mental disorder that caused him to believe that his expertise in aviation made him an expert on other subjects. This wasn't the crazy part. Stephenson's stooge went on to say that the Lindbergh baby was alive and being held in a secret location.

65

DURING THE SUMMER of 1941 Roosevelt beat the drum of defiance to Nazism more loudly than ever. He missed no opportunity to assert that Hitler was bent on world conquest and that anything less than full commitment to the German regime's destruction was disloyalty to American ideals. "In 1776 we waged war in behalf of the great principle that government should derive its just powers from the consent of the governed," he said on the Fourth of July. "In other words, representation chosen in free elections. In the century and a half that followed, this cause of human freedom swept across the world. But now, in our generation—in the past few years—a new resistance, in the form of several new practices of tyranny, has been making such headway that the fundamentals of 1776 are being struck down abroad and definitely they are threatened here."

Astonishingly, not all could see this obvious fact. Some prominent individuals said America could survive in its own hemisphere regardless of what happened beyond. They cited America's founders to this effect. "Yet all of us who lie awake at night—all of us who study and study again—know full well that in these days we cannot save freedom with pitchforks and muskets alone, after a dictator combination has gained control of the rest of the world. We know too that we cannot save freedom in our own midst, in our own land, if all around us our neighbor nations have lost their freedom."

Loyal Americans must make common cause against the deceivers. And they must do more. "We need not the loyalty and unity alone;

we need speed and efficiency and toil, and an end to backbiting, and an end to the sabotage that runs far deeper than the blowing up of munitions plants."

Again: American freedom demanded the defense of freedom everywhere. "I tell the American people solemnly that the United States will never survive as a happy and fertile oasis of liberty surrounded by a cruel desert of dictatorship." Americans must be willing to make sacrifices, including the greatest of all. "And so it is that when we repeat the great pledge to our country and to our flag, it must be our deep conviction that we pledge as well our work, our will and, if it be necessary, our very lives."

Three days later Roosevelt announced that American troops would be occupying Iceland. The government there had been persuaded that if the Americans didn't grab that strategically located island, the Germans would. And the Americans were less dangerous. "The United States cannot permit the occupation by Germany of strategic outposts in the Atlantic to be used as air or naval bases for eventual attack against the Western Hemisphere," Roosevelt said. America had nothing against Iceland's independence; it merely needed to secure the North Atlantic against the insatiable aggression of Germany. "We have no desire to see any change in the present sovereignty of those regions. Assurance that such outposts in our defense frontier remain in friendly hands is the very foundation of our national security and of the national security of every one of the independent nations of the New World. . . . It is, therefore, imperative that the approaches between the Americas and those strategic outposts, the safety of which this country regards as essential to its national security, and which it must therefore defend, shall remain open and free from all hostile activity or threat thereof."

In late July Roosevelt asked Congress to extend the one-year term of service of conscripts in the American military. When the law authorizing the draft had been passed in 1940, the threat to America had been grave. Matters had changed only for the worse. "The international situation is not less grave but is far more grave than it was a year ago," Roosevelt said. "It is so grave, in my opinion, and in the opinion of all who are conversant with the facts, that the Army should be maintained in effective strength and without diminution of its effective numbers in a complete state of readiness." Congress must not be misled by appeasers and defeatists. "Occasional individuals, basing their opinions on unsupported evidence or on no evidence at all, may with honest intent assert that the United States need fear no attack on its own territory or on the other nations of this hemisphere by aggressors from without." They were woefully wrong. "It is the well-nigh unanimous opinion of those who are daily cognizant, as military and naval officers and as government servants in the field of international relations, that schemes and plans of aggressor nations against American security are so evident that the United States and the rest of the Americas are definitely imperiled in their national interests."

IN AUGUST, ROOSEVELT met with Winston Churchill in Placentia Bay, Newfoundland. Since the beginning of the year, American and British officers had been collaborating on war plans in the event the United States joined the conflict. For political reasons, Roosevelt insisted that the existence of the planning, let alone its content, be a closely guarded secret. The president monitored the work and quietly approved its essential premise: that should the United States become involved in a war with both Germany and Japan, America would focus first on Germany.

The collaboration deepened during the following months. Churchill encouraged the American occupation of Iceland. "We cordially welcome your taking over Iceland at the earliest possible moment, and will hold ourselves and all our resources there at your disposal as may be found convenient," he wrote to Roosevelt. Churchill and Roosevelt compared notes as their intelligence bureaus warned of the impending German invasion of Russia. "From every source at my disposal including some most trustworthy it looks as if a vast German onslaught on the Russian frontier is imminent," Churchill wrote in mid-June. "Not only are the main German armies deployed from Finland to Roumania but the final arrivals of air and armoured forces are being completed." The prime minister explained what this would mean for British policy and potentially for American. "Should this new war break out, we shall of course give all encouragement and any help we can spare to the Russians, following the principle that Hitler is the foe we have to beat."

Churchill put the sentiment more memorably after the invasion began. "If Hitler invaded Hell, I would at least make a favourable reference to the Devil in the House of Commons," he said. He added, in language he thought Roosevelt could use, "The Russian danger is, therefore, our danger, and the danger of the United States, just as the cause of any Russian fighting for his hearth and home is the cause of free men and free peoples in every quarter of the globe."

Roosevelt agreed, but only in private. A reporter sought a public statement. "Mr. President, is the defense of Russia essential to the defense of the United States?"

"Oh, ask me a different type of question," Roosevelt said. "You know I never answer those." Yet he answered another, more pressing question about Russia. "We are going to give all the aid that we possibly can to Russia," Roosevelt said.

To this point in the war, Roosevelt's correspondence with Churchill had emphasized military and naval affairs and been essentially bilateral. But with the Soviets now de facto allies of Britain, and America a de facto ally of Britain, the relationship became trilateral. And it grew more complicated. Both Roosevelt and Churchill thought they would benefit from a face-to-face meeting.

A meeting entailed risks—from a German submarine, for example. So Roosevelt and Churchill arranged a secret shipboard rendezvous. "Looking forward so much to our meeting," Roosevelt wrote to Churchill on August 5. Noting the date, he remarked, "It is 27 years ago today that the Huns began their last war. We all must make a good job of it this time. Twice ought to be enough."

The Atlantic Conference, as the huddle of Roosevelt and Churchill was soon dubbed, became known to the world only when the two leaders issued separate communiqués and a joint declaration after its end. "The President of the United States and the Prime Minister, Mr. Churchill, representing His Majesty's Government in the United Kingdom, have met at sea," the statement from the White House declared. "They have been accompanied by officials of their two Governments, including high ranking officers of their military, naval, and air services." The meetings alternated between the American warship the president arrived on and the British vessel carrying Churchill. "They have considered the dangers to world civilization arising from the policies of military domination by conquest upon which the Hitlerite Government of Germany and other Governments associated therewith have embarked, and have made clear the steps which their countries are respectively taking for their safety in the face of these dangers."

While the uniformed officers discussed military strategy and tactics, Roosevelt and Churchill devised a joint political vision for the future. They proposed eight principles, constituting what came to be called the Atlantic Charter. "First, their countries seek no aggrandizement, territorial or other. Second, they desire to see no territorial changes that do not accord with the freely expressed wishes of the peoples concerned. Third, they respect the right of all peoples to choose the form of government under which they will live; and they wish to see sovereign rights and self-government restored to those who have been forcibly deprived of them. Fourth, they will endeavor, with due respect for their existing obligations, to further the enjoyment by all states, great or small, victor or vanquished, of access, on equal terms, to the trade and to the raw materials of the world which are needed for their economic prosperity. Fifth, they desire to bring about the fullest collaboration between all Nations in the economic field with the object of securing, for all, improved labor standards, economic advancement, and social security. Sixth, after the final destruction of the Nazi tyranny, they hope to see established a peace which will afford to all Nations the means of dwelling in safety within their own boundaries, and which will afford assurance that all the men in all the lands may live out their lives in freedom from fear and want. Seventh, such a peace should enable all men to traverse the high seas and oceans without hindrance. Eighth, they believe that all of the Nations of the world, for realistic as well as spiritual reasons, must come to the abandonment of the use of force. Since no future peace can be maintained if land, sea, or air armaments continue to be employed by Nations which threaten, or may threaten, aggression outside of their frontiers, they believe, pending the establishment of a wider and permanent system of general security, that the disarmament of such Nations is essential."

The two leaders revealed that they had written a letter to Stalin. Praising the "splendid defense" the Soviets were belatedly making against Germany, Roosevelt and Churchill expressed a desire to be as helpful as possible. "We are at the moment cooperating to provide you with the very maximum of supplies that you most urgently need. Already many shiploads have left our shores and more will leave in the immediate future. We must now turn our minds to the consideration of a more long-term policy, since there is still a long and hard path to be traversed before there can be won that complete victory without which our efforts and sacrifices would be wasted."

The three countries must work together in the common interest. They must apportion responsibilities in the fight against Germany and parcel out supplies. "We suggest that we prepare for a meeting to be held at Moscow, to which we would send high representatives who could discuss these matters directly with you," Roosevelt and Churchill said. "We realize fully how vitally important to the defeat of Hitlerism is the brave and steadfast resistance of the Soviet Union and we feel, therefore, that we must not in any circumstances fail to act quickly and immediately in this matter on planning the program for the future allocation of our joint resources."

66

ROOSEVELT REVEALED MORE to reporters the next day. "Could you tell us where this conference with Mr. Churchill was held?" one asked.

"I cannot, for obvious reasons." The Germans might review radio intercepts and draw inferences about the British code. Roosevelt acknowledged that he had been there on the *Augusta* and Churchill on the *Prince of Wales*. "But outside of that, nothing about ships, nothing about times, dates, and nothing about locations."

Deprived of facts, the reporters wanted impressions. "I think the first thing in the minds of all of us was a very remarkable religious service on the quarterdeck of the *Prince of Wales* last Sunday morning," Roosevelt offered. "There was their own ship's complement, with three or four hundred bluejackets and marines from American ships, on the quarterdeck, completely intermingled, first one uniform and then another uniform. The service was conducted by two chaplains, one English and one American, and, as usual, the lesson was read by the captain of the British ship. They had three hymns that everybody took part in, and a little ship's altar was decked with the American flag and the British flag. The officers were all intermingled on the fantail." Roosevelt let the image of Anglo-American unity sink in. "The point is, I think everybody there, officers and enlisted men, felt that it was one of the great historic services. I know I did."

Reporters asked about the origins of the conference. "Was it your idea, sir?"

"I should say it was our joint idea."

Reporters pressed for details of what was discussed.

Roosevelt declined, then expanded. "Put it this way: that the conferences were primarily an interchange of views relating to the present and the future—a swapping of information, which was eminently successful. I think one of the subjects which perhaps all overlooked, both in the statements and comments, was the need for an exchange of what might be called views relating to what is happening to the world under the Nazi regime, as applied to other nations. The more that is discussed and looked into, the more terrible the thought becomes of having the world as a whole dominated by the kind of influences which have been at work in the occupied or affiliated nations. It's a thing that needs to be brought home to all of the democracies, more and more."

"Are we any closer to entering the war?"

"I should say, no."

"May we quote directly?"

"No, you can quote indirectly."

ROOSEVELT HAD REASON for not letting himself be quoted directly. He wanted to convey the impression that his talks with Churchill had not carried America closer to war. The vote in Congress on renewal of the draft was approaching, and he hoped to give political cover to supporters in antiwar districts. But he didn't want to have the words placed in his own mouth, because he knew they weren't true.

Churchill told his cabinet as much in strictest confidence on the prime minister's return to London. Roosevelt had been making such a point of the global danger to democracy in part because he wanted to link Japanese aggression in Asia to German aggression in Europe. Japan posed the lesser threat to American interests, it being a lesser power than Germany, and Asia being less important to the American economy than Europe. Moreover, American isolationists were less sensitive about Japan than about Germany, no Americans having died in war against Japan. Roosevelt thought he could pressure Japan in a way that would compel Tokyo to retreat or to strike out. Retreat would be beneficial on its merits; striking out would produce the trigger for war Roosevelt was seeking.

Churchill described the president's strategy to his cabinet colleagues. "The President had proposed to Japan some time ago the neutralization of Indo-China and Siam under a joint guarantee of the United States, Britain, China and others, but there had been a number of conditions which were unacceptable to the Japanese," Churchill said, in the paraphrasing employed in minutes of British cabinet meetings. "The President's idea was to negotiate about these unacceptable conditions and thus procure a moratorium of 30 days, during which we might improve our position in Singapore and the Japanese would have to stand still. At the end of the note which the President proposed to hand to the Japanese Ambassador was a passage to the effect that any further encroachment by Japan in the South-west Pacific would produce a situation in which the United States Government would be compelled to take counter measures even though this might lead to war between the United States and Japan."

Amid the cabinet meeting Churchill was handed a telegram just in from Roosevelt. The president had spoken with the Japanese ambassador. "The President said that the statement he had made to the Ambassador was no less vigorous and substantially similar to that already agreed with the Prime Minister," Churchill told the cabinet. Roosevelt continued to tighten the screws on Japan; America was nearer to war than ever.

ROOSEVELT DELIVERED HIS public report on the Atlantic Conference in a message to Congress. He reiterated the reasons for the conference having been held in secret. He relayed the eight principles of the Atlantic Charter. He recounted the letter he and Churchill had sent to Stalin.

And he declared that those who questioned the policy of the administration were fellow travelers with the Nazis. "The declaration of principles at this time presents a goal which is worthwhile for our type of civilization to seek," Roosevelt said. "It is so clear cut that it is difficult to oppose in any major particular without automatically admitting a willingness to accept compromise with Nazism; or to agree to a world peace which would give to Nazism domination over large numbers of conquered nations. Inevitably such a peace would be a gift to Nazism to take breath—armed breath—for a second war to extend the control over Europe and Asia to the American Hemisphere itself."

During the following weeks, Roosevelt relentlessly assailed those who challenged him. In late August he warned reporters not to be taken in by the appeasers and Nazi collaborators. "There can be no doubt that there is an organized campaign to spread rumors, distortions or half-truths, and I fear falsehoods—you probably know the word—being launched by certain forces to sabotage the program of aid to opponents of Hitlerism."

He continued to fan fears of Hitler and Nazi control of the world. On Labor Day he praised the workers in factories producing Lend-Lease munitions. "Why are we doing this?" he asked rhetorically. "Why are we determined to devote our entire industrial effort to the prosecution of a war which has not yet actually touched our own shores? We are not a warlike people. We have never sought glory as a nation of warriors. We are not interested in aggression. We are not interested—as the dictators are—in looting. We do not covet one square inch of the territory of any other nation. Our vast effort, and the unity of purpose that inspires that effort, are due solely to our recognition of the fact that our fundamental rights—including the rights of labor—are threatened by Hitler's violent attempt to rule the world."

He rang the tocsin against "the enemies who believed that they could divide us and conquer us from within." For the moment these enemies were at bay, but they never rested. Loyal Americans must not underestimate the challenge. "I give solemn warning to those who think that Hitler has been blocked and halted, that they are making a very dangerous assumption. When in any war your enemy seems to be making slower progress than he did the year before, that is the very moment to strike with redoubled force, to throw more energy into the job of defeating him, to end for all time the menace of world conquest and thereby end all talk or thought of any peace founded on a compromise with evil itself."

Americans must rally behind their president. "We cannot hesitate, we cannot equivocate in the great task before us. The defense of America's freedom must take precedence over every private aim and over every private interest." The path to safety wasn't easy. "Yes, we are engaged on a grim and perilous task. Forces of insane violence have been let loose by Hitler upon this earth. We must do our full part in conquering them. For these forces may be unleashed on this nation as we go about our business of protecting the proper interests of our country."

Vigilance against traitors must be unceasing. "The task of defeating Hitler may be long and arduous. There are a few appeasers and Nazi sympathizers who say it cannot be done. They even ask me to negotiate with Hitler, to pray for crumbs from his victorious table. They do, in fact, ask me to become the modern Benedict Arnold and betray all that I hold dear: my devotion to our freedom, to our churches, to our country."

The traitors would not win. "This course I have rejected; I reject it again. Instead, I know that I speak the conscience and determination of the American people when I say that we shall do everything in our power to crush Hitler and his Nazi forces."

67

O N SEPTEMBER 11 Roosevelt went on the radio to relate an important development in the war. "The Navy Department of the United States has reported to me that on the morning of September 4th, the United States destroyer *Greer*, proceeding in full daylight toward Iceland, had reached a point southeast of Greenland. She was carrying American mail to Iceland. She was flying the American flag. Her identity as an American ship was unmistakable. She was then and there attacked by a submarine. Germany admits that it was a German submarine. The submarine deliberately fired a torpedo at the *Greer*, followed later by another torpedo attack. In spite of what Hitler's propaganda bureau has invented, and in spite of what any American obstructionist organization may prefer to believe, I tell you the blunt fact that the German submarine fired first upon this American destroyer without warning, and with deliberate design to sink her.

"Our destroyer, at the time, was in waters which the government of the United States had declared to be waters of self-defense, surrounding outposts of American protection in the Atlantic."

Once again the Nazis had shown their disregard for international law and human decency, Roosevelt said. "This was piracy—piracy legally and morally. It was not the first nor the last act of piracy which the Nazi government has committed against the American flag in this war. For attack has followed attack." Roosevelt cited the sinking of the *Robin Moor*. "No apology, no allegation of mistake, no offer of reparations has come from the Nazi government." He described an encounter in which a submarine periscope was spotted by the crew of an American battleship. "No British or American submarines were within hundreds of miles of this spot at the time, so the nationality of the submarine is clear." An American-owned ship flying the flag of Panama had been torpedoed and shelled near Greenland. "In view of the established presence of German submarines in this vicinity, there can be no reasonable doubt as to the identity of the flag of the attacker." An American merchant ship had been sunk by a German warplane in the Red Sea.

America had shown remarkable restraint in the face of this provocation. "We Americans are keeping our feet on the ground," Roosevelt said. "Our type of democratic civilization has outgrown the thought of feeling compelled to fight some other nation by reason of any single piratical attack on one of our ships. We are not becoming hysterical or losing our sense of proportion."

Yet patience had limits. "It would be inexcusable folly to minimize such incidents in the face of evidence which makes it clear that the incident is not isolated, but is part of a general plan. The important truth is that these acts of international lawlessness are a manifestation of a design which has been made clear to the American people for a long time. It is the Nazi design to abolish the freedom of the seas, and to acquire absolute control and domination of these seas for themselves."

Why did the Nazis want control of the seas? "With control of the seas in their own hands, the way can obviously become clear for their next step: domination of the United States." Before Hitler, the Atlantic had been a blessing to America. No longer, if the Nazi dictator had his way. "The Atlantic Ocean which has been, and which should always be, a free and friendly highway for us would then become a deadly menace to the commerce of the United States, to the coasts of the United States, and even to the inland cities of the United States."

Roosevelt took yet another opportunity to warn of Hitler's agents within. "It is time for all Americans, Americans of all the Americas, to stop being deluded by the romantic notion that the Americas can go on living happily and peacefully in a Nazi-dominated world." He was sure the great majority of Americans were too perceptive and honest for that. "No tender whisperings of appeasers that Hitler is not interested in the Western Hemisphere, no soporific lullabies that a wide ocean protects us from him, can long have any effect on the hard-headed, far-sighted, and realistic American people."

Roosevelt this evening was working toward an announcement of a change in American naval policy. "The Nazi danger to our Western world has long ceased to be a mere possibility. The danger is here now—not only from a military enemy but from an enemy of all law, all liberty, all morality, all religion. There has now come a time when you and I must see the cold, inexorable necessity of saying to these inhuman, unrestrained seekers of world conquest and permanent world domination by the sword: 'You seek to throw our children and our children's children into your form of terrorism and slavery. You have now attacked our own safety. You shall go no further.'"

America would now use force to ensure freedom of the seas. "No matter what it takes, no matter what it costs, we will keep open the line of legitimate commerce in these defensive waters." Employing an analogy that would lead the coverage of his speech, Roosevelt said, "When you see a rattlesnake poised to strike, you do not wait until he has struck before you crush him. These Nazi submarines and raiders are the rattlesnakes of the Atlantic."

Getting specific, Roosevelt declared, "American naval vessels and American planes will no longer wait until Axis submarines lurking under the water, or Axis raiders on the surface of the sea, strike their deadly blow." American ships and planes would shoot on sight. Lest Hitler and his evil allies have any doubt regarding the new policy, the president said, "Let this warning be clear. From now on, if German or Italian vessels of war enter the waters the protection of which is necessary for American defense, they do so at their own peril."

DAVID WALSH HAD been suspicious of government explanations of attacks on American warships since the *Maine* blew up in Havana harbor and provided William McKinley occasion for war against Spain in 1898. As a beginning politician in Massachusetts, Walsh had joined the anti-imperialist wing of the Democratic party, and with William Jennings Bryan he denounced the payoff of the Spanish-American War: the American annexation of the Philippines. By 1914 he was governor of Massachusetts, the first Irish Catholic to hold that office, and he opposed American entry into the World War, seeing no reason why American soldiers should die in defense of British imperialism.

In 1941 he remained as distrustful of American involvement in foreign wars as ever. He also chaired the Senate committee on naval affairs, and from that perch he determined to probe Roosevelt's account of the *Greer* incident. He scheduled a hearing and summoned Admiral Harold Stark, Roosevelt's chief of naval operations.

Stark tried to evade the summons. He knew Roosevelt's account wouldn't survive scrutiny, and he didn't want to be the one squirming in the witness seat before the committee. Stark submitted a written statement regarding the *Greer* affair, hoping it would answer the chairman's questions.

Stark's account revealed that Roosevelt hadn't lied, exactly, but had left out information that put the affair in a crucially different light. "On September 4, 1941, at 0840 G. C. T., the U.S.S. *Greer*, while en route to Iceland with United States mail and passengers and some freight, was informed by a British plane of the presence of a submerged submarine, distance about 10 miles directly ahead," Stark's statement said. "This British plane continued in the vicinity of the submarine until 1052"—more than two hours—"when she departed. Prior to her departure, at 1032, she dropped four depth charges in the vicinity of the submarine. Acting on the information from the British plane, the *Greer* proceeded to search for the submarine, and at 0920 she located the submarine directly ahead by her underwater sound equipment. The *Greer* proceeded then to trail the submarine and broadcasted the submarine's position. This action taken by the *Greer* was in accordance with her orders, that is, to give out information but not to attack."

In other words, the *Greer* served as the spotter for the British plane, which initiated the exchange of fire with its depth charges. The *Greer* maintained its pursuit of the German submarine following the departure of the British plane. Eventually the submarine turned to face its pursuer. It was then that the submarine fired a torpedo, which passed behind the *Greer*. The *Greer* responded with eight depth charges. The submarine fired a second torpedo, which likewise missed. The submarine tried to escape. The *Greer* lost sound contact and began searching. Two hours later it detected a submarine, perhaps the same one, perhaps another. It dropped depth charges against the target.

"In neither of the *Greer's* attacks did she observe any results which would indicate that the attacks on the submarine had been effective," Stark said. The navy chief added, "At no time did the *Greer* sight the submarine's periscope. The weather was good. The commander of the Atlantic Fleet corroborates the above report in detail, and further states that the action taken by the *Greer* was correct in every particular in accordance with her existing orders."

What Roosevelt had portrayed as an unprovoked attack by the German submarine upon the *Greer* had in fact been provoked by the *Greer's* assisting the British plane depth-charging the German submarine. And the *Greer's* action had been in keeping with existing orders that Roosevelt had not revealed to the American public.

68

Luckily for Roosevelt, the revelations about the *Greer* coincided with a storm about Lindbergh, whose campaigning against the war carried him to Iowa in early September. "Lunch with about twenty-five Des Moines citizens representing both sides of the war controversy," Lindbergh wrote in his journal for September 11. He had come for an America First rally. His celebrity preceded him, and his midwestern roots attracted men and women of all political persuasions to meet this famous son of the heartland. "Interesting and pleasant; no formal speeches, but we discussed war trends and conditions here and abroad."

The rally was set for the evening, but so, as it happened, was the radio address by Roosevelt about the *Greer*. Given the time difference, Lindbergh decided to let the president go first. "Afternoon spent reading over my address, and in conferences," Lindbergh wrote. "All sorts of people came in during the afternoon. One, a preacher, said a prayer as he left. Another had a religious prophecy he wanted to tell me about. One man had a new economic plan. A fourth wanted to show me his collection of magazine and newspaper records of 'undercover British dealings.' Several 'old friends' came to call, most of whom I had apparently met *once* many years ago at a time when I was meeting thousands of people every week. They recalled the circumstances surrounding our meeting 'fourteen years ago,' and expected me to then remember all details connected with it. The unfortunate part is that the real friends you would like to see stay away because they are afraid of intruding when you are busy, and you are left surrounded by people who push themselves forward claiming to be friends."

The coincidence of speeches—Roosevelt's and Lindbergh's—happened at least partly by chance. Roosevelt had originally scheduled his talk on the *Greer* for several days earlier, but his mother died and he postponed it to September 11. Lindbergh's Des Moines hosts thereupon considered postponing *their* rally, also scheduled for September 11, but decided to stick with the published schedule. Quite possibly Roosevelt's staff realized that the president's new date would disrupt Lindbergh's rally; if so, their strategy worked. The Des Moines organizers felt obliged to put Roosevelt on the sound system in the meeting hall. The rally would commence immediately after.

"I felt very doubtful about this arrangement," Lindbergh remarked. "But it had already been announced when I learned of it, and there was nothing to do." Lindbergh and the other speakers had to decide whether to sit on stage while Roosevelt spoke, or wait backstage. They chose the latter. "Since the President is an able speaker, and since he has the ability to arouse crowds, it gave us about as bad a setting as we could have had for our meeting."

The start of the program was inauspicious. "The curtain went up and we filed onto the platform. We were met by a mixture of applause and boos—it was the most unfriendly crowd of any meeting to date, by far. Also, the opposition had been organized and there were groups of hecklers in the galleries strategically located to be effective for the microphones. We learned after the meeting that these groups contained paid 'shouters.' Confusion was increased by the improper functioning of the loudspeakers during the first several minutes."

The opening speaker was Janet Fairbank, a Chicago author and activist for women's rights and nonintervention. "She did a very good job under very difficult conditions," Lindbergh said. "Before long we began to win over the crowd, and the clapping and cheering of our supporters overcame the cries of our opposition." Hanford MacNider, a decorated veteran of the World War, former head of the American Legion and former ambassador to Canada, came next. "MacNider made a strong address and was well received."

Lindbergh was the main attraction. "I spoke for twenty-five minutes. It seemed that over eighty per cent of the crowd was with us by the time I finished; but the ice had been well broken before I started, by the previous speakers."

A more artful politician than Lindbergh would have worked a riposte to Roosevelt's speech that evening into his prepared remarks. But Lindbergh disdained politics, priding himself on his refusal to reckon the political consequences of what he said. Sticking to his script, he plunged ahead.

"It is now two years since this latest European war began," he said. "From that day in September 1939, until the present moment, there has been an ever-increasing effort to force the United States into the conflict. That effort has been carried on by foreign interests, and by a small minority of our own people; but it has been so successful that today our country stands on the verge of war."

These last words revealed for the first time that Lindbergh understood his side was losing the debate, if it hadn't lost already. He was convinced the American public remained opposed to war, yet Roosevelt and the advocates of war had manipulated affairs so as to make American involvement nearly inevitable. How had this happened? And could anything be done at this eleventh hour to keep the country from going into the abyss?

Lindbergh paused to point out a difference between the war party and the antiwar party. "If you will look back over the record, you will find that those of us who oppose intervention have constantly tried to clarify facts and issues, while the interventionists have tried to hide facts and confuse issues. We ask you to read what we said last month, last year, and even before the war began. Our record is open and clear, and we are proud of it. We have not led you on by subterfuge and propaganda. We have not resorted to steps short of anything, in order to take the American people where they did not want to go. What we said before the elections, we say again and again, and again today. And we will not tell you tomorrow that it was just campaign oratory. Have you ever heard an interventionist, or a British agent, or a member of the administration in Washington ask you to go back and study a record of what they have said since the war started?" They did not, for they knew their record would not stand inquiry. Time and again they had said they were trying to keep America out of the war, yet their actions carried America ever closer to war. They should be judged not by what they said but by what they had accomplished.

And what they had accomplished was to delude the American people into thinking American safety required entanglement in a distant war. "When this war started in Europe, it was clear that the American people were solidly opposed to entering it," Lindbergh said. "Why shouldn't we be? We had the best defensive position in the world; we had a tradition of independence from Europe; and the one time we did take part in a European war left European problems unsolved and debts to America unpaid."

Lindbergh reminded his listeners that polls taken of Americans at the outset of the fighting showed fewer than ten Americans in a hundred in favor of American involvement. "But there were various groups of people, here and abroad, whose interests and beliefs necessitated the involvement of the United States in the war," Lindbergh continued. "I shall point out some of these groups tonight, and outline their methods of procedure. In doing this, I must speak with the utmost frankness, for in order to counteract their efforts, we must know exactly who they are."

He paused, perhaps weighing for a final time whether he should take the fateful step. He had been thinking about this for months but always held his tongue in public. He knew he would spark a furor. He knew that what he was about to say would ruin his reputation and kill any hopes anyone had of a political career for him.

Yet he was already being called a traitor by the president, a proxy for Hitler by the president's men, and an enemy of freedom by members of Congress and many others who took the president's cues. What had he done to merit such treatment? He had simply exercised his constitutional right to challenge the president's interpretation of world affairs and American interests. If Roosevelt and the war party had been able to win the argument over the war on the merits of their case, they wouldn't have had to stoop to such personal slander. But they hadn't, and they did. And they were carrying the country swiftly to war. Lindbergh concluded he had no choice but to speak out as strongly as he could.

"The three most important groups who have been pressing this country toward war are the British, the Jewish and the Roosevelt administration," he said. "Behind these groups, but of lesser importance, are a number of capitalists, Anglophiles, and intellectuals who believe that the future of mankind depends upon the domination of the British empire. Add to these the Communistic groups who were opposed to intervention until a few weeks ago, and I believe I have named the major war agitators in this country."

Lindbergh made clear he referred to small groups of people. "I am speaking here only of war agitators, not of those sincere but misguided men and women who, confused by misinformation and frightened by propaganda, follow the lead of the war agitators. As I have said, these war agitators comprise only a small minority of our people, but they control a tremendous influence. Against the determination of the American people to stay out of war, they have marshaled the power of their propaganda, their money, their patronage."

He examined the war lobbies one by one. "First, the British. It is obvious and perfectly understandable that Great Britain wants the United States in the war on her side. England is now in a desperate position. Her population is not large enough and her armies are not strong enough to invade the continent of Europe and win the war she declared against Germany." This last point was important: Britain had declared war on Germany, not vice versa. And Britain had done so unprepared to fight. "Her geographical position is such that she cannot win the war by the use of aviation alone, regardless of how many planes we send her. Even if America entered the war, it is improbable that the Allied armies could invade Europe and overwhelm the Axis powers. But one thing is certain. If England can draw this country into the war, she can shift to our shoulders a large portion of the responsibility for waging it and for paying its cost."

Britain had persuaded America to rescue it from its folly once before. "As you all know, we were left with the debts of the last European war, and unless we are more cautious in the future than we have been in the past, we will be left with the debts of the present case. If it were not for her hope that she can make us responsible for the war financially as well as militarily, I believe England would have negotiated a peace in Europe many months ago, and be better off for doing so."

The British were hoping America had *not* learned from its previous experience. They hoped that what had worked in the past would work again. "England has devoted, and will continue to devote every effort to get us into the war. We know that she spent huge sums of money in this country during the last war in order to involve us. Englishmen have written books about the cleverness of its use. We know that England is spending great sums of money for propaganda in America during the present war."

Lindbergh stressed that there was nothing nefarious in this, from the British point of view. "If we were Englishmen, we would do the same. But our interest is first in America; and as Americans, it is essential for us to realize the effort that British interests are making to draw us into their war."

Lindbergh's second group was American Jews. Again, he held nothing against them for the position they took. Indeed, it would be nearly impossible for them to think otherwise than they did. "It is not difficult to understand why Jewish people desire the overthrow of Nazi Germany. The persecution they suffered in Germany would be sufficient to make bitter enemies of any race. No person with a sense of the dignity of mankind can condone the persecution of the Jewish race in Germany."

But again, the question was the interest of America as a whole. And, considering the backlash in America after the previous war, Lindbergh wondered if the Jewish advocates of war understood what they were getting into. "No person of honesty and vision can look on their pro-war policy here today without seeing the dangers involved in such a policy both for us and for them. Instead of agitating for war, the Jewish groups in this country should be opposing it in every possible way, for they will be among the first to feel its consequences." After the previous war, angry Americans had vilified bankers and arms-makers, who were seen as having suckered the country into war. Jews had trouble enough in America without making themselves similar targets. "Tolerance is a virtue that depends upon peace and strength. History shows that it cannot survive war and devastations. A few far-sighted Jewish people realize this and stand opposed to intervention. But the majority still do not."

Jews were a small minority in America. But they had influence beyond their numbers. "Their greatest danger to this country lies in their large ownership and influence in our motion pictures, our press, our radio and our government," Lindbergh said.

Lindbergh emphasized yet again that he had nothing against the

British or the Jews. "I am not attacking either the Jewish or the British people. Both races, I admire. But I am saying that the leaders of both the British and the Jewish races, for reasons which are as understandable from their viewpoint as they are inadvisable from ours, for reasons which are not American, wish to involve us in the war. We cannot blame them for looking out for what they believe to be their own interests, but we also must look out for ours. We cannot allow the natural passions and prejudices of other peoples to lead our country to destruction."

Lindbergh had less sympathy for the Roosevelt administration, his third and most sinister faction pushing for war. "Its members have used the war emergency to obtain a third presidential term for the first time in American history," Lindbergh reminded his listeners. "They have used the war to add unlimited billions to a debt which was already the highest we have ever known. And they have just used the war to justify the restriction of congressional power, and the assumption of dictatorial procedures on the part of the president and his appointees." Extending aid to Russia and launching a naval war against Germany, both without consulting Congress, were the most egregious instances.

Lindbergh perceived an ironic symmetry between Roosevelt's policy and the policies of the governments the president criticized. "The power of the Roosevelt administration depends upon the maintenance of a wartime emergency." Certainly Roosevelt couldn't have been elected a third time without the war. And there was nothing to stop him from being elected to a fourth term, as long as the war lasted. On present trends, such was in store for America. Like the dictators, the president operated by misdirection. "The danger of the Roosevelt administration lies in its subterfuge. While its members have promised us peace, they have led us to war heedless of the platform upon which they were elected."

The three factions worked together, Lindbergh said. "If any one of these groups—the British, the Jewish, or the administration—stops agitating for war, I believe there will be little danger of our involvement. I do not believe that any two of them are powerful enough to carry this country to war without the support of the third. And to these three, as I have said, all other war groups are of secondary importance."

The war factions had labored patiently. "When hostilities commenced in Europe, in 1939, it was realized by these groups that the American people had no intention of entering the war. They knew it would be worse than useless to ask us for a declaration of war at that time. But they believed that this country could be entered into the war in very much the same way we were entered into the last one. They planned: first, to prepare the United States for foreign war under the guise of American defense; second, to involve us in the war, step by step, without our realization; third, to create a series of incidents which would force us into the actual conflict. These plans were of course, to be covered and assisted by the full power of their propaganda.

"Our theaters soon became filled with plays portraying the glory of war. Newsreels lost all semblance of objectivity. Newspapers and magazines began to lose advertising if they carried anti-war articles. A smear campaign was instituted against individuals who opposed intervention. The terms 'fifth columnist,' 'traitor,' 'Nazi,' 'anti-Semitic' were thrown ceaselessly at any one who dared to suggest that it was not to the best interests of the United States to enter the war." Lindbergh's listeners knew he had been labeled all those things.

"Men lost their jobs if they were frankly anti-war. Many others dared no longer speak. Before long, lecture halls that were open to the advocates of war were closed to speakers who opposed it. A fear campaign was inaugurated. We were told that aviation, which has held the British fleet off the continent of Europe, made America more vulnerable than ever before to invasion. Propaganda was in full swing. There was no difficulty in obtaining billions of dollars for arms under the guise of defending America. Our people stood united on a program of defense. Congress passed appropriation after appropriation for guns and planes and battleships, with the approval of the overwhelming majority of our citizens. That a large portion of these appropriations was to be used to build arms for Europe, we did not learn until later. That was another step."

Lindbergh gave an example from his own area of expertise. "In 1939, we were told that we should increase our air corps to a total of 5,000 planes. Congress passed the necessary legislation. A few months later, the administration told us that the United States should have at least 50,000 planes for our national safety. But almost as fast as fighting planes were turned out from our factories, they were sent abroad, although our own air corps was in the utmost need of new equipment; so that today, two years after the start of war, the American army has a few hundred thoroughly modern bombers and fighters—less, in fact, than Germany is able to produce in a single month. Ever since its inception, our arms program has been laid out for the purpose of carrying on the war in Europe, far more than for the purpose of building an adequate defense for America."

American neutrality was eroded by this deception, Lindbergh said. "England and France would win if the United States would only repeal its arms embargo and sell munitions for cash, we were told. And then began a refrain that marked every step we took toward war for many months. 'The best way to defend America and keep out of war,' we were told, was 'by aiding the Allies.' First, we agreed to sell arms to Europe; next, we agreed to loan arms to Europe; then we agreed to patrol the ocean for Europe; then we occupied a European island"—Iceland—"in the war zone. Now, we have reached the verge of war."

The advocates of war had carried the country to the brink. "We have become involved in the war from practically every standpoint except actual shooting. Only the creation of sufficient 'incidents' yet remains; and you see the first of these already taking place"—this reference to the *Greer* episode was Lindbergh's one nod to what Roosevelt had just said—"according to plan, a plan that was never laid before the American people for their approval."

Lindbergh hadn't given up hope, which was why he had come to Des Moines. "Men and women of Iowa: only one thing holds this country from war today. That is the rising opposition of the American people. Our system of democracy and representative government is on test today as it has never been before. We are on the verge of a war in which the only victor would be chaos and prostration. We are on the verge of a war for which we are still unprepared, and for which no one has offered a feasible plan for victory—a war which cannot be won without sending our soldiers across the ocean to force a landing on a hostile coast against armies stronger than our own.

"We are on the verge of war, but it is not yet too late to stay out. It is not too late to show that no amount of money, or propaganda, or patronage can force a free and independent people into war against its will. It is not yet too late to retrieve and to maintain the independent American destiny that our forefathers established in this new world." The opponents of war must make their voices heard. "We can still make our will known. And if we, the American people, do that, independence and freedom will continue to live among us, and there will be no foreign war."

PART SIX

Opposition Undone

69

F EW SPEECHES HAVE had a more enduring effect on American history, and none of those worked so opposite the speaker's intention. In the space of twenty-five minutes in Des Moines, Charles Lindbergh not only destroyed his own reputation—he expected this—but simultaneously discredited the antiwar movement and killed any plausible alternative to the globalist vision of Franklin Roosevelt. Indeed, if evidence had been required that Lindbergh was *not* the German agent his foes alleged him to be, the fact that his speech made American armed intervention *more* likely should have been exhibit A.

But Lindbergh's enemies weren't looking for evidence. They wanted a weapon to beat him with. And he gave it to them in his Des Moines speech. Interventionists who previously had to answer Lindbergh's arguments that entering the war would enmesh America inextricably in European politics no longer had to do so; they called him an anti-Semite and left it at that. To his warnings that Roosevelt was amassing too much power and thereby threatening American democracy, they gave the same answer. Ditto to his characterization as deliberately alarmist the president's contention that Germany posed a pressing danger to the American homeland. Likewise his observation that a war in alliance with imperial Britain and communist Russia would be no war for democracy.

Neither did Lindbergh leave much ground for other opponents of war to make those arguments, which were as valid after the Des

Moines debacle as they had been before. If the headline speaker for
the leading antiwar group was such a poor excuse for a human being,
what hope did the lesser members of the movement have? Burton
Wheeler and Gerald Nye might carry on the battle, but all their critics had to say was "Lindbergh," and ears closed to their arguments.

THE CONDEMNATIONS OF Lindbergh were immediate and overwhelming. The *New York Herald Tribune* called Lindbergh's comments profoundly un-American. "The Des Moines speech, marking
the climax of a series of innuendoes and covert allusions by isolationist leaders, opens new and ugly vistas and seeks to inject into
open debate subjects which all good Americans should pray might
be confined to the pages of the 'Voelkischer Beobachter' and the
addresses of one Adolf Hitler," the paper's editors declared. "To be
sure, Mr. Lindbergh did not counsel anti-Semitism. He warned the
Jews that they may suffer from it in the event of war—and provided
anti-Semites with fuel for their anti-Semitism. He asserted, after the
fashion of anti-Semites everywhere, that the Jews were dangerous
to the United States because of their 'large ownership and influence
in our motion pictures, our press, our radio and our government.' To
state that Jews exert an influence in this country out of proportion to
their numbers is to state what is unproved and unprovable; to state
that their influence is exerted as Jews and not as American citizens is
to libel not only the Jews but the whole American system."

The *New York Post* said Lindbergh had lost his moorings. "So
deep does Mr. Lindbergh's anti-Semitism go that he can look upon
a world in which almost half the human race has suffered intolerable outrage against its independence and dignity, and decide that
somehow the chief villain in the piece is the Jew. This is no shallow, surface anti-Semitism, no mere petulance or passing bar-room
anger; this is a deep, dark, mystical current, Teutonic, if not in inspiration, quite obviously in coloration and content. Only a feeling that
has climbed to the level of obsession, only a fury among emotions
can explain such an analysis of recent events. To look upon a nation
which has responded to an obvious peril by taxing and straining itself
for a fifty-billion-dollar defense program, and to conclude that its
future would be bright if only the Jews would cease to make war, is

to tell us more about the speaker than about the world in which he lives."

The *Philadelphia Inquirer* noted the bad company Lindbergh was keeping. "Anti-Semitism is a cardinal Nazi doctrine. Without urging anti-Semitism in so many words, Lindbergh virtually accuses Jewish citizens in the United States of being dangerous to its peace and safety. Place the most striking passages from Lindbergh's and Hitler's speeches side by side and they are as alike as Tweedledum and Tweedledee."

The *Cincinnati Enquirer* said much the same thing. "Lindbergh took the chapter and verse of his speech from official German propaganda. It was not the first time this has occurred, but never before so strikingly as when he said that America was being driven to war by three groups—the British, the Jews, and the Roosevelt Administration. Characteristically, there was not a word of criticism of the Nazis in his speech. Anti-Semitism, Hitler's staple commodity, showed itself repeatedly in Lindbergh's speech."

The *Detroit Free Press* had had quite enough of Lindbergh. "No more need be said. He should not only keep that Nazi medal Goring pinned on him. He should use it as a decoration for a Ku Klux Klan nightshirt when he is also given that 'honorary' decoration."

The *Kansas City Times* offered one of the more thoughtful critiques of Lindbergh's speech. "As an American citizen, Charles A. Lindbergh has an undeniable right freely to express his opinion concerning the foreign policy of his government. He shares that right with some 130,000,000 other persons. If he wishes to charge the Roosevelt administration, as a whole, or any individual member of it, from the President on down, with conspiring to drive this country into war against the will of a majority of the American people, we may disagree, but we cannot legitimately object. If he wants to say we are being made the victims of a British plot, the purpose of which is to render us financially and militarily responsible for the future conduct of the war, again it is his privilege and one in which he must be rigorously protected, however much we may dispute his interpretation of the fact.

"But when Mr. Lindbergh publicly accuses a racial group among his fellow countrymen of warmongering, as he did on Thursday night in Des Moines, then he goes beyond the rights of an American citizen. Lindbergh may not have meant to play upon race prejudice when he described the Jews of the United States as anxious to bring this country into the conflict, out of sympathy for the plight of the Jews in Germany. That remains, however, the incontestable effect of what he said."

Civic groups joined the chorus of condemnation. The Committee to Defend America asserted, "Mr. Lindbergh may say that 'no person with a sense of the dignity of mankind can condone the persecution of the Jewish race in Germany.' But he should know that this persecution was brought about in Germany by exactly the kind of thing he said in Des Moines."

A spokeswoman for Hadassah, the Women's Zionist Organization of America, denounced what she called Lindbergh's "effort to besmirch a loyal group of American citizens." Mrs. David de Sola Pool added, "Coming at a time when we must close our ranks and present a united front against the aggressors who would divide and bedevil us, the speech of Mr. Lindbergh is a warning to all who remember the anti-Jewish campaigns of the Nazis and the use to which they were put."

The editor of the *Protestant Digest* asserted that Lindbergh's speech showed the "true nature of those guiding the destinies of the America First Committee through his open appeal to anti-Semitism as a political principle." The editor said it was essential for Christians in America to speak out against Lindbergh. "The past decade has written large what we Christians have long known, that anti-Semitism is anti-Christianity. American Christians dare not repeat the mistake of German Christians who failed to speak forth their condemnation clearly and unequivocally when this evil first raised its head in that unhappy land." The *Protestant Digest* circulated a letter condemning Lindbergh; it was signed by seven hundred Protestant churchmen from across the country.

The Loyal Americans of German Descent wrote Lindbergh an open letter disavowing him and embracing Roosevelt. "As loyal Americans who truly love the land from which our forebears or we ourselves have come, we stand behind President Roosevelt's foreign policy in order to bring about the defeat of Hitlerism and thereby insure justice, equality and freedom for the entire world. We think that most Americans agree with that position. Therefore, we respectfully suggest that when you mention those who do not share your attitude toward Hitler and his program you will be good enough to include us."

The American Socialist party lambasted Lindbergh's Des Moines address as "at once a serious blow to democracy and to the movement to keep the United States out of war." The party's national executive committee concluded a three-day meeting by saying, "Although it is true that Lindbergh recognized and condemned Nazi cruelty to the Jews, that fact cannot undo the harm done by his other statements." The compulsions toward war weren't the work of the Jews or any other race or nationality, the Socialists said. "They have their roots, instead, in an economic system"—capitalism.

New York mayor Fiorello La Guardia had been asked by the Council Against Intolerance for a comment on Lindbergh's speech. La Guardia responded, "No American should read at a public meeting at any time from a carbon copy of a Nazi paper."

Thomas Dewey, the district attorney of New York, called Lindbergh profoundly un-American. "Charles A. Lindbergh, in a national broadcast, injected religious and racial prejudice into a discussion of our foreign policy," Dewey said. "That, I declare, is an inexcusable abuse of the right of freedom of speech which 130,000,000 Americans, regardless of their views, will wholly reject. When the religion or race of any individual or group is made a part of the discussion of domestic or foreign policy, that is a challenge to our freedoms."

Alabama congressman Luther Patrick waved a copy of *Mein Kampf* in the House of Representatives and said, "It sounds just like Charles A. Lindbergh."

Senator Claude Pepper hinted at a power grab by Lindbergh. The Florida Democrat described Lindbergh as part of a shadowy group who were "looking forward to the day when, out of the nation's misery, they can set up their own kind of dictatorship." Pepper added, "There comes a time when disloyalty to one's president is disloyalty to one's country. There comes a time when men must forget differences of opinion about methods and stand together for the common cause."

The Texas House of Representatives warned Lindbergh to stay out of the Lone Star State. "Lindbergh ought to be shipped back to Germany to live with his own people," one Texas lawmaker said.

An antiwar rival to the America First Committee slammed Lindbergh. "The Keep America Out of War Congress most deeply regrets and disagrees with Mr. Lindbergh's implication that the American citizens of Jewish extraction or religion are a separate group, apart from the rest of the American people, or that they react as a separate group, or that they are unanimously for our entrance into the European war."

LINDBERGH WASN'T ABANDONED entirely, at least not at once. Gerald Nye told an audience in Ohio, "I agree with Charles Lindbergh that the Jewish people are a large factor in our movement toward war. There is no evasion of the truth that the Jewish people are among the leaders in this movement. I do not say they are the largest factor, but they certainly are one of the leading factors. This is only natural, for the Jewish people have suffered under the Nazi regime." Burton Wheeler, in the friendly confines of his home state, mentioned Lindbergh in a speech without condemning him. The Montanan had several eggs thrown at him.

The America First Committee came to Lindbergh's defense tepidly and impersonally. In a statement that carried no signatures, the committee declared, "Ever since the nationwide effort to keep America out of war began, the interventionists have sought to hide the real issue by flinging false charges at the America First Committee and at every leader who has spoken out against our entry into the European conflict. The present attack on Colonel Lindbergh is merely another case in point. Colonel Lindbergh and his fellow members of the America First Committee are not anti-Semitic. We deplore the injection of the race issue into the discussion of war or peace. It is the interventionists who have done this. America First, on the other hand, has invited men and women of every race, religion and national origin to join this committee, provided only that they are patriotic citizens who put the interests of their country ahead of any other nation. We repeat that invitation. At least 80 percent of the American people oppose our entry into the war. The America First Committee has supplied to these millions of citizens a leadership which has thus far helped to avert disaster. Consequently, the aim of the war-makers is to destroy the America First Committee. Behind a smoke screen of groundless charges this nation is being led to war in violation of the Constitution of the United States. There is but one real issue—the issue of war. From this issue we will not be diverted. We will carry on the fight until it is won."

70

EW YORK TIMES carries bitter attacks on my address from Jewish and other organizations and from the White House," Lindbergh wrote in his journal two days after the Iowa speech. This didn't surprise him. What *did* surprise him was the response from America First. "My Des Moines address has caused so much controversy that General Wood has decided to hold a meeting of the America First National Committee in Chicago. I must, of course, attend." He would explain that he had spoken carefully. The *Times* and the other critics were overreacting. "The very mention of the word 'Jew' is cause for a storm." But one couldn't solve problems without confronting them. "I feel that the only hope for a moderate solution lies in an open and frank discussion."

He flew to Chicago. "Bob Stuart and Page Hufty were waiting for me at the airport. We drove to the Chicago Club. General Wood and Dick Moore were there. We ate supper while we discussed tomorrow's meeting. General Wood suggested the possibility of adjourning the America First Committee! His plan would be to state that since the President had already involved us seriously in war, the committee saw nothing gained by continuing its activities at this time and would adjourn until the congressional elections next year."

Lindbergh hadn't been expecting this. Wood had another engagement and left Lindbergh and the others to consider his suggestion. "We all felt the committee should continue its activities unless and until Congress declares war, or unless it becomes obvious that we are no longer being effective—which is far from the case today."

Stuart had brought telegrams that had arrived from America First chapters around the country. "Ninety per cent or more of them are in accord with what I said. Apparently the only strong opposition comes from one portion of the New York City chapter."

Lindbergh was Wood's guest that night. "Half hour's conference with the general before bed. I suggest that the American First Committee continue for the present and until the war situation shows more definitely its trend. Much is unforeseen, and I prefer to go down fighting for what we believe in, if we must go down at all."

The conversation with Wood continued at breakfast. "I told him 1) that I felt it was not the time for the committee to adjourn; and 2) that while I was not willing to repudiate or modify any portion of my Des Moines address, I would, if the committee wished, issue a statement to the effect that the address represented my personal opinion and not the policy of the committee. I told General Wood that the latter course seemed to me inadvisable." Wood responded noncommittally.

Lindbergh returned to the Chicago Club. John Flynn approached him first. "Flynn says he does not question the truth of what I said at Des Moines, but feels it was inadvisable to mention the Jewish problem." Lindbergh was exasperated. "It is difficult for me to understand Flynn's attitude. He feels as strongly as I do that the Jews are among the major influences pushing this country toward war. He has said so frequently, and he says so now. He is perfectly willing to talk about it among a small group of people in private. But apparently he would rather see us get into the war than mention in public what the Jews are doing, no matter how tolerantly and moderately it is done."

Lindbergh lunched by himself. "I thought it best not to attend the meeting of the committee, since the discussion will center largely around my Des Moines address." Stuart called at quarter past two, asking Lindbergh to come to the home where the committee was meeting. "When I arrived, General Wood, Amos Pinchot, Mrs. Fairbank, Ed Webster, John Flynn, Page Hufty, Dick Moore, Bob Stuart, and several others were there. I found that the majority of the committee wanted to issue a statement backing up my Des Moines address, but that Flynn had objected so strongly it was decided to issue a statement that really took no stand at all."

Discussion turned to the offer Lindbergh had made to Wood to say the Des Moines speech represented his views alone. "I reaffirmed my willingness to do this, and at the same time said I thought it would be a mistake. A vote was taken, and everyone was against it except Flynn. Flynn said afterward that certain rules should be laid down for America First speakers."

Lindbergh responded that the committee could lay down rules, but it ought to do so before inviting speakers, and then it should stick by them.

He could see where this was going. In fact, he had seen it months before. "I knew this type of situation would arise in connection with America First, and it was among my reasons for refusing to accept the national chairmanship when it was offered to me last spring."

The committee remained split. "The friction between Webster and Flynn continues to develop," Lindbergh wrote. "Webster is too far 'right' for Flynn, and Flynn is too far 'left' for Webster. I tried to explain to Webster that America First could never be a powerful organization if it alienated the liberal groups represented by such men as John T. Flynn. I told Webster that an organization which went too far to the right would lose the spark and incentive of the liberal mind, while one which went too far to the left would lose stability and direction."

LINDBERGH SOLDIERED ON. He traveled to Fort Wayne, Indiana, a city unusual in having a newspaper that backed America First. "We have become so accustomed to an opposition press that it is a strange and pleasant experience to pick up a local paper which carries friendly headlines and editorials," Lindbergh wrote. The other major paper was hostile. "The opposition paper here is carrying a large advertisement in which statements are attributed to me which I never made," Lindbergh remarked after a read. "As far as the 'war party' is concerned, what I actually say seems to be of little importance. They quote me as saying what they *wish* or *think* that I said. They do not bother to refer to my addresses, which are all available; at best, they refer to some garbled newspaper account. The result is that I am often quoted as saying things which I not only never said, but which I never believed."

The Fort Wayne audience was small but supportive. Lindbergh touched old themes while avoiding the recently inflamed nerve. "The crowd was with us from the beginning. There was no opposition during the entire meeting." He was a bit disappointed. "I think some opposition is a good thing."

Afterward John O'Brien of Notre Dame came up to Lindbergh. "Father O'Brien showed me a telegram he had just received, to the effect that a poll of the Catholic hierarchy showed that ninety per cent were opposed to entering the war."

He met Robert Wood in Chicago on the way home. "We discussed, among other matters, the possibility of adjourning the America First Committee until the congressional campaigns begin in 1942. I took the stand that an adjournment at this time would not be understood by our members, that they would feel we were showing weakness at the very moment we should be fighting the hardest. The noninterventionist forces in this country have placed their confidence in us and their support behind us. We have accepted their confidence and support—in fact, we have asked for it. Now, we cannot let these people down at the very moment they have a right to expect us to stand firm."

Wood agreed in principle but wondered whether continued resistance to the increasingly inevitable would do more harm than good.

Lindbergh didn't question Wood's right to a rest. "General Wood has given a tremendous amount of his time and effort to the America First Committee. He is working much too hard for a man of his age and looks tired. He sees the country being led closer and closer to war in spite of anything we do."

Lindbergh hadn't changed his mind about the forces propelling the country toward war. "The amazing thing is not that we are so close to war but that we have been able to hold the war forces back as long as we have. Their ranks include the American government, the British government, the Jews, and the major portion of the press, radio, and motion-picture facilities of the country. We have on our side the mass of the people, but it is a question of how long the people can withstand the flood of propaganda with which the country is being covered. They have no accurate source of information to which to turn."

At this point, the fate of the country—and of much of the world—was in the hands of Roosevelt. "Regardless of the attitude of our people, it is a question as to whether the President will force us into war by actions and incidents which will make it unavoidable. He is in a position where he can force war on us whether we want it or not."

Like Wood, Lindbergh longed for a respite from the strife of opposition. He wished to get back to writing and the study of aviation. And he wanted to find a quiet home for Anne and the children. "Anne deserves one, and the children need one."

Yet this was probably a vain hope. "If we get into the type of war Roosevelt is headed for, there probably won't be any opportunity for writing or research or a permanent home for years at best."

He had no choice but to persevere. "No matter what sacrifice it involves, I feel my time is well spent in opposing our participation in this war. And even aside from a personal standpoint, I simply could not stand idly by and watch my country follow a leadership I think is so dishonest, so incompetent, and so wrong."

In New York, Herbert Hoover explained the facts of life to Lindbergh. The former president said the question of war or peace for America was beyond the influence of the antiwar movement. It was in the hands of Roosevelt and the events he had set in motion. And Lindbergh hadn't helped matters lately. "Hoover told me he felt my Des Moines address was a mistake (the mention of the Jews in connection with the war-agitating groups). I told him I felt my statements had been both moderate and true. He replied that when you had been in politics long enough you learned not to say things just because they are true."

Lindbergh didn't object aloud, saving his riposte for his journal. "I am not a politician—and that is one of the reasons why I don't wish to be one. I would rather say what I believe when I want to say it than to measure every statement I make by its probable popularity."

71

On October 9 Roosevelt sent a message to Congress requesting revision of the existing neutrality law. He observed that the original neutrality law of 1935 had been modified in response to changing circumstances. Each revision had been overtaken by events. The last major modification was in 1939. At the time of revision, the new provisions seemed reasonable. "But so did the Maginot Line," Roosevelt said. "Since then, in these past two tragic years, war has spread from continent to continent; very many nations have been conquered and enslaved; great cities have been laid in ruins." The future would be like the recent past, only worse, unless America did something to change it. "The pattern of the future, the future as Hitler seeks to shape it—is now as clear and as ominous as the headlines of today's newspapers."

Roosevelt said that Americans had never been neutral in thought. "We have never been indifferent to the fate of Hitler's victims. And, increasingly, we have become aware of the peril to ourselves, to our democratic traditions and institutions, to our country, and to our hemisphere. We have known what victory for the aggressors would mean to us."

Americans understood the importance of defense in depth, Roosevelt said. "We know that we could not defend ourselves in Long Island Sound or in San Francisco Bay. That would be too late. It is the American policy to defend ourselves wherever such defense becomes necessary under the complex conditions of modern warfare."

Isolationists, alarmists and fifth columnists would protest any change in the law, Roosevelt said. They would say he was asking for a declaration of war. They would be wrong. "The revisions which I suggest do not call for a declaration of war any more than the Lend-Lease Act called for a declaration of war." But certain provisions of the existing neutrality law severely handicapped America's ability to defend itself. "The repeal or modification of these provisions will not leave the United States any less neutral than we are today, but will make it possible for us to defend the Americas far more successfully, and to give aid far more effectively against the tremendous forces now marching toward conquest of the world."

The key change Roosevelt sought would allow the arming of merchant ships. Such a change would simply restore historical practice, the president said. "Through our whole history"—until 1937—"American merchant vessels have been armed whenever it was considered necessary for their own defense. It is an imperative need now to equip American merchant vessels with arms. We are faced not with the old type of pirates but with the modern pirates of the sea who travel beneath the surface or on the surface or in the air destroying defenseless ships without warning and without provision for the safety of the passengers and crews."

The American government owed the ships this historic right. It would be no guarantee of safety, but it would give them a fighting chance. "In the event of an attack by a raider they have a chance to keep the enemy at a distance until help comes. In the case of an attack by air, they have at least a chance to shoot down the enemy or keep the enemy at such height that it cannot make a sure hit. If it is a submarine, the armed merchant ship compels the submarine to use a torpedo while submerged, and many torpedoes thus fired miss their mark. The submarine can no longer rise to the surface within a few hundred yards and sink the merchant ship by gunfire at its leisure."

Roosevelt reemphasized the global stakes of the current conflict. "I cannot impress too strongly upon the Congress the seriousness of the military situation that confronts all of the nations that are combating Hitler," he said. "The ultimate fate of the Western Hemisphere lies in the balance." Congress must act swiftly. "We cannot permit the affirmative defense of our rights to be annulled and diluted by sections of the Neutrality Act which have no realism in the light of unscrupulous ambition of mad-men."

The American people demanded the changes. "We Americans have determined our course. We intend to maintain the security and the integrity and the honor of our country. We intend to maintain the policy of protecting the freedom of the seas against domination by any foreign power which has become crazed with a desire to control the world. We shall do so with all our strength and all our heart and all our mind."

CONGRESS GAVE ROOSEVELT the revisions he wanted. Meanwhile he maintained his rhetorical offensive. "Every school child knows what our foreign policy is," he told the Foreign Policy Association in late October. "It is to defend the honor, the freedom, the rights, the interests and the well-being of the American people. We seek no gain at the expense of others. We threaten no one, nor do we tolerate threats from others. No nation is more deeply dedicated to the ways of peace; no nation is fundamentally stronger to resist aggression."

Strength required vigilance, against enemies within as well as enemies abroad. "There are a few persons in this country who seek to lull us into a false sense of security, to tell us that we are not threatened, that all we need to do to avoid the storm is to sit idly by—and to submit supinely if necessary. The same deadly virus has been spread by Hitler's agents and his Quislings and dupes in every country which he has overrun."

The American people weren't fooled. "They are hardheaded realists and they fear no one." They were deliberate but not timid. "We reach decisions slowly, but when they are made they are backed by the determination of 130 million free Americans and are inexorable." Americans had decided what to do about Germany. "They are constantly becoming more determined that Hitler's threat to everything for which we stand must be struck down." To date this determination had given rise to aid to the countries fighting Hitler.

Yet aid was a means, not the end. "The real end, the inescapable end, is the destruction of the Hitler menace. In achieving that end, our responsibility is fully as great as that of the peoples who are fighting and dying for it. I know that our country will not shrink from that responsibility nor quail before whatever sacrifices it may demand."

ROOSEVELT REPORTED A new incident involving an American warship. The destroyer *Kearny* had been ordered from Iceland to the aid of a British convoy that encountered German submarines. The *Kearny* joined the fray, dropping depth charges and incurring torpedo damage that killed eleven and wounded nearly two dozen others.

In an address marking Navy Day—October 27—Roosevelt put the blame on Hitler. "We have wished to avoid shooting," he said. "But the shooting has started. And history has recorded who fired the first shot. In the long run, however, all that will matter is who fired the last shot."

The attack was bigger than one ship. "America has been attacked. The U.S.S. *Kearny* is not just a Navy ship. She belongs to every man, woman, and child in this nation. Illinois, Alabama, California, North Carolina, Ohio, Louisiana, Texas, Pennsylvania, Georgia, Arkansas, New York, and Virginia—those are the home states of the honored dead and wounded of the *Kearny*. Hitler's torpedo was directed at every American, whether he lives on our sea coasts or in the innermost part of the country, far from the seas and far from the guns and tanks of the marching hordes of would-be conquerors of the world."

Roosevelt employed the occasion of the *Kearny* attack to drop a bombshell of his own. "I have in my possession a secret map made in Germany by Hitler's Government—by the planners of the new world order," Roosevelt said. "It is a map of South America and a part of Central America, as Hitler proposes to reorganize it. Today in this area there are fourteen separate countries. But the geographical experts of Berlin have ruthlessly obliterated all existing boundary lines; they have divided South America into five vassal states, bringing the whole continent under their domination. And they have also so arranged it that the territory of one of these new puppet states includes the Republic of Panama and our great life line—the Panama Canal."

There was more. "Your Government has in its possession another document, made in Germany by Hitler's Government. It is a detailed plan, which, for obvious reasons, the Nazis did not wish and do not wish to publicize just yet, but which they are ready to impose, a little later, on a dominated world—if Hitler wins. It is a plan to abolish all existing religions—Catholic, Protestant, Mohammedan, Hindu, Buddhist, and Jewish alike. The property of all churches will be seized by the Reich and its puppets. The cross and all other symbols of religion are to be forbidden. The clergy are to be forever liquidated, silenced under penalty of the concentration camps, where even now so many fearless men are being tortured because they have placed God above Hitler. In the place of the churches of our civilization, there is to be set up an International Nazi Church—a church which will be served by orators sent out by the Nazi Government. And in the place of the Bible, the words of *Mein Kampf* will be imposed and enforced as Holy Writ. And in the place of the cross of Christ will be put two symbols—the swastika and the naked sword. The god of Blood and Iron will take the place of the God of Love and Mercy."

Roosevelt warned his listeners against the denials sure to come from Hitler and his apologists. "These grim truths which I have told you of the present and future plans of Hitlerism will of course be hotly denied tonight and tomorrow in the controlled press and radio of the Axis powers. And some Americans—not many—will continue to insist that Hitler's plans need not worry us—that we should not concern ourselves with anything that goes on beyond rifle shot of our own shores."

Americans must shut their ears to these traitors even as they prepared for battle. In language suited to his Navy Day audience, Roosevelt said, "We Americans have cleared our decks and taken our battle stations. We stand ready in the defense of our nation and in the faith of our fathers to do what God has given us the power to see as our full duty."

"Mr. President, I am instructed by the *New York Times* to ask if you will release for publication that map and document you mentioned last night," a reporter said at Roosevelt's press conference the next day.

"No," Roosevelt replied. "And for a very good reason. The map has on it—it's in my basket at the present time—it has on it certain manuscript notations, which if they were reproduced would in all probability disclose how—where the map came from. And on account of these manuscript notations it might be exceedingly unfair to a number of people. It might also dry up the source of future information."

"Mr. President, if you have had time to read the German comment—Berlin comment—you may have noticed that they were accusing you of having faked the map. They speak of the map as a fraud, a forgery."

"Good stuff that has come out of Berlin today," Roosevelt said mockingly. "It's a scream." He waved some teletype copy from his desk. "Of course it sounds better in German."

Roosevelt got the laugh he wanted, but his questioner persisted. "What would you say to the charge of the suspicion that the map had been foisted on you in some way?"

"Well—"

"They make that very serious claim."

"Well, you know they made the serious claim about ten days ago that I had torpedoed the *Kearny*," Roosevelt said. "I suppose that is as good an answer as I can make."

The reporter wouldn't let go. He started to put his question again.

Roosevelt cut him off. "It comes from a source which is undoubtedly reliable. There is no question about that."

"Mr. President, have you had occasion to make that map available to the Latin American nations concerned?"

"No. It would only be done in the very strictest confidence. The kind of a confidence that would be—I suppose so that they could not trace the poor devil that we got it from."

Roosevelt never did show the map to the Latin American governments or to anyone else. And he never mentioned it again. The possibility of forgery certainly occurred to him. The American government had received the map from British intelligence, which had an obvious interest in helping the president argue his case that Hitler posed an imminent danger to the Americas. The British had been clever at forging documents to entice America into the World War, as Americans had learned after that war. The discovery that they had been fooled fed the isolationist backlash of the interwar decades. There was no reason to think the British were less clever this time around.

In fact, the map *was* a forgery, produced by William Stephenson's British propaganda crew and delivered to Roosevelt by Stephenson's American partner in deception, William Donovan.

Roosevelt might have known or suspected as much. He might not have. In either case, the map served his purpose of stirring American wrath against Hitler. He himself had said that who fired the first shot would matter less than who fired the last one. By the time America fired those last shots, no one would care about the fiddly provenance of a dodgy map.

AMERICA FIRST DIDN'T silence Lindbergh but it did ration his appearances. On October 30 he spoke again in New York. "We drove to Madison Square Garden behind the usual and apparently unavoidable police escort. The place was jammed when we arrived—every seat filled and a large crowd in the street outside. The final police estimate placed the crowd outside at between 20,000 and 30,000, making a total attendance of more than 40,000 people, more than 50,000 if there were 30,000 outside the building."

Lindbergh shared the stage with Burton Wheeler and two others. Wheeler got the prime closing slot. But the audience let Lindbergh know they still liked him, even if a lot of other people didn't. "This was in many ways the most successful meeting we have yet held. The only ones that would compare to it in size are the first meeting we held at Madison Square Garden last May and the meeting we held at the Hollywood Bowl in June. And we have never before had quite such enthusiasm at so large a meeting. I was unable to start speaking for six minutes after I was introduced! There is no better indication of how people feel about this war."

Lindbergh took particular encouragement from the fact that such a crowd appeared in the heart of enemy territory. "All of us who spoke took turns in going outside to speak briefly to the people who were not able to get inside the building. A small wooden stand had been built for this purpose on the sidewalk, and loudspeakers had been installed. The entire block in front of Madison Square Garden was jammed with people—both street and sidewalks. And the next block west was jammed as far as I could see!"

He had expected hecklers, at least outside the building. "The amazing thing was that we had the same reception from the people in the street as from those in the Garden. I had expected strong vocal opposition outside. There was *none.* It seemed as though every man and woman in the crowd was behind us! During the entire meeting there were only two instances of individuals trying to cause trouble, and they occurred at the time Flynn was opening the meeting. First, someone shouted out something I could not hear. A little later a man shouted, 'Hang Roosevelt.' The latter was almost certainly an opposition 'plant.' They will say that there were demands to hang the President at our meeting. But with over 40,000 people present those were the only two incidents that took place within my sight or hearing."

73

I s there anything you can tell us, sir, about these Japanese
negotiations?" a reporter asked at Roosevelt's press conference
on November 28.

While the president had been haranguing Hitler for years and
applying naval pressure for months, he had said little publicly about
Japan and had looked to economic leverage to modify that country's
behavior. The administration imposed an embargo on scrap metal
after Japanese troops occupied French Indochina in 1940, and a year
later it added petroleum products to the banned list. Imported met-
als and oil were crucial to Japan's economy and especially its military
machine. The Japanese agreed to negotiations even as they considered other options.

"I think I'd better not," Roosevelt answered the reporter. He
reconsidered. "It has been based on an American policy of infinite
patience."

"Well, Mr. President, could you say, sir, whether these negotiations
have broken down temporarily?"

"No. They have not."

"Mr. President, can you tell when the next meeting will be held
with the Japanese?"

"I don't know."

"Can you tell us, sir, if there were any new developments in your
talks with the Japanese different from those that they have had from
Mr. Hull?"

"No. I would say just exactly the same." Again Roosevelt added a bit. "I think I could tell you, for background—but only for background—that the situation seems serious, because our one desire has been peace in the Pacific, and the taking of no steps to alter the prospects of peace, which of course has meant non-aggression. It really boils down to that.

"And also—as background—I was, last spring, talking along the line of general peace for the Pacific, based on a settlement of the war between China and Japan, the restoration of peace there, plus a permanent arrangement for non-aggression in the Pacific, and the restoration of normal economic relations, access to raw materials."

Roosevelt continued to elaborate. "As you know, the Secretary of State, with even more patience than I have—which is saying a whole lot—had been holding conversations from, I think it was, April. And in the middle of them came the Japanese expedition to Indo-China, which is very far afield, and caused us very great concern, because it seemed to show a reasonable parallel with the Hitler methods in Europe. As, for example, the infiltration, over a period of several months, of the German armies into Rumania and Hungary, placing themselves in the position where strategically they were all set to attack Yugoslavia and Greece. And of course the drawing of the parallel made peacefully inclined people over here wonder whether this occupation, with a limited number of troops in Indo-China, was the beginning of a similar action in the Far East, placing obvious American interests in great jeopardy if the drawing of such a parallel was justified."

The chief American interest in the region was the Philippines, still an American possession although scheduled for independence in a few years. The Philippines were being encircled by the Japanese, Roosevelt said. "Even before the Japanese went into Indo-China, one might almost say that the Philippines were located in a horse-shoe, with Japanese military control over the coasts of China, all the way down to the southern border of China, and Japanese military control on the opposite side—the east—over the mandated islands, so called." These were Pacific islands placed under Japanese administration by the League of Nations.

Again Roosevelt linked Japan to Hitler. "A study of the map would be advisable for all of us, because the Hitler method has always been aimed at a little move here and a little move there, by which complete encirclement, or the obtaining of essential military points, was merely a prelude to the extension of aggression to other places. It's a perfectly obvious historical fact today. And we are of course thinking not only about the American flag in the Philippines, not only about certain vital defense needs which come from that open end of the horseshoe, but we are thinking about something even more important, and that is the possible extension of control by aggression into the whole of the Pacific area. And we are thinking about what it would mean to this country if that policy were to be used against us in the whole Pacific area."

"Mr. President, would this mean that we are working for the status quo?"

"Yes, we have been for a long time." Roosevelt again reconsidered. "Wait a minute. I wouldn't say working for the status quo, because we have got to leave China out of the status quo. We are certainly not working for the status quo in China." Parts of China had been occupied by Japanese forces for a decade. "Or Indo-China, for that matter." That French colony had been recently occupied by the Japanese.

"Against further aggression?"

"Against further aggression. And we are working to remove the present aggression."

"The Chinese situation is absolutely solid and set, is it not?" Roosevelt had demanded that Japan evacuate China.

"Absolutely."

"No chance of compromise?"

"No."

ROOSEVELT ADDED CONTEXT at a press conference a few days later. "Since last April, we have been discussing with the Japanese Government some method to arrive at an objective. The objective was permanent peace in the whole area of the Pacific. It seemed at times as if progress were being made toward that objective. And during that whole period, up to I think it was the end of June, we assumed that as both nations were negotiating toward that objective, that there would be no act which would be contrary to the desired end of peace.

"We were therefore somewhat surprised, the end of June, when the Japanese government sent troops—I think to a specified over-all total, in other words, a number which would not be exceeded—into Indo-China, after very brief negotiations with the French Vichy government. At the conclusion of this arrangement the Vichy government let it be understood rather clearly that they had agreed to this number of troops, principally because they were powerless to do anything else.

"Sometime thereafter, after the troops had gone there, the conversations were resumed between Japan and the United States, and for a while they seemed to be making progress. But again we made it perfectly clear that the objective which we were seeking meant the taking of no additional territory by anybody in the Pacific area.

"And the other day we got word from various sources that already, in Indo-China, there were large additional bodies of Japanese forces—various kinds of forces: naval, air, and land—and that other forces were on the way; and that even before these other forces had arrived, the number of forces already there had greatly exceeded, in Indo-China, the original amount which the French Government had agreed to, and that the forces that were on the way would still more greatly exceed the original number.

"And the question was asked this morning of the Japanese government, at my request, very politely, as to what the purpose of this was—what the intention of the Japanese Government in doing this was, as to the future; and eliminating, of course, the possibility that it was for the policing of Indo-China, which was an exceedingly peaceful spot beforehand. And we hope to get a reply to that very simple question shortly."

"Was there any time limit put on it?"

"No, no. That's a silly question. One doesn't put a time limit on things any more. That's the last century. We are at peace with Japan. We are asking a perfectly polite question."

TWO DAYS LATER the *Chicago Tribune* ran a story that was anything but polite. "F.D.R.'s War Plans!" the headline shouted. "Goal Is 10 Million Armed Men. Half to Fight in A.E.F."

Robert McCormick was as certain as Lindbergh that Roosevelt was maneuvering America into the war, and the *Tribune* publisher had investigative resources Lindbergh lacked. The paper's Washington correspondent had acquired a secret plan prepared for the joint board of the army and navy. The essence of the story was that the administration wasn't intending merely to assist in the defeat of the fascists; it was intending to take the leading role. "Germany and her European satellites cannot be defeated by the European powers now fighting against her," the report said, per the article's quote. "If our European enemies are to be defeated, it will be necessary for the United States to enter the war, and to employ a part of its armed forces offensively in the Eastern Atlantic and in Europe and Africa." The new American Expeditionary Force would number five million, and it would lead a major offensive against Germany in the summer of 1943.

The White House declined to comment. Others in the administration eventually conceded that the report was authentic, but they remarked that plans were simply plans. They didn't bind the government to anything. The *Tribune's* scoop was much ado about little.

THE BIGGER STORY came on December 7. Roosevelt had just finished lunch in the Oval Office that Sunday when he learned that an attack on Pearl Harbor in Hawaii was underway. Roosevelt thought there must be a mistake. He had expected a Japanese attack—that was the point of the pressure he had been applying for months. But not at Pearl Harbor. The resources the Japanese needed to replace what America had embargoed lay in the opposite direction. Hawaii was thousands of miles out of the way, besides being fearsomely defended. The Philippines seemed a more logical target.

On second thought, the very illogicality of an attack on Pearl Harbor might make it a *likelier* target. It was the last place the Americans would be expecting to be hit, and their guard would be lax. Apparently the Japanese had more in mind than replacing resources; they wanted a showdown with America.

Roosevelt wanted a showdown, too, although not chiefly with Japan. Roosevelt wanted a war against Germany. Whether the first would lead to the second, no one could say. Germany had an alliance with Japan, but the agreement mandated co-belligerence only if Japan were attacked. Besides, Hitler's word wasn't exactly to be relied on.

Roosevelt would deal with that later. At the moment he had a crisis on his hands. He shortly learned that the attack at Pearl Harbor had been devastating: more than two thousand Americans dead and nearly a score of ships destroyed or damaged, including the heart of America's Pacific battleship fleet.

Under other circumstances, the president could have expected searching questions as to how the commander in chief—Roosevelt himself—had let such a thing happen. But after two years in which Americans had wondered whether they were going to war, after two years of arguing about whether they *should* go to war, the news that war had begun, without America having to make a decision, brought a distracting relief from the uncertainty.

Roosevelt made the most of the moment. He summoned the leaders of Congress to the White House. He shared the grim news from Hawaii. They demanded to know if he would be requesting a declaration of war.

He said he hadn't decided.

They didn't believe him. Some said if he didn't ask for a declaration, they'd go to war without it.

He savored the irony. During those two years he had been accused of pushing America toward war. Now he was the reluctant one. Of course he was going to ask for a declaration, but he wanted to let the tension build a bit more.

He addressed a joint session of Congress the next day. His words were terse and grim. "Yesterday, December 7, 1941—a date which will live in infamy—the United States of America was suddenly and deliberately attacked by naval and air forces of the Empire of Japan," he told the senators and representatives. "The distance of Hawaii from Japan makes it obvious that the attack was deliberately planned many days or even weeks ago. During the intervening time the Japanese Government has deliberately sought to deceive the United States by false statements and expressions of hope for continued peace."

By this time the Japanese had launched attacks elsewhere in the Pacific region—on the Philippines, Hong Kong, Malaya, Guam and Wake and Midway islands. "Japan has, therefore, undertaken a surprise offensive extending throughout the Pacific area." The facts were unmistakable. "Hostilities exist. There is no blinking at the fact that our people, our territory, and our interests are in grave danger."

Roosevelt knew Congress and the American people would rise to the challenge. "With confidence in our armed forces, with the unbounded determination of our people, we will gain the inevitable triumph. So help us God."

Almost as an afterthought: "I ask that the Congress declare that since the unprovoked and dastardly attack by Japan on Sunday, December 7, 1941, a state of war has existed between the United States and the Japanese Empire."

Congress approved the request overwhelmingly. The vote was 82 to 0 in the Senate and 388 to 1 in the House.

Epilogue

S OONER OR LATER, countries get the foreign policies they can afford. This is as close to a law of history as the uncertain study of human idiosyncrasy allows. Poor countries bend before the gales of world affairs; rich countries change the global climate. As poor countries grow rich, they seek to protect their riches. And their riches afford them the capacity—by trade, diplomacy and war—to do so. The process takes time. Typically the assertion of power trails years or decades behind the power itself. But the assertion inevitably comes.

The United States began national life as a poor country by comparison with the great powers of the eighteenth-century Atlantic world: Britain, France, Spain. America's foreign policy was commensurately modest. But America's economy grew, until by the end of the nineteenth century it was the most powerful on the planet. America tested its new strength in war against Spain in 1898 and Germany in 1917. Yet many Americans, whose expectations of the world had been learned in earlier times, retained modest ambitions for their country, preferring that its horizons not extend beyond their continent or hemisphere.

The American economy continued to grow. The older generation passed from the scene. Younger Americans were willing to assert themselves and their country in a broader arena. Franklin Roosevelt, who came of age amid the war against Spain and held his first national office during the war against Germany, understood what America's industrial power permitted. He concluded before most of his generation that America need not accommodate rogue nations like Nazi Germany but could destroy them. And because it could, and because Hitler's regime offended Roosevelt's and America's standards of decent international behavior, America *must* destroy Germany.

Charles Lindbergh was twenty years younger than Roosevelt but an older soul. For all his virtuosity on the aeronautical edge of technology, Lindbergh thought like a premodern. He resented cities and the complexities of industrial life. He longed to escape to the countryside and implicitly to the past. As his own life grew more complicated, the attraction of earlier, simpler times grew stronger.

Lindbergh wasn't alone. The sentiments that moved him inspired the isolationism of interwar America. The country's economy had outgrown its hemisphere, which fact helped explain the duration of the Great Depression, when overseas markets for American products collapsed; yet Lindbergh and the other reactionaries refused to believe this mattered. Lindbergh's personal circumstances—the wealth he acquired by expertise, fame and marriage—enabled him to ignore mundane matters of economics, but few others could afford such freedom.

Lindbergh was fighting a losing battle, as he eventually realized. He was asking Americans to pretend they didn't have the power to settle the affairs of Europe on America's terms. He was counseling them to behave as timidly as they had had to act a century earlier. He was urging them to ignore events they found abhorrent—that even *he* found abhorrent—on the now specious ground they couldn't do anything about them.

Lindbergh got much right in his campaign against modernity. He understood that if America waded into European affairs again, there would be no getting out. Eighty years later, his prediction held true. He saw that Britain was a shadow of its former self. Within two decades of when he spoke, Britain had lost the empire that had made it more than a couple of islands on the European periphery. He argued that a war on the side of Russia would be no war for democracy. The war delivered half of Europe to communism. He feared that if Roosevelt succeeded in using the war to get elected a third time, he would become president for life. Roosevelt died in office during his fourth term. Lindbergh contended that if Congress and the American people failed to resist Roosevelt, the legislative control over war-making decreed by the Constitution would be lost forever. America fought five wars in the eight decades after World War II, and not one was declared by Congress.

But Lindbergh got the one big thing wrong. He thought the American people would be willing to settle for the modest American role that had suited their grandfathers. He believed they could be persuaded to ignore Roosevelt's call to American greatness. He supposed they could see through the deceptive incrementalism Roosevelt employed to make war increasingly likely until it became an accomplished fact. He judged that they would recoil from the sacrifices another European war exacted from them, as they had recoiled after the first war, and would regret their being deceived.

But they didn't recoil, and they showed few regrets. America became the great power Lindbergh warned the American people against, and they were entranced by their country's might. Roosevelt was shrewd, but not original, in casting American greatness in moral terms; power always wraps itself in the mantle of justice. Eighty years later Americans still looked on World War II as the "good war," despite the scores of millions it killed, and despite its ending with the use by the United States of the most terrible weapon ever invented. After World War II Americans fought on battlefields ever more distant and ever more tenuously related to America's immediate defense.

Lindbergh saw the path ahead and found it appalling. Americans trod the path and found it irresistible.

"Mr. President, what's this about Japan?" Churchill had heard of the attack on Hawaii and hastened to call Roosevelt.

"It's quite true," Roosevelt replied. "They have attacked us at Pearl Harbor. We are all in the same boat now."

"This certainly simplifies things," Churchill said.

Roosevelt and Churchill were getting ahead of themselves. Japan's attack on Pearl Harbor, and its nearly simultaneous attacks on the British colonial territories of Hong Kong, Malaya and Singapore, meant that America and Britain were fighting a common enemy in the Pacific region. But America still wasn't fighting Germany.

Indeed, American belligerence against Japan potentially *compli-cated* things. Roosevelt wanted a war against Germany; what he got was a war against Japan. If Germany didn't rally to the aid of Japan, Roosevelt might find it harder rather than easier to take America to war against Germany. The sudden change in American thinking about the war had everything to do with having been attacked; the American anger against Japan might diminish concern about Germany.

Roosevelt wrestled with the problem for three days. American war planning had supposed a two-front conflict, with primacy given to the European theater. This thinking might have to be dramatically revised. Roosevelt wondered if he could—or should—keep provoking Germany in the Atlantic while preparing to retaliate against Japan.

Then Hitler did Roosevelt a tremendous favor. The German leader, after scant consultation with his generals and admirals, declared war on America. Citing the unneutral behavior of the United States, most recently the shoot-on-sight policy and incidents to which it gave rise, Hitler had his foreign minister tell the American chargé d'affaires in Berlin that a state of war existed between Germany and the United States.

Likely Hitler had concluded that Roosevelt wouldn't rest until he got the war he wanted, and decided to seize the initiative by moving first. Doubtless he underestimated the capacity of America to fight two wars at once. Whatever Hitler's reasons, as of December 11 the United States was a full participant in World War II.

"So we had won after all," Churchill remembered thinking. "The United States was in the war, up to the neck and in to the death."

LINDBERGH LISTENED TO Roosevelt's request for a war declaration against Japan and to the roll call in favor. "What else was there to do?" he wrote regarding the decision. "We have been asking for war for months. If the President had asked for a declaration of war before, I think Congress would have turned him down with a big majority. But now we have been attacked, and attacked in home waters. We have brought it on our own shoulders; but I can see nothing to do under these circumstances except to fight. If I had been in Congress, I certainly would have voted for a declaration of war."

He called Robert Wood of the America First Committee. "His first words were, 'Well, he got us in through the back door.'" After the German declaration of war, Wood announced the decision of the America First Committee to disband. "The time for military action is here," the retired general explained. "There is no longer any question about our involvement in the conflict in Europe and Asia. We are at war. Today, though there may be many important subsidiary considerations, the primary objective is not difficult to state. It can be completely defined in one word: victory."

Lindbergh made his own public statement. "We have been stepping closer to war for many months," he said. "Now it has come and we must meet it as united Americans regardless of our attitude in the past toward the policy our government has followed. Whether or not that policy has been wise, our country has been attacked by force of arms, and by force of arms we must retaliate. Our own defenses and our military position have already been neglected too long. We must now turn every effort to building the greatest and most efficient Army, Navy and Air Force in the world. When American soldiers go to war, it must be with the best equipment that modern skill can design and that modern industry can build."

Lindbergh hadn't changed his mind about Roosevelt or the president's policies. "We are in a war which requires us to attack if we are to win it," he wrote to himself. "We must attack in Asia and in Europe, in fact, all over the world. That means raising and equipping an army of many millions and building shipping, which we have not now got. And after that, if we are to carry through our present war aims, it probably means the bloodiest and most devastating war of all history. And then what? We haven't even a clear idea of what we are fighting to attain." America's allies were a colonialist empire and a communist dictatorship; what might come of that collaboration? "Where is it leading us to, and when will it end?" Lindbergh couldn't say, and he didn't think anyone else could either.

He had fought the good fight against the war, and had lost. He knew his duty—and his desire. "Now that we are at war I want to contribute as best I can to my country's war effort. It is vital for us to carry on this war as intelligently, as constructively, and as successfully as we can, and I want to do my part."

His instinct was to write to the president offering his services. "But the trouble is that I have no confidence in President Roosevelt," he recorded. "It is not only my own experience and judgment, but I do not know a single man who has known Roosevelt, friend or enemy, who trusts what he says from one week to the next. And the President has the reputation, even among his friends, for being a vindictive man. If I wrote to him at this time, he would probably make what use he could of my offer from a standpoint of politics and publicity and assign me to some position where I would be completely ineffective and out of the way."

Instead he wrote to Hap Arnold. The air general passed Lindbergh's letter to Henry Stimson, the secretary of war. Stimson summoned Lindbergh to a meeting. Lindbergh expressed his hope to serve the country wherever he could; the air corps was the obvious place.

"Stimson said he would speak with complete frankness, that he would be extremely hesitant to put me into any position of command because of the views I had expressed about the war," Lindbergh wrote after the meeting. "He said he did not think anyone who had held such views should be in a position of command in this war because he did not believe such a person could carry on the war with sufficient aggressiveness." Stimson said he doubted that Lindbergh had changed his views.

"I replied that I had not changed them and that I felt it had been a mistake for this country to get into the war, but that now we were in the war my stand was behind my country, as I had always said it would be, and that I wanted to help in whatever way I could be most effective."

Stimson was unmoved. He'd had a long career in Washington, serving as secretary of war under William Howard Taft and then secretary of state under Herbert Hoover, before his current stint. He was a Republican in a Democratic administration. Whether on his own or with a nod from Roosevelt, he made it clear that Lindbergh wasn't wanted in the air corps. The last thing Roosevelt needed was for his sharpest critic to become a war hero.

So the Lone Eagle had his wings clipped. Officially, that is. Rejected by Roosevelt's War Department, Lindbergh enlisted as consultant with companies that designed and built airplanes for the army, including Ford Motor and United Aircraft. He talked United into sending him to the Pacific to observe its planes in combat. There he suggested improvements in the tuning of the airplane engines and in the techniques of flight. He demonstrated the latter to the combat pilots, eventually accompanying them on missions against the Japanese. He flew some fifty missions in all, and scored at least one kill of his own.

His service impressed Douglas MacArthur, the Allied commander in the southwestern Pacific, and Dwight Eisenhower, who as president summoned him back to the military, as a brigadier general of the Air Force Reserve. Lindbergh's rehabilitation included a Pulitzer Prize for his 1953 book, *The Spirit of St. Louis*, about the famous transatlantic flight.

The criticism of Lindbergh by then had faded. If Eisenhower, the hero of the war against Germany, didn't question Lindbergh's loyalty, few others felt inclined to do so. Lindbergh's warning that communism was a more abiding danger than fascism seemed prescient as the Cold War took shape. The charge of anti-Semitism lost purchase for lack of new evidence. And after the liberation of the death camps revealed the monstrousness of Nazi anti-Semitism, the stereotyping in Lindbergh's Des Moines speech seemed venial by comparison.

Yet some of the stigma remained. The discovery of the death camps cemented in American minds the idea that their country's participation in the war had been morally righteous. Eisenhower called his account of the war *Crusade in Europe*, and Americans almost as one embraced the characterization. They looked on the anti-interventionists as not merely mistaken but wicked. Isolationism was evil and must be shunned.

Lindbergh died in 1974, but his inadvertent legacy lived on. Fifty years later—eight decades after his dramatic fall from grace—isolationism remained a concept approachable only at peril to one's reputation for seriousness in foreign policy. Donald Trump revived the label "America First" in his 2016 campaign, and he adopted policies as president that echoed the anti-interventionist themes of Lindbergh and the committee of that name. In doing so Trump brought upon himself the derision of the heirs of Lindbergh's critics. The keepers of the Rooseveltian consensus sighed relief when Trump lost to Joe Biden in 2020, and they applauded America's reversion to interventionist form during Biden's presidency.

But the debate wasn't over. Sooner or later, countries get the foreign policies they can afford. In the 1940s and for half a century afterward, America could afford the most ambitious foreign policy in the world. Its economy bestrode the planet, funding victory in the two-hemisphere war against fascism, global containment of communism during the Cold War, and a reshaping of international trade and finance. At the same time the American economy allowed a steady expansion of the social programs pioneered by the New Deal. But economic power is a comparative concept, and eight decades after America entered World War II, the country's lead over its international rivals had shrunk dramatically, even as those domestic programs increasingly strained the government budget. In the age of the Roosevelt consensus, Americans had never had to choose between guns and butter. They might yet postpone the choice for some years or even decades, but not forever. Roosevelt and Lindbergh lived only in memory, but the arguments they made had resonance still.

Sources

PART ONE: THE ALLURE OF NEUTRALITY

I.

8 "I am personally": *New York Times*, Mar. 3, 1932.
9 "No crime": Ibid., May 14, 1932.
9 "Every agency": Thomas Doherty, *Little Lindy Is Kidnapped* (2020), 86.
11 "This will elect me": H. W. Brands, *Traitor to His Class: The Privileged Life and Radical Presidency of Franklin Delano Roosevelt* (2008), 259.

2.

13 On one occasion: A. Scott Berg, *Lindbergh* (1998), 339.
14 "Colonel Charles A. Lindbergh": *New York Times*, Dec. 23, 1935.
15 "brought into play . . . increased armaments": *Report of the Special Committee on Investigation of the Munitions Industry* (1936), 3–4.
17 "The political situation . . . search for peace": Roosevelt speech, Oct. 5, 1937, American Presidency Project, presidency.ucsb.edu. Roosevelt speeches and messages cited below are from this archive unless otherwise indicated.

3.

20 "He discussed": Kennedy diary, Feb. 22, 1938, in *Hostage to Fortune: The Letters of Joseph P. Kennedy*, edited by Amanda Smith (2001), 236.
21 "In taking up . . . its own citizens": Kennedy speech, Mar. 18, 1938, in *New York Times*, Mar. 19, 1939.

4.

25 "Papers carry reports": Entry for Mar. 12, 1938, in *The Wartime Journals of Charles A. Lindbergh* (1970). This source will be referred to below as "Lindbergh journal."

25 "Will there be": Ibid., Apr. 1, 1938.

26 "The contrast . . . military aircraft": Ibid., Apr. 2, 1938.

26 "When an Englishman": Ibid., Apr. 5, 1938.

26 "There is a combination": Ibid., Apr. 27, 1938.

26 "It was one": Ibid., May 5, 1938.

27 "Trippe said . . . accept the position": Ibid., June 3, 1938.

27 "France seems": Ibid., June 23, 1938.

28 "Great change . . . modern war": Ibid., Aug. 17–20, 1938.

28 "Sikorsky expects": Ibid., Oct. 15, 1938.

29 "He asked . . . from Russia": Ibid., Sept. 3–4, 1938.

5.

30 "Talked with Ambassador Kennedy . . . Sudeten territory": Ibid., Sept. 21, 1938.

31 "I venture . . . protect themselves": Kennedy to Hull, Sept. 22, 1938, *Foreign Relations of the United States* (*FRUS*), 1938, vol. 1, doc. 38.

6.

33 "The fabric of peace . . . good of humanity": Roosevelt to Hitler, Sept. 26, 1938, ibid., doc. 631.

34 "In 1918 . . . peace or war": Hitler to Roosevelt, received Sept. 27, 1938, *FRUS* 1938, vol. 1, doc. 643.

7.

36 "Went to Morgan Grenfell": Lindbergh journal, Sept. 23, 1938.

36 "News seems . . . he is insane": Ibid., Sept. 24, 1938.

37 "To get to . . . felt better": Ibid., Sept. 25, 1938.

37 "Opinion is hardening": Ibid., Sept. 26, 1938.

37 "Everyone depressed": Ibid., Sept. 27, 1938.

37 "Kept waking up . . . no hope": Ibid., Sept. 28, 1938.

38 "Everything is . . . about the crisis": Ibid., Sept. 29, 1938.

38 "peace with honor": *New York Times*, Oct. 1, 1938.

38 "They should know": Churchill speech in House of Commons, Oct. 5, 1938, *Hansard* 339:373.

8.

40 "Seems very strange . . . dying nation": Lindbergh journal, Sept. 30, 1938.

41 "Those who take part": Ibid., Oct. 3, 1938.

41 "I suggested . . . regard to them": Ibid., Oct. 1, 1938.

41 "The most amazing": Ibid., Oct. 2, 1938.

42 "Berlin has greatly changed": Ibid., Oct. 12, 1938.

42 "This is an excellent": Ibid., Oct. 17, 1938.

42 "The plane handled": Ibid., Oct. 21, 1938.

42 "They are to take": Ibid., Oct. 24, 1938.

42 "I am anxious": Ibid., Oct. 25, 1938.

42 "He said": Ibid., Oct. 16, 1938.

43 "Marshal Goering . . . religious problem": Ibid., Oct. 18, 1938.

9.

45 "A wave of destruction . . . legislation and ordinance": *New York Times*, Nov. 11, 1938.

46 "I do not understand": Lindbergh journal, Nov. 13, 1938.

47 "Milch told me": Ibid., Dec. 20, 1938.

47 "During the days": Ibid., Dec. 22, 1938.

47 "I told la Chambre": Ibid., Dec. 23, 1938.

48 "I think it": Ibid., Jan. 7, 1939.

48 "European affairs": Ibid., Jan. 27, 1939.

48 "Lord Astor asked . . . disarmament program": Ibid., Feb. 24, 1939.

49 "amazingly young": Ibid., Feb. 25, 1939.

50 "He has just come . . . are themselves": Ibid., Feb. 26, 1939.

50 "Said it was essential . . . not external": Ibid., Feb. 28, 1939.

50 "Cliveden gives": Ibid., Feb. 26, 1939.

51 "I cannot help . . . European war": Ibid., Feb. 27, 1939.

52 "The acting": Ibid., Feb. 28, 1939.

52 "I think that . . . resorted to": Ibid., Mar. 7, 1939.

10.

54 In January 1939: *New York Times*, Feb. 5, 1939.

54 "Mr. Roosevelt": Ibid.

55 "A great many . . . Yes": Roosevelt press conference, Feb. 3, 1939.

11.

58 "Hundreds of millions . . . years to come": Roosevelt to Hitler, Apr. 14, 1939, *FRUS*, 1939, vol. 1, doc. 120.

60 "The present Greater . . . to my people": Hitler speech of Apr. 28, 1939, translated by German News Agency, in *New York Times*, Apr. 29, 1939.

12.

63 "If England . . . seem desperate": Lindbergh journal, Mar. 31, 1939.

64 "This man": Ibid., Apr. 2, 1939.

64 "Both sides": Ibid., Apr. 14, 1939.

65 "Discussed military aviation . . . not be for long": Ibid., Apr. 20, 1939.

66 "The meeting room . . . of our aircraft": Ibid.

67 "America's number one . . . this condition": *New York Times*, Apr. 30, 1939.

68 "He gave us": Ibid., May 18, 1939.

68 "But during": Ibid., June 13, 1939.

68 "Flew over": Lindbergh journal, May 11, 1939.

69 "The high peaks": Ibid., July 2, 1939.

69 "Taxi to Capitol . . . save it for democracy": Ibid., June 30, 1939.

70 "Do you mind . . . pretty definite objective)": Ibid., June 7, 1939.

13.

71 "European crisis becoming": Lindbergh journal, Aug. 18 and 20, 1939.

72 "There is talk": Ibid., Aug. 23, 1939.

72 "We discussed": Ibid., Aug. 24, 1939.

72 "Constantly thinking": Ibid., Aug. 30, 1939.

73 "General Arnold": Ibid., Aug. 31, 1939.

PART TWO: DISTANT GUNS

14.

77 "The war has . . . of our lives": Lindbergh journal, Sept. 1, 1939.

78 "The radio commentators . . . leave affairs chaotic": Ibid., Sept. 2, 1939.

15.

79 "I think probably . . . Yes": Roosevelt press conference, Sept. 1, 1939.

79 "Tonight my single . . . toward that end": Roosevelt radio address, Sept. 3, 1939.

16.

82 "It was a better talk": Lindbergh journal, Sept. 3, 1939.

82 "It is impossible": Charles A. Lindbergh (Sr.), *Why Is Your Country at War, and What Happens to You After the War* (1917), 8. A few copies had been printed before the censors arrived.

83 "I have now written": Lindbergh journal, Sept. 7, 1939.

84 "The matter . . . that statement": Lindbergh journal, Sept. 14, 1939.

85 "He told me . . . 'Of course not'": Lindbergh journal, Sept. 15, 1939.

85 "That means complete": Lindbergh journal, Sept. 14, 1939.

86 "They were very considerate": Lindbergh journal, Sept. 15, 1939.

86 "In times . . . in the conflagration": Lindbergh radio address, Sept. 15, 1939, in *New York Times*, Sept. 16, 1939.

17.

89 "I was not well satisfied": Lindbergh journal, Sept. 15, 1939.

89 "About forty": Ibid. Sept. 16, 1939.

89 "The papers": Ibid., Sept. 20, 1939.

89 "We talked . . . most committees": Ibid., Sept. 21, 1939.

90 "We discussed": Ibid., Sept. 22, 1939.

91 "He brought . . . France lose": Ibid., Sept. 26, 1939.

92 "I liked him": Ibid., Sept. 27, 1939.

92 "He stood up . . . for this country": Ibid., Sept. 27, 1939.

18.

94 "Because I am . . . out of this war": Roosevelt address to Congress, Sept. 21, 1939.

19.

97 "We are met . . . now proposed": *New York Times*, Sept. 15, 1939.

98 "From here on": Ibid., Sept. 14, 1939.

99 "We are now . . . their followers": Ibid., Sept. 17, 1939.

99 "We did not": Ibid.

100 "No such grave . . . out of war": Ibid., Oct. 3, 1939.

20.

102 "Herbert Hoover . . . of the British fleet": Lindbergh journal, Oct. 2, 1939.

103 "When I arrived . . . tense atmosphere": Ibid., Oct. 3, 1939.

105 "I speak again . . . to take action": Lindbergh radio address, Oct. 13, 1939, *Washington Star*, Oct. 14, 1939.

21.

109 "Colonel Charles Lindbergh . . . a school boy": Harold Nicolson, "People and Things," *The Spectator*, Oct. 19, 1939.

22.

113 "The most unfortunate part": *New York Times*, Oct. 15, 1939.

113 "I condemn": Ibid., Oct. 21, 1939.

113 "He has a passion": Dorothy Thompson, "On the Record," *Washington Post*, Sept. 20, 1939.

114 "She sensed": Eleanor Roosevelt, "My Day," Oct. 19, 1939, Eleanor Roosevelt Papers Project, George Washington University, https://erpapers.columbian.gwu.edu/.

114 "Radio listeners . . . into a truth": Roosevelt radio address, Oct. 26, 1939.

23

116 "Opened some": Lindbergh journal, Oct. 16, 1939.

116 "Morning papers": Ibid., Oct. 22, 1939.

116 "Threatening letters": Ibid., Oct. 24, 1939.

117 "Of course, I am": Ibid., Oct. 7, 1939.

117 "Borah and I . . . ever held one": Ibid., Oct. 11, 1939.

118 "Anne and I . . . day to day": Lindbergh journal, Dec. 9, 1939.

119 "I talked to Ford . . . collecting the juice": Lindbergh journal, Dec. 28, 1939.

PART THREE: A SPECIAL RELATIONSHIP

24.

123 "With earnest best wishes": Churchill inscription to Roosevelt, Oct. 8, 1933, *Churchill and Roosevelt: The Complete Correspondence*, edited by Warren F. Kimball (1984). Unless otherwise noted, all messages between Roosevelt and Churchill are from this collection.

124 "My dear Churchill": Roosevelt to Churchill, Sept. 11, 1939.

125 "There remains": Notes of Churchill telephone conversation with Roosevelt, Oct. 5, 1939.

125 "We don't believe": *New York Times*, Oct. 6, 1939.

126 "We quite understand": Churchill to Roosevelt, Oct. 5, 1939.

126 "We have been hitting": Churchill to Roosevelt, Oct. 16, 1939.

127 "I am very sorry . . . in right way": Churchill to Roosevelt, Dec. 25, 1939.

25.

129 "As the Congress . . . to be preserved": Roosevelt State of the Union address, Jan. 3, 1940.

131 "economic royalists . . . within our gates": Roosevelt acceptance speech, June 27, 1936.

131 "Lunch with Harry Byrd . . . within a few days": Lindbergh journal, Mar. 27, 1940.

133 "Lundeen knew": Lindbergh journal, Mar. 28, 1940.

134 "Down with Hitler . . . imperfect world": *New York Times*, May 18, 1934.

135 Viereck's activities: In 1943 Viereck was convicted of violating the Foreign Agents' Registration Act. He served almost four years in federal prison before being paroled.

26.

136 "A large hole": Enclosure in Churchill to Roosevelt, Jan. 7, 1940.

136 "Ever so many thanks": Roosevelt to Churchill, Feb. 1, 1940.

138 "At the time": Roosevelt to Churchill, Feb. 1, 1940.

27.

139 "Even the most . . . military history": Lindbergh journal, Apr. 11, 1940.

139 "Our papers": Ibid., Apr. 12, 1940.

140 "Drove to New York": Ibid., Apr. 15, 1940.

140 "We discussed the war": Ibid., Apr. 18, 1940.

140 "Took a taxi": Ibid., Apr. 19, 1940.

141 "There were fifteen": Ibid., Apr. 29, 1940.

141 "I was very . . . yet experienced": Ibid., May 3, 1940.

142 "How interesting": Ibid., Apr. 30, 1940.

142 "After lunch . . . nearby countryside": Ibid., May 3, 1940.

28.

144 "After crossing...in this area": "The Blitzkrieg in Belgium: A Newsman's Eyewitness Account," *Wisconsin Magazine of History*, Summer 1967, 337–42.
145 "The scene...way convenient": Churchill to Roosevelt, May 15, 1940.
147 "I have just...luck to you": Roosevelt to Churchill, May 16, 1940.
148 "Many thanks": Churchill to Roosevelt, May 18, 1940.
149 "I understand...German will": Churchill to Roosevelt, May 20, 1940.

29.

151 "These are ominous days...future may hold": Roosevelt address to Congress, May 16, 1940.

30.

154 "Antwerp has fallen...(and that is true)": Lindbergh journal, May 18, 1940.
155 "The German advance...for their offer": Ibid., May 19, 1940.
156 "The power of aviation...crisis is at hand": Lindbergh radio address, May 19, 1940, *Washington Post*, May 20, 1940.

31.

159 "Mr. President...I don't know": Roosevelt press conference, May 21, 1940.
160 "I think the country": Ibid.
160 "unprecedented gravity...march behind you": Roosevelt conference with Business Advisory Council, May 23, 1940, in Roosevelt Press Conferences.
163 "There are many...across our vision": Roosevelt fireside chat, May 26, 1940.

32.

165 "We are told...back to England": Murrow broadcast for May 31, 1940, in *This Is London*, edited by Elmer Davis (1941).
167 "The evacuation...troop trains": Ibid., June 1, 1940.
167 "I spent...to go again": Ibid., June 2, 1940.
168 "We are told": Ibid., June 3, 1940.
168 "I sat...and gravity": Ibid., June 4, 1940.

33.

171 "I understand": Churchill to Roosevelt, June 1, 1940.
172 "Every generation...every defense": Roosevelt address, June 10, 1940.

34.

175 "We all listened...should be lost": Churchill to Roosevelt, June 11, 1940.

PART FOUR: DISSENT OR DISLOYALTY?

35.

179 "I had lunch . . . laughing at me": James A. Farley, *The Jim Farley Story: The Roosevelt Years* (1948), 237–52.

36.

183 "The German Army . . . demagogic as usual": Lindbergh journal, June 10, 1940.

184 "We discussed . . . give me time": Lindbergh journal, June 12, 1940.

184 "I have asked . . . is now heading": Lindbergh radio address, June 15, 1940, *Los Angeles Times*, June 16, 1940.

37

188 "It appears . . . its military matters": Key Pittman radio address, June 16, 1940, *New York Times*, June 17, 1940.

189 "Mr. President Roosevelt": Anonymous letter to Roosevelt, May 21, 1940, FBI file on Lindbergh, vault.fbi.gov/Charles Lindbergh.

189 "I don't understand . . . Special Agent in Charge": Various letters in FBI file on Lindbergh.

38.

194 "For six days . . . too late": Reynaud to Roosevelt, June 10, 1940, in Bullitt to Hull, *FRUS*, 1940, vol. 1, doc. 208.

195 "The practical point . . . now is the time": Churchill to Roosevelt, June 12, 1940.

196 "Your message of June 10": Roosevelt to Reynaud, June 13, 1940, in *FRUS*, 1940, vol. 1, doc. 210.

196 "When this message": Ibid.

196 "Ambassador Kennedy . . . end of the day": Churchill to Roosevelt, June 14, 1940.

197 "Four days . . . awaited salvation": Reynaud to Roosevelt, June 14, 1940, *FRUS*, 1940, vol. 1, doc. 215.

198 "I am very much . . . possible misunderstanding": Roosevelt to Churchill, June 14, 1940.

199 "I am sending you . . . such commitments": Roosevelt to Reynaud, June 15, in *FRUS*, 1940, vol. 1, doc. 217.

200 "I understand . . . these destroyers": Churchill to Roosevelt, June 15, 1940.

39.

202 "German tanks today . . . civilian force": United Press, June 14, 1940.

203 "An hour or so . . . Thor": Lindbergh journal, June 8, 1940.

204 "I have decided": Ibid., June 12, 1940.

204 "We discussed politics": Ibid., June 14, 1940.

204 "All but three": Ibid., June 15, 1940.

204 "The radio announces . . . to Philadelphia": Ibid., June 17, 1940.

205 "The shore": Ibid., June 18, 1940.

205 "I went . . . Spent the evening": *Why Is Your Country at War?*" Ibid., June 21, 1940.

206 "I think": Ibid., June 22, 1940.

206 "He agreed": Ibid., June 27, 1940.

206 "I showed Ford": Ibid., June 28, 1940.

206 "We discussed": Ibid., June 29, 1940.

206 "A large number": Ibid., July 10, 1940.

207 "Something is wrong": Ibid., July 22, 1940.

207 "I told Howard . . . in it instead": Ibid., July 26, 1940.

40.

209 "Senator Clark's secretary": Lindbergh journal, July 31, 1940.

209 "It will not be popular": Ibid., Aug. 2, 1940.

209 "Several weeks . . . our desires": Lindbergh address, Aug. 4, 1940, *Washington Post*, Aug. 5, 1940.

41.

214 "the chief": Pepper speech excerpted in *Los Angeles Times*, Aug. 6, 1940.

214 "I was not only . . . great American flier": Lucas address, Aug. 5, 1940, *New York Times*, Aug. 6, 1940.

215 "There is widespread": Birkhead letter excerpted in *New York Times*, Aug. 7, 1940.

215 "Colonel Lindbergh thinks . . . worse still, captured": Lippmann syndicated column in *Washington Post*, Aug. 6, 1940.

216 "It may be possible . . . non-American nation": Roosevelt to Churchill, Aug. 13, 1940.

217 "I need not . . . impossible contingency": Churchill to Roosevelt, Aug. 15, 1940.

217 "Could you tell us . . . the present time": Roosevelt press conference, Aug. 6, 1940.

218 "Can you give . . . won't tell you": Ibid., Aug. 9, 1940.

218 "This has nothing . . . make that clear": Ibid., Aug. 16, 1940.

219 "The right . . . acquire them": Roosevelt message to Congress, Sept. 3, 1940.

42.

220 "Ostensibly private business . . . certain specific ways": *British Security Coordination: The Secret History of British Intelligence in the Americas, 1940–45* (1998), xxiii–xxvii, 3–25, 56–60, 69–84.

43.

224 "During the last . . . real enough": Murrow, Aug. 16, 1940.

226 "I've spent the day . . . happens next": Murrow, Sept. 9, 1940.

227 "This is London . . . to the shelter": Murrow, Sept. 13, 1940.

44.

230 "The Republican Party . . . United States": Republican party platform, June 24, 1940, Presidency Project.

231 "The American people . . . mechanized army": Democratic party platform, July 15, 1940.

232 "I find myself . . . of appeasement": Roosevelt radio acceptance speech, July 19, 1940.

45.

235 "The country will": *New York Times*, Sept. 4, 1940.

235 "You must remember": Ibid., Sept. 5, 1940.

236 "This trade": Ibid., Sept. 7, 1940.

236 "If I am president": Ibid., Sept. 8, 1940.

236 "I want to ask": Ibid., Oct. 9, 1940.

236 "If his promise": Ibid., Oct. 23, 1940.

236 "I promise": Ibid., Nov. 5, 1940.

237 "I hate war": Roosevelt address, Sept. 11, 1940.

237 "There is one . . . days of my life": Roosevelt speech, Oct. 23, 1940.

237 "While I am talking": Roosevelt speech, Oct. 30, 1940.

238 "I had a conversation . . . 'I need it'": James Roosevelt with Bill Libby, *My Parents: A Differing View* (1976), 160–63.

46.

240 "1. The United States": Principles of the America First Committee, *Washington Post*, Jan. 5, 1941.

241 "The party": *New York Times*, Sept. 9, 1940.

241 "We discussed the Chicago": Lindbergh journal, Sept. 4, 1940.

241 "I arrived . . . get it personally": Ibid., Sept. 16, 1940.

242 "Stuart says": Ibid., Oct. 1, 1940.

243 "We discussed the America . . . a little time": Ibid., Oct. 3, 1940.

243 "I asked his advice": Ibid., Oct. 4, 1940.

47.

245 "As I read . . . lay plans for one": Lindbergh journal, Oct. 10, 1940.

48.

250 "The newsreels again . . . hot lights": Lindbergh journal, Oct. 14, 1940.

251 "I come before you . . . and to war": Lindbergh speech, Oct. 14, 1940, *Washington Post*, Oct. 15, 1940.

PART FIVE: EXECUTIVE UNBOUND

49.

257 "I did not": Churchill to Roosevelt, Nov. 6, 1940.

257 "As we reach . . . our common purpose": Churchill to Roosevelt, Dec. 7, 1940.

50.

261 "This is not . . . greatly succeed": Roosevelt radio address, Dec. 29, 1940.

51.

266 "I feel it my duty": Churchill to Roosevelt, Jan. 1, 1941.

266 "Roosevelt demands": Lindbergh journal, Dec. 30, 1940.

266 "She was thrown . . . camps were shown": Ibid., Jan. 1, 1941.

267 "The pall of the war": Ibid., Jan. 6, 1941. The Gallup results were reported in *Washington Post*, Dec. 29, 1940.

267 "I address you . . . and our pledge": Roosevelt annual message to Congress on the state of the Union, Jan. 6, 1941.

272 "We were sitting . . . neighbors now": Samuel I. Rosenman, *Working with Roosevelt* (1952), 262–64.

52.

275 "Roosevelt has asked . . . very wise": Lindbergh journal, Jan. 7, 1941.

275 "to promote the defense . . . any defense article": H.R. 1776, 55 Stat. 31.

276 "The first thing": *New York Times*, Jan. 11, 1941.

276 "The president's so-called": Ibid.

276 "the first step": Ibid., Jan. 12, 1941.

277 "Never before": Ibid., Jan. 13 and 15, 1941.

277 "not *short* of war . . . drifting into war": Ibid., Jan. 20 and 25, 1941.

277 "machinery of": Ibid., Mar. 5, 1941.

278 "Wall Street": Ibid., Feb. 1, 1941.

53.

279 "Colonel . . . from foreign attack": *Lend-Lease Bill*, Hearings before the Committee on Foreign Affairs, House of Representatives, Jan. 15–18, 21–25, 29, 1941, 371–74.

281 "Colonel Lindbergh . . . a war abroad": Ibid., 374–81.

284 "Do you not think . . . Yes, sir": Ibid., 382–94.

286 "Colonel Lindbergh's appearance": *New York Times*, Jan. 24, 1941.

287 "Colonel Lindbergh . . . committee rising": *Lend-Lease* Hearings, 435–36.

54.

288 "courageous": *New York Times*, Jan. 25, 1941.
288 "Certain statements": Roosevelt press conference, Jan. 24, 1941.
288 "The most untruthful": Ibid., Jan. 14, 1941.
289 "Don't you think . . . Vatican navy!": Ibid., Jan. 17, 1941.
289 "The Senate hearing": Lindbergh journal, Feb. 6, 1941.
289 "He told me": Ibid., Feb. 25, 1941.
290 "I went to . . . in the air": Ibid., Feb. 24, 1941.
290 "The table . . . somewhat beyond": Ibid., Feb. 27, 1941.
291 "Phoned Senator Byrd": Ibid., Feb. 28, 1941.
291 "The decisions . . . call us blessed": Roosevelt speech, Mar. 15, 1941.

55.

294 "Thank God": Lindbergh journal, Mar. 12, 1941.
294 "One of the men": Ibid., Mar. 28, 1941.
294 "Ed Webster": Ibid., Mar. 30, 1941.
295 "They said": Ibid., Apr. 1, 1941.
295 "We discussed": Ibid., Apr. 2, 1941.
295 "It is essential": Ibid., Apr. 7, 1941.
295 "We discussed": Ibid., Apr. 16, 1941.
295 "Arrived at auditorium": Ibid., Apr. 17, 1941.

56.

297 "There are many . . . need it now": Lindbergh speech, Apr. 23, 1941, *New York Times*, Apr. 24, 1941.

57.

301 "Mr. President . . . Yes": Roosevelt press conference, Apr. 25, 1941.

58.

305 "Lyman phoned . . . going to be": Lindbergh journal, Apr. 25, 1941.
306 "He is just back": Ibid., Apr. 26, 1941.
306 "If I did not tender": Ibid., Apr. 27, 1941.
307 "My dear Mr. President . . . Charles A. Lindbergh": Lindbergh to Roosevelt, Apr. 28, 1941, in *New York Times*, Apr. 29, 1941.

59.

308 "To smear": *New York Times*, Apr. 28, 1941.
308 "Col. Charles Lindbergh . . . is to prevail": Ibid., Apr. 30, 1941.
309 "Read Dostoevsky . . . many others": Ibid., May 1, 1941.
309 "The prime minister . . . in opposition": Lindbergh speech, May 3, 1941, in *New York Times*, May 4, 1941.

310 "There were about": Lindbergh journal, May 3, 1941.

310 "I suddenly realized": Ibid., May 5, 1941.

311 "It is strange": Ibid., May 10, 1941.

311 "I was given . . . and his courage": Ibid., May 10, 1941.

312 "Mr. Appel": Ibid., May 11, 1941.

312 "Some of my friends . . . this country today": Ibid., May 18, 1941.

312 "No man has served . . . at an end": Wheeler speech, May 23, 1941, in *New York Times*, May 24, 1941.

60.

315 "We cannot afford . . . power and authority": Roosevelt radio address, May 27, 1941.

61.

319 "Boy, he's got . . . is all right": *Washington Post*, May 28, 1941.

320 "very forceful . . . to death of Hitler": Ibid., May 28, 1941.

320 "We listened": Lindbergh journal, May 27, 1941.

321 "It seems . . . says the next": Ibid., May 28, 1941.

321 "Can you explain . . . after a while": Roosevelt press conference, May 28, 1941.

322 "Suppose the Germans . . . new leadership?": Lindbergh speech, May 29, 1941, in *New York Times*, May 30, 1941.

323 "In some ways . . . his nationality": Lindbergh journal, May 29, 1941.

324 "Hoover thinks . . . to which I agree": Ibid., May 31, 1941.

62.

326 "The sinking . . . propose to yield": Roosevelt message to Congress, June 20, 1941.

328 "We arrived": Lindbergh journal, June 20, 1941.

63.

329 "I would a hundred . . . at peace": Lindbergh speech, July 1, 1941, in *Los Angeles Times*, July 2, 1941.

331 "It was clear . . . still Hitler": *New York Times*, July 15, 1941.

332 "Secretary of the Interior . . . utmost effect": Lindbergh journal, July 16, 1941.

333 "My Dear Mr. President . . . Charles A. Lindbergh": Lindbergh to Roosevelt, July 17, 1941, in *New York Times*, July 18, 1941.

64.

335 "He had phoned . . . additional information": Lindbergh journal, July 7, 1941.

336 "Through cut-outs . . . Fascist Number Two": *British Security Coordination*, 59–65, 102–5.

65.

339 "In 1776 . . . our very lives": Roosevelt address, July 4, 1941.

340 "The United States cannot": Roosevelt message, July 7, 1941.

340 "The international situation": Roosevelt message, July 21, 1941.

341 "We cordially welcome": Churchill to Roosevelt, May 29, 1941.

341 "From every source": Churchill to Roosevelt, June 14, 1941.

342 "If Hitler invaded Hell": Churchill, *The Grand Alliance* (1948), 331–33.

342 "Mr. President . . . can to Russia": Roosevelt press conference, June 24, 1941.

342 "Looking forward": Roosevelt to Churchill, Aug. 5, 1941.

342 "The President . . . is essential": White House statement on Atlantic Charter meeting, and declaration of principles, Aug. 14, 1941.

343 "splendid defense . . . joint resources": Roosevelt and Churchill to Stalin, Aug. 15, 1941.

66.

345 "Could you tell us . . . quote indirectly": Roosevelt press conference, Aug. 16, 1941.

347 "The President had . . . the Prime Minister": Cabinet minutes, Aug. 19, 1941, CAB 65, 84(41), National Archives, United Kingdom. https://www .nationalarchives.gov.uk/cabinetpapers/cabinet-gov/cab65-second-world-war -conclusions.htm.

347 "The declaration": Roosevelt message to Congress, Aug. 21, 1941.

348 "There can be no doubt": Roosevelt press conference, Aug. 26, 1941.

348 "Why are we doing . . . his Nazi forces": Roosevelt radio address, Sept. 1, 1941.

67.

350 "The Navy Department . . . their own peril": Roosevelt radio address, Sept. 11, 1941.

353 "On September 4 . . . existing orders": Stark to Walsh, Sept. 20, 1941, in *Congressional Record*, vol. 87, part 8 (1941), 8314–15.

68.

355 "Lunch with about . . . previous speakers": Lindbergh journal, Sept. 11, 1941.

357 "It is now two years . . . no foreign war": Lindbergh speech, Sept. 11, 1941, charleslindbergh.com.

PART SIX: OPPOSITION UNDONE

69.

368 "The Des Moines speech . . . 'honorary' decoration": Editorials excerpted in Jewish Telegraph Agency *Daily News Bulletin*, Sept. 15, 1941.

369 "As an American citizen . . . what he said": *Kansas City Times* editorial excerpted in *Los Angeles Times*, Sept. 20, 1941.

370 "Mr. Lindbergh may say . . . unhappy land": *New York Times*, Sept. 12, 1941.

370 "As loyal Americans": Ibid., Sept. 13, 1941.

371 "at once a serious": *Los Angeles Times*, Sept. 22, 1941.

371 "No American": Ibid., Sept. 19, 1941.

371 "Charles A. Lindbergh": Ibid., Sept. 15, 1941.

371 "It sounds": *New York Times*, Sept. 20, 1941.

371 "looking forward": *Washington Post*, Sept. 20, 1941.

371 "Lindbergh ought": *Los Angeles Times*, Sept. 17, 1941.

372 "The Keep America Out of War Congress": *Washington Post*, Sept. 21, 1941.

372 "I agree with Charles Lindbergh": Ibid., Sept. 21, 1941.

372 several eggs: *Los Angeles Times*, Sept. 17, 1941.

372 "Ever since the nationwide": *New York Times*, Sept. 25, 1941.

70.

374 "*New York Times*": Lindbergh journal, Sept. 13, 1941.

374 "My Des Moines address": Ibid., Sept. 15 1941.

374 "Bob Stuart . . . go down at all": Ibid., Sept. 17, 1941.

375 "I told him . . . last spring": Ibid., Sept. 18, 1941.

376 "The friction": Ibid., Oct. 2, 1941.

376 "We have become": Ibid.

376 "The opposition paper . . . entering the war": Ibid., Oct. 3, 1941.

377 "We discussed . . . so wrong": Ibid., Oct. 4, 1941.

378 "Hoover told me . . . probable popularity": Ibid., Oct. 6, 1941.

71.

379 "But so did . . . all our mind": Roosevelt message, Oct. 9, 1941.

381 "Every school child knows . . . it may demand": Roosevelt message, Oct. 25, 1941.

382 "We have wished . . . our full duty": Roosevelt address, Oct. 27, 1941.

383 "Mr. President . . . we got it from": Roosevelt press conference, Oct. 28, 1941.

385 the map *was* a forgery: Nicholas John Cull, *Selling War: The British Propaganda Campaign Against American "Neutrality" in World War II* (1995), 170–73.

72.

386 "We drove . . . sight or hearing": Ibid., Oct. 30, 1941.

73.

388 "Is there anything . . . No": Roosevelt press conference, Nov. 28, 1941.

390 "Since last April . . . polite question": Roosevelt press conference, Dec. 2, 1941.

391 "F.D.R.'s War Plans! . . . summer of 1943": *Chicago Tribune*, Dec. 4, 1941.

393 "Yesterday . . . Japanese Empire": Roosevelt address, Dec. 8, 1941.

EPILOGUE

397 "Mr. President . . . simplifies things": Churchill, *The Grand Alliance* (1948),
     605–6.
398 "So we had won": Ibid., 606.
398 "What else was there . . . back door": Lindbergh journal, Dec. 8, 1941.
399 "The time for military action": Ibid., Dec. 12, 1941.
399 "We have been stepping": Lindbergh statement, *New York Times*, Dec. 9, 1941.
399 "We are in a war": Lindbergh journal, Dec. 11, 1941.
399 "Now that we . . . out of the way": Ibid., Dec. 12, 1941.
400 "Stimson said . . . most effective": Ibid., Jan. 12, 1942.
401 Lindbergh died in 1974: A quarter century after he died, Lindbergh's legacy
     was complicated by the revelation that starting in the late 1950s, and while
     he was still married to Anne, he had romantic relationships with three other
     women, with each of whom he had multiple children. The mothers withheld
     Lindbergh's true identity from the children as long as he was alive, but eventu-
     ally they found out. "Lindbergh's Double Life," Minnesota Historical Society;
     mnhs.org/lindbergh/learn/family/double-life.

Index

Illustration Credits

Page 1, Library of Congress
Page 2, top: Library of Congress
Page 2, bottom: Library of Congress
Page 3, top: Library of Congress
Page 3, bottom: Minnesota Historical Society
Page 4, top: National Archives
Page 4, bottom: Library of Congress
Page 6, top: Library of Congress
Page 6, bottom: Library of Congress
Page 7, Library of Congress
Page 8, National Archives
Page 9, top: Library of Congress
Page 9, bottom: Library of Congress
Page 10, Library of Congress
Page 11, National Archives
Page 12, Library of Congress
Page 13, top: FDR Library
Page 13, bottom: Library of Congress
Page 14, top: Library of Congress
Page 14, bottom: Library of Congress
Page 14, bottom: Harry Ransom Center, University of Texas at Austin
Page 15, Library of Congress
Page 16, National Archives

ABOUT THE AUTHOR

H. W. BRANDS holds the Jack S. Blanton Sr. Chair in History at the University of Texas at Austin. He has written histories and biographies that include *The General vs. the President*, a *New York Times* bestseller, and *Founding Partisans*, his most recent book. Two of his biographies, *The First American* and *Traitor to His Class*, were finalists for the Pulitzer Prize.